Facing Segregation

Facing Segregation

HOUSING POLICY SOLUTIONS FOR
A STRONGER SOCIETY

Edited by Molly W. Metzger and Henry S. Webber

OXFORD
UNIVERSITY PRESS

OXFORD
UNIVERSITY PRESS

Oxford University Press is a department of the University of Oxford. It furthers
the University's objective of excellence in research, scholarship, and education
by publishing worldwide. Oxford is a registered trade mark of Oxford University
Press in the UK and certain other countries.

Published in the United States of America by Oxford University Press
198 Madison Avenue, New York, NY 10016, United States of America.

© Oxford University Press 2019

All rights reserved. No part of this publication may be reproduced, stored in
a retrieval system, or transmitted, in any form or by any means, without the
prior permission in writing of Oxford University Press, or as expressly permitted
by law, by license, or under terms agreed with the appropriate reproduction
rights organization. Inquiries concerning reproduction outside the scope of the
above should be sent to the Rights Department, Oxford University Press, at the
address above.

You must not circulate this work in any other form
and you must impose this same condition on any acquirer.

Library of Congress Cataloging-in-Publication Data
Names: Metzger, Molly W., 1979- editor | Webber, Henry S., editor.
Title: Facing segregation : housing policy solutions for a stronger society /
edited by Molly W. Metzger and Henry S. Webber.
Description: New York, NY : Oxford University Press, [2019] | Includes
bibliographical references and index.
Identifiers: LCCN 2018030331 (print) | LCCN 2018033092 (ebook) | ISBN
9780190862312 (updf) | ISBN 9780190862329 (epub) | ISBN 9780190862336
 (Online Component) | ISBN 9780190862305 (jacketed : alk. paper)
Subjects: LCSH: Discrimination in housing—United States. | Housing
policy—United States. | Segregation—United States.
Classification: LCC HD7288.76.U5 (ebook) | LCC HD7288.76.U5 F33 2019 (print) |
DDC 363.5/9—dc23
LC record available at https://lccn.loc.gov/2018030331

9 8 7 6 5 4 3 2 1

Printed by Sheridan Books, Inc., United States of America

CONTENTS

List of Illustrations   vii
Foreword   ix
Acknowledgments   xiii
About the Editors   xv
List of Contributors   xvii
List of Abbreviations   xix

PART I Facing the Causes and Consequences of Segregation

1. Segregation: A Threat to Americans' Shared Goals   3
   MOLLY W. METZGER AND HENRY S. WEBBER

2. *De Facto* Segregation: A National Myth   15
   RICHARD ROTHSTEIN

3. The Siting Dilemma: Race and the Location of Federal Housing Projects   35
   LANCE FREEMAN

4. The Enduring Significance of Segregation   58
   JASON Q. PURNELL

PART II The Policy Agenda

5. Affirmatively Furthering Fair Housing and the *Inclusive Communities Project* Case: Bringing the Fair Housing Act into the Twenty-First Century   77
   PHILIP D. TEGELER

6. Enabling More Families with Housing Vouchers to Access Higher-Opportunity Neighborhoods   92
   BARBARA SARD

7. The Community Reinvestment Act as a Catalyst for Integration and an Antidote to Concentrated Poverty   120
   JOHN TAYLOR AND JOSH SILVER

8. Promoting Poverty Deconcentration and Racial Desegregation through Mixed-Income Development   146
   MARK L. JOSEPH

9. Market-Savvy Housing and Community Development Policy: Grappling with the Equity-Efficiency Trade-off   173
TODD SWANSTROM

10. Financing Affordability: Tax Increment Financing and the Potential for Concentrated Reinvestment   197
SARAH L. COFFIN

11. Beyond Education Triage: Building Brain Regimes in Metropolitan America   215
WILLIAM F. TATE IV

12. Concluding Thoughts on an Agenda for Solving Segregation   233
HENRY S. WEBBER AND MOLLY W. METZGER

Index   243

ILLUSTRATIONS

Boxes

6.1   The Low-Income Housing Tax Credit Could Do More to Provide Access to High-Opportunity Areas   103
11.1   Brain Regime Strategies   225

Table

9.1   Market-Savvy Housing and Community Development Policies   189

Figures

4.1   Life Expectancy for Select Zip Codes in St. Louis, Missouri   59
4.2   African American Population, Poverty, and Cardiovascular and Cancer Mortality, by Zip Code in St. Louis, Missouri   61
9.1   A Typology of Market Strength   176
9.2   The Equity-Efficiency Trade-off: Targeting Need or Leveraging Private Investment   178
10.1   Municipal Distress in 2012, St. Louis County, Missouri   204
10.2   Percentage of Nonwhites in Population by Municipality in 2012, St. Louis County, Missouri   205

FOREWORD

I am writing these words in my home in a quiet middle-class neighborhood in St. Louis, Missouri. Houses in this neighborhood are sound and maintained, and people of all ages are walking and using the park for sports. But I can travel a very short distance to a part of our city that looks quite different: unemployment and poverty are high, many buildings are abandoned and boarded up, outdoor spaces have few people in them. My neighborhood is mostly white, and the other is mostly African American. Because of my job, I am very familiar with the other neighborhood—and certainly the authors in this book know urban landscapes well—but the vast majority of Americans travel little outside their segregated daily living patterns.

Why does this matter? Over several decades of applied social research, engaged in many social and economic issues, I have observed a distinct trend: sharp segregation in residential real estate has arisen again and again as a key issue. I have come to view segregation as America's most fundamental social problem. Many other challenges—in education, employment, public services, transportation, health, crime, and civic engagement—are exacerbated by racial and class segregation. The empirical outcome is predictable and shameful. Location of residence is a strong predictor of child outcomes.[1] Segregation leads to millions of diminished lives and lost potential. The nation as a whole is weakened, yet segregation continues year after year with little change.

This book is about the residential segregation of Americans, the harms that follow from this division, and what can and should be done to reduce it. The title, *Facing Segregation,* is clear: it is oriented toward positive action, and it is hopeful.

In an excellent recent book, we are reminded by Richard Rothstein, a contributor in this volume, that public policies purposefully created US racial segregation.[2] In this fundamental respect, the nation has not yet fully recovered from slavery. Indeed, I sometimes wonder whether that recovery has only barely started. Given the role of government in engineering racial segregation in neighborhoods, schools, prisons, and elsewhere, it is logical to suggest that these public policies should be actively reversed. New policies should support freedom and opportunity in residence for everyone.

Indeed, I would go further. It is desirable—and would be historically just—to enact public policies that proactively encourage racially integrated neighborhoods—in other words, housing policies that go beyond freedom of choice at the individual level to express the *social value* of integration by class and race. This is a policy direction we might call *living together*, though the meaning is deeper than these simple words. Living together is not only about being decent to human beings and benefitting from cultural diversity. It is also a practical necessity. With the transition to a white minority population in the next few decades, and with rising inequality, the future vitality and functioning of the United States depends on raising all of our children well, so that people of every color and creed, and people from every economic background, can reach their full potential. As a nation, we can no longer afford to have millions of undereducated people, much less millions of incarcerated people. The waste is too great. In economic terms alone, the cost is too high. And social strain and instability accompany economic decline. Achieving social stability and a sound economy in the twenty-first century depends fundamentally on figuring out how to conceive, test, and accomplish *living together*. The United States is not ready for this policy today, but applied scholars can lay the groundwork that may put it on the table for consideration.

A short time ago, I urged my colleague Molly Metzger to plan and organize a conference on *inclusive housing*, which is her primary area of study. Molly is a great contributor on our faculty and in the community. Her applied research agenda is engaged and productive. She is an effective and popular teacher. Molly was joined by Hank Webber as co-editor and conference organizer. Hank is the executive vice chancellor and chief administrative officer at Washington University. His career is a very productive mixture of university administration, urban scholarship, and community development. In their hands, it was not surprising that Inclusive Housing: A Symposium for Policy Action, held at Washington University in St. Louis, was a highly successful event. The Center for Social Development in the Brown School of Social Work was the major organizer and sponsor, along with many other partners. The center also provided editorial support for revisions of the conference papers, which now make up this book. Chris Leiker very capably handled the copy-editing.

The authors in *Facing Segregation* are experienced and highly regarded. The book is noteworthy for its emphasis on application with a vision of social change. This is not a book that focuses only on how bad things are (we always have many of these). Instead, the editors and authors aim more ambitiously, as the title shows. The book offers reasoning, concepts, strategies, and empirical evidence regarding potential solutions. *Facing Segregation* illuminates constructive pathways forward.

As a nation, and as residents in our own communities, we cannot afford to accept the sharply segregated residence patterns in much of America today. The editors and authors of this volume believe we can do better, and most of them are devoting their careers to this goal. They know that the challenge is huge. They know that innovation and knowledge building are always long hauls, and successes are hard to achieve. Yet they are steady and determined in their work, making notable progress. In *Facing Segregation*, the authors explain what they have learned about achieving inclusive housing and offer evidence-based implications for more effective policies and practices.

Michael Sherraden
George Warren Brown Distinguished University Professor
Washington University in St. Louis
September 17, 2017

Notes

1. For example, Raj Chetty and Nathaniel Hendren, *The Impacts of Neighborhoods on Intergenerational Mobility: Childhood Exposure Effects and County-Level Estimates* (Cambridge, MA: Harvard University and National Bureau of Economic Research, 2015).

2. Richard Rothstein, *The Color of Law: A Forgotten History of How Our Government Segregated America* (New York: W.W. Norton, 2017).

ACKNOWLEDGMENTS

A conference hosted by the Center for Social Development (CSD) at Washington University in St. Louis was a critical step in launching this book project. We are so grateful for the support of CSD and the participation of all who attended. Participants included most of the contributing authors, as well as Paul Brophy, Bryan Greene, Sandra Moore, Luke Tate, and Rev. Starsky Wilson. Thanks to each of you for helping us to get this project off the ground.

Jodie Lloyd and Ryan Haas both contributed to the introductory chapter; thank you for crucial help at the eleventh hour. Special thanks as well to Chris Leiker, our steadfast editor at CSD, and Dana Bliss, our editor at Oxford University Press. It has been a pleasure working with both of you!

This book would not have been possible without funding from several entities at Washington University in St. Louis. Thanks to Michael Sherraden at CSD, Washington University Provost Holden Thorp, and former Brown School Dean Eddie Lawlor for supporting our work.

Finally, we wish to acknowledge those on the front lines of fair housing: tenants, organizers, lawyers, public servants, and others. In our home base of St. Louis, some of these advocates—especially Glenn Burleigh, Kalila Jackson, and Elisabeth Risch at the Metropolitan St. Louis Equal Housing and Opportunity Council—have been critical thought partners in recent years. We are inspired by your work, and we strive to do work that might complement yours in powerful ways.

ABOUT THE EDITORS

Molly W. Metzger is assistant professor at the Brown School at Washington University in St. Louis. She received her BA in women's studies from Carleton College in 2001 and her PhD in human development and social policy from Northwestern University in 2012. Metzger's research focuses on public policy, structural racism, and residential segregation in the United States. She is a community-engaged scholar, working with housing advocates in the St. Louis region to bring an evidence-based approach to activism.

Henry S. (Hank) Webber is executive vice chancellor and chief administrative officer at Washington University in St. Louis. He is also professor of practice at the Brown School and the School of Architecture and Urban Design. Mr. Webber oversees a wide variety of administrative and external affairs functions with combined budgets of over $400 million annually. Mr. Webber also teaches courses on topics including community development, health policy, strategic management, and social welfare policy. His research and writing center on community development, mixed-income housing, racial and economic segregation, and the role of anchor institutions in urban development.

CONTRIBUTORS

Sarah L. Coffin, PhD, is associate professor and director of the Urban Planning and Development program in the School of Social Work at Saint Louis University. Her research focuses on the intersection of economic development and environmental planning in postindustrial cities as well as on framing redevelopment for the benefit of distressed communities.

Lance Freeman, PhD, is a professor and director of the Urban Planning program at Columbia University. His research focuses on affordable housing, gentrification, ethnic and racial stratification in housing markets, and the relationship between the built environment and well-being. He teaches courses on community development, housing policy, and research methods.

Mark L. Joseph is the Leona Bevis and Marguerite Haynam Associate Professor of Community Development in the Jack, Joseph, and Morton Mandel School of Applied Social Sciences, and founding director, National Initiative on Mixed-Income Communities, at Case Western Reserve University.

Jason Q. Purnell is associate professor in the Brown School at Washington University in St. Louis. He is trained in applied psychology and public health and focuses his research on health equity, social determinants of health, and community mobilization for population health improvement.

Richard Rothstein is the author of *The Color of Law: A Forgotten History of How Our Government Segregated America* (2017), from which the chapter in this volume was adapted. He is a research associate of the Economic Policy Institute, where he works on issues involving education and race.

Barbara Sard, Vice President for Housing Policy at the Center on Budget and Policy Priorities, is a leading expert on the Housing Choice Voucher program, rental assistance, and housing and welfare policy. She has served as Senior Advisor for Rental Assistance to Secretary of Housing and Urban Development Shaun Donovan.

Michael Sherraden is the George Warren Brown Distinguished University Professor and founding director of the Center for Social Development at the Brown School of Social Work at Washington University in St. Louis. In testing innovations to improve social and economic well-being, he has defined asset building as a new policy direction and contributed to the creation of AmeriCorps.

Josh Silver is senior advisor at the National Community Reinvestment Coalition (NCRC). He has more than 25 years of experience in housing and community development, including 19 years as Vice President of Research and Policy with NCRC as well as doing housing-market analysis and program evaluation with the Urban Institute.

Todd Swanstrom is E. Desmond Lee Professor of Community Collaboration and Public Policy Administration at the University of Missouri–St. Louis. A specialist in urban politics and public policy, Swanstrom has authored and edited several books. His current research focuses on neighborhood change in older industrial cities.

William F. Tate IV is dean of the Graduate School, vice provost for Graduate Education, and Edward Mallinckrodt Distinguished University Professor at Washington University in St. Louis. His research interests include social stratification, community psychology, and epidemiological and geospatial approaches to the study of education and health.

John Taylor is president and CEO of the National Community Reinvestment Coalition. A recipient of numerous awards, he has served on several national boards, including the Consumer Advisory Council of the Federal Reserve Bank Board, the Fannie Mae Housing Impact Division, and the Freddie Mac Housing Advisory Board.

Philip D. Tegeler is the executive director of Poverty & Race Research Action Council, a civil-rights policy organization based in Washington, DC. The Council's mission is to promote research-based advocacy on structural inequality issues, with a focus on the causes and consequences of housing and school segregation.

ABBREVIATIONS

AFFH	affirmatively furthering fair housing
AFH	Assessment of Fair Housing
AMI	area median income
CRA	Community Reinvestment Act
CSD	Center for Social Development
ECAP	ethnically concentrated area of poverty
FHA	Fair Housing Act
FMR	Fair Market Rent
HCV	housing choice voucher
HUD	US Department of Housing and Urban Development
ICP	Inclusive Communities Project
IRS	Internal Revenue Service
LIHTC	Low-Income Housing Tax Credit
LMI	low and moderate income
MTO	Moving to Opportunity
NAACP	National Association for the Advancement of Colored People
NCRC	National Community Reinvestment Coalition
OCC	Office of the Comptroller of the Currency
PHA	public housing agency
PILOT	payment in lieu of taxes
PWA	Public Works Administration
Q&A	question and answer
QAP	Qualified Allocation Plan
RCAP	racially concentrated area of poverty
SAFMR	Small Area Fair Market Rent
SEMAP	Section 8 Management Assessment Program
SES	socioeconomic status
TIF	tax increment financing

Facing Segregation

PART I

Facing the Causes and Consequences of Segregation

1

Segregation
A THREAT TO AMERICANS' SHARED GOALS
Molly W. Metzger and Henry S. Webber

> Discrimination and segregation have long permeated much of American life; they now threaten the future of every American.
>
> This deepening racial division is not inevitable. The movement apart can be reversed. Choice is still possible. Our principal task is to define that choice and to press for a national resolution.
>
> To pursue our present course will involve the continuing polarization of the American community and, ultimately, the destruction of basic democratic values.
>
> The alternative is not blind repression or capitulation to lawlessness. It is the realization of common opportunities for all within a single society.
>
> This alternative will require a commitment to national action—compassionate, massive, and sustained, backed by the resources of the most powerful and the richest nation on this earth. From every American it will require new attitudes, new understanding, and, above all, new will.
>
> —Report of the National Advisory Commission on Civil Disorders[1]

As of this writing, 54 years have passed since President Lyndon B. Johnson signed the Civil Rights Act of 1964.[2] The legislation marked a major victory for the civil rights movement, but it was incomplete: the 1964 act failed to address the movement's central goal of open housing, and it failed to end racial discrimination in housing laws and real estate practices. Presidential support for opening housing was withheld for several years. Only after the uprisings—the so-called urban riots that occurred in dozens of cities during the summer of 1967—the assassination of Dr. Martin Luther King Jr., and the civil disorder that followed his assassination did President Johnson express support for open housing by signing the Fair Housing Act into law (Sugrue 2018).[3] The act outlawed discrimination on the basis of race, religion, or national origin in the rental, sale, or financing of housing. Subsequent amendments added gender, disability, and families with children to the list of classes protected from discrimination (National Low Income Housing Coalition 2014).

Since 1968, the Fair Housing Act has served as a critical tool for dismantling the structures that divide people in the United States into separate and unequal neighborhoods. Yet despite the gains won with the act, US metropolitan areas remain segregated along the lines of race, ethnicity, and social class. It is not unusual for metro areas to have racial dissimilarity values above 70—that is, more than 70 percent of the white households in such an area would have to move for whites to be perfectly interspersed among people of color (Frey n.d.). In recent decades, however, many metro areas have seen modest declines in racial segregation (Massey 2015). Economic segregation, not only the concentration of poverty but also—and particularly—the self-segregation of affluent households, continues to be high and is rising (Reardon and Bischoff 2011; Reeves 2017).

Now 50 years after the uprisings that preceded the 1968 Fair Housing Act, we see a renewed pattern of protest across US cities. In the wake of police killings of black men, women, and children, the movement has been reborn in Ferguson, Missouri; Baltimore, Maryland; Minneapolis, Minnesota; New York City, and elsewhere. This movement has brought us to a new crossroads with regard to racial and economic justice in the United States. The choices before us resemble the scenarios identified in the 1968 Kerner Commission report: one choice leads further down the current path of polarization and inequity, and the alternative is to pursue a path toward "the realization of common opportunities for all within a single society" (National Advisory Commission on Civil Disorders 1968, 1).

This book presents a set of policy solutions aimed at the commission's single-society alternative, focusing specifically on addressing the interlinked problems of racial and economic segregation in housing. Our goal in editing this book has been, quite simply, to contribute to making the United States a country where people live together in neighborhoods that are racially and economically diverse. This introductory chapter (alongside the other chapters in Part I of this book) articulates our motivations for pursuing this long-fought goal of housing justice. We argue that the threat posed by our segregated living patterns is not limited to households in high-poverty, low-resource areas; segregation affects us all, individually and collectively. This introduction proceeds with a demographic snapshot of US metro areas, paying attention to continuity and change since the 1960s. We then discuss the ways in which segregation undermines the shared goals of economic prosperity, democracy, and equality of opportunity. We conclude the introduction by describing the unique contributions of this edited volume, which focuses on policy solutions to segregation in the United States.

US Demographics and Living Patterns from the 1960s to Now

RACIAL, ETHNIC, AND ECONOMIC COMPOSITION

In the more than 50 years since the passage of the Fair Housing Act, the population of the United States has become significantly more diverse. In 1965, 84 percent of Americans were white, 11 percent were black, 4 percent were Latino, less than 1 percent were Asian American, and less than 1 percent were from all other groups combined (Pew Research Center 2015a).[4] By 2015, 62 percent were white, 12 percent were black, 18 percent were Latino, 6 percent were Asian American, and 2 percent were from all other groups combined (Pew Research Center 2015a).

As the country's racial and ethnic makeup has evolved, the distributions of income and wealth have become significantly more polarized. Income inequality in the United States is high compared with levels in other Western countries and has risen at a sharp rate since 1970 (Piketty and Saez 2014). Nearly 50 percent of annual earnings in the United States accrue to the top 10 percent of earners (Piketty and Saez 2014). Wealth inequality remains even more extreme. The wealthiest 10 percent of households now control more than 70 percent of assets in the United States, and that figure has also risen steadily since 1970 (Piketty and Saez 2014). The 10 percent of households at the bottom of the wealth distribution provide a point of contrast. From 1963 to 2016, they moved from having zero assets, on average, to being $1,000 in debt. Moreover, wealth inequality remains starkly racialized: as of 2016, the median wealth held by white households was more than seven times that held by black households and more than five times that held by Latino households (McKernan et al. 2015).

RESIDENTIAL SEGREGATION

During the decades succeeding passage of the Fair Housing Act, black–white segregation has decreased modestly in some metropolitan areas and increased in others (Logan and Stults 2011), while still others have showed patterns of "stalled integration" (Rugh and Massey 2014, 219). By 2010, a third of all African Americans in US cities lived in communities that were hypersegregated by race (Massey 2015).[5] The segregation of metropolitan Hispanic and Asian Americans also increased over the period from 1970 through 2010. The average Latino lived in a census tract that was 27 percent Latino in 1970 and 47 percent Latino in 2010; the average Asian American lived in a census tract that was 9 percent Asian American in 1970 and 20 percent Asian American in 2010 (Massey 2015, 580).

One trend of the past 15 years has been a movement of high-income suburban residents to previously distressed urban cores and the displacement of poorer minority populations from central-city communities to inner-ring suburban neighborhoods (Hyra 2012). This reverse migration of white professionals to city centers has shifted the pattern of racially segregated geography while intensifying the racial wealth gap. Socioeconomic disparities by race were particularly aggravated by the Great Recession and the implosion of the housing, labor, and stock markets that caused it. Overall, minority net worth was disproportionately damaged by the ensuing foreclosures and job losses (Pfeffer, Danziger, and Schoeni 2013).

Moreover, where wealthy communities have increasingly concentrated in urban cores, they have consolidated access to the improved urban features made possible by the increased tax base associated with their residence there: a process that some have characterized as "opportunity hoarding" (Reeves 2017, 13). Between 2000 and 2009, income segregation in US metropolitan areas grew more rapidly than it had in several decades (Spader et al. 2017).

Reversal of white flight and the subsequent consolidation of economic power in wealthy urban enclaves have made it so that economic growth in cities no longer correlates with cities' population growth. Many people disadvantaged by the Great Recession and growing income inequality have also been deterred by the cost of living in urban areas where wages are highest and economic opportunities most accessible; such costs discourage them from relocating in those areas (Schleicher 2017). At a macroeconomic level, these patterns have generated economic segregation between and within US regions. High-income housing markets in particular have prevented the kind of labor migration to cities that often occurred during the previous urban booms (Ganong and Shoag 2017).

Therefore, despite the increasing racial and ethnic diversity of the US population as a whole, significant barriers continue to impede the successful integration of those diverse populations at the neighborhood level. Moreover, if we widen the lens through which segregation is assessed, considering not just patterns within metro areas but also patterns between metro areas, racial segregation and economic segregation both appear to be increasing (Lichter, Parisi, and Taquino 2015).

Segregation Harms Us All

The case for anti-segregation policy action often focuses on segregation's impact on the poor and people of color. It is certainly true that segregation brings fundamental disadvantages to these communities in terms of physical and mental health, education, income, and wealth. Ta-Nehisi Coates (2014, para. 12) characterizes housing discrimination, the driver of segregation, as follows:

> If you sought to advantage one group of Americans and disadvantage another, you could scarcely choose a more graceful method than housing discrimination. Housing determines access to transportation, green spaces,

decent schools, decent food, decent jobs, and decent services. Housing affects your chances of being robbed and shot as well as your chances of being stopped and frisked. And housing discrimination is as quiet as it is deadly. It can be pursued through violence and terrorism, but it doesn't need it. Housing discrimination is hard to detect, hard to prove, and hard to prosecute. Even today most people believe that Chicago is the work of organic sorting, as opposed segregationist social engineering. Housing segregation is the weapon that mortally injures, but does not bruise.

All of this is true, and the harms of segregation do not end with the list that Coates provides. Segregation harms us all, not just those residing in disadvantaged communities. It stifles economic growth in our metropolitan areas, threatens the functioning of our democracy, and calls into question fundamental ideals—such as the principle of equality of opportunity—that contribute to many Americans' definition of what makes our country great.

SEGREGATION STIFLES ECONOMIC GROWTH

A recent set of studies demonstrates the harm that segregation may present to the economies of US metro areas. Some of the strongest evidence comes from work by Huiping Li, Harrison Campbell, and Steven Fernandez (2013), who found that racial segregation is negatively associated with economic growth in the United States. Across a number of time frames, geographies, and statistical models, they found that racial segregation emerges as a consistent, negative predictor of annual growth in per capita income (Li, Campbell, and Fernandez 2013).

Gregory Acs and colleagues (2017) found mixed results regarding the connection between segregation and economic trends within commuting zones, although one result suggests that economic segregation predicts household median income for whites as well as for blacks. Chris Benner and Manuel Pastor (2015a) focused not on growth rates but on sustained growth, which they measured as the length of growth spells within regions. Their findings suggest that greater economic inequality within a region is associated with shorter growth spells, and they identified some evidence that racial segregation also shortens periods of growth. In short, research appears to suggest that greater levels of regional equality and integration foster stronger and more sustained growth.

SEGREGATION UNDERMINES DEMOCRATIC PROCESS

Residential segregation also threatens the functioning of our democracy. The United States is fragmented not only along lines of race, ethnicity, and socioeconomic status; our living patterns are increasingly divided along lines of political ideology and political party (Pew Research Center 2015b). In 1976, roughly a quarter of Americans lived in a "landslide" county—that is, a county in which a presidential candidate won the ticket by more than 20 percentage points (Bishop 2008, 9). Over 50 percent of Americans now reside in such counties (Benner and Pastor 2015b). Increasingly surrounded by like-minded individuals, we are less likely to deliberate and more likely to rely on ideology. Sheryll Cashin (2017, 3–4) observes: "The average Republican congressperson represents a district that mirrors the overwhelmingly white America of 1972, while the average Democrat represents a district that looks like the projected diversity of America in 2030. The end result is a clash of distinctly different worldviews. . . . In a segregated nation where many people and the leaders who represent them get little practice at pluralism, democracy is broken."

Homogeneity breeds extremism (Sunstein 2009). As such, the shift toward politically homogenous living patterns poses a threat to both major political parties and to the country as a whole. The election of Donald Trump—a polarizing figure who emerged from a polarized electorate—is a case in point.

Benner and Pastor (2015b, 14) observe that complex problems, such as those facing our metropolitan areas, are best solved by "diverse and dynamic epistemic communities." In a landscape in which the political left and right interact less and less, we are moving further from such a community.

SEGREGATION CALLS INTO QUESTION A SHARED AMERICAN IDEAL

American identity is fragmented. Americans are sharply divided in our attitudes toward issues fundamental to who we are as a nation, issues such as our country's increasing diversity, the role of immigration in society, and the importance of religion in daily life (Associated Press–NORC Center for Public Affairs Research 2017). Yet one issue that we all tend to agree on is the goal of equal opportunity.

A recent poll suggested that 86 percent of Americans agreed with the statement, "Our society should do what is necessary to make sure that everyone has an equal opportunity to succeed" (Pew Research Center n.d.). Regardless of their political party, gender, age, race, education, income, and religion, Americans endorse the statement at consistently high rates. Since 1987, endorsement of the item has never dropped below 75 percent for any group and is typically closer to 90 percent. And yet segregation, much of which is rooted in governmental action, undercuts this fundamental American ideal.

As detailed by Richard Rothstein and others in this volume, our current patterns of racial and economic segregation are direct results of public policy decisions. These divisions have serious implications for equality of opportunity in this country. Racial and economic segregation have been identified as significant predictors of upward mobility within American commuting zones (Chetty et al. 2014; Sharkey and Graham 2013). The evidence is clear: the more segregated the region, the lower the level of intergenerational social mobility.

The belief that the United States is the land of opportunity, and the fact that opportunity remains sharply unequal across neighborhoods, may create cognitive dissonance for Americans, especially white and affluent Americans. The knowledge of unearned privilege can lead to two very different responses. One possible response is the denial or downplaying of the injustice (DiAngelo 2011). Another possible response is acknowledgment of injustice and action toward a fairer society. It is our deep hope that this volume inspires the latter.

Outline of the Book

The book complements other works on segregation by focusing explicitly on policy solutions to racial and economic segregation. Contributors consider both *mobility strategies*, which are designed to help families move to higher-opportunity areas, and *investment strategies*, which are intended to make every neighborhood an opportunity area (Crowley and Pelletiere 2012; powell and Menendian 2018).

PART I: FACING THE CAUSES AND CONSEQUENCES OF SEGREGATION

The chapters in Part I, "Facing the Causes and Consequences of Segregation," document key points in the history of segregation and provide frameworks for understanding its evolving role in the United States of the twenty-first century. Drilling down into segregation and concentrated poverty, these chapters analyze the historical and contemporary determinants of their dynamics, including pro-suburbanization policies, racialized politics, and issues of social psychology. The chapters also demonstrate the need for policy action and the delineation of the effects of segregation on health outcomes, educational attainment, rates of employment, and civic engagement.

Chapters by Richard Rothstein and Lance Freeman provide complementary assessments of the history of segregation in the United States. In "*De facto* Segregation: A National Myth" (Chapter 2), Rothstein examines policies that purposefully contributed to segregation but have never been remedied because policymakers are unfamiliar with their history and the obligations they entail. Believing that segregation is *de facto*—that is, resulting mostly from private prejudice and income differences—policymakers have failed to consider aggressive initiatives that are constitutionally required to remedy state-sponsored *de jure* segregation. In "The Siting Dilemma: Race and the Location of Federal Housing Projects" (Chapter 3), Freeman traces a similar history: from the Great Depression until the 1970s, housing assistance in the form of the Public Housing Program was planned and developed in a way that reinforced existing patterns of residential segregation by race. Freeman chronicles black responses to this program and considers the implications of those responses for past, present, and future public policy. In Chapter 4, "The Enduring Significance of Segregation," Jason Purnell uses examples from the St. Louis metropolitan area to detail how segregation has affected population health. His analysis draws from social psychology and other fields to explore obstacles to integration.

PART II: THE POLICY AGENDA

The chapters in Part II provide constructive critiques and proposals for reform of policies implicated in maintaining segregation. Identifying specific policy alternatives, contributors map paths for reform of both federal efforts and local strategies; their goal is to identify, within the current policy landscape, a package of innovations to reduce segregation.

A timely chapter by Philip Tegeler, "Affirmatively Furthering Fair Housing and the *Inclusive Communities Project* Case: Bringing the Fair Housing Act into the Twenty-First Century" (Chapter 5), focuses on the regulatory history of the Affirmatively Furthering Fair Housing provision of the Fair Housing Act. This provision has been consistently interpreted by the courts as the act's pro-integration clause, requiring the US Department of Housing and Urban Development and its grantees to take affirmative action to promote residential integration.

Chapters by Barbara Sard, John Taylor and Josh Silver, and Mark Joseph provide a vision for a major federal program or policy. In Chapter 6, Sard provides a targeted reform agenda for the Housing Choice Voucher program, which helps 2.1 million low-income households pay for modestly priced, decent-quality homes in the private market. This chapter discusses ways in which state and local housing authorities can incentivize better locational choices by voucher recipients. In Chapter 7, Taylor and Silver focus on the Community Reinvestment Act, a federal policy intended to promote fair lending toward the goals of homeownership and business development. Taylor and Silver provide a vision for improving enforcement of the act. In "Promoting Poverty Deconcentration and Racial Desegregation through Mixed-Income Development" (Chapter 8), Mark Joseph examines the achievement, limitations, and outlook of mixed-income development, weighing the approach's effectiveness as an anti-poverty strategy and suggesting targets for program improvement.

In "Market-Savvy Housing and Community Development Policy: Grappling with the Equity-Efficiency Trade-off" (Chapter 9), Todd Swanstrom argues that the gentrification of "middle" neighborhoods represents as much opportunity as threat. Among other policies, this chapter proposes that housing subsidies should be targeted to these high-opportunity places in order to guarantee affordable workforce housing while land prices are still relatively low.

Sarah Coffin examines tax increment financing (TIF) in Chapter 10. TIF is often offered as a politically attractive solution to complicated development scenarios in underresourced urban neighborhoods—not, however, without controversy over the ultimate beneficiaries of TIF projects. Coffin's chapter explores ways in which the tool can be used to promote inclusionary development practices and support creative affordable housing strategies.

Finally, the chapter by William F. Tate IV, "Beyond Education Triage: Building Brain Regimes in Metropolitan America" (Chapter 11), explores the important link between housing and education. Many social scientists have argued that, for students experiencing segregation, high-quality educational opportunities are linked to better life-course outcomes. Education can therefore be viewed as a potential intervention to address segregation. This chapter asserts that the predominant approach to educational reform is analogous to triage in medicine but that the failures of such triage-based policies are reinforcing segregation. Instead, Tate argues, we need to develop a different approach to education and youth development, an approach that takes an intergenerational perspective on education achievement, attainment, and youth development in our nation's most segregated communities.

We close the volume with a chapter focusing on recommendations for action to create a more just housing policy. Such efforts are challenging. It will take strong action by governments at all levels and by organizations, including organizations represented by some of the contributors to this volume. Our hope is that readers will weigh the arguments provided by the contributing authors and consider (or reconsider) their own strategies for contributing to housing policy solutions that can reduce segregation.

Notes

1. National Advisory Commission on Civil Disorders (1968, 1).
2. Civil Rights Act of 1964, Pub L. No. 88–352, 78 Stat. 241 (1964).
3. Fair Housing Act of 1968, Pub. L. No. 90-284, title VIII, 82 Stat. 81 (1969) (codified as amended at 42 U.S.C. §§ 3533, 3535, 3601–3631 (2012)).
4. Michael Omi (1997) and others have described the inconsistency and inadequacy of standard racial and ethnic groupings. We use terms such as "white," "black," "Latino," and "Asian American" in this introduction while acknowledging that these terms oversimplify a more complex and dynamic mix of ethnicities.
5. According to Douglas Massey (2015), a metropolitan area is *hypersegregated* if at least four out of five spatial measures of racial segregation show that the area is highly segregated.

References

Acs, Gregory, Rolf Pendall, Mark Treskon, and Amy Khare. 2017. *The Cost of Segregation: National Trends and the Case of Chicago, 1990–2010*. Research Report. Washington, DC: Urban Institute. http://www.urban.org/sites/default/files/ publication/89201/the_cost_of_segregation_final.pdf.

Associated Press–NORC Center for Public Affairs Research. 2017. "The American Identity: Points of Pride, Conflicting Views, and a Distinct Culture." Report. Chicago: Associated Press–NORC Center for Public Affairs Research. http://www.apnorc.org/projects/Pages/HTML%20Reports/points-of-pride-conflicting-views-and-a-distinct-culture.aspx.

Benner, Chris, and Manuel Pastor. 2015a. "Brother, Can You Spare Some Time? Sustaining Prosperity and Social Inclusion in America's Metropolitan Regions." *Urban Studies* 52 (7): 1339–56. doi:10.1177/0042098014549127.

Benner, Chris, and Manuel Pastor. 2015b. *Equity, Growth, and Community: What the Nation Can Learn from America's Metro Areas*. Oakland: University of California Press.

Bishop, Bill. 2008. *The Big Sort: Why the Clustering of Like-Minded America Is Tearing Us Apart*. New York: Houghton Mifflin.

Cashin, Sheryll. 2017. "Integration as a Means of Restoring Democracy and Opportunity." Cambridge, MA: Joint Center for Housing Studies at Harvard University. http://www.jchs.harvard.edu/sites/jchs.harvard.edu/files/a_shared_future_integration_restoring_democracy_0.pdf.

Chetty, Raj, Nathaniel Hendren, Patrick Kline, and Emmanuel Saez. 2014. "Where Is the Land of Opportunity? The Geography of Intergenerational Mobility in the United States." *Quarterly Journal of Economics* 129 (4): 1553–1623. doi:10.1093/qje/qju022.

Coates, Ta-Nehisi. 2014. "This Town Needs a Better Class of Racist." *The Atlantic*, May 1. https://www.theatlantic.com/politics/archive/2014/05/This-Town-Needs-A-Better-Class-Of-Racist/361443/.

Crowley, Sheila, and Danilo Pelletiere. 2012. *Affordable Housing Dilemma: The Preservation vs. Mobility Debate*. Report. Washington, DC: National Low Income Housing Coalition. http://nlihc.org/library/other/periodic/dilemma.

DiAngelo, Robin. 2011. "White Fragility." *International Journal of Critical Pedagogy* 3 (3): 54–70.

Frey, William H. n.d. "New Racial Segregation Measures for Large Metropolitan Areas: Analysis of the 1990–2010 Decennial Censuses, Race Segregation for Largest Metro Areas (Population over 500,000)." Accessed February 5, 2018. http://censusscope.org/2010Census/Segregation.html.

Ganong, Peter, and Daniel Shoag. 2017. "Why Has Regional Income Convergence in the U.S. Declined?" *Journal of Urban Economics* 102: 76–90. doi:10.1016/j.jue.2017.07.002.

Hyra, Derek S. 2012. "Conceptualizing the New Urban Renewal: Comparing the Past to the Present." *Urban Affairs Review* 48 (4): 498–527. doi:10.1177/1078087411434905.

Li, Huiping, Harrison Campbell, and Steven Fernandez. 2013. "Residential Segregation, Spatial Mismatch and Economic Growth across US Metropolitan Areas." *Urban Studies* 50 (13): 2642–60. doi:10.1177/0042098013477697.

Lichter, Daniel T., Domenico Parisi, and Michael C. Taquino. 2015. "Toward a New Macro-Segregation? Decomposing Segregation within and between Metropolitan

Cities and Suburbs." *American Sociological Review* 80 (4): 843–73. doi:10.1177/0003122415588558.

Logan, John R., and Brian J. Stults. 2011. "The Persistence of Segregation in the Metropolis: New Findings from the 2010 Census." Census Brief, March 24. Providence, RI: Brown University, US2010 Project. https://s4.ad.brown.edu/Projects/Diversity/Data/Report/report2.pdf.

Massey, Douglas S. 2015. "The Legacy of the 1968 Fair Housing Act." *Sociological Forum* 30 (Suppl. 1): 571–88. doi:10.1111/socf.12178.

McKernan, Signe-Mary, Caroline Ratcliffe, C. Eugene Steuerle, Caleb Quakenbush, and Emma Kalish. 2015. "Nine Charts about Wealth Inequality in America." Accessed January 1, 2018. http://datatools.urban.org/Features/wealth-inequality-charts/.

National Advisory Commission on Civil Disorders. 1968. *Report of the National Advisory Commission on Civil Disorders*. Otto Kerner, Chairman. New York: New York Times Company.

National Low Income Housing Coalition. 2014. "40 Years Ago: Fair Housing Act Amended to Prohibit Discrimination on Basis of Sex." Accessed February 5, 2018. http://nlihc.org/article/40-years-ago-fair-housing-act-amended-prohibit-discrimination-basis-sex.

Omi, Michael. 1997. "Racial Identity and the State: The Dilemmas of Classification." *Law and Inequality* 15 (1): 7–23.

Pew Research Center. n.d. "American Values Survey: Question Database." Accessed January 1, 2018. http://www.people-press.org/values-questions/q40c/society-should-ensure-all-equal-opportunity-to-succeed.

Pew Research Center. 2015a. *Modern Immigration Wave Brings 59 Million to U.S., Driving Population Growth and Change Through 2065: Views of Immigration's Impact on U.S. Society Mixed*. Report. Washington, DC: Pew Research Center. http://www.pewhispanic.org/files/2015/09/2015-09-28_modern-immigration-wave_REPORT.pdf.

Pew Research Center. 2015b. *Political Polarization in the American Public: How Increasing Ideological Uniformity and Partisan Antipathy Affect Politics, Compromise and Everyday Life*. Report. Washington, DC: Pew Research Center. http://www.people-press.org/2014/06/12/political-polarization-in-the-american-public/.

Pfeffer, Fabian T., Sheldon Danziger, and Robert F. Schoeni. 2013. "Wealth Disparities before and after the Great Recession." *Annals of the American Academy of Political and Social Science* 650: 98–123. doi:10.1177/0002716213497452.

Piketty, Thomas, and Emmanuel Saez. 2014. "Inequality in the Long Run." *Science* 344 (6186): 838–43. doi:10.1126/science.1251936.

powell, John A., and Stephen Menendian. 2018. "Opportunity Communities: Overcoming the Debate over Mobility versus Place-Based Strategies." In *The Fight for Fair Housing: Causes, Consequences and Future Implications of the 1968 Federal Fair Housing Act*, edited by Gregory D. Squires, 207–27. New York: Routledge.

Reardon, Sean F., and Kendra Bischoff. 2011. "Income Inequality and Income Segregation." *American Journal of Sociology* 116 (4): 1092–1153. doi:10.1086/657114.

Reeves, Richard V. 2017. *Dream Hoarders: How the American Upper Middle Class Is Leaving Everyone Else in the Dust, Why That Is a Problem, and What to Do about It*. Washington, DC: Brookings Institution.

Rugh, Jacob S., and Douglas S. Massey. 2014. "Segregation in Post-Civil Rights America: Stalled Integration or End of the Segregated Century?" *Du Bois Review: Social Science Research on Race* 11 (2): 205–32. doi:10.1017/S1742058X13000180.

Schleicher, David. 2017. "Stuck! The Law and Economics of Residential Stagnation." *Yale Law Journal* 127 (1): 78–154.

Sharkey, Patrick, and Bryan Graham. 2013. *Mobility and the Metropolis: How Communities Factor into Economic Mobility*. Economic Mobility Project Report. Washington, DC: Pew Charitable Trusts.

Spader, Jonathan, Shannon Rieger, Christopher Herbert, and Jennifer Molinsky. 2017. *Fostering Inclusion in American Neighborhoods*. Report. Cambridge, MA: Joint Center for Housing Studies at Harvard University. http://www.jchs.harvard.edu/sites/jchs.harvard.edu/files/a_shared_future_fostering_inclusion.pdf.

Sugrue, Thomas J. 2018. "From Jim Crow to Fair Housing." In *The Fight for Fair Housing: Causes, Consequences and Future Implications of the 1968 Federal Fair Housing Act*, edited by Gregory D. Squires, 14–27. New York: Routledge.

Sunstein, Cass R. 2009. *Going to Extremes: How Like Minds Unite and Divide*. New York: Oxford University Press.

2

De Facto Segregation*
A NATIONAL MYTH
Richard Rothstein

The Fair Housing Act of 1968 prohibits discrimination in the sale or rental of housing,[1] and it requires jurisdictions receiving federal funds to affirmatively further the purposes of the act—primarily, the prevention of discrimination. It has been interpreted by the courts and the executive branch to prohibit acts or policies that, though not provably discriminatory, have an avoidable, discriminatory effect ("disparate impact").[2]

If fully enforced, the Fair Housing Act would permit anyone, regardless of race, ethnicity, or disability, to purchase or rent housing in any neighborhood where he or she can afford what the market offers. But even if fully enforced, the act could do little to dismantle the landscape of racial segregation that characterizes every metropolitan area in the United States. And segregation is deepening.

An important reason for the Federal Housing Act's inability to desegregate our metropolitan areas is the persistence of a myth that was initially perpetrated by the Supreme Court and subsequently adopted by policymakers, political leaders, and influential opinion makers. The myth is that the nation is characterized by *de facto* segregation, a result of private prejudices and forces for which there is no obvious remedy. This view was expressed succinctly in Justice Potter Stewart's 1974 concurring opinion in *Milliken v. Bradley*. In that case, the court ruled that the suburbs of Detroit bore no legal responsibility for segregation in the city proper. Justice Stewart wrote that black students were concentrated in the city, not spread throughout Detroit's suburbs, because of

---

*This chapter includes material previously published in articles by the author, including his book, *The Color of Law: A Forgotten History of How Our Government Segregated* America (New York: Liveright, 2017). Other articles are posted at http://www.epi.org/people/richard-rothstein/.

"unknown and perhaps unknowable factors such as in-migration, birth rates, economic changes, or cumulative acts of private racial fears."[3]

This has become the consensus view of American jurisprudence, a view reflected again in Chief Justice John Roberts's plurality opinion in the court's 2007 *Parents Involved* decision. There, the court prohibited school districts in Louisville, Kentucky, and Seattle, Washington, from accounting for a student's race as part of very modest school-integration plans. The chief justice acknowledged that racially identifiable housing patterns in these cities, leading to racial homogeneity of neighborhood schools, might result from what he termed "societal discrimination," but he said that the goal of remedying discrimination "not traceable to [government's] own actions" can never justify a constitutionally acceptable, racially conscious remedy.[4] "The distinction between [*de jure*] segregation by state action and [*de facto*] racial imbalance caused by other factors has been central to our jurisprudence. . . ." Later in the decision, the chief justice quoted approvingly from a previous court decision: "Where [racial imbalance] is a product not of state action but of private choices, it does not have constitutional implications."[5]

The view that we have a segregation of private choices and market forces was endorsed by dissenters in *Parents Involved*. Led by Justice Stephen Breyer, the dissenters agreed with the distinction Roberts made. Breyer mostly accepted that the isolation of black students in Louisville and Seattle was not the result of *de jure* segregation and thus that the school districts were not constitutionally required to desegregate. But he argued that school districts should be permitted to address *de facto* racial homogeneity by implementing voluntary integration plans, even if not constitutionally required to do so.

In June 2015, however, the possibility emerged that a belief in *de facto* segregation would become less central to our jurisprudence. A hint that more than private choices might have been involved came from a different court majority. In the remarkable majority opinion he wrote in *Texas Department of Housing and Community Affairs v. Inclusive Communities Project* (the "disparate impact" case), Justice Kennedy noted that the "vestiges [of *de jure* residential segregation by race] remain today, intertwined with the country's economic and social life."[6] "In the mid-20th century," he added, "various practices were followed, sometimes with governmental support, to encourage and maintain the separation of the races."[7] This passage was remarkable for two reasons.

First, the acknowledgment that the vestiges of *de jure* segregation persist opened the door to a much more aggressive desegregation policy than policymakers had previously entertained. Of course, the acknowledgment runs contrary to understandings of the Roberts, Rehnquist, and even the Burger courts, which saw unfortunate *de facto* residential segregation, not unconstitutional *de jure* residential segregation, in the United States of the late twentieth and early twenty-first centuries.

Second, having acknowledged the ongoing effects of *de jure* segregation, Justice Kennedy stepped back, grossly understating how powerful those effects remain. He did so because of what is apparently a naive understanding of our history; that naiveté is almost universally shared. In characterizing efforts to separate the races since the 1917 *Buchanan v. Warley* decision banned explicit racial zoning, Justice Kennedy misrepresented our history. The record shows that government did not merely *sometimes* support private discrimination but that federal, state, and local governments were leading actors, inextricably involved with and frequently directing racially motivated housing policy. The historical record also shows that the effects of these governmental policies have been powerful and that what remains is no mere vestige. But for unconstitutional residential race policy by government, we would not have the racially segregated landscape we experience today. Remedying unconstitutional race policy requires much more than the Fair Housing Act's prohibitions of ongoing discrimination, as the following discussion shows.

Public Housing

During the administrations of Franklin D. Roosevelt, Harry S Truman, and Dwight D. Eisenhower, public housing programs purposely concentrated African Americans in urban ghettos.

Civilian public housing began during the New Deal to address a great civilian housing shortage. Builders were then constructing homes only for the affluent. Intended to remedy the shortage by providing options for working- and middle-class white families, public housing became the most desirable housing available. The program was led by Interior Secretary and Public Works Administration (PWA) Director Harold Ickes, the most liberal member of Franklin Roosevelt's cabinet and "brain trust." In the 1920s, Ickes had been president of the Chicago branch of the National Association for the Advancement of Colored People. Alongside Eleanor Roosevelt, he argued in the administration for better treatment of African Americans.

Because of Ickes's efforts, African Americans occupied one-third of public housing units by 1940, and the government commitment to their housing needs was greater than ever. But Ickes also established a "neighborhood composition rule": public housing projects could not alter the racial composition of neighborhoods in which they were located. Projects in white areas could house only white tenants, those in black areas could house only black tenants, and projects in integrated neighborhoods could be integrated. African Americans were housed in 21 fully segregated projects and 6 technically mixed ones, but tenants in the mixed developments were segregated internally by building (Hirsch [1983] 1998, 14; 2000*a*; 2005, 59; Fishel 1964–65, 116; Miller 1964, 65).

The PWA established segregation in neighborhoods where there was no previous pattern. In the 1930s many urban neighborhoods housed both black and white (mostly immigrant) low-income families; workers of both races had to live within walking distance of downtown factories. Despite Ickes's composition rule, the PWA designated such integrated neighborhoods as either white or black. The public housing program made the government's designation self-fulfilling.

The first PWA project, Techwood Homes, opened in Atlanta, Georgia, in 1935. It was built on land cleared by demolishing the Flats, a low-income neighborhood that was adjacent to downtown and had been home to 1,600 families, about 450 of which were African American. Techwood replaced the neighborhood with 604 units for white families and made no provision for relocating those displaced. Some of the African Americans eventually found housing in a second public housing project that opened 3 years later on the city's west side and was for blacks only (Holliman 2016).

In 1934, the City of St. Louis, Missouri, proposed razing the DeSoto-Carr area, a racially integrated low-income tenement neighborhood on the near-north side. The population there was about 55 percent white and 45 percent black. The city said that it would construct a whites-only low-rise project for two-parent families with steady employment. When the PWA objected that the city's plan failed to accommodate African Americans, St. Louis proposed an additional blacks-only project that would be removed from the white one but also located in the previously integrated area. This met the federal government's conditions for nondiscriminatory funding, conditions insisted upon by liberals and civil rights leaders. Before the projects were built, however, the city revised its plans to increase the distance between the all-black and all-white projects. It designated the DeSoto-Carr project (renamed Carr Square Village) for African Americans only and located the all-white Clinton-Peabody project south of downtown (Heathcott 2011, 89–90, 94).[8]

In 1937, the United States Housing Act replaced the PWA as the federal government's public housing instrument.[9] As war production accelerated, the military also built worker housing. Segregation was the rule. At the insistence of the Ohio Congressional delegation, public housing constructed in Cleveland during the war was only open to white workers (Weaver [1948] 1967, 171–72). In Newark, New Jersey, three projects were reserved for whites and three others admitted blacks but assigned them to units in segregated sections (Weaver [1948] 1967, 203). In Jersey City, New Jersey, the housing authority demolished buildings in an integrated neighborhood to construct a new, whites-only project (Weaver [1948] 1967, 204). In New York City and Boston, federally sponsored public housing authorities built separate projects for white and black families (Bloom 2008; Vale 2002). Franklin Roosevelt's biographer, James MacGregor Burns (1970, 466), concluded that cities "in which prewar segregation was virtually unknown . . . received segregated housing, starting a new 'local custom' still in force many years later."

In San Francisco, the local housing authority constructed a massive project to house workers at the Hunter's Point Dry Dock and announced that units would be leased on a first-come, first-served basis, without regard for race. The Navy objected, the city bowed to the Navy's demand, and the project was segregated. Because the need for housing was more desperate among black migrant war workers than among their white counterparts (who had more private-housing choices), the policy resulted in many vacant units in the white sections while the housing needs of black workers (and later black veterans) were not met. This pattern—vacant units in white-designated projects with long waiting lists for black-designated projects—characterized public housing nationwide (Weaver [1948] 1967, 199–200).

The civilian housing shortage persisted through the war and in the years that followed, worsening as veterans returned and formed families. In 1949, newly elected President Truman proposed legislation for a massive public effort. Republican opponents of any public involvement in the private housing market attempted to saddle the Truman bill with a "poison pill" amendment prohibiting racial discrimination in public housing. They knew that southern Democrats would kill the legislation if the amendment were adopted, despite general Democratic support for public housing. The legislation's liberal proponents, led by Minnesota Senator Hubert Humphrey and Illinois Senator Paul Douglas, had to choose between enacting a segregated public housing program and enacting no program at all. On the Senate floor, Senator Douglas proclaimed: "I should like to point out to my Negro friends what a large amount of housing they will get under this act."[10] He continued: "I am ready to appeal to history and to time that it is in the best interest of the Negro race that we carry through this housing program as planned, rather than to put in the bill an amendment which will inevitably defeat it."[11] The Senate and House then considered and defeated proposed amendments that would have prohibited segregation and racial discrimination in federally funded public housing programs. As adopted, the 1949 Housing Act established a principle that local authorities design separate public housing projects for blacks and whites, and to segregate blacks and whites within purportedly integrated projects (Davies 1966, 108; Julian and Daniel 1989, 668–69; Hirsch 2000b, 400–401).[12]

With funds from the 1949 act, massive segregated projects were built nationwide. St. Louis, for example, constructed the Pruitt-Igoe towers in the early 1950s, with Pruitt designated for blacks and Igoe for whites. But by the time the projects opened in the mid-1950s, few whites were interested in urban public housing; as happened in so many other places, there were vacancies in Igoe but long waiting lists for Pruitt. Igoe was then opened to African Americans, and Pruitt-Igoe became an African American ghetto (Orfield 1981, 37–38; Gordon 2008, 99).

All of this was openly explicit racial policy. Racially motivated public housing segregation continued for years. It was *de jure* segregation even by the narrowest definition of state action. It played the leading role in creating black low-income neighborhoods, mostly in central cities. Most continue to exist, with barely a dent made in them by modest settlements in cases like *Gautreaux* in Chicago and *Thompson* in Baltimore.[13] In 1984, investigative reporters from the *Dallas Morning News* visited federally funded public housing projects in 47 cities nationwide. The reporters found that the nation's nearly 10 million public housing residents were almost always segregated by race, with facilities, amenities, services, and maintenance in every predominantly white-occupied project being superior to those in predominantly black-occupied projects (Flournoy and Rodrigue 1985).

Black families today do not live in these segregated concentrations by choice or because of demographic trends. They were herded there by the federal government, and the policy has never been remedied.

White Suburbanization

Why were the white tenants of public housing able to leave for the private housing market while the black tenants were not? Was this the result of private discrimination, or did the federal government prohibit African American families from suburbanizing as white families did?

A prohibition by the federal government was, in fact, the cause.

As the housing shortage eased and material was freed for civilian purposes after World War II, the federal government not only built public housing but also implemented a racially explicit policy to subsidize relocation of whites to suburbs and prohibit similar relocation of blacks. The Federal Housing Administration (FHA) recruited a nationwide cadre of mass-production builders to construct whites-only suburban developments. Banks advanced capital for 100 percent of the subdivisions' construction costs, and the FHA guaranteed those loans. A condition of the FHA guarantees was that builders must refuse sales to African Americans. FHA support was the only means by which large-scale production of suburban single-family homes could have been financed; without it, the suburbanization of metropolitan areas could not have taken place. By 1948, most housing in the United States was being constructed with this racially guided government financing. Federally segregated suburbs included places like Levittown on Long Island, New York; Lakewood, Panorama City, and Westlake (Daly City) in California; and subdivisions in numerous other metropolises between the coasts (Jackson 1985, 238; Larrabee 1948, 85–87; "Construction Financing" 1948, 12–13).

To obtain FHA support, builders' plans required approval of the FHA. The agency then determined the appraised values on which loans were made, the construction materials that could be used, the specifications of home design, and the neighborhood zoning restrictions to prohibit industry or commercial development that might reduce home values (Steinberg 1949; Checkoway 1980, 28). The FHA also deemed home values protected if deeds included clauses (restrictive covenants) prohibiting resale or rental to African Americans and if no African Americans resided in nearby neighborhoods; the FHA saw such residents as harbingers of future racial change (Clark 1938, 112).

The prohibition on African American residence in FHA-subsidized developments was systematic and nationwide. In a survey of 300 subdivisions developed from 1935 to 1947 in the suburban New York counties of Queens, Nassau, and Westchester, 83 percent of those with 75 or more units had racially restrictive covenants. Deeds typically included language like the following: "Whereas the Federal Housing Administration requires that the existing mortgages on the said premises be subject and subordinated to the said restrictions" (Dean 1947, 430). The racial provision followed, usually with an exception for domestic live-in servants, whose presence was not seen as a violation of the prohibition or as a factor that increased the risk of mortgage insurance (Dean 1947).

Following World War II, Stanford University recruited the renowned novelist Wallace Stegner to teach. Unable to find housing, he helped organize a 150-family cooperative to purchase a large tract adjoining the campus. The co-op hired architects and builders, but construction had barely begun when it learned that the FHA would withhold guarantees because three African American families were co-op members. Faced with a choice between expelling these members or disbanding the co-op, Stegner and other leaders chose the latter. The tract was then resold to a private developer who constructed a whites-only subdivision of homes with FHA-guaranteed mortgages and deeds prohibiting resales to African Americans (Stegner 1947; Benson 1996; Grier and Grier 1960; Friend and Lund [1974] 1989).

In addition to guaranteeing construction loans taken out by mass-production developers of all-white suburbs, the FHA also issued federal insurance for individual mortgages. A racially explicit policy governed appraisals of risk: mortgages for African Americans in white neighborhoods were deemed to be too risky for such insurance. Mortgages even to whites in neighborhoods that the FHA considered subject to possible future integration were considered to carry too high a risk. Although the Supreme Court's 1948 ruling in *Shelley v. Kraemer* barred courts from enforcing racial deed restrictions,[14] the restrictions themselves were deemed lawful for another 30 years, and the FHA knowingly continued, until the Fair Housing Act was adopted in 1968, to finance developers who constructed suburban developments that openly barred African Americans.[15]

This was *de jure* segregation. There was nothing *de facto* about it. The public housing policy that concentrated African Americans in urban ghettos and the federal suburbanization policy that subsidized white relocation to new communities were the primary means by which the segregated metropolitan landscape was created. These were not, as Justice Kennedy described them, private policies that sometimes had government support. They were federal policies with private participation.

Other Public Policies and Practices to Enforce Segregation

Numerous other federal, state, and local policies supported and contributed to a *de jure* system of residential racial segregation with equally explicit intent. Bank regulators from the Federal Reserve, Comptroller of the Currency, Office of Thrift Supervision, and other agencies knowingly approved "redlining" policies by banks and savings institutions, which denied loans to black families in white suburbs on the premise that the risk of underwriting those loans was too high. In most cases, the institutions used the same premise to deny mortgages for black families in black neighborhoods. Such denials led to the deterioration and ghettoization of those neighborhoods (US Commission on Civil Rights 1961). In 1961, Federal Reserve Board Chairman William McChesney Martin told the U.S. Commission on Civil Rights that "neither the Federal Reserve nor any other bank supervisory agency has—or should have—authority to compel officers and directors of any bank to make any loan against their judgment" (US Commission on Civil Rights 1961, 45). If a black family was denied a loan because of race, Martin smugly asserted, "the forces of competition" ensured that another bank would come forward to make the loan (46). With his regulatory authority over all banks that were members of the Federal Reserve System, and with all such banks engaging in similar discriminatory practices, Martin surely knew (or should have known) that his claim was patently false.

Federal and state courts also allowed tax-exempt institutions to enforce racial segregation. The practice was pervasive among universities, churches, hospital complexes, and other nonprofit organizations.

The University of Chicago, for example, organized property owners' associations to prevent black families from moving into neighborhoods surrounding the university. The university not only subsidized the associations themselves, but spent $100,000 from 1933 to 1947 on legal services to defend the associations' restrictive covenants and evict African American residents who moved to the neighborhoods in violation of the covenants (Hirsch [1983] 1998, 144–45; Plotkin 1999, 122–25).

In 1948, the Supreme Court concluded in *Shelley v. Kraemer* that restrictive covenants were unenforceable by courts. The covenant in question had been sponsored by the Cote Brilliante Presbyterian Church (2011) in St. Louis, and its trustees provided funds from the church treasury to finance Ms. Kraemer's lawsuit, which sought to enforce the covenant. Leadership by tax-favored churches in racially purposed property owners' associations was commonplace. In Detroit in 1941, racially explicit opposition to a public housing project was led by a homeowners association headquartered in a local Catholic church whose priest represented the association in appeals asking the US Housing Authority to cancel the project. The opposition eventually escalated into violence and riots by white neighbors who opposed construction (Long and Johnson 1947, 53, 83; Funigiello 1978, 98).

Despite the Supreme Court's 1917 ban, explicit racial zoning was enforced in some municipalities until the 1960s. Several cities interpreted the *Buchanan* ruling as inapplicable to their racial zoning laws because the measures only prohibited black residence in white neighborhoods, not ownership. Some cities, Miami, Florida, for example, continued to include racial zones in their master plans and issued development permits accordingly, even though neighborhoods themselves were not explicitly zoned for racial groups. In Austin, Texas, a 1928 city plan specified boundaries for a Negro district on the east side and closed segregated schools, parks, and libraries elsewhere in the city to create powerful incentives for the African American population to relocate (Koch and Fowler [1928] 1957).

In Baltimore, following the Supreme Court's 1917 *Buchanan* ruling, the mayor organized a municipal Committee on Segregation to maintain racial zones without an explicit ordinance that would violate the ruling. The committee was headed by the city attorney. In addition to organizing restrictive covenants, the committee coordinated the efforts of the city's building and health inspectors to deem black residences in white neighborhoods uninhabitable.

Urban renewal programs of the mid-twentieth century were often designed to force low-income black residents away from universities, hospital complexes, or business districts and into new ghettos. Displaced residents received no help with relocation to stable and integrated neighborhoods; in most cases, those whose homes were razed relocated into housing of diminished quality; public housing high-rises or overcrowded neighborhoods were the only options for many. No disparate-impact theory was necessary to prove the unconstitutionality of displacements whose purposes were racially explicit, as often they were.

Interstate highways also served as tools of segregation. Federal and local officials routed interstates to raze or separate integrated and mostly black neighborhoods from white communities and key commercial districts (Mohl 2000).

State regulatory authorities also abetted *de facto* segregation practices. Real estate is a highly regulated industry. State governments require brokers to take exams and courses in ethics to keep their licenses. State commissions suspend or even lift licenses for professional and personal infractions—from mishandling escrow accounts to failing to pay personal child support. But although real estate agents openly enforced segregation through steering and other practices, state authorities did not punish brokers for racial discrimination until very late in the twentieth century. Indeed, some licenses were suspended for abuse of professional ethics because the real estate agents sold homes in white neighborhoods to black purchasers. This misuse of regulatory authority contributed to *de jure* segregation (US Commission on Civil Rights 1970).

Police and prosecutorial powers were used to enforce racial boundaries in localities across the United States. Illustrations are legion. In the Chicago area, police forcibly evicted blacks who moved into an apartment in a white neighborhood (Rubinowitz and Perry 2002, 351–52); in Louisville, the city where, in 2007, the Supreme Court found only a history of *de facto* segregation,[16] the state prosecuted and convicted a white seller for sedition after he sold his home in a white neighborhood to a black family (Braden 1958). Everywhere—North, South, East, and West—police stood by while thousands of mobs set fire to and stoned homes that blacks purchased in white neighborhoods. Prosecutors almost never charged well-known and easily identifiable mob leaders, who were often the officers of neighborhood associations (Rubinowitz and Perry 2002). ("Thousands" of mobs is not an exaggeration.)

Private prejudice undeniably played a very large role in segregation. But unconstitutional government action helped to create and sustain private prejudice. In part, white homeowners' resistance to black neighbors was fed by deteriorating ghetto conditions, and state action sparked that deterioration. Slum conditions were largely created and exacerbated by overcrowding that was due almost entirely to federal restrictions on access to the housing supply beyond ghetto boundaries. Because of these restrictions, African Americans paid higher rents than whites paid for similar accommodations. Without access to FHA or Veterans Administration financing, African Americans paid exorbitant interest rates on mortgages or were forced to buy homes on contract, without the opportunity for equity accumulation. To make payments, families doubled up or subdivided their homes and took in renters. The overcrowding was made more intolerable by municipalities' discriminatory denial of adequate public services. Garbage was collected too infrequently in black neighborhoods; predominantly African American areas were rezoned for mixed, industrial, or even toxic use; streets remained unpaved, and street lighting was not provided or not maintained. Water, power, and sewer services were often not provided. The racially discriminatory motivation for these service shortfalls was frequently unhidden.

Seeing slum conditions invariably associated with African Americans, and unsophisticated about the causes, white homeowners had an understandable fear: if African Americans moved into their neighborhoods, these refugees from urban slums would bring the slum conditions with them. White homeowners came to see slum conditions as characteristics of black residents themselves, not as the results of racially motivated municipal policy. White flight when black homeowners moved nearby was, at least in part, the result of government-sponsored conditions.

Enduring Effects

As Justice Kennedy's 2015 opinion acknowledged, "vestiges" of *de jure* residential segregation remain in the country's economic and social life. Consider the whites-only suburbs created by the FHA in the mid-twentieth century—suburbs like Levittown, Westlake, and Lakewood. In the late 1940s and early 1950s, builders sold the houses there to lower-middle and working-class white families for $7,000 to $10,000. At the time, the price was about two and a half times the national median family income; in today's dollars, it would perhaps come to $125,000. White veterans could get Veterans Administration loans with no down payment. Their monthly carrying charges were no more (and often less) than the rents they were paying in urban public housing or apartments. Today, these homes typically sell for $400,000 or more, about eight times the national median income, and mortgages typically require 20 percent down.

The 1968 Fair Housing Act said, in effect, okay African Americans, you are no longer prohibited from living in Levittown, Westlake, or Lakewood. Go ahead. But the act's invitation was mostly an empty one. Levittown, for example, has become unaffordable for working-class families, and so only a few African Americans now live there. White Levittowners benefitted from a half-century of equity appreciation, gaining wealth that enabled their children, and their children's children, to attend college and join the middle class. Their racially exclusive access to this wealth enabled them to retire in comfort, relieving their children of the need to divert income in order to support parents in old age. African Americans of the same postwar generation were denied access to this community and thousands like it nationwide; instead, most were relegated to urban rentals for a half century, and they are less able to easily send children to college or to retire in comfort.

Nationwide, black median family income is now about 60 percent of white median family income, but black median household wealth is an astonishingly low 10 percent of white median household wealth. For middle-class families, the black–white wealth ratio is about 25 percent (Economic Policy Institute 2012, 2014; Shapiro, Meschede, and Osoro 2013).[17] Most families' wealth consists of home equity or of liquid assets converted from home equity. The enormous differential in black–white wealth is, to a considerable extent, the direct result of unconstitutional federal racial housing policy, which greatly limited the ability of large numbers of African Americans to purchase homes in middle-class suburbs. Even in the absence of ongoing discrimination, those effects would remain.

Where Do We Go from Here?

The myth that segregation is wholly (or even primarily) *de facto* limits our imagination when we attempt to conceive policies to desegregate metropolitan areas. As long as this myth, this misrepresentation of our racial history, is widely shared, any proposals to desegregate by remedying *de jure* segregation will be politically inconceivable, notwithstanding their constitutional necessity. So the first step in any remedial desegregation campaign must be education, not action: familiarizing the American public, and especially its opinion leaders, with the reality of our racial past.

This history is well known to scholars and even to many undergraduates (before they forget it), but not to the general public. Kenneth Jackson's *Crabgrass Frontier* (1985) and Douglas Massey's and Nancy Denton's *American Apartheid* (1993), are the best-known surveys of many of the policies described in this chapter. Numerous city-specific studies are also well known. Most notable among them are Arnold Hirsch's *Making the Second Ghetto* (on Chicago; [1983] 1998) and Thomas Sugrue's *Origins of the Urban Crisis* (on Detroit; 1996). The nation requires a renewed effort to teach our racial history—an effort that draws upon these works. Absent such an effort, the next generation will be as unprepared as the present one to remedy our *de jure* system of segregation.

And it should begin in our schools. Elementary- and secondary-school curricula typically ignore or, worse, misstate this story. For example, in over 1,200 pages of McDougal Littell's widely used high school textbook, *The Americans*, a single paragraph is devoted to twentieth century "Discrimination in the North." It devotes one passive-voice sentence to residential segregation, stating that "African Americans found themselves forced into segregated neighborhoods," with no further explanation of how public policy was responsible (Danzer et al. 2007, 494). *United States History*, another widely used textbook published by Pearson Education and Prentice Hall, also attributes segregation to mysterious forces: "In the North, too, African Americans faced segregation and discrimination. Even where there were no explicit laws, *de facto* segregation, or segregation by unwritten custom or tradition, was a fact of life. African Americans in the North were denied housing in many neighborhoods" (Lapsansky-Werner et al. 2010, 916–17). *History Alive!*, a popular textbook published by the Teachers' Curriculum Institute (2008), explains that segregation was a Southern problem: "Even New Deal agencies practiced racial segregation, especially in the South." The book fails to make any reference to the New Deal's embrace of residential segregation nationwide. Avoidance of our racial history is pervasive, and we are ensuring the persistence of that avoidance for subsequent generations.

Following the racially motivated 2015 massacre of African American churchgoers in Charleston, South Carolina, national attention turned to ways in which the nation has sanitized its history of slavery and the Civil War.

There was broad acknowledgment and condemnation of the depiction of the Confederacy as a movement to stand for abstract "states rights" principles, rather than for a state's right to permit, protect, and promote the ownership and exploitation of human slaves. Although some statues of confederate leaders have lost their places of honor, scholars, educators, and political leaders have not paid similar attention to how we describe the Jim Crow era in both the North and South. They should challenge school districts to abandon mendacious curricula for one that faces the truth about twentieth-century racial history.

If a national consensus is ever reached on the necessity to remedy unconstitutionally created residential segregation, programs should subsidize the movement of African Americans into predominantly white suburbs. Proposals discussed in this book's other chapters focus primarily on creating mobility for the lowest-income families and on preventing ongoing discrimination (e.g., on preventing racial steering by real estate agents). But more than prevention of discrimination is needed to undo the legacy of *de jure* segregation and to integrate metropolitan areas. Purposeful mobility incentives are necessary for working- and middle-class families, not only those with low income.

Consider the Levittown example discussed earlier and the thousands of federally segregated suburbs like it. In 2010, African Americans comprised only about 1 percent of Levittown's population, in a New York metropolitan area whose African American population was about 25 percent. To remedy its constitutional violations, the federal Department of Housing and Urban Development could purchase 25 percent of Levittown homes at market prices ($400,000 and above), reselling them to qualified African Americans—those who, like the white returning war veterans in the late 1940s and 1950s, have steady jobs and working-class incomes. The homes could be sold for $125,000, the price (in present dollars) their grandparents would have paid for such a home if permitted to purchase one. The terms of the sales would require the purchaser to remain for a period of time in Levittown or in the many other communities for which similar remedies could be fashioned, absent extraordinary circumstances. Or perhaps not: if the purchasers turned around and resold their homes to gain an equity profit of nearly $300,000, they would be doing no differently than their white peers.

Admittedly, such a proposal is fanciful. But some sort of subsidies to African American homeowners may be necessary to remedy segregation, and should not be given only for suburban purchases. Offering them in gentrifying urban areas would permit working-class African Americans to remain in these communities and prevent the neighborhoods from becoming new white enclaves.

Certainly, such subsidy programs would provoke resentment and bitterness; some whites will feel that the subsidies are unjustified and unfair. The reactions would likely have political consequences. That's why proposals to subsidize middle- and working-class African Americans are fanciful. They can become less fanciful only to the extent that racial history is widely taught and widely discussed. Ultimately, those solutions will become feasible when ownership of that history is generally shared.

Along with subsidies for working- and middle-class African Americans, other policies are also constitutionally required. Many suburban jurisdictions maintain exclusionary zoning ordinances banning apartments or town houses, or requiring large lot sizes, minimum square footages, excessive setbacks, and other devices purportedly motivated only by economic elitism. But, in fact, many also were designed to achieve racial exclusion. Indeed, the 1926 Supreme Court case that upheld such economic zoning was appealed from a district court that opined, "The blighting of property values and the congesting of the population, whenever the colored or certain foreign races invade a residential section, are so well known as to be within the judicial cognizance."[18]

In some cases, municipalities made zoning decisions for which racial motivation was so transparent that courts could not look the other way.[19] In one, after a town refused to grant a zoning variance for a multi-unit dwelling following a barrage of racially explicit public complaints, a federal appeals court observed: "Although the Planning Commission did not use race as the official basis of its permit denial . . . [if] proof of a civil right violation depends on an open statement by an official of an intent to discriminate, the Fourteenth Amendment offers little solace to those seeking its protection."[20]

Given the evidence, a national inclusionary zoning requirement—for example, a requirement conditioning approvals of new developments on their incorporation of some low- and moderate-income units—should pass constitutional muster. Such a requirement would permit construction of modest single-family homes and multi-unit residential structures.

It is too late to undo the racially segregating effect of interstate highway routing. But racially motivated public transportation policy has also contributed to segregation and can be remedied. In many cities, light rail, subway, and bus lines, as well as highways, are designed to bring (white) suburbanites to downtown jobs but not to provide access to employment for residents of African American ghettos. In some cases, plans for rail lines were purposely drawn to avoid stops in white communities and to prevent African Americans without automobiles from accessing those communities (e.g., *Baltimore Sun* 1975). Future public transportation should be designed with a desegregation purpose.

Chapters 5 and 6 in this volume describe necessary reforms in housing assistance programs for low-income and poor families. The reforms are designed to ensure that the programs do not reinforce or exacerbate segregation and do not concentrate low-income families in low-opportunity neighborhoods. However, the Housing Choice Voucher program has insufficient appropriations: the number of eligible families far exceeds the number of vouchers for which funds are appropriated. As long as appropriations continue to fall short of demand from eligible applicants, African American families willing to locate to high-opportunity neighborhoods should have some priority.

Critics charge that such proposals are a form of "social engineering," a pejorative term, in their view. Only when the history of *de jure* segregation becomes known and is widely shared will defenders be able to explain that the proposals merely attempt to undo a century of social engineering designed to create a segregated society.

No proposal mentioned here forces African Americans to integrate, but they should be offered incentives to do so. Many African Americans have no interest in leaving racially homogenous communities. And many would like to live in communities that they identify as integrated but that consist of a substantially greater share of African Americans than would be consistent with truly integrated metropolitan areas (Charles 2003). A lack of interest in integration, however, stems at least in part from the violence and hostility African Americans have historically encountered in white neighborhoods. Although police-supported firebombings are no longer the norm when African Americans move to white communities, the collective memory of this violence still persists. And police suspicion of African Americans in predominantly white, middle-class neighborhoods—a presumption that they don't belong—continues to this day. Were that environment to disappear, a reluctance to integrate would likely diminish.

Some African Americans invoke the accessibility of cultural resources in black neighborhoods—churches, hairdressers, and restaurants—as a reason to reject residential desegregation. Yet many other ethnic groups initially confronted similar challenges when integrating into American middle-class society. The integration of each of these groups required pioneers who frequently traveled back to their former communities for cultural support. But it did not take a cluster of many before supermarkets dedicated aisles to ethnic food and other familiar institutions branched out. This was certainly the case when African Americans left the ghetto for inner-ring suburbs; cultural institutions moved long before such neighborhoods became heavily black. If there comes a time when all neighborhoods are open to whites and blacks alike, African American cultural institutions will again move with the populations they serve, branching out to new areas as African Americans relocate. If all neighborhoods are open, African Americans will no longer have to concentrate in only a few.

Integration and Diversity

In America today, economic inequality is extreme. Not only is income unequal, but so too is housing. In metropolitan areas, a growing number of families of all races and ethnicities live in neighborhoods where poverty is prevalent and income low. Children in these neighborhoods have fewer successful, well-educated, middle-class adults to serve as role models. Schools are more challenged by the concentration of academic and behavioral problems, and have less time or attention to devote to even the most talented students. These neighborhoods provide less adequate healthcare to residents and subject residents to greater stress arising from disorder and violence. These neighborhoods have less access to jobs or to the transportation that could connect residents to jobs. In short, these neighborhoods typically offer fewer opportunities for intergenerational mobility, economic or geographic.

As a matter of good social and economic policy, great efforts should be made to increase family mobility from low-opportunity neighborhoods to high-opportunity ones. Many of the proposals discussed in this book's other chapters are necessary to support this mobility of all families, whatever their race or ethnicity.

But we should be clear about the distinction between good social policy and constitutionally required remedy. Good social policy requires housing mobility and improvement for all residents of low-opportunity neighborhoods. African Americans will benefit from such policy, as will others, but African Americans are also entitled to special remedies to compensate for their *de jure* segregation.

Native Americans also have inherited the effects of government discrimination and exploitation. They too are entitled to remedies that supplement good social policy; such remedies are beyond the scope of this chapter, as are the remedies due in compensation for the experiences of Chinese and Japanese Americans.

Latinos share a unique experience. They have suffered from some *de jure* segregation but to a lesser extent than African Americans. In part, this is because most Latino immigrants came to the United States after the era when *de jure* segregation, with its enduring effects, became the norm—exceptions include Puerto Ricans in New York and Mexican Americans in California, Texas, and the rest of the Southwest. And even for Latino immigrants in that era, *de jure* segregation in California and the Southwest was less extreme than that experienced by African Americans.

For example, in cities like Austin, Texas, public housing constructed under the 1937 United States Housing Act was segregated, with separate projects for whites, African Americans, and Latinos. But as described earlier in this chapter, African Americans not in public housing were also herded into Austin's Eastside ghetto. Mexican Americans were not; those living in private housing remained scattered throughout the city. In California, restrictive covenants sometimes excluded Latinos as well as African Americans from neighborhoods. Although many covenants nominally prohibited sales or rental to both groups, courts upheld those excluding African Americans but found that covenants excluding Latinos were unenforceable. Indeed, in several cases, courts enforced the rights of Latinos to exclude African Americans from their neighborhoods.

For the most part, and especially for the wave of Mexican and Central American immigration of the late twentieth and early twenty-first centuries, Latinos have concentrated in low-income, ethnically homogenous neighborhoods, not because they have been restricted to such places by *de jure* segregation policies but because low-wage immigrants have always settled in such neighborhoods. In addition to the support of relatives, other native-language speakers, and familiar institutions, those neighborhoods typically offer less costly (albeit less adequate) housing. Past immigrant groups have tended to leave such neighborhoods by the third generation. Many Latinos, like previous immigrant groups, continue to do so today. But such mobility is now blocked in a way that it was not for previous immigrant groups: inequality, not *de jure* segregation policies, now impedes immigrants' residential mobility.

There are similarities in the inadequate mobility of "black and brown" families. Full enforcement of the nondiscrimination provisions of the Fair Housing Act, its prohibition of avoidable policies and practices whose disparate impacts impede mobility, and reform of programs like the Housing Choice Voucher program and Low-Income Housing Tax Credit will benefit not only African Americans but also Latinos and others. Some policies that are constitutionally required because of the legacy of African Americans' *de jure* segregation, but that are also advisable for reasons of good social policy, will incidentally benefit Latinos and others—a national inclusionary zoning policy, for example.

It remains important, however, to preserve the distinction between good social and economic policy intended to enhance equality and mobility, and remedial policy intended to undo the vestiges of *de jure* segregation of African Americans. We will be unable to keep this distinction in mind if there is no concerted effort to reacquaint Americans with the truth of our racial history.

Notes

1. Fair Housing Act of 1968, Pub. L. No. 90-284, title VIII, 82 Stat. 81 (1969) (codified as amended at 42 U.S.C. §§ 3533, 3535, 3601–31 (2012)).
2. Texas Department of Housing and Urban Affairs v. Inclusive Communities Project, No. 13-1371, slip op. at 1 (U.S. June 25, 2015), https://www.supremecourt.gov/opinions/14pdf/13-1371_8m58.pdf.
3. Milliken v. Bradley, 418 U.S. 717, 756 (1974).
4. Parents Involved in Community Schools v. Seattle School District No. 1, 551 U.S. 701, 731–32 (2007).
5. *Parents Involved*, 551 U.S. at 736.
6. *Inclusive Communities*, slip op. at 5.
7. *Inclusive Communities*, slip op. at 5–6.
8. Davis v. St. Louis Hous. Auth., Civ. No. 8637, E.D. Mo. (1955) (1 *Race Rel. L. Rep.* (1956), 353–55, at 354–55).

9. United States Housing Act of 1937, Pub. L. No. 75-412, 50 Stat. 888 (1937).

10. 95 Cong. Rec. 4852 (1949).

11. 95 Cong. Rec. 4855 (1949).

12. Housing Act of 1949, Pub. L. No. 81-171, 63 Stat. 413 (1950) (codified as amended at 42 U.S.C. § 1441a et seq. (2012)).

13. Hills v. Gautreaux, 425 U.S. 284 (1976); Thompson v. HUD, Civ. No. MJG-95-309 (D. Md.).

14. Shelley v. Kraemer, 334 U.S. 1 (1948).

15. Mayers v. Ridley, 465 F.2d 630 (D.C. Cir., 1972). http://openjurist.org/465/f2d/630/mayers-v-s-ridley. See also Fair Housing Act of 1968, Pub. L. No. 90-284, 82 Stat. 81 (1969) (codified as amended at 42 U.S.C § 3601 et seq. (2012)).

16. *Parents Involved,* 551 U.S. at 701.

17. Thomas Shapiro, email correspondence with author, May 3, 2014.

18. Village of Euclid v. Amber Realty Corporation, 272 U.S. 365 (1926).

19. For example, United States v. City of Black Jack, Missouri, 508 F. 2d 1179 (1974).

20. Willie Mae Dailey and Columbia Square, Inc. v. City of Lawton, Oklahoma, 425 F.2d 1037 (1970).

References

Baltimore Sun. 1975. "Transit Fears in Anne Arundel." Editorial. April 22, 14.
Benson, Jackson J. 1996. *Wallace Stegner: His Life and Work.* New York: Viking.
Bloom, Nicholas Dagen. 2008. *Public Housing That Worked: New York in the Twentieth Century.* Philadelphia: University of Pennsylvania Press.
Braden, Anne. 1958. *The Wall Between.* New York: Monthly Review Press.
Burns, James MacGregor. 1970. *Roosevelt: The Soldier of Freedom, 1940–1945.* New York: Harcourt Brace Jovanovich.
Charles, Camille Zubrinsky. 2003. "The Dynamics of Racial Residential Segregation." *Annual Review of Sociology* 29: 167–207. doi:10.1146/annurev.soc.29.010202.100002.
Checkoway, Barry. 1980. "Large Builders, Federal Housing Programmes, and Postwar Suburbanization." *International Journal of Urban and Regional Research* 4 (1): 21–44. doi:10.1111/j.1468-2427.1980.tb00350.x.
Clark, Charles D. 1938. "Federal Housing Administration Standards for Land Subdivision." *Journal of the American Institute of Planners* 4 (5): 109–12. doi:10.1080/01944363808978792.
"Construction Financing: Let's Take a Good Clear Look at FHA's Title VI and See How We Can Really Get What We Want." 1948. *Architectural Forum* 88 (2): 12–15.
Cote Brilliante Presbyterian Church. 2011. "History." Accessed 2011. http://cbpc.ministrytoolboxonline.com/?action=1917495344&sectionID=2885.
Danzer, Gerald A., Jorge Klor de Alva, Larry S. Krieger, Louis E. Wilson, and Nancy Woloch. 2007. *The Americans.* Evanston, IL: McDougal Littell.
Davies, Richard O. 1966. *Housing Reform during the Truman Administration.* Columbia: University of Missouri Press.
Dean, John P. 1947. "Only Caucasian: A Study of Race Covenants." *Journal of Land & Public Utility Economics* 23 (4): 428–32. doi:10.2307/3158842.

Economic Policy Institute. 2012. "Median Household Wealth, by Race and Ethnicity, 1983–2010 (2010 dollars)." State of Working America. http://www.stateofworkingamerica.org/chart/swa-wealth-figure-6e-median-household-wealth/.

Economic Policy Institute. 2014. "Black Median Family Income, as a Share of White Median Family Income, 1947–2013." State of Working America. http://www.stateofworkingamerica.org/charts/ratio-of-black-and-hispanic-to-white-median-family-income-1947-2010/.

Fishel, Leslie H., Jr. 1964–65. "The Negro in the New Deal Era." *Wisconsin Magazine of History* 48 (2): 111–26.

Flournoy, Craig, and George Rodrigue. 1985. "Separate and Unequal: Illegal Segregation Pervades Nation's Subsidized Housing." *Dallas Morning News*, February 10, 1A.

Friend, Hallis, and Nancy Lund. (1974) 1989. *Ladera Lore*. Reprint by Maureen Hamner. San Francisco: Grubb & Ellis Real Estate.

Funigiello, Philip J. 1978. *The Challenge to Urban Liberalism: Federal-City Relations during World War II*. Knoxville: University of Tennessee Press.

Gordon, Colin. 2008. *Mapping Decline: St. Louis and the Fate of the American City*. Philadelphia: University of Pennsylvania Press.

Grier, Eunice, and George Grier. 1960. *Privately Developed Interracial Housing: An Analysis of Experience*. Berkeley: University of California Press.

Heathcott, Joseph. 2011. "'In the Nature of a Clinic': The Design of Early Public Housing in St. Louis." *Journal of the Society of Architectural Historians* 70 (1): 82–103. doi:10.1525/jsah.2011.70.1.82.

Hirsch, Arnold R. (1983) 1998. *Making the Second Ghetto: Race and Housing in Chicago, 1940–1960*. Reprint. Chicago: University of Chicago Press.

Hirsch, Arnold R. 2000a. "Choosing Segregation: Federal Housing Policy between *Shelley* and *Brown*." In *From Tenements to the Taylor Homes: In Search of an Urban Housing Policy in Twentieth-Century America*, edited by John F. Bauman, Roger Biles, and Kristin M. Szylvian, 206–25. University Park: Pennsylvania State University Press.

Hirsch, Arnold R. 2000b. "Searching for a 'Sound Negro Policy': A Racial Agenda for the Housing Acts of 1949 and 1954." *Housing Policy Debate* 11 (2): 393–441.

Hirsch, Arnold R. 2005. *"The Last and Most Difficult Barrier": Segregation and Federal Housing Policy in the Eisenhower Administration, 1953–1960*. Report. Washington, DC: Poverty & Race Research Action Council. http://www.prrac.org/pdf/hirsch.pdf.

Holliman, Irene V. 2016. "Techwood Homes." In *New Georgia Encyclopedia*, edited by New Georgia Encyclopedia staff, October 6. Georgia Humanities Council. http://www.georgiaencyclopedia.org/articles/arts-culture/techwood-homes.

Jackson, Kenneth T. 1985. *Crabgrass Frontier: The Suburbanization of the United States*. New York: Oxford University Press.

Julian, Elizabeth K., and Michael M. Daniel. 1989. "Separate and Unequal: The Root and Branch of Public Housing Segregation." *Clearinghouse Review* 23: 666–76.

Koch and Fowler. (1928) 1957. *City Plan for Austin, TX*. Reprint with new preface, Austin: City of Austin, Department of Planning.

Lapsansky-Werner, Emma J., Peter B. Levy, Randy Roberts, and Alan Taylor. 2010. *United States History*. Upper Saddle River, NJ: Pearson Education and Prentice Hall.

Larrabee, Eric. 1948. "The Six Thousand Houses That Levitt Built." *Harper's Magazine*, September, 79–88.

Long, Herman H., and Charles S. Johnson. 1947. *People vs. Property. Race Restrictive Covenants in Housing*. Nashville, TN: Fisk University Press.

Massey, Douglas, and Nancy Denton. 1993. *American Apartheid: Segregation and the Making of the Underclass*. Cambridge, MA: Harvard University Press.

Miller, Loren. 1964. "Government's Responsibility for Residential Segregation." In *Race and Property*, edited by John H. Denton, 58–76. Berkeley, CA: Diablo Press.

Mohl, Raymond A. 2000. "Planned Destruction: The Interstates and Central City Housing." In *From Tenements to the Taylor Homes: In Search of an Urban Housing Policy in Twentieth-Century America*, edited by John F. Bauman, Roger Biles, and Kristin M. Szylvian, 226–45. University Park: Pennsylvania State University Press.

Orfield, Gary. 1981. *The Housing Issues in the St. Louis Case: A Report to Judge William L. Hungate, U.S. District Court, St. Louis Missouri*. Mimeo of report to judge in Liddell v. Board of Education, City of St. Louis, April 21.

Plotkin, Wendy. 1999. "Deeds of Mistrust: Race, Housing, and Restrictive Covenants in Chicago, 1900–1953." PhD diss., University of Illinois at Chicago.

Rubinowitz, Leonard S., and Imani Perry. 2002. "Crimes without Punishment: White Neighbors' Resistance to Black Entry." *Journal of Criminal Law and Criminology* 92 (2): 335–428.

Shapiro, Thomas, Tatjana Meschede, and Sam Osoro. 2013. "The Roots of the Widening Racial Wealth Gap: Explaining the Black-White Economic Divide." Research and Policy Brief, February. Waltham, MA: Brandeis University, Institute on Assets and Social Policy. http://iasp.brandeis.edu/pdfs/Author/shapiro-thomas-m/racialwealthgapbrief.pdf.

Stegner, Wallace. 1947. "Four Hundred Families Plan a House." *'47: The Magazine of the Year* 1 (2): 63–67.

Steinberg, Alfred. 1949. "FHA—Profits before Housing." *The Nation* 168 (January 1): 11–13.

Sugrue, Thomas. 1996. *The Origins of the Urban Crisis: Race and Inequality in Postwar Detroit*. Princeton, NJ: Princeton University Press.

Teachers' Curriculum Institute. 2008. *History Alive! Pursuing American Ideals*. Palo Alto, CA: Teachers' Curriculum Institute.

US Commission on Civil Rights. 1961. *Housing*. Vol. 4, *1961 United States Commission on Civil Rights Report*. Washington, DC: Government Printing Office.

US Commission on Civil Rights. 1970. *Hearing before the United States Commission on Civil Rights. Hearing held in St. Louis, Missouri, January 14–17, 1970*. Washington, DC: US Government Printing Office. http://babel.hathitrust.org/cgi/pt?id=mdp.39015027012205.

Vale, Lawrence J. 2002. *Reclaiming Public Housing: A Half Century of Struggle in Three Public Neighborhoods*. Cambridge, MA: Harvard University Press.

Weaver, Robert C. (1948) 1967. *The Negro Ghetto*. Reprint. New York: Russell and Russell.

3

The Siting Dilemma
RACE AND THE LOCATION OF FEDERAL HOUSING PROJECTS

Lance Freeman

Among the challenges in building government-sponsored affordable housing, the question of where to build such housing has been one of the most vexing. Race has played an outsized role in creating this vexation. Public housing, the earliest manifestation of government-sponsored affordable housing, is often held up as an example of a failed social policy that confined poor blacks in vertical ghettos (see, e.g., Vale 2013). On this dimension, the scholarly portrayal is consistent: public housing served to isolate and segregate poor blacks. Moreover, policy elites created this reality by choosing where to site public housing and how to populate those developments (Hirsch 1983; Bickford and Massey 1991; Goering, Kamely, and Richardson 1997; Rohe and Freeman 2001).

This chapter argues that the aforementioned narrative, although true, is incomplete. Most notably, the narrative leaves out the role blacks played in the siting of government-sponsored affordable housing and their reactions to siting policy. Although the political position of blacks was relatively weak, their actions and potential for action influenced the implementation of the Public Housing Program as well as its evolution. Public housing provided affordable and decent housing as well as employment opportunities—important resources in the ghetto. Moreover, the ensuing segregation fostered institutions within the ghetto, and those institutions would complicate efforts to undo segregated affordable housing once state-sanctioned segregation became illegal. Thus, the siting of affordable housing poses a choice between bringing important resources to disadvantaged neighborhoods and using such housing to break down the walls of the ghetto. This is what I call the "siting dilemma."

A narrative that examines the role of black agency in the implementation and evolution of the Public Housing Program is necessary for historical accuracy. Analyzing the role of black agency and power, however, does more than set the historical record straight. The analytical framework that elucidates how blacks shaped the siting of public housing also sheds light on project-based housing assistance programs that succeeded the Public Housing Program. Although public housing is perhaps the most well-known project-based housing assistance program in the United States, it is no longer the largest, and many observers would describe it as the least successful (Hunt 2001; Bloom 2012).

The Low-Income Housing Tax Credit (LIHTC) has come to the fore as the primary mechanism through which affordable housing is built. Unlike public housing, LIHTC is largely viewed as a success. It has produced more than two million units of affordable housing to date (US Department of Housing and Urban Development 2015). Although LIHTC's siting practices are not as stigmatized as those of public housing, the two sets of practices mirror each other in many ways. In particular, developments are disproportionately sited in poor, minority neighborhoods (Freeman 2004). Moreover, as I discuss in detail, blacks have often been instrumental in the siting of LIHTC developments within predominantly black neighborhoods. Blacks' reactions to siting policy and the concomitant dilemma therefore continue to bedevil decisions about where affordable housing is built in the twenty-first century.

This chapter briefly documents housing conditions in black communities, chronicles blacks' reactions to public housing from the New Deal to the present, and details the dilemma these reactions created for opponents of segregation. The chapter then traces evolution over time in blacks' reactions to the siting of public and other affordable housing, examining how they have influenced project-based housing assistance policy to this day.

Housing in Black Communities in the Early Twentieth Century

Prior to the Great Migration, the bulk of the black population resided in the rural South. Those blacks who did live in urban areas faced significant housing discrimination and tended to be clustered together. Because of their small numbers, blacks in most cities lived in neighborhoods with a significant number of whites nearby. Blacks' poverty, combined with discrimination, relegated them to the worst slums in the industrial era (Logan et al. 2015).

Commencing during World War I, the Great Migration of blacks to the urban North brought hundreds of thousands to Northern cities and turned the small "black belts" into the modern all-black ghettos that have persisted for a century. Housing discrimination intensified, and blacks typically sought housing where their kinfolk and other black institutions were already located. This led to overcrowding in ghetto neighborhoods where housing was already in poor condition (Chicago Commission on Race Relations 1922; Kusmer 1978; Washington 1920; Weaver 1948).

By the 1920s, housing conditions in the ghetto were deplorable. In *The Negro in Chicago*, the Chicago Commission on Race Relations (1922, 191) reported that, among Negroes, "There were about as many homes without as with bathrooms." T. J. Woofter's (1928) study of 14 cities found that only 33.6 percent of all black renters had indoor toilet facilities. Summarizing these and other studies, the Hoover administration's Committee on Negro Housing concluded, "There is no escaping the general [poor] aspect of the bulk of this housing" (Gries and Ford 1932, 12). Only a small portion of blacks' housing in the urban North was in good condition. Consequently, even W. E. B. Dubois (1934), perhaps the most prominent agitator against segregation in the early twentieth century, spoke approvingly of segregated housing developments because of the desperate need for decent housing.

Although ghettoization and overcrowding contributed to deplorable housing conditions, the resulting neighborhoods spawned "black metropolises" where a segregated black population supported and sustained black institutions that served the interests of the race. With ghettoization, blacks were able to send politicians to Congress for the first time since Reconstruction, support larger business enterprises, and foster a cultural movement that sought to prove the humanity of blacks—the Negro Renaissance. Some blacks, while abhorring discrimination, accepted that some degree of self-segregation was not necessarily problematic; they were not eager to dismantle the ghetto and disperse the population that supported black institutions and politicians. In a debate over residential segregation carried out in the pages of *Current History* in 1927, Kelly Miller wrote:

> The negro is developing his own business enterprises to meet the needs of a segregated population. . . . Every negro community in our large cities has business streets where one sees encouraging indications of negro business in the future. . . .
>
> Whatever political power the negro exerts derives from segregation. . . . The negro has established his own dance halls, theatres and places of amusement. (831)

Other elite blacks stood fast by the principle of integration and refused to countenance any segregation. James Weldon Johnson of the National Association for the Advancement of Colored People (NAACP) criticized Miller for acquiescing to segregation (Miller 1927). Elite blacks, too, had much to lose from residential segregation because they were the ones with the means to afford the better housing typically found in white neighborhoods.

Thus arose tension in attitudes toward residential segregation. All participants in this debate aggressively opposed discrimination, but there were competing and sometimes ambivalent views concerning the resulting segregation. This tension and duality in feelings would color blacks' reactions to the siting of public and (later) other affordable housing for the next nine decades.

The New Deal Era

In the 1930s, the tragedy of the Great Depression pushed the federal government to intervene broadly in the housing sector. One prong of a multipronged approach was the Public Housing Program, which would stimulate the construction industry by providing jobs for unemployed construction workers and replace some of the dreadful slums in the nation's cities with affordable and decent housing (Marcuse 1995).[1]

As it did in virtually all features of public life, race played a role in determining the contours of the Public Housing Program. But the role of race was different in an almost revolutionary way. The Roosevelt administration, in a manner heretofore unseen since the days of Reconstruction, aimed to give blacks their due in public housing and other parts of the New Deal.

The Roosevelt administration did not set out to champion the rights of blacks. But several influential individuals close to the president were at least sympathetic to black interests. These included the president's wife, Eleanor, and Secretary of the Interior Harold Ickes, who were longtime supporters of blacks' civil rights. Ickes was a member of the NAACP. As Secretary of the Interior, Ickes had a say in how public housing was built, first under the Public Works Administration (PWA) and then under the US Housing Authority. Moreover, the Roosevelt administration's focus on "the forgotten man" predisposed it to helping the downtrodden, including blacks. Because of housing discrimination and their low economic status, blacks were among the most ill-housed Americans, and they were in desperate need of public housing.

While the Roosevelt administration often failed in its attempts to treat blacks fairly—for example, large numbers of Southern blacks were excluded from the Social Security program—the administration was successful in ensuring that blacks received their due with public housing. Indeed, a disproportionate share of public housing was targeted toward blacks because of the condition of the housing in their communities (*Chicago Defender* 1938).

The Roosevelt administration's relative friendliness toward blacks did not mean that it championed integration, a goal which many blacks saw as the sine qua non of the incipient civil rights movement. Public housing was to be segregated, with separate developments for blacks and whites. Moreover, developments would be targeted so that the race of tenants in developments would match the predominant race in the surrounding neighborhoods.

But rather than dwell on the Jim Crow nature of the Public Housing Program, the Roosevelt administration deftly used segregation to create the image that it was the first since the Civil War to target resources by race. Public housing was presented to blacks as a works program that would provide new, decent, and affordable housing; construction jobs for unemployed laborers; and employment for black professionals in the planning and design of the developments. Indeed, this is how John Murchison, the Department of the

Interior's assistant adviser on the economic status of Negroes, sold the program to blacks:

> Now, what are the specific benefits of the program to Negroes? In the first place, because of the very insanitary and ugly housing now provided for Negroes throughout the country, they more than likely will receive about one-fourth of the total to be allotted by the Division for low-rent projects. Then, too, it can be added here that continuous employment of the groups to be housed is essential to the success of the program. To date, a proportion of the housing payroll, equal to the occupational distribution as between white and colored workers of the building trades as shown by the 1930 census, has gone to Negro skilled and unskilled workers.... Negroes... will be employed as architects, engineers, project analysts, social planners, project accountants and auditors, project managers and supervisors and rehousing engineers. This employment will mean that the program of the Housing Division is based on policies and practices of doing things *with* Negroes rather than *for* Negroes.... Low-rent housing projects, which provide for Negro participation, have been announced in (1) Atlanta, Georgia, (2) Chicago, Illinois, (3) Cincinnati, Ohio, (4) Cleveland, Ohio, (5) Detroit, Michigan, (6) Indianapolis, Indiana, (7) Montgomery, Alabama, and (8) Nashville, Tennessee.... These projects will provide about 23,000 rooms for about 6,175 Negro families, and about 9,500,000 direct man hours of labor. (Murchison 1935, 210; italics in original)

Thus, the new Public Housing Program was presented not as a bulwark of segregation but as a source of opportunity. The *New York Amsterdam News*, a leading black newspaper, described the program as a "boon" to blacks and opined as follows:

> The Roosevelt administration has not only gone ahead with the first federal housing program in the history of the nation for both colored and white wage earners, but it has, through Harold L. Ickes, Secretary of the Interior and PWA administrator, refused to permit the construction of housing projects with federal funds for whites unless a similar project was constructed for Negroes whenever it was needed.... The health, educational and financial benefits accruing to the Negro citizens of America as a result of the Roosevelt administration's enlightened housing and other building programs are enormous. (Winston 1936, 11)

Upon the federal announcement of the Public Housing Program, the black-owned *Pittsburgh Courier* (1933, 10) described it as an effort "that should be hailed by Negroes, who suffer more than any other citizens from bad housing." The black press also proudly reported the role blacks played in planning and developing government-sponsored projects: "The largest housing project in New Jersey for Negroes is being erected in the third ward of

Newark. The manager will be a Negro college graduate and he will have Negro assistants in all the six buildings" (*Crisis* 1933, 257). A later headline from the *Pittsburgh Courier* (1938a, 1) blared, "Fourth of 30,496 New U.S. Homes Open to Race." The *Philadelphia Tribune* (1935, 20), which trumpeted itself as being "live" but not "yellow" in its vigorous support of every worthwhile movement for the betterment of Negroes, vigorously advocated for the construction of public housing within the ghetto as a way to improve the deplorable housing conditions of the race.

The extent to which public housing was viewed as an advancement for the race rather than an edifice of Jim Crow is revealed in New York City Mayor Fiorello La Guardia's response to urban unrest stemming from a case of police brutality in Harlem on March 19, 1935. An investigation by Mayor La Guardia identified poor housing conditions as one cause of the disturbance (*New York Amsterdam News* 1935, 1). The Harlem River Houses, the first public housing targeted to blacks in New York City, would be a balm to help soothe the burning anger that led to the riot.

For the common black man, debates about integration had to take a back seat to accessing affordable, decent housing at a time when blacks were still being ravaged by the Depression. Anyone would prefer to have a choice in where to live, but segregated public housing offered an option much superior to segregated substandard housing. In the Harlem River project, people voted with their feet: 10,000 applications were submitted for only 574 units. The response suggests that public housing, however segregated, was a popular proposition (*New York Amsterdam News* 1936, 19).

Those fortunate enough to secure a place in public housing felt themselves lucky and upwardly mobile. A former resident of public housing in Cleveland expressed this succinctly: "We really moved to the projects because at that time Outhwaite Homes was supposed to be something very special. It's hard to believe that now. But it was the place to live. In fact, you know, your friends would say, 'Oh, my,' you know, 'you have moved up in the world'" (Cleveland State University 2010, 0:10–0:28).

Such enthusiasm is not surprising. The first public housing developments were far superior to what was available to people of modest means at that time. As Hall of Fame pitcher Bob Gibson (1968, 5) put it, "Later we moved to the government housing project and even though it was in the ghetto, it was a step up in class because we had heat and electricity." The new developments were clean and relatively spacious. They had attractive landscaping and amenities, such as refrigerators, that were uncommon for the time (*Cleveland Plain Dealer* 1937; Plunz 1990). Public housing had none of the stigma associated with the "projects" of the late twentieth century. Families submitted to screening that evaluated both their "financial status" and "social desirability" (*New York Times* 1936, 14).

The positive response of the black community toward the first public housing does not mean there were no objections to the segregated nature of most developments. Not surprisingly, the NAACP, which remained "opposed both to the principle and the practice of enforced segregation of human beings on the basis of race and color," also opposed the idea of segregated public housing developments (DuBois 1934, 149). The Cleveland City Council's Special Housing Committee accused the federal government of segregating Cleveland developments by race, a charge the federal government denied (Simmons 1937).

But the benefits of the new public housing posed a dilemma. In 1942, the *Pittsburgh Courier* celebrated that Sojourner Truth Homes, once targeted for white occupancy, were reserved for blacks after strong and organized protests from the black community (1942, 6; see also Simmons 1937). Yet, in a remarkably prescient piece published only 4 years earlier, the same paper editorialized:

> It has long been apparent that this is the purpose of Negro housing projects. As a general rule white people are barred from them while Negroes cannot usually rent apartments in buildings in so-called white neighborhoods....
>
> Negroes themselves are partly responsible for this condition because they have registered no strong and nationwide complaint against it. They have been hypnotized by eight or ten housing projects "exclusively for Negroes" and failed to note what this portended for the future.
>
> Segregation begets more segregation. First it was the all-Negro housing projects. Now it is the effective efforts of the FHA [Federal Housing Administration] to keep Negroes living where prejudiced white folks think they ought to live.
>
> What will it be tomorrow if we continue to play ostrich? (*Pittsburgh Courier* 1938b, 10)

Another writer asserted, "The Philadelphia Housing Authority, by its method of designating types of tenants in the various Housing projects, is fostering a policy of segregation and discrimination only a little less vicious than the traditional southern brand" (Fauset 1941, 4; see also King 1938; *Pittsburgh Courier* 1938b).

Thus, there were ambivalent feelings about the segregated nature of the Public Housing Program. This ambivalence found its origins in the Great Depression and in the New Deal programs that arose as responses to the economic crisis. Blacks saw public housing as a positive and much-needed resource for the race. They saw the opportunities in planning, developing, and building public housing, opportunities due to federal largesse. After decades of the federal government turning a blind eye to the disenfranchisement and murder of black people, the development of federally funded public housing for black people was interpreted as a small but important step toward full inclusion in the body politic. This was true despite the Jim Crow nature of the first public housing developments. The ambivalence of blacks toward segregated public housing set a pattern that would persist for several decades.

The Postwar Years: 1945 to 1960

Wartime economic controls diverted resources from housing construction to the war industries, and little housing was built in the early 1940s. As the housing stock aged, workers migrated to the cities in search of work at wartime plants, and an incredible housing shortage emerged. In the wake of the Second World War, two housing-related problems absorbed the attention of black leaders: overcrowding in slum housing and confinement to the ghetto due to discrimination and restrictive covenants (Weaver 1948). The first problem persisted despite efforts made through the New Deal, and the second was never a target of the Roosevelt administration's interventions.

The housing shortage also affected whites, albeit in different ways, and made them all the more resistant to blacks moving into their neighborhoods. Aside from white mobs, the restrictive covenant was seen as the primary impediment that prevented blacks from breaking out of the ghetto.[2]

In *Shelley v. Kraemer*, the NAACP successfully convinced the Supreme Court to rule that the enforcement of such covenants was unconstitutional.[3] Other black elites endorsed the construction of integrated public housing outside of the ghetto, preferably in areas with no history of racial antagonism, as a way to address both overcrowding and segregation. Integrated public housing was consistent with democratic ideals, and it would demonstrate that blacks and whites could live together. Siting it outside of the ghetto would provide opportunities for at least some blacks to move out, thereby reducing overcrowding there (Weaver 1948).

But one key concession made during the 1930s would play out again and again in the postwar years: when tension arose between the need for decent housing and the ideal of integration, decent housing typically won the day. An article in the *New York Amsterdam News* is telling: "At the outset 'urban development' plans were welcomed by Negro business and community leaders." The article went on to state, "The central theme of slum clearance is highly acceptable to most Negroes" (Jarrett 1952, 36). The black poet Langston Hughes even penned a poem singing the praises of the public housing towers arising in Harlem in the early 1950s. The first few lines are as follows:

> There's a new skyline in Harlem,
> > It's tall and proud and fine.
> > At night its walls are gleaming
> > Where a thousand windows shine. (Hughes 2001, 207)

To the extent that blacks expressed concerns about public housing, the concerns generally centered on people displaced by the slum clearance: where the displaced would go, whether those with higher incomes would be eligible for the new housing, whether displaced homeowners would get a fair price for their properties, and when black businesses and institutions were displaced (White 1947; Woods 1948; *Los Angeles Sentinel* 1950; *Chicago Defender* 1953). Blacks were also concerned about the roles that black professionals (e.g., architects, appraisers, and contractors) would play in the redevelopment. Although there was concern that blacks would "be forced into the already over-crowded ghettos," worries that public housing would recreate the ghetto were muted in the black press (Jarrett 1952, 36).

Even as late as 1960, some public housing projects in the ghetto were described in glowing terms: "Open space, which includes sitting areas, private yards, playground and wading pools, is eye-pleasing with flower gardens and greenery. . . . Teenager or golden ager (senior resident), whatever one's pleasure, some form of it is available at Richard Allen [Homes]. Activities run the gamut from jazz to symphonies" (Rolen 1960, 9). And local black politicians could build a platform around the removal of the slums. Rev. Marshal L. Shepard and Thomas McIntosh, both members of the Philadelphia City Council, told the *Philadelphia Tribune* that the elimination of slum housing was their primary concern in 1960 (Peters 1960).

This is not to say that the black community was uniform in praising the continued development of public housing in the ghetto during this era. Although the NAACP supported slum clearance, it argued that "slum clearance alone is not the sole solution"; Negroes deserved access to all private housing they could afford, and the ghetto should ultimately be eliminated (*Philadelphia Tribune* 1956, 2). The NAACP branch in Pittsburgh went so far as to assert that "no future sites should be acquired by the [Pittsburgh Housing] Authority in predominantly Negro areas" (*Pittsburgh Courier* 1956, 1).

In addition, during World War II and accelerating thereafter, another powerful interest rose in the black community with strong opinions on the siting of public housing: middle- and upper-class blacks. Blacks were caught in the slipstream of the economic boom that spanned the war and postwar eras. As a consequence, their economic fortunes began to splinter sharply. Many blacks obtained secure, well-paying jobs and were able to afford the accoutrements of middle-class status, including homeownership in solidly middle-class, albeit segregated, neighborhoods. In general, black homeowners did not see their interests advanced by public housing. Occasionally, when public housing was directed toward their neighborhoods, the black middle class arose in opposition. This opposition was exemplified in the efforts of the Citizens Committee of West Chesterfield, a black neighborhood in Chicago. The committee's members vociferously opposed a proposal to build a public housing project in their midst, fearing that the "slum project" would threaten their property values and lead to the "deterioration of the community" (Smith 2012, 48). Given the relatively small, albeit growing, size of the black middle class and its low rates of homeownership, however, such resistance was a relatively rare occurrence.

Others have chronicled the failures of efforts to address overcrowding and segregation through construction of integrated public housing outside of the ghetto (Meyerson and Banfield 1955; Hirsch 1983). Instead, public housing reinforced the walls of the ghetto in the post–World War II era. Although integrationist-minded blacks opposed all forms of segregation, black response to segregation was often muted. For many, the desperate need for decent housing and elation at having a modern home, as encapsulated in Langston Hughes' poem, outweighed concerns about segregation. And public housing was seen as a threat to the interests of the black middle class, a small but growing segment of the black populace. Decent but segregated public housing continued to be the dilemma posed by then extant siting policy.

The Civil Rights Era

In the wake of the Second World War—when hundreds of thousands of Americans died to rid the world of fascism and notions of a "master race"—America, prodded by the civil rights movement, began a slow retreat from white supremacy in ideology and policy. By the 1960s, the civil rights movement was at its zenith, and housing was not immune to the changes brought about by this movement. Evidence of such change was reflected in the cessation of state-sanctioned housing segregation. Led by Massachusetts and Colorado, in 1959, states began outlawing housing discrimination (Collins 2004). In 1962, Executive Order 11063 forbade discrimination in housing owned or operated by the federal government as well as in housing provided with federal funds.[4] In 1967, the US Department of Housing and Urban Development (HUD) began directing housing authorities to seek a balanced distribution of public housing projects in their locality, including areas outside the ghetto (Lev 1981). The 1968 Civil Rights Act outlawed discrimination in privately owned housing.[5] In 1970, under Secretary George Romney, HUD began withholding categorical grants to suburban localities that refused to develop affordable housing within their boundaries. The march away from segregated public housing culminated with HUD's introduction of site and neighborhood standards in 1972. The standards forbade the development of public housing in the ghetto unless there was an "overriding need" (Lev 1981, 209). The federal government had pivoted 180 degrees and was now a force for siting affordable housing in an integrated fashion.

The growing black middle class continued to exert influence over the siting of affordable housing, often acting to protect perceived class interests by opposing the construction of public housing in its midst. The opposition was organized in groups like the West Logan Community Civic Association in Philadelphia. The association's leader said that plans for a 14-unit public housing development would "destroy" his community (*Philadelphia Tribune* 1970, 5). He also indicated that efforts to continue peaceful integration and neighborhood stabilization would "go down the drain" (5). In other instances, the justifications for opposition mirrored those offered by whites. Black homeowners organized the Concerned Citizens of the Eighth District to oppose public housing construction in a neighborhood on the southwest side of Los Angeles, and the group's attorney asserted that "it is unfair to concentrate low-income housing in an area that is already economically depressed," as serious problems with crime, traffic, pollution and falling property values would soon follow (Brown 1983, D1). The *Pittsburgh Courier* described opposition by residents of a "predominantly Black East Hills neighborhood" to a new subsidized housing development (Webster 1980, 2). Although the proposed development was ostensibly for low- and moderate-income homeowners, residents were concerned that it would "deteriorate our community" through the introduction of rental or subsidy housing (Webster 1980, 2).

It therefore appeared that forces were aligning to prevent the development of affordable housing in black neighborhoods. Those where poor blacks resided were off limits by HUD dictate, and middle-class blacks were mobilizing to prevent public housing from encroaching in their neighborhoods.

Middle-class blacks with nationalist leanings and those with interests in the segregated ghetto lamented the changing policy climate because it seemed that resources like public housing would be diverted out of the ghetto. For example, Roy Innis of the Congress of Racial Equality argued, "The integrationists would have us disperse to the suburbs. Many of us are resisting that because we feel that we cannot maximize our power that way. Those who want to go to the suburbs—we will fight for their right to do that. But we would oppose any massive program to move us there" (Wyche 1972, 10). A well-known black clergyman, the Reverend A. I. Dunlap, observed wryly: "We have to move toward building up our own communities. . . . The federal freeze is just trying to force us out toward the suburbs, and black people don't want that any more than whites welcome our coming" (McClory 1972*b*, 4).

Thus, by the dusk of the civil rights era, a completely altered landscape shaped the siting of affordable housing. The poorest blacks, whose concerns were often overlooked, still needed affordable housing wherever it was to be provided. Integrationists in the black community and their white allies had succeeded in persuading the federal government to avoid public housing development in the ghetto. But this would prove a pyrrhic victory. Suburban jurisdictions chose to decline federal funds rather than to allow the construction of public housing in their communities, and they pressured the Nixon administration to stop trying to force integration. A confluence of factors would lead to these suburban jurisdictions getting their wish.

First, by the 1970s, public housing's reputation was lower than perhaps it had ever been. The demolition of the Pruitt-Igoe public housing complex because of the deteriorated conditions there in 1972, when the complex was not even two decades old, seared public housing's damaged reputation in the public's imagination. Public housing's declining reputation made it unpopular to build HUD-sponsored housing almost anywhere (Montgomery 1985). Second, around this time, HUD was rocked by scandals associated with several of its other new construction programs (Orlebeke 2000). Finally, a presidential report concluded that a lack of physically decent housing was no longer the primary housing problem for poor people. The swaths of physically sound central-city housing being abandoned suggested affordability was now the major problem. Building more low-income housing could, in some instances, accelerate the already worrisome trends in abandonment (Nixon 1971).

These problems, along with the politically charged issue of where to build subsidized housing, led the Nixon administration to issue a moratorium on the construction of federally financed affordable housing (Bonastia 2000). With virtually no new housing being built, the contentious issue of where to place subsidized housing became moot.

For those who favored using federal resources to redevelop the ghetto, the threat was not integration in the suburbs but the evaporation of federal resources altogether. *Black Enterprise* reported concerns about the adverse impacts of the Nixon administration's moratorium, noting that HUD construction projects were the only projects they could get because they were "the last ones on the construction scene" (Johnson 1974, 19).

The *Chicago Daily Defender* put the situation as follows in reporting the assertions of black real estate developer Dempsey Travis:

> The freeze combined with new Federal Housing Authority regulations prohibiting federal subsidies to potential buyers and renters in black neighborhoods, causes a growing punishment of black people.
>
> "As it is," [Travis] said, "the onus of solving the problem is put on the blacks, but they're not the ones who created it. We could use 10,000 new homes a year in the black neighborhoods for the next ten years, but federal restrictions make that impossible. The result is that whites in the suburbs are the only ones able to take advantage of middle-income housing subsidies, and blacks can't do a thing." (McClory 1972*b*, 3)

Some black developers went as far as to accuse HUD of "a conspiracy to deprive the black community of all decent low-income housing" (McClory 1972*a*, 4). A report of comments by Travis regarding Chicago housing development exemplifies this assessment: "The HUD density factor and site selection criteria make it impossible for new low or middle-income buildings to be built in the inner city. As a result, he argued, properties in Englewood, Woodlawn, and throughout the South side [of Chicago] lie deserted awaiting the total black evacuation of the area. Wealthy private developers, mostly white, he maintained, will then be able to purchase the land for a song and erect, with their private money, huge Lake-Point-Towers type buildings, for a white clientele" (McClory 1972a, 4). The *Daily Defender* continued, paraphrasing Travis: "By insisting that no more than 25 units per acre be built and by requiring that three units of subsidized housing be constructed in white neighborhoods for every one in black, says Travis, developers like himself are hog-tied" (McClory 1972a, 4).

By the 1970s, blacks' position toward public housing had evolved considerably. In contrast to their predecessors in the New Deal era, blacks in the 1970s were less likely to view public housing as an unalloyed benefit. Though blacks were still highly segregated, the ghetto had expanded physically, and overcrowded ghettos were largely a thing of the past. Indeed, with whites fleeing to the suburbs, there was *too much* housing available in inner cities. Where densely packed ghettos had once stood, wide swaths of land lay depopulated and abandoned (National Urban League 1973). Housing affordability and quality continued to be problems for the poor, but units were available for those with the means to afford them. Thus, newly constructed affordable housing was the object of less enthusiasm.

Integrationists won half of their battle. They were able to reshape government policy so that public housing developments with high concentrations of poor blacks were to be built in the ghetto only in special circumstances. Less successful were their attempts to open up white areas to affordable housing occupied by blacks. Despite these developments, public housing continued to be an important source of contracts for black developers, as I have noted.

Thus, in the post–civil rights era, the siting of affordable housing continued to pose a dilemma, but the nature of this dilemma had evolved: the urge to dismantle the ghetto stood in tension with the improved housing, economic benefits, and other important resources that housing could bring to the ghetto. Another transformation marked the housing landscape in this era: President Nixon's moratorium represented a paradigm shift in the federal government's role in affordable housing. Thereafter the private and nongovernmental sectors would play much more significant roles in the provision of affordable housing. This shift to the market would come to define the neoliberal era.

The Neoliberal Era

The most significant developments in this shift toward the market were housing vouchers and LIHTC. Vouchers were introduced in 1974 as a way to help the poor, and the Reagan administration introduced LIHTC a little over a decade later. The housing voucher program (known as Section 8, for the section of the federal code authorizing the program) paid the difference between 25 percent of the tenant's income and the "fair market rent" for a given area.[6]

The shift from public housing to vouchers dramatically altered the nature of subsidized housing's benefits for blacks. Gone were the large-scale, tangible projects that served as symbols of government accountability and responsiveness to blacks as citizens. Gone, too, were the development contracts and professional jobs that were part of the Public Housing Program. Instead, vouchers represented a program targeted to a specific slice of the black populace: the very needy. This targeting was restricted further by funding. Vouchers were not an entitlement and only reached a small segment of the eligible population (Cutts and Olsen 2002). Consequently, the voucher program, though desperately needed by some blacks, has never been seen as a boon for the entire race.

The shift from public housing to LIHTC fostered a subtler shift in blacks' perspectives concerning subsidized housing. Adopted in legislation co-sponsored by Harlem Congressman Charles Rangel in 1986, LIHTC provided developers with a tax credit in exchange for the development of low-income housing.[7] Unlike public housing, LIHTC is highly decentralized. Because the subsidy derives from a tax credit, politicians cannot take credit for tangible government funds or the associated expenditures. Moreover, LIHTC developments have typically been at a much smaller scale than public housing and therefore typically have had commensurately smaller impacts on the population's imagination.

But in other ways, the forces that motivated blacks' claims on public housing worked the same way with regard to LIHTC. Just as public housing represented brand new housing in the ghetto when most blacks were overcrowded in substandard slums, LIHTC represented new or refurbished housing in places that had seen little in the way of new development for years, if not decades. Because of white flight and inner-city depopulation during the post–World War II era, many black communities had virtually no new development other than government-sponsored projects. Consider the perceived impact of LIHTC in Harlem, where "the development of more than 6,000 units of housing in less than ten years [the 1990s] had the effect of stabilizing Harlem and jumpstarting its revitalization in other areas" (Wright 2002, 11). The Abyssinian Development Corporation was one of the organizations that used the credit to develop properties in Harlem. Rev. Calvin O. Butts, one of the corporation's founders, noted: "The transformation of this neighborhood from an area known for having the highest concentration of city-owned abandoned buildings into a viable, economically integrated and socially healthy community is under way" (Ravo 1991, R3).

Across the nation, black churches, long serving as pillars of civil society within black America, have used LIHTC to develop affordable housing and rebuild devastated black communities (Owens 2007). Community development corporations, disproportionately located in black neighborhoods (Berndt 1977), have also used LIHTC as a major source of revenue to rebuild their communities and fund their primary activity, the development of affordable housing (Stoutland 1999). Indeed, Congressman Rangel is said to have brought "the tax bacon home" for his role in authoring the legislation that authorized LIHTC (Anekwe 1986, 4).

A program administered by the Internal Revenue Service, LIHTC is not subject to the site and neighborhood standards that govern HUD-sponsored developments and that have restrained the extent to which HUD projects perpetuate segregation. It is up to each state, through its Qualified Allocation Plan, to develop the equivalent of site and neighborhood standards for meeting the respective state's priorities.[8] Only three states prioritize racial desegregation. And while a number of states do aim to deconcentrate poverty or promote income mixing, federal guidelines provide incentives to develop LIHTC in high-poverty census tracts (Poverty & Race Research Action Council 2015).

Given the LIHTC program's meager emphasis on desegregation, it is not surprising that LIHTC developments have been disproportionately sited in minority neighborhoods. Our best guess is that the racial identity of their occupants mirrors that of the surrounding neighborhoods. LIHTC projects appear to be continuing the patterns of segregation that characterize the Public Housing Program, albeit in a less extreme form (Bickford and Massey 1991; Goering, Kamely, and Richardson 1997; Horn and O'Regan 2011). This pattern, like the segregated pattern that characterized the earlier public housing years, has not always been loudly denounced. Although public housing helped reinforce the segregated ghetto, with all the concomitant disadvantage that entails, such segregation also helped foster a sense of community that many blacks cherished. Some people valued these neighborhoods in spite of their segregated nature.

This sentiment has not disappeared. During a 2015 forum broadcast on the Brian Lehrer radio show, an unidentified audience member expressed that view aptly: "I would love for people of color to know our value . . . to have knowledge of the value of our spaces of our communities" (Lehrer 2015, 10:50–10:59). Houston Mayor Sylvester Turner also articulated this sentiment during his ongoing battle with HUD over the siting of a LIHTC development in a predominantly white neighborhood in his city. Whereas a HUD investigation found the city likely violating Title VI of the 1964 Civil Rights Act, which disallows federal funding for initiatives that discriminate based on the race of the occupants, Mayor Turner refused to support developing the project in the white neighborhood, preferring to site the development in a predominantly black neighborhood. He argued, "When you no longer build affordable housing in these low-income communities, then you are participating in the closing and consolidation of these schools, which impacts communities. You don't get that growth and that development with the people there, maintaining that history, that culture, that personality of those neighborhoods, and so you force people out (Elliott 2017, under "Housing Demand Unmet," para. 11).

These sentiments can also be found in some of the public comments on HUD's long-awaited Affirmatively Furthering Fair Housing rule.[9] The statements underscore the importance of ensuring that ghetto residents have the option to stay where they are and improve their community. For example, one commenter wrote that the option to "stabilize and revitalize neighborhoods that constitute racially/ethnically concentrated areas of poverty" should not be taken off the table.[10] Another wrote, "The final rule must clearly indicate throughout (not only in the statement of purpose) that affirmatively furthering fair housing may entail devoting resources to improve areas of concentrated racial and ethnic poverty by funding activities and implementing policies that foster mixed-race/mixed-income occupancy, and that augment access to essential community assets for protected class residents who wish to remain in their communities."[11]

The precise extent to which LIHTC is segregating blacks and minorities remains unclear. Extensive data on the occupancy characteristics of LIHTC developments have not been disseminated as of this writing. But we do know that, relative to LIHTC developments for older adults, the developments for families are more likely to be located in minority communities, and those family developments serve a population that is disproportionately composed of minority occupants (Poverty & Race Research Action Council 2004). Moreover, one study based on tenant data in four states found that "developments in areas with higher minority concentration themselves house more minorities" (Horn and O'Regan 2011, 455). Thus, the available evidence suggests that LIHTC developments, though perhaps not as segregated as public housing, are nevertheless continuing existing patterns of segregation.

Conclusion

Like much of American society, project-based housing assistance bears the scars of America's racist past. The channeling of blacks into segregated housing developments represents a missed opportunity to attempt integration and has served to strengthen the ghetto's walls. For blacks, segregated affordable housing created a dilemma: whether to accept accommodations that were affordable and of decent quality (at least initially) or to pursue integration, the hallmark of racial equality. Indeed, many blacks fled to the North to escape the clutches of Jim Crow segregation in the South (Wilkerson 2010). Segregated public housing was a large, visible, and federal endorsement of Jim Crow. But it was also much better than the housing that blacks of modest means could have ever hoped for. With it came jobs for black workers and resources for forlorn ghettos. This dilemma has persisted through the civil rights era and the neoliberalization of federal public housing policy.

A skeptic might argue that the dilemma confronting blacks was, and is, inconsequential. As Arnold Hirsch (2003) argued in his article, "Second Thoughts on the Second Ghetto," it was whites who had the power and ultimately bore the responsibility for creating the second ghetto, which included segregated public housing. The skeptic would argue that it was unlikely that blacks could have materially influenced siting policy during the New Deal era or in the ensuing decades. To the extent that blacks valued integration over decent housing—a Hobson's choice indeed—there might have been more all-white developments and a few integrated ones. But many thousands of blacks would have been left without decent housing.

But blacks did not merely acquiesce to the development of segregated public housing. There were instances where militant black protest groups demanded such housing in the ghetto. For example, in the 1930s, the Consolidated Tenants League of Harlem demanded a public housing development for Harlem, and the National Negro Congress likewise demanded such a project for the Negro section of Los Angeles (Roster 1936; *Los Angeles Sentinel* 1939; Schwartz 1986).

Blacks also successfully fought the establishment of *de jure* segregated public schools in the North, using boycotts and lawsuits to voice their displeasure (Douglas 2005; *Chicago Defender* 1930). Moreover, in 1941, blacks used the threat of a march on Washington to persuade President Roosevelt to issue Executive Order 8802, which forbade discrimination by defense contractors on the basis of "race, creed, color or national origin." They also prompted him to create a Committee on Fair Employment Practices, which served to ensure compliance with the order (Associated Press 1943). Thus, depicting blacks as completely impotent in the face of whites' power is probably a mischaracterization. In other spheres, such as public schools in the North or the defense industries, blacks vocally fought segregation and achieved some success. This suggests that the motivation to fight segregated public housing was perhaps not as great. And perhaps the Public Housing Program could have evolved differently but for the siting dilemma.

Today, the choices presented by the siting dilemma might be less Hobsonian. In many housing markets, the most efficient way to address housing affordability is through vouchers (Weicher 1990). Vouchers also appear to do a better job at promoting economic and racial integration than does public housing or LIHTC (McClure and Johnson 2015).[12] Focusing affordable housing policy almost exclusively on vouchers could actually reduce the affordability crisis.

Although LIHTC has become the primary federal program for developing affordable housing, its provisions for promoting integration are modest at best. In fact, because larger subsidies are offered for development in the poorest neighborhoods, the credit probably exacerbates segregation, though some state Qualified Allocation Plans provide incentives that could promote integration. Except for the objections raised by a few fair housing groups, there has been relatively little outcry over this oversight in federal fair housing policy. Indeed, as I have noted, there was significant outcry over the initial proposal for the Affirmatively Furthering Fair Housing rule and over fears that it would restrict the development of additional affordable housing in the ghetto. These criticisms prompted revisions to indicate that HUD would approve of a balanced approach and that "affirmatively furthering fair housing" could mean "taking actions that . . . address significant disparities in housing needs."[13] One could imagine a low-income black neighborhood where households had high rent burdens and thus a high need for affordable housing. A new affordable housing development that targets low-income households and is likely to attract few whites could still be classified as affirmatively furthering fair housing because it would address a disparity in housing needs. One would be hard-pressed to distinguish this outcome from the earlier segregation of blacks in public housing. Then, as now, interests within the ghetto wanted new housing built there. Then, and now, poor communities were home to many who had no desire to leave. Thus, the siting dilemma persists and shapes policy to this day.

Notes

1. Whether demolishing slums made a big difference in terms of public housing's impact on the housing market remains unclear. The number of units built, at least initially, was relatively small.

2. Restrictive covenants were clauses on property deeds that restricted the race of the occupant. They were ruled unenforceable by the Supreme Court in the *Shelley v. Kraemer* decision of 1948 (334 U.S. 1 (1948)).

3. 334 U.S. 1 (1948).

4. Exec. Order No. 11063, 3 C.F.R. § 261 (1963).

5. Pub. L. No. 90-284, 82 Stat. 73 (1969).

6. The fair market rent was the equivalent of the 40th percentile for all local rents in a specified area. These guidelines would subsequently be changed to use the 45th percentile for area rents and 30 percent of the tenant's income.

7. Tax Reform Act of 1986, §252, Pub. L. No. 99-514, 100 Stat. 2085, 2189 (1989) (codified as amended at I.R.C. § 42 (2015)).

8. Each state is required to develop a Qualified Allocation Plan that details how it will administer the state's allocation of tax credits (I.R.C. § 42(m)(1)(B) (2016); 26 C.F.R. 1.42–5 (2016)).

9. Affirmatively Furthering Fair Housing, 80 Fed. Reg. 42,272 (July 16, 2015) (codified at 24 C.F.R. pts. 5, 91, 92, 570, 574, 576, 903 (2016)).

10. Matt Oglander, Fair Housing of Marin, comment on proposed federal rule re. Affirmatively Furthering Fair Housing (Docket No. FR-5173-P-01, September 19, 2013), http://www.regulations.gov/#!documentDetail;D=HUD-2013-0066-0853.

11. Michael Anderson, Center for Community Change, comment on proposed rule re. Affirmatively Furthering Fair Housing (Docket No. FR-5173-P-01, September 13, 2013), http://www.regulations.gov/#!documentDetail;D=HUD-2013-0066-0504. See also Sorauf (1960).

12. As I noted, we cannot be sure of the extent of segregation among LIHTC developments because tenant data for this program have not been disseminated.

13. 80 Fed. Reg. at 42,316.

References

Anekwe, Simon. 1986. "Rangel, People's Man Brings Home Tax Bacon." *New York Amsterdam News*, August 23, 4, 22.

Associated Press. 1943. "The President's Order." *New York Times*, May 29, 6.

Berndt, Harry Edward. 1977. *New Rulers in the Ghetto: The Community Development Corporation and Urban Poverty*. Westport, CT: Greenwood.

Bickford, Adam, and Douglas S. Massey. 1991. "Segregation in the Second Ghetto: Racial and Ethnic Segregation In American Public Housing, 1977." *Social Forces* 69 (4): 1011–36. doi:10.1093/sf/69.4.1011.

Bloom, Nicholas Dagen. 2012. "Learning from New York: America's Alternative High-Rise Public Housing Model." *Journal of the American Planning Association* 78 (4): 418–31. doi:10.1080/01944363.2012.737981.

Bonastia, Chris. 2000. "Why Did Affirmative Action in Housing Fail during the Nixon Era? Exploring the 'Institutional Homes' of Social Policies." *Social Problems* 47 (4): 523–42. doi:10.2307/3097133.

Brown, Nick. 1983. "Residents Oppose Housing Projects: Protest March Set for Jan. 22." *Los Angeles Sentinel*, January 20, A1, D1.

Chicago Commission on Race Relations. 1922. *The Negro in Chicago: A Study of Race Relations and a Race Riot*. Chicago: University of Chicago Press.

Chicago Defender. 1930. "Fight Segregation of Indiana Students." September 6, 3.

Chicago Defender. 1938. "Race Gets One-Fourth Benefits from Approved Federal Housing Projects." August 6, 3.

Chicago Defender. 1953. "Hunt for Homes on in Chicago." October 10, 11.

Cleveland Plain Dealer. 1937. "U.S. Government Installs 1853 Westinghouse Refrigerators in Low Rent Housing Projects." June 6, 11A.

Cleveland State University, Center for Public History + Digital Humanities. 2010. "Outhwaite Homes: 'Growing up at Outhwaite'." Video, 1:12. Posted February 24. https://youtu.be/F6qq-txe1fQ.

Collins, William J. 2004. "The Housing Market Impact of State-Level Anti-Discrimination Laws, 1960–1970." *Journal of Urban Economics* 55 (3): 534–64. doi:10.1016/j.jue.2003.11.003.

Crisis: A Record of the Darker Races. 1933. "Housing." Along the Color Line, November, 257.

Cutts, Amy Crews, and Edgar O. Olsen. 2002. "Are Section 8 Housing Subsidies Too High?" *Journal of Housing Economics* 11 (3): 214–43. doi:10.1016/S1051-1377(02)00102-X.

Douglas, Davison M. 2005. *Jim Crow Moves North: The Battle over Northern School Segregation, 1865–1954*. New York: Cambridge University Press.

DuBois, W. E. B. 1934. "The Board of Directors on Segregation." Postscript. *The Crisis: A Record of the Darker Races*, May, 149.

Elliott, Rebecca. 2017. "Turner, Feds Clash over Affordable Housing Policies." *Houston Chronicle*, January 28. http://www.houstonchronicle.com/news/politics/houston/article/Turner-feds-clash-over-affordable-housing-10891783.php.

Fauset, Arthur Huff. 1941. "Instruct Your Housing Authority. I Write as I See," *Philadelphia Tribune*, March 6, 4.

Freeman, Lance. 2004. *Siting Affordable Housing: Location and Neighborhood Trends of Low Income Housing Tax Credit Developments in the 1990s*. Census 2000 Survey Series Report. Washington, DC: Brookings Institution, Center on Urban and Metropolitan Policy.

Gibson, Bob. 1968. *From Ghetto to Glory: The Story of Bob Gibson*. Englewood Cliffs, NJ: Prentice Hall.

Goering, John, Ali Kamely, and Todd Richardson. 1997. "Recent Research on Racial Segregation and Poverty Concentration in Public Housing in the United States." *Urban Affairs Review* 32 (5): 723–45. doi:10.1177/107808749703200506.

Gries, John S., and James Ford, eds. 1932. *Negro Housing: Report of the Committee on Negro Housing*. Washington, DC: President's Conference on Home Building and Home Ownership.

Hirsch, Arnold R. 1983. *Making the Second Ghetto: Race and Housing in Chicago, 1940–1960*. London: Cambridge University Press.

Hirsch, Arnold R. 2003. "Second Thoughts on the Second Ghetto." *Journal of Urban History* 29 (3): 298–309. doi:10.1177/0096144202250385.

Horn, Keren M., and Katherine M. O'Regan. 2011. "The Low Income Housing Tax Credit and Racial Segregation." *Housing Policy Debate* 21 (3): 443–73. doi:10.1080/10511482.2011.591536.

Hughes, Langston. 2001. "Hope for Harlem." In *The Poems: 1951–1967*, edited by Arnold Rampersad, 207. Vol. 3 of *The Collected Works of Langston Hughes*. Columbia: University of Missouri Press.

Hunt, D. Bradford. 2001. "What Went Wrong with Public Housing in Chicago? A History of the Robert Taylor Homes." *Journal of the Illinois Historical State Society* 94 (1): 96–117.

Jarrett, Vernon. 1952. "Slum Clearance—Is It 'Negro Clearance?' R. Foley to Present Govt. Case." *New York Amsterdam News*, October 4, 36.

Johnson, Herschel. 1974. "Housing Policy at the Crossroads. The People's Forum." *Black Enterprise*, February, 17–20.

King, Truxton. 1938. "Reader Just Raves over 'His' Tribune." *Philadelphia Tribune*, July 21, 4.

Kusmer, Kenneth L. 1978. *A Ghetto Takes Shape: Black Cleveland, 1870–1930*. Urbana: University of Illinois Press.

Lehrer, Brian. (2015). "Gentrification and Integration of Our Public Schools." *The Brian Lehrer Show*, audio, 33:11. December 14, 2015. WNYC. http://www.wnyc.org/story/gentrification-and-integration-our-local-schools/.

Lev, Steven. 1981. "HUD Site and Neighborhood Selection Standards: An Easing of Placement Restrictions." *Urban Law Annual* 22: 199–225.

Logan, John R., Weiwei Zhang, Richard Turner, and Allison Shertzer. 2015. "Creating the Black Ghetto: Black Residential Patterns before and during the Great Migration."

Annals of the American Academy of Political and Social Science 660: 18–35. doi:10.1177/0002716215572993.
Los Angeles Sentinel. 1939. "Negro Congress Says Slum Project Here Assured." October 12, 5.
Los Angeles Sentinel. 1946. "Overcrowding, Sanitation Lack, High Rents in 'Ghetto' Districts Create Scandalous Situation." January 3, 3.
Los Angeles Sentinel. 1950. "Public Housing Problem." *Los Angeles Sentinel*, August 31, A8.
Marcuse, Peter. 1995. "Interpreting 'Public Housing' History." *Journal of Architectural and Planning Research* 12 (3): 240–58.
McClory, Robert. 1972a. "HUD Denies Black Housing Plot." *Chicago Daily Defender*, April 29–May 5, 4.
McClory, Robert. 1972b. "Row over Austin Rule: Blacks Trapped in Housing Fight." *Chicago Daily Defender*, March 7, 3–4.
McClure, Kirk, and Bonnie Johnson. 2015. "Housing Programs Fail to Deliver on Neighborhood Quality, Reexamined." *Housing Policy Debate* 25 (3): 463–96. doi:10.1080/10511482.2014.944201.
Meyerson, Martin, and Edward C. Banfield. 1955. *Politics, Planning and the Public Interest: The Case of Public Housing in Chicago*. Glencoe, IL: Free Press.
Miller, Kelly. 1927. "The Causes of Segregation." *Current History* 25 (6): 827–31.
Montgomery, Roger. 1985. "Pruitt-Igoe: Policy Failure or Societal Symptom." In *The Metropolitan Midwest: Policy Problems and Prospects for Change*, edited by Barry Checkoway and Carl V. Patton, 229–43. Urbana: University of Illinois Press.
Murchison, John P. 1935. "The Negro and Low-Rent Housing." *Crisis: A Record of the Darker Races*, July, 199–200, 210.
National Urban League. 1973. "Summary of the National Survey of Housing Abandonment." In *Abandonment*, edited by US Department of Housing and Urban Development, 39–40. Washington, DC: US Government Printing Office.
New York Amsterdam News. 1935. "$4,700,000 for Housing Here: New Project Will Provide Rooms at $8." July 6, 1.
New York Amsterdam News. 1936. "Housing Project Flooded by Applicants: Modern Units and Low Rents Draw Crowds." November 14, 19.
New York Times. 1936. "Would Pick Tenants by Point System." January 29, 14.
Nixon, Richard. 1971. *Third Annual Report on National Housing Goals*. House Doc. 92–136. Washington, DC: Government Printing Office.
Orlebeke, Charles J. 2000. "The Evolution of Low-Income Housing Policy, 1949 to 1999." *Housing Policy Debate* 11 (2): 489–520. doi:10.1080/10511482.2000.9521375.
Owens, Michael Leo. 2007. *God and Government in the Ghetto: The Politics of Church-State Collaboration in Black America*. Chicago: University of Chicago Press.
Peters, Art. 1960. "Slum Clearance Prime Objective of Councilmen Shepard, McIntosh." *Philadelphia Tribune*, January 5, 1, 2.
Philadelphia Tribune. 1935. "The Heart of Any Good Newspaper Is Its Editorial Policy." January 17, 20.
Philadelphia Tribune. 1956. "NAACP Blasts Effort to Shackle Philly with Biased Housing." July 31, 2.

Philadelphia Tribune. 1970. "Logan Group Says 'Project' Will Ghetto-ize Them: Claim 20th & Rockland Units Will Shatter Peaceful Integration." August 15, 5.

Pittsburgh Courier. 1933. "Federal Housing." October 21, 10.

Pittsburgh Courier. 1938a. "Fourth of 30,496 New U.S. Homes Open to Race: Weaver Shows Quota for Race in Housing Plan." August 6, 1.

Pittsburgh Courier. 1938b. "Perpetuating Segregation." October 22, 10.

Pittsburgh Courier. 1942. "The Lesson of Sojourner Truth." May 9, 6.

Pittsburgh Courier. 1956. "NAACP Unhappy about Housing 'Integration'." May 5, sec. 2, 1.

Plunz, Richard. 1990. *A History of Housing in New York City: Dwelling Type and Social Change in the American Metropolis.* New York: Columbia University Press.

Poverty & Race Research Action Council. 2004. *Civil Rights Mandates in the Low Income Housing Tax Credit (LIHTC) Program.* Washington, DC: Poverty & Race Research Action Council and Lawyers Committee for Civil Rights.

Poverty & Race Research Action Council. 2015. *Building Opportunity II: Civil Rights Best Practices in the Low Income Housing Tax Credit Program (2015 Update).* Report. Washington, DC: Poverty & Race Research Action Council.

Ravo, Nick. 1991. "Tax Credit Program on Borrowed Time." *New York Times,* November 24, R3.

Rohe, William M., and Lance Freeman. 2001. "Assisted Housing and Residential Segregation: The Role of Race and Ethnicity in the Siting of Assisted Housing Developments." *Journal of the American Planning Association* 67 (3): 279–92. doi:10.1080/01944360108976236.

Rolen, Ruth. 1960. "City's Largest Housing Project: The Richard Allen Apts. Called Home by 6,100 Residents." *Philadelphia Tribune,* September 13, 9.

Roster, Edgar W. 1936. "New Deal Ignored Negro Needs Congress Charges." *Philadelphia Tribune,* October 22, 1.

Schwartz, Joel. 1986. "The Consolidated Tenants League of Harlem: Black Self-Help vs. White, Liberal Intervention in Ghetto Housing, 1934–1944." *Afro-Americans in New York Life and History* 10 (1): 31–52.

Simmons, Clarence L. 1937. "Cleveland Committee Charges Race Jim-Crow in Gov't Housing Projects." *Pittsburgh Courier,* October 23, 12.

Smith, Preston H., II. 2012. *Racial Democracy and the Black Metropolis: Housing Policy in Postwar Chicago.* Minneapolis: University of Minnesota Press.

Sorauf, Frank J. 1960. "The Silent Revolution in Patronage." *Public Administration Review* 20 (1): 28–34. doi:10.2307/974064.

Stoutland, Sara E. 1999. "Community Development Corporations: Mission, Strategy, and Accomplishments." In *Urban Problems and Community Development,* edited by Ronald F. Ferguson and William T. Dickens, 193–240. Washington, DC, Brookings Institution Press.

US Department of Housing and Urban Development. 2015. "Low-Income Housing Tax Credits." Last modified June 18, 2015. Accessed December 17, 2015. http://www.huduser.gov/portal/datasets/lihtc.html.

Vale, Lawrence J. 2013. *Purging the Poorest: Public Housing and the Design Politics of Twice-Cleared Communities.* Chicago: University of Chicago Press.

Washington, Forrester B. 1920. *The Negro in Detroit: A Survey of the Conditions of a Negro Group in a Northern Industrial Center during the War Prosperity Period*. Detroit: Associated Charities of Detroit.

Weaver, Robert C. 1948. *The Negro Ghetto*. New York: Harcourt, Brace.

Webster, Gary. 1980. "E. Hill Residents Alarmed over New Housing." *Pittsburgh Courier*, September 13, 2.

Weicher, John C. 1990. "The Voucher/Production Debate." In *Building Foundations: Housing and Federal Policy*, edited by Denise DiPasquale and Langley C. Keyes, 263–92. Philadelphia: University of Pennsylvania Press.

White, Gennan S. 1947. "Writes On Housing." Letter to the editor, *Chicago Defender*, February 1, 14.

Wilkerson, Isabel. 2010. *The Warmth of Other Suns: The Epic Story of America's Great Migration*. New York: Random House.

Winston, Smith. 1936. "Better Housing for Negroes Gift of New Deal: Slum Dwellers Seen Getting 'Break' from Low-Rental Project." *New York Amsterdam News*, September 19, 11.

Woods, Howard B. 1948. "NAACP Girds for Battle against 'Slum Clearance' in St. Louis." *Chicago Defender*, July 24, 2.

Woofter, T. J., Jr. 1928. *Negro Problems in Cities*. Garden City, NY: Doubleday, Doran.

Wright, Charilyn. 2002. "A Visual Explosion in Harlem." *International Review of African American Art* 18 (4): 3–23.

Wyche, Paul H., Jr. 1972. "An Analysis of New Separatism." *Philadelphia Tribune*, March 25, 10.

4

The Enduring Significance of Segregation
Jason Q. Purnell

> In the name of the greatest people that have ever trod this earth, I draw the line in the dust and toss the gauntlet before the feet of tyranny, and I say segregation now, segregation tomorrow, segregation forever.
> —Alabama Governor George Wallace, *inaugural address, January 14, 1963*
>
> I have a dream that one day . . . the sons of former slaves and the sons of former slave owners will be able to sit down together at the table of brotherhood.
> —Dr. Martin Luther King, Jr., *keynote address at the March on Washington for Jobs and Freedom, August 28, 1963*

A little over 2 months prior to the 2014 shooting death of Michael Brown and subsequent protests that drew national attention to the small St. Louis suburb of Ferguson, Missouri, a report was released documenting many of the racial disparities that would be noted in the coverage of those events (Purnell, Camberos, and Fields 2015). One of the most striking figures from *For the Sake of All: A Report on the Health and Well-Being of African Americans in St. Louis—and Why It Matters for Everyone* was a map of life expectancy by selected St. Louis zip codes (Figure 4.1).[1] The largest gap—18 years—was noted between the affluent, predominantly white, suburban zip code of 63105, and the low-income, mostly African American zip code of 63106 in the city of St. Louis. The areas delimited by these zip codes are less than 10 miles apart, but they are characterized by vastly different conditions. At the time of the 2010 decennial census, the median income in 63105 was $90,000, six times the $15,000 median income in 63106. The rate of poverty was just 7 percent in 63105 but 54 percent in 63106, and the unemployment rate was six times higher in 63106 (24 percent vs. 4 percent in 63105). In 2010, the population of 63105 was 9 percent African American and 78 percent white. The population of 63106 was 95 percent African American and 2 percent white.

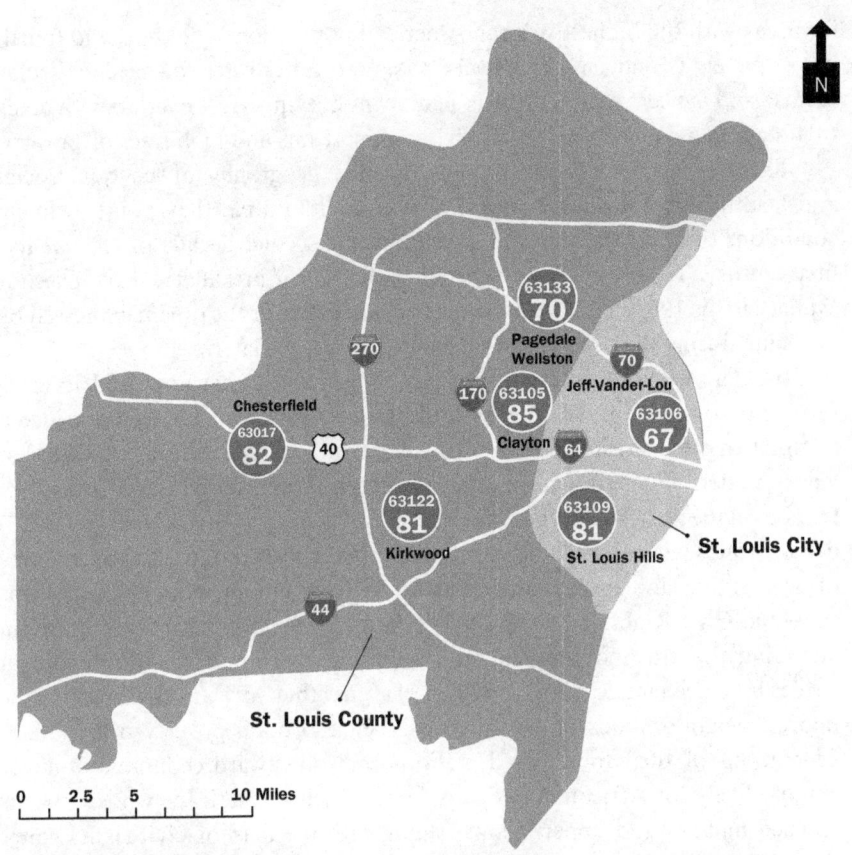

Source: City of St. Louis Department of Health-Center for Health Information, Planning, and Research; Census 2010; MODHSS, Death MICA 2010

Notes: Life expectancies were constructed using a calculator developed by the City of St. Louis Department of Health-Center for Health Information, Planning, and Research; Zip code life expectancies were derived using population counts from Census 2010 and deaths from Death MICA 2010

FIGURE 4.1 Life expectancy for select zip codes in St. Louis, Missouri. Adapted from Jason Q. Purnell, Gabriela J. Camberos, and Robert P. Fields, eds., *For the Sake of All: A Report on the Health and Well-Being of African Americans in St. Louis and Why It Matters for Everyone* (St. Louis, MO: Washington University and Saint Louis University, 2015), 27.

The report also included another series of maps (Purnell, Camberos, and Fields 2015, 30; Goodman and Gilbert 2013, 3), which are shown in Figure 4.2. The first map, in panel A of the figure, shows the percentage of African Americans in the population (roughly 30 percent of the total population) by zip code for the city of St. Louis and the surrounding St. Louis County (the city and county are politically distinct entities). The highest concentrations are in the northern portion of the city and the northeastern quadrant of the county: African Americans make up 45 to 97 percent of the population in those zip codes. The second map, in panel B, shows the percentage of the population living in poverty by zip code for the same geography, with significant overlap for areas with the highest African American population. The third and fourth maps, panels C and D, respectively, show mortality rates for cardiovascular disease and cancer. Again, there is significant but imperfect overlap with areas that have high concentrations of African Americans and high rates of poverty.

These maps do more than illustrate the geography of unequal social and health outcomes in a major US metropolitan area; they point to living conditions that remain segregated well into the second decade of the twenty-first century. They seem to suggest that the vision articulated by Governor Wallace in his 1963 inaugural address has won out over the dream expressed by Dr. King during the March on Washington 7 months later.

In "The Making of Ferguson," another analysis that appeared in close proximity to the events of August 2014, Richard Rothstein (2014a) provided a comprehensive historical overview of the federal, state, and local policies that led to modern-day segregation in St. Louis and that focused international attention on the area. At the national level, scholarship by Patrick Sharkey (2013) demonstrates with disquieting clarity the utter lack of progress made in terms of segregation and the concentration of poverty among African Americans since the Civil Rights Movement. The lack of progress belies the optimism attending the era and the general population's assumption that significant strides have been made. Sharkey (2013, 9) argues that African Americans in the poorest neighborhoods have "inherited" neighborhood poverty from several generations of their forebears. He shows that downward economic mobility is more likely for African Americans, even African Americans whose parents reached middle- and upper-income status with the help of civil rights gains, than for their similarly situated white counterparts. The cumulative disadvantage of multigenerational poverty and the social isolation of decades of residential segregation exact an economic toll and assault the body, producing poor health outcomes.

This chapter uses St. Louis in the age of Ferguson as a point of departure to explore the making of modern segregation and its social, economic, and health consequences. Although St. Louis is also marked by the economic segregation that now characterizes residential patterns in the United States, this chapter focuses specifically on racial residential segregation. Often missing from discussions of segregation are its psychological root causes. The chapter attempts to address this gap by examining the social psychology of intergroup relations as a means of understanding modern segregation. The chapter ends by considering possible remedies and policy implications.

The Development and Impact of Modern Segregation

Urban segregation was the result of an explicit set of formal policies and practices that led to the creation of African American ghettos in cities across

A

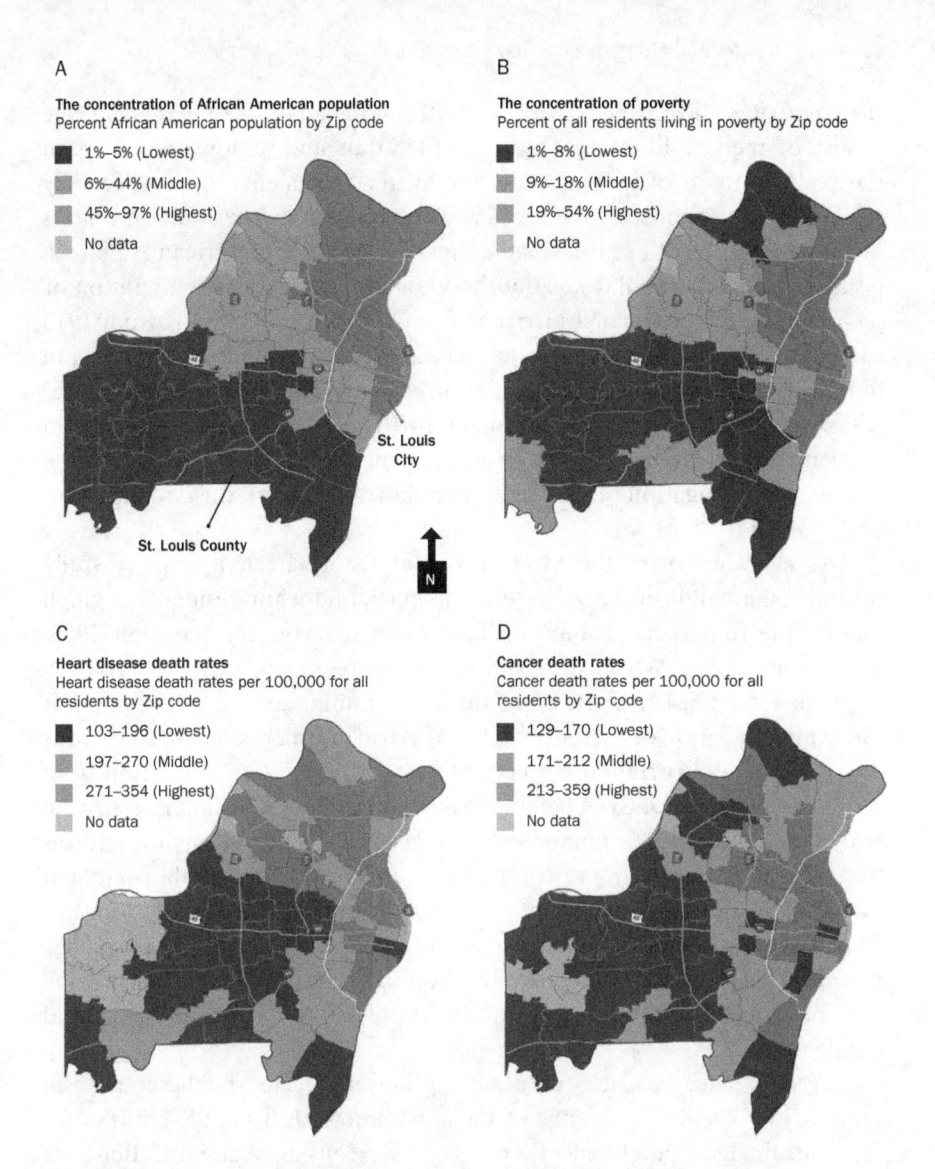

The concentration of African American population
Percent African American population by Zip code

- ■ 1%–5% (Lowest)
- ■ 6%–44% (Middle)
- ■ 45%–97% (Highest)
- ■ No data

B

The concentration of poverty
Percent of all residents living in poverty by Zip code

- ■ 1%–8% (Lowest)
- ■ 9%–18% (Middle)
- ■ 19%–54% (Highest)
- ■ No data

C

Heart disease death rates
Heart disease death rates per 100,000 for all residents by Zip code

- ■ 103–196 (Lowest)
- ■ 197–270 (Middle)
- ■ 271–354 (Highest)
- ■ No data

D

Cancer death rates
Cancer death rates per 100,000 for all residents by Zip code

- ■ 129–170 (Lowest)
- ■ 171–212 (Middle)
- ■ 213–359 (Highest)
- ■ No data

Death rates were age-adjusted using the US 2000 Standard population. Rates were not included for Zip codes with less than 20 deaths due to heart disease or cancer.

FIGURE 4.2 African American population, poverty, and cardiovascular and cancer mortality, by zip code in St. Louis, Missouri. Adapted from Jason Q. Purnell, Gabriela J. Camberos, and Robert P. Fields, eds., *For the Sake of All: A Report on the Health and Well-Being of African Americans in St. Louis and Why It Matters for Everyone* (St. Louis, MO: Washington University and Saint Louis University, 2015), 30.

A. The concentration (percentage) of African Americans in the population by zip code. Source: US Census 2010.

B. The concentration (percentage) of residents living in poverty by zip code. Source: American Community Survey 2007–2011, 5-year estimates.

C. Heart disease death rates per 100,000 residents by zip code. Source: Chronic Disease MICA (Missouri Information for Community Assessment) 2009–2010.

D. Cancer death rates per 100,000 residents by zip code. Source: Chronic Disease MICA (Missouri Information for Community Assessment) 2009–2010.

the country. As Rothstein (2014b, 6) notes in his analysis of Ferguson, the "cause of metropolitan segregation in St. Louis and nationwide has been the explicit intents of federal, state, and local governments to create racially segregated metropolises." While many northern and southern urban centers of the late nineteenth century had a highly concentrated African American population in a particular neighborhood or district, it was the migration of large numbers of African Americans from rural to urban areas from 1915 to 1970 that occasioned what would become the largely uninterrupted and unique segregation of a single racial or ethnic group in the United States (Massey and Denton 1993; Wilkerson 2010). St. Louis turns out to be a particularly instructive example because of the various "innovations" in the practice of segregation made there since shortly after the turn of the twentieth century.

As early as 1916, the St. Louis Real Estate Exchange successfully introduced a ballot initiative to separate black and white residents through one of the first racial zoning ordinances in the country (Gordon 2008; Rothstein 2014a). When such ordinances were struck down by the US Supreme Court in 1917,[2] St. Louis turned to similar zoning tactics that left out explicit mention of race, often placing African American neighborhoods near planned industrial development to create a buffer of separation from white neighborhoods. Even before the passage of zoning ordinances, private real estate professionals, homeowners, and even churches and civic organizations had begun adopting restrictive covenants, whereby neighbors entered into contractual agreements not to sell their homes to African Americans. Though ruled unconstitutional by the Supreme Court in the 1948 *Shelley v. Kraemer* decision,[3] the practice lived on in the formal regulations of the new Federal Housing Administration created as part of the New Deal (Rothstein 2014a).

By the 1940s, as blacks were moving into segregated public housing in central cities like St. Louis (one of the most notorious being St. Louis's own failed Pruitt-Igoe development), the Federal Housing Administration was massively subsidizing the movement of whites out of cities and into new suburban developments. As but one example of the racial exclusion of that era, only 0.05 percent (or 35) of the 70,000 units built in the city of St. Louis and St. Louis County between 1947 and 1952 were available for purchase by African Americans; the combined effects of Federal Housing Administration regulations, restrictive covenants, and private real estate industry practices severely limited their housing options (Rothstein 2014a).

During the 1960s, zoning re-emerged as a favored tool for reinforcing segregation in the new suburban communities of St. Louis; it remained so well into the 1990s. The most famous example comes from Black Jack, an all-white suburb in an unincorporated part of St. Louis County. In 1969, plans to build integrated housing for low- and moderate-income residents prompted the community's hurried incorporation as a city and the enactment of a zoning ordinance to prohibit the construction. The motivation for the ordinance was explicitly racial, and a suit was filed against it; by the time of the 1974 ruling from the Court of Appeals for the Eighth Circuit,[4] developers had lost interest in the project (Rothstein 2014a). More recent incorporations in St. Louis County have been less explicit in their racial intent but achieved the same racial outcome. This history of exclusion and isolation of African Americans through policies in the St. Louis region helped to produce the map (Figure 4.2, panel A) depicting the concentrations of the African American population. In many ways, it also helped to produce the life expectancy map in Figure 4.1. Understanding the latter requires an examination of the impact of residential segregation.

Douglas Massey and Nancy Denton (1993, 2) assert in *American Apartheid* that residential segregation "systematically undermines the social and economic well-being of blacks in the United States." It does this by creating areas of concentrated poverty that lack the jobs, educational opportunities, services, and amenities taken for granted in other communities. Indeed, the black ghetto has become a recognizable section of most major metropolitan areas with significant African American populations. It is characterized by disinvestment and the associated social disadvantage. Residential segregation and concentrated poverty have created what some sociologists call the "underclass," a subpopulation divorced from economic opportunity, its prospects for advancement so far out of reach that norms and structures supporting achievement have broken down (e.g., Wilson [1987] 2012, 3). Moreover, even African Americans who are able to make it into the middle class are more likely than similarly situated whites to live in or near areas of concentrated poverty (Pattillo-McCoy 1999).

Indeed, the analyses presented by Sharkey (2013) show that successful escape from areas of concentrated poverty has been exceedingly rare for African Americans. Sharkey finds that the proportion of African Americans who grew up in high-poverty neighborhoods (i.e., neighborhoods with poverty rates of 20 percent or more) was higher among those born between 1985 and 2000 than among their counterparts born between 1955 and 1970 (66 percent vs. 62 percent). In contrast, a very small fraction of white children were raised in high-poverty neighborhoods during those periods (4 percent vs. 6 percent; Sharkey 2013). White poverty (which is greater in absolute magnitude) also tends to be dispersed throughout urban metropolitan areas, not concentrated in the way that African American poverty is (Wilson [1987] 2012). This means that, in comparison with poor African Americans, poor whites are often better able to take advantage of the resources, such as well-resourced schools, safe streets, and high-quality recreational programs, available in more affluent neighborhoods.

The negative effects of residential segregation on health status have been long recognized as a particular challenge. In the roughly $17 trillion US economy, 17.5 percent of gross domestic product (or $3 trillion) is spent annually on healthcare (Martin et al. 2016). Racial and ethnic disparities are a national public health priority, and there is a powerful economic imperative to address them. An analysis by the Urban Institute estimated that health disparities will have cost $337 billion in the 10 years from 2009 through 2018 (Waidmann 2009); another analysis that considered healthcare costs as well as the indirect costs of segregation to society placed the estimate at $1.24 trillion over the 4 years from 2003 through 2006 (LaVeist, Gaskin, and Richard 2011). Clearly, intervening to eliminate disparities must be part of any serious strategy to contain the outsized costs of healthcare.

In an important review, David Williams and Chiquita Collins (2001, 404) note the following:

> Segregation is a primary cause of racial differences in socioeconomic status (SES) by determining access to education and employment opportunities. SES in turn remains a fundamental cause of racial differences in health. Segregation also creates conditions inimical to health in the social and physical environment. . . . Effective efforts to eliminate racial disparities in health must seriously confront segregation and its pervasive consequences.

The review goes on to explore the ways in which segregation limits educational and employment opportunities, leading to well-known disparities in SES that drive differences in individual-level health outcomes such as activity limitations and self-rated health. Segregation also has negative impacts on health at the level of neighborhoods and communities, results that persist in analyses controlling for the individual effects of SES. For example, residential segregation is associated with an elevation in the risk for heart disease morbidity, cause-specific and overall adult mortality, infant mortality, and tuberculosis (Williams and Collins 2001). Several explanations have been offered for segregation's negative neighborhood-level effects: inadequate and poorly maintained physical infrastructure, poor housing quality, underfunded municipal services, and exposure to certain environmental elements such as toxins and pollutants. Concerns about safety, the expense or unavailability of goods and services, and targeted advertisements for tobacco and alcoholic beverages also pose challenges because they are community-level factors associated with health behaviors that are key drivers of chronic disease. Finally, the authors suggest that segregation of urban African Americans is implicated in poor access to high-quality medical care as well as in the higher incidence of crime in general and of homicide mortality in particular. There is one notable exception to the largely negative findings concerning segregation's impact on health: residing in ethnic enclaves is reported to have protective effects for mental health (Williams and Collins 2001).

A more recent review by Michael Kramer and Carol Hogue (2009) covers much of the same conceptual ground as that traversed by Williams and Collins (2001) but focuses with greater specificity on various indices used to measure segregation. Kramer and Hogue also explore the possibility that differences in segregation's effects on health depend on which dimension of segregation is measured. They offer a useful conceptual framework to explain the potential pathways through which segregation exerts its influence on health. According to this model, racial residential segregation has its indirect impact on health outcomes by influencing individual-level SES (e.g., education, employment, and income), neighborhood SES (concentrated poverty, crime, infrastructure decay), social capital (e.g., black political power, social support networks), and individual exposure and behaviors (e.g., stress, discrimination, substance use, nutrition). Each of these mediating factors also interacts with others in the model.

Most of the 39 studies reviewed by Kramer and Hogue (2009) used the dissimilarity index, which estimates the proportion of the minority group that would have to move to another neighborhood in order to achieve complete integration. The authors suggest that the index may be the weakest measure for uncovering segregation's effects on health. They assert that measures of isolation (i.e., the probability that two individuals randomly drawn from the same neighborhood are of the same race) and concentration (i.e., the spatial density of a minority group in an area) better capture unhealthy environments and exposure (Kramer and Hogue 2009). On balance, however, Kramer and Hogue (2009) affirm prior findings that residential segregation has negative effects on the health of African Americans, particularly on pregnancy outcomes and adult mortality. Their review also finds that clustering—the grouping of racially similar neighborhoods in space—has a protective effect, which persists in results from analyses that account for social and economic isolation.[5] The finding is similar to the one on ethnic enclaves in the review by Williams and Collins (2001). Largely corroborating these findings, additional reviews have emphasized the need for theoretical development, explication of causal pathways (including the use of biological data to examine such pathways), better measurement of key constructs, exploration of resilience, movement beyond black–white segregation to include segregation of other ethnic groups, and attention to the nativity status of blacks and other ethnic groups (Acevedo-Garcia et al. 2003; Landrine and Corral 2009; White and Borrell 2011).

This section has traced the development of modern segregation and discussed its effects on social, economic, and health outcomes. However, a full understanding of modern segregation requires insights that go beyond these observations and associations. Part of that fuller rendering can be provided by insights from social psychology, which are discussed in the following section.

The Psychology of Group Interaction

Though the social science and public health literatures offer considerable evidence of the development and impact of segregation, two key questions remain largely unanswered: why did segregation emerge as a response to the reality of race in America, and why has it been so enduring even in the face of significant social and cultural change? Indeed, the legal and legislative victories of the Civil Rights Movement and the election of the first black president of the United States in Barack Obama would seem to suggest that segregation is obsolete, yet it persists. While segregation is certainly an institutional expression of racial bias, it is ultimately perpetuated by individuals and groups. Understanding the persistence of segregation among individuals and groups requires an understanding of the social psychology of intergroup relations.[6]

"Intergroup relations," as Michael Hogg understands the term, "refers to the way in which people who belong to social groups or categories perceive, think about, feel about, and act towards and interact with people in other groups" (Hogg 2013, 533). One of the most basic precepts of the social psychology of intergroup relations is that intergroup behavior is both competitive and ethnocentric. In other words, individuals within groups tend to seek advantages over other groups and to view their own group as the norm or standard by which groups should be evaluated. This drive toward group competitiveness was exploited in Muzafer Sherif's (1966) now-classic study, the Robbers Cave experiment. Sherif was able to create meaningful identities and considerable intergroup conflict between boys at a camp who were divided into groups (the Rattlers and the Eagles) and made to compete for valuable prizes. The researchers were able to reverse some of the highly negative attitudes that emerged toward the respective out-group (i.e., Rattlers toward Eagles and vice versa) by engaging the boys in cooperative activities whereby members of both groups stood to gain. The results helped Sherif to formulate realistic-conflict theory (or interdependence theory), which holds that conflict will emerge in a zero-sum competition between groups with similar goals but that more harmonious relations can develop where shared goals can be accomplished by working together. In a related vein, the concept of intergroup social dilemma describes a situation in which "a group has to sacrifice its own benefits for the sake of a larger collective that includes out-groups" (Hogg 2013, 539). In the face of such dilemmas, in-groups tend to pursue their own goals rather than collective good (Brewer and Schneider 1990; Hogg 2007). While superordinate goals seem to be powerful motivators for intergroup cooperation and harmony, other forces make conflict the much more frequent circumstance between groups. (Superordinate goals are subsequently discussed further in relation to contact theory.) Without intentional intervention to create conditions for cooperation, such competitive dynamics are likely to be the norm. Several of the forces driving conflict merit close discussion here.

The fundamental and largely automatic cognitive processes involved in social categorization militate against harmonious group interactions. In laboratory simulations of "minimal groups," which have no real-life social basis and do not carry any meaning beyond the experimental condition, individuals who believe themselves to be members of these groups "discriminate in favor of their group, show evaluative ingroup bias [i.e., rate their group more favorably], and indicate that they feel a sense of belonging to their group, and similarity to and liking for their anonymous fellow ingroup members" (Hogg 2013, 539). If such strong feelings of attachment can be elicited from an anonymous group whose members have no actual contact or history, it is easy to imagine the strength with which actual group affiliations are felt. Indeed, much social categorization is not only strong but happens outside of consciousness, and distinctive visual cues cause categorization of people who are associated with cognitive schemas for a given group. The physical markers commonly associated with race are highly visual cues, and the stereotypes linked with race seem to be activated automatically. While the effects of categorization can be mitigated through perspective taking and reductions in prejudice, the evidence unfortunately suggests that the association between the social category and the stereotype is actually strengthened when people are asked to consciously think about it—a phenomenon known as the "stereotype rebound effect" (Hogg 2013, 540).

There are also important implications for social categorization in individuals' perceptions of themselves and in the related social identities that are part of their self-concepts. Group membership and affiliation are crucial aspects of identity, and social identity theory suggests that "people define and evaluate themselves in terms of the groups to which they belong" (Hogg 2013, 542). Therefore, there is a strong drive to identify one's group membership as superior to membership in other groups. In the process of social categorization, the self is categorized as a prototypical member of the relevant social group. In other words, when one conceives of oneself as a group member, individual distinctiveness gives way to the characteristics of a prototypical category through a process called "depersonalization" (2013, 542). One of the primary motives for maintaining social identity and categorizing oneself in such a way is to provide certainty about modes of thought, behavior, and interaction in the social world. People often go to extremes to guard against identity uncertainty and seek to align themselves with groups that have very specific and cohesive attributes (Hogg 2013).

In light of these processes, it is not surprising that prejudice and discrimination are often the results of intergroup interactions. There are strong drives to maintain a positive self-image and to protect the status of one's in-group. Interestingly, prejudice (an attitude) does not always result in discrimination (a behavior), and this is in keeping with overall findings on attitude-behavior consistency. Modern forms of prejudice are seldom voiced explicitly because social norms proscribe such behavior. This impedes efforts to measure prejudice, and social psychologists have been forced to rely on implicit measures. Just as prejudiced attitudes need not (and often do not) lead to overt discrimination, discrimination itself follows an interesting pattern called the "positive-negative asymmetry effect": people will discriminate against out-groups (and in favor of in-groups) when distributing rewards but not when distributing punishments, unless the in-group is perceived to be under threat (Hogg 2013, 547; Mummendey and Otten 1998). Discrimination, then, is more about protecting resources and advantages for the in-group than it is about harming the out-group. Indeed, most in-groups view discrimination as a mark of loyalty and commitment to the group (Hogg 2013).

This brief overview of relevant social psychological principles points to the significant challenges to intergroup harmony posed by cognitive, motivational, and identity-based factors. Most in-groups not only perceive their members to be superior to other groups but will actively discriminate in favor of their group, especially when resources are believed to be finite or when they are under threat. Certainly the resources that are associated with neighborhoods and the deeply personal choice of housing for oneself and one's family can be conceived in this way. Policy is without question responsible for segregation in the United States, but those policies are enacted and supported by individuals and groups with relatively consistent patterns of behavior in the face of racial and ethnic difference.

Policy Implications

William Julius Wilson, Douglas Massey and Nancy Denton, and Patrick Sharkey have all offered several policy prescriptions for addressing the impact of residential segregation. Wilson argues for a broad policy agenda that would touch all segments of the US population and include some elements specifically targeted by race. The agenda would emphasize economic growth, the competitiveness of American goods and services, and maintenance of tight and adaptable labor markets. It would also offer support for families: an allowance program, guaranteed child support, and child care (Wilson [1987] 2012). Wilson's seminal work on concentrated poverty among urban blacks was a primary inspiration for the HOPE VI program and the subsequent Choice Neighborhoods program, though such inspiration was apparently not his intent. Both programs led to the elimination of traditional public housing and the development of mixed-income housing; both programs were seen as means to broaden economic integration (Wilson [1987] 2012). Interestingly, in the second edition of *The Truly Disadvantaged*, Wilson retreats from his original political calculation that a mostly race-neutral and color-blind framing is needed to secure passage of his policy agenda. This chapter returns later to a discussion on the wisdom of that retreat.

Massey and Denton (1993) also offer policy prescriptions, but most of the proposals in *American Apartheid* center on strengthening the US Department of Housing and Urban Development's enforcement of the Fair Housing Act.[7] The proposals include providing financial support for local fair housing agencies; creating a permanent testing program to identify violations by realtors; increasing enforcement of discrimination in lending; fostering desegregation in public housing through rental vouchers; and speeding up the judicial review of fair-housing complaints (Massey and Denton 1993). Though discrimination in housing remains a persistent problem more than 25 years after these recommendations were made, the Department of Housing and Urban Development's recent rules clarify the mandate to "affirmatively further fair housing" and a Supreme Court ruling preserved the disparate-impact provisions of the Fair Housing Act. Though their durability remains in question at this writing, these developments would seem to be in keeping with the recommendations.[8]

Interestingly, Sharkey (2013) takes a slightly more indirect approach to the problem of concentrated, multigenerational poverty in segregated urban neighborhoods: he calls for a "durable urban policy" approach (23), arguing that investment, policies, and programs have to be substantial enough in their magnitude and duration to have meaningful impact. His argument largely sidesteps contemporary debates about whether approaches ought to be place-based or regional (he holds that they must be both) and whether moving families out of urban ghettos to areas of greater opportunity is better than investing in distressed neighborhoods (he asserts that residents of the most distressed neighborhoods should be supported in leaving but that massive relocation is not feasible). He focuses instead on providing guaranteed employment through a public service program along the lines of New Deal–era efforts such as the Works Progress Administration and the Civilian Conservation Corps. Drawing motivation from the Harlem Children's Zone and its federal offshoot, the Promise Neighborhoods program, he calls for heavy investments in the development of children living in urban areas (Sharkey 2013). Support for such policies was evident in the Obama administration, but Sharkey worries that the durability of these policies is threatened both by their relatively limited reach and their vulnerability to shifting political priorities. He believes a political strategy is therefore necessary in order to secure the foundations of a durable urban policy powerful enough to address decades-long disinvestment and disadvantage among the urban poor.

All of these policy prescriptions have value, however hard it is to make progress in the current federal political climate. But the challenges are not merely political. The intergroup relations literature cited previously should give policymakers pause in designing programs to ameliorate segregation's impact. Reducing segregation means increasing intergroup contact. Most groups, especially groups that have a history of negative interaction, will approach intergroup contact with anxiety. Integration will require combating this anxiety.

Social psychology has not just explored the dynamics of conflict between groups but has also undertaken study of the conditions under which groups can cooperate and prejudice can be reduced. The most influential work in this field was done more than 60 years ago by Gordon Allport (1954), and his contact theory continues to influence the study of intergroup harmony today. Allport suggested that four conditions must be satisfied in order for intergroup contact to result in positive attitude change: group members must (1) meet as equals; (2) share common (or superordinate) goals; (3) cooperate in reaching goals; and (4) have the support of authorities, laws, and norms (Allport 1954; Pettigrew and Tropp 2006). Mere contact alone, evidence suggests, is woefully inadequate to the task of achieving intergroup harmony. Studies over several decades have corroborated Allport's basic claims, but meeting these conditions in the real world has proven exceptionally difficult (Pettigrew and Tropp 2006). This is due in part to the anxiety that intergroup contact provokes: out-group members are the subjects of negative stereotypes, and both groups fear rejection. But the difficulty in satisfying Allport's conditions also stems from conflicts (real or perceived) over finite resources and from actual differences in values and beliefs (Stephan and Stephan 2000). Moreover, positive intergroup contact threatens the identity of both groups, and those threats even persist during recategorization, which is one of the primary processes by which bias is reduced as a result of contact. When two formerly disparate groups attempt to recategorize themselves as members of a new superordinate group (e.g., through assimilation), there are very real concerns about relinquishing the distinctiveness of the original groups and the social identities attached to them. For this reason, it may be optimal to simultaneously maintain subgroup distinctiveness and superordinate group membership. Thomas Pettigrew's (1998) conceptualization of contact theory suggests that there may also be a developmental trajectory for contact: first interpersonal contact and individual tolerance, then broad acceptance of out-group members within superordinate groups. However, both laboratory and field research by Samuel Gaertner and John Dovidio (2005) suggests that racial bias can be reduced when a common in-group identity can be formed.

The applications of these principles to experiments like Moving to Opportunity are clear. Moving to Opportunity is a federal program that encourages poor families living in public housing to move to low-poverty, high-opportunity neighborhoods. The program has had success in improving the prospects of the youngest children at the time of the move and the mental health of some adults. Those interested in enhancing such efforts have focused on the need to provide services and resources for families. Those offerings are likely necessary but not sufficient to ensure the success of efforts at meaningful integration. Evidence from social psychology suggests that an attempt should be made to meet all of Allport's (1954) conditions for positive intergroup contact, but at a minimum, cooperation toward superordinate goals might be useful. In other words, efforts should be made to engage families in the life of their new community (e.g., through an explicit set of welcoming gestures or activities or encouragement of shared decision-making in neighborhood or block associations) and to develop enough attachment to it that it is incorporated into their sense of identity. Just as important will be inculcating a sense of shared identity with existing residents. Gaertner and Dovidio's (2005) applied research suggests that interventions with school-aged children may be particularly promising both in establishing a common in-group identity and reducing bias. It will also be important for arriving families to maintain connections to long-held affiliations and group memberships; these connections offer protection from the identity threats posed by radical recategorization, which can be triggered by relocation to a new community. For instance, we might expect relocating families to become involved in their new community while maintaining ties to their previous neighborhood, which may have been home to multiple generations (Sharkey 2013). Compared with programs that focus only on movement out of disadvantaged neighborhoods, programs that have this dual focus—acclimation as well as maintenance of other important aspects of identity—may be better at fostering successful integration.

Second, as Sharkey (2013) notes, reductions in concentrated urban poverty among African Americans occurred when immigrant groups entered predominantly black neighborhoods, not when gentrification brought an influx of middle- and upper-income whites. This suggests that effective policy remedies for segregation may be helped by a broad vision of intergroup relations that extends beyond the familiar black–white binary to include Latino, Asian, and even black Caribbean and African populations. It is likely that the dynamics between these groups and African Americans in urban areas of concentrated poverty will look very different than those dynamics emerging from the movement of small numbers of low-income African Americans to more affluent, mostly white neighborhoods, or from the entry of middle- and upper-class whites into historically poor black neighborhoods. It is possible that intergroup conflict and competition will be the outcome of an influx of immigrant groups into majority black neighborhoods—and there are several examples of this in places like Los Angeles, Miami, and New York City. Just because the dominant group may lump "minorities" into a single category does not mean that the same distrust of out-groups will not be present when minority groups encounter one another. Common in-group identity may be just as critical to establish among these groups, and it is unclear whether shared "minority" status will be sufficient for its development.

Finally, social psychology offers an important lesson on the politics of policies to counter residential segregation by race. The social psychology literature suggests that Wilson (1987) may have been correct in his initial inclination to downplay race in framing a policy agenda. In light of the fundamentally ethnocentric and competitive nature of intergroup relations, it would seem ill-advised to highlight race in the redistribution of resources or even the intensification of programmatic efforts.

For all of the obvious challenges, political attempts to build a multiracial class agenda that promotes the life chances of all poor Americans may be important to reconsider. The direction of activism in the past several years has been toward racial identity, not away. The events in Ferguson have morphed into a national Black Lives Matter movement, and one wonders whether Wilson's approach could gather much support today. But the record of history and the results of behavioral science should make policymakers and advocates far from sanguine that the Black Lives Matter movement will lead to the durable urban policy that Sharkey envisions. Regardless, the challenges will be formidable. In particular, the unique social isolation of African Americans over the course of US history will not be easily diminished even under the best of circumstances. More than 50 years after Wallace and King first offered their competing visions for the nation, it remains to be seen which vision will win: Wallace's permanent segregation or King's superordinate goal of a common table for all.

Notes

1. In June 2018, the For the Sake of All project became Health Equity Works, signaling its deep commitment to translating data and research into collaborative community action to advance health equity, particularly in the St. Louis region.

2. Buchanan v. Warley, 245 U.S. 60 (1917).

3. Shelley v. Kraemer, 334 U.S. 1 (1948).

4. United States v. City of Black Jack, 508 F.2d 1179 (8th Cir. 1974), *cert. denied*, 422 U.S. 1042 (1974).

5. The distinction between clustering and isolation centers on the level of analysis. Isolation is the probability of encountering someone of the same race/ethnicity in a random encounter *within* a neighborhood. Clustering is about whether groups of racially/ethnically homogenous neighborhoods are contiguous with each other.

6. A full review of the vast psychological literature on intergroup relations is beyond the scope of this chapter, but discussion of some key concepts may explain the persistence of segregation and shed light on ways to combat it. For much of this discussion, I rely on a review by Hogg (2013), though other reviews are available.

7. Fair Housing Act, 42 U.S.C. §§ 3533, 3535, 3601–3631 (2012).

8. For the fair housing rule, see Affirmatively Furthering Fair Housing, 80 Fed. Reg. 42,272 (July 16, 2015) (codified at 24 C.F.R. pts. 5, 91, 92, 570, 574, 576, 903 (2016)). For the high court's 2015 rule on disparate impact, see Texas Department of Housing and Community Affairs v. Inclusive Communities Project, No. 13-1371, slip op. (U.S. June 25, 2015). https://www.supremecourt.gov/opinions/14pdf/13-1371_8m58.pdf.

References

Acevedo-Garcia, Dolores, Kimberly A. Lochner, Theresa L. Osypuk, and S. V. Subramanian. 2003. "Future Directions in Residential Segregation and Health Research: A Multilevel Approach." *American Journal of Public Health* 93 (2): 215–21. doi:10.2105/AJPH.93.2.215.

Allport, Gordon W. 1954. *The Nature of Prejudice*. Reading, MA: Addison Wesley.

Brewer, Marilynn B., and Sherry K. Schneider. 1990. "Social Identity and Social Dilemmas: A Double-Edged Sword." In *Social Identity Theory: Constructive and Critical Advances*, edited by Dominic Abrams and Michael A. Hogg, 169–84. London: Harvester Wheatsheaf.

Gaertner, Samuel L., and John F. Dovidio. 2005. "Understanding and Addressing Contemporary Racism: From Aversive Racism to the Common Ingroup Identity Model." *Journal of Social Issues* 61 (3): 615–39. doi:10.1111/j.1540-4560.2005.00424.x.

Goodman, Melody S., and Keon L. Gilbert. 2013. "Segregation: Divided Cities Lead to Differences in Health." For the Sake of All Brief 4, November. St. Louis, MO: Washington University and Saint Louis University. https://forthesakeofall.org/wp-content/uploads/2016/06/FSOA_policybrief_4.pdf.

Gordon, Colin. 2008. *Mapping Decline: St. Louis and the Fate of the American City*. Philadelphia: University of Pennsylvania Press.

Hogg, Michael A. 2007. "Social Identity and the Group Context of Trust: Managing Risk and Building Trust through Belonging." In *Trust in Cooperative Risk Management: Uncertainty and Scepticism in the Public Mind*, edited by Michael Siegrist, Timothy C. Earle, and Heinz Gutscher, 51–71. London: Earthscan.

Hogg, Michael A. 2013. "Intergroup Relations." In *Handbook of Social Psychology*, 2nd ed. Edited by John DeLamater and Amanda Ward, 533–61. Dordrecht, Netherlands: Springer Netherlands.

Kramer, Michael R., and Carol R. Hogue. 2009. "Is Segregation Bad for Your Health?" *Epidemiologic Reviews* 31 (1): 178–94. doi:10.1093/epirev/mxp001.

Landrine, Hope, and Irma Corral. 2009. "Separate and Unequal: Residential Segregation and Black Health Disparities." *Ethnicity and Disease* 19 (2): 179–84.

LaVeist, Thomas A., Darrel J. Gaskin, and Patrick Richard. 2011. "The Economic Burden of Health Inequalities in the United States." Fact Sheet. Washington, DC: Joint Center for Political and Economic Studies.

Martin, Anne B., Micah Hartman, Joseph Benson, Aaron Catlin, and the National Health Expenditure Accounts Team. 2016. "National Health Spending in 2014: Faster Growth Driven by Coverage Expansion and Prescription Drug Spending." *Health Affairs* 35 (1): 150–60. doi:10.1377/hlthaff.2015.1194.

Massey, Douglas S., and Nancy A. Denton. 1993. *American Apartheid: Segregation and the Making of the Underclass*. Cambridge, MA: Harvard University Press.

Mummendey, Amélie, and Sabine Otten. 1998. "Positive–Negative Asymmetry in Social Discrimination." *European Review of Social Psychology* 9 (1): 107–43. doi:10.1080/14792779843000063.

Pattillo-McCoy, Mary. 1999. *Black Picket Fences: Privilege and Peril among the Black Middle Class*. Chicago: University of Chicago Press.

Pettigrew, Thomas F. 1998. "Intergroup Contact Theory." *Annual Review of Psychology* 49: 65–85. doi:10.1146/annurev.psych.49.1.65.

Pettigrew, Thomas F., and Linda R. Tropp. 2006. "A Meta-Analytic Test of Intergroup Contact Theory." *Journal of Personality and Social Psychology* 90 (5): 751–83. doi:10.1037/0022-3514.90.5.751.

Purnell, Jason Q., Gabriela J. Camberos, and Robert P. Fields, eds. 2015. *For the Sake of All: A Report on the Health and Well-Being of African Americans in St. Louis and Why It Matters for Everyone*. St. Louis, MO: Washington University in St. Louis and Saint Louis University.

Rothstein, Richard. 2014a. "The Making of Ferguson." *American Prospect* 25 (5): 46–53.

Rothstein, Richard. 2014b. *The Making of Ferguson: Public Policies at the Root of Its Troubles*. Report. Washington, DC: Economic Policy Institute.

Sharkey, Patrick. 2013. *Stuck in Place: Urban Neighborhoods and the End of Progress toward Racial Equality*. Chicago: University of Chicago Press.

Sherif, Muzafer. 1966. *In Common Predicament: Social Psychology of Intergroup Conflict and Cooperation*. Boston: Houghton Mifflin.

Stephan, Walter S., and Cookie White Stephan. 2000. "An Integrated Threat Theory of Prejudice." In *Reducing Prejudice and Discrimination*, edited by Stuart Oskamp, 23–45. Mahwah, NJ: Lawrence Erlbaum.

Waidmann, Timothy A. 2009. *"Estimating the Cost of Racial and Ethnic Health Disparities."* Policy Brief. Washington, DC: Urban Institute.

White, Kellee, and Luisa N. Borrell. 2011. "Racial/Ethnic Residential Segregation: Framing the Context of Health Risk and Health Disparities." *Health and Place* 17 (2): 438–48. doi:10.1016/j.healthplace.2010.12.002.

Wilkerson, Isabel. 2010. *The Warmth of Other Suns: The Epic Story of America's Great Migration*. New York: Random House.

Williams, David R., and Chiquita Collins. 2001. "Racial Residential Segregation: A Fundamental Cause of Racial Disparities in Health." *Public Health Reports* 116 (5): 404–16. doi:10.1093/phr/116.5.404.

Wilson, William Julius. 1987. *The Truly Disadvantaged: The Inner City, the Underclass, and Public Policy*. Chicago: University of Chicago Press.

Wilson, William Julius. (1987) 2012. *The Truly Disadvantaged: The Inner City, the Underclass, and Public Policy*, 2nd ed. Chicago: University of Chicago Press.

PART II

The Policy Agenda

5

Affirmatively Furthering Fair Housing and the *Inclusive Communities Project* Case[*]

BRINGING THE FAIR HOUSING ACT INTO
THE TWENTY-FIRST CENTURY

Philip D. Tegeler

The Supreme Court's powerful 2015 decision in *Texas Department of Housing and Community Affairs v. Inclusive Communities Project* (hereinafter *ICP v. Texas*) affirmed the principle that policies with a significant disparate impact on the basis of race can be challenged under the Fair Housing Act.[1] The ruling, coming in the aftermath of racial uprisings in Ferguson, Missouri, and Baltimore, Maryland, emphasized the anti-segregation origins of the Fair Housing Act of 1968 for a new generation. The Court reflected on a period of "social unrest in the inner cities" during the 1960s, and for the first time since 1990,[2] cited the Kerner Commission report of President Johnson's National Advisory Commission on Civil Disorders (1968): "The [Fair Housing Act] must play an important part in avoiding the Kerner Commission's grim prophecy that '[o]ur Nation is moving toward two societies, one black, one white—separate and unequal'. . . . The Court acknowledges the Fair Housing Act's continuing role in moving the Nation toward a more integrated society."[3]

A few months after the Court's decision, the federal government finalized a comprehensive new regulation implementing the original pro-integration clause of the Fair Housing Act.[4] The new rule, titled "Affirmatively Furthering Fair Housing" (AFFH), echoes the *ICP* case with its focus on the structural forces that drive segregation. But the rule also acknowledges the ways in which our understanding of fair housing and structural discrimination has evolved. It

---

[*] I am grateful for insightful comments from Megan Haberle and Heather Smitelli, and indebted to the many colleagues we have worked with in the development of the AFFH rule and on the amicus campaign in support of the *ICP v. Texas* case in the Supreme Court.

focuses on the need for equalization of resources and assets in racially isolated communities, and it recognizes that the goals of fair housing include equal access to quality education, transportation, and healthy environments. The new rule looks at race and poverty intersectionally, affirming that "racially concentrated areas of poverty" are a particular fair housing concern.[5] Moreover, the rule marks a shift from a private, complaint-based model of fair housing enforcement to one with a greater reliance on administrative oversight and compliance.

Disparate impact analysis has been part of American civil rights law from the beginning, but the pendency of the *ICP* case had temporarily put this principle in question under the Fair Housing Act. It is not surprising that the US Department of Housing and Urban Development (HUD) waited for the Supreme Court's ruling before releasing the final AFFH rule because the new HUD rule goes "all in" on the court's structural approach to racial segregation and disparities. Throughout the rule and its accompanying reporting tool, there is an emphasis on segregation outcomes and disparities in access to resources across different racial and ethnic groups. Largely framed in terms of nonintentional policies, the causes of these disparities are explored, as are the societal structures that create racial segregation and disparities in access to opportunity. For example, of the 40 "potential contributing factors" listed in HUD's *AFFH Rule Guidebook* (US Department of Housing and Urban Development 2015a, 205), only two ("private discrimination" and "community opposition") fit the traditional intentional-discrimination framework. The remaining factors, which are also reflected in the Assessment of Fair Housing tool, are largely structural: issues like "access to financial services," "admissions and occupancy policies," "displacement of residents due to economic pressures," "lack of affordable, accessible housing in a range of unit sizes," "lack of public investment in specific neighborhoods," "location of environmental health hazards," "location of proficient schools and school assignment policies," "occupancy codes and restrictions," "siting selection policies," and so on (2015a, 205–19).

Taken together, the *ICP* case and the AFFH rule have brought the Fair Housing Act back to its roots as an anti-segregation tool, but they also represent a much-needed modernization of the federal government's approach to fair housing, an approach that acknowledges segregation's role in driving the persistent racial and economic disparities in American society.

A Brief History of the AFFH Rule

In an editorial marking the release of the AFFH rule, the *New York Times* reflected on how many years it had taken HUD to effectively implement the Fair Housing Act's anti-segregation provision:

The fact that it has taken nearly 50 years since the law's passage for these common-sense changes to materialize is all the more distressing, given that federally sanctioned housing discrimination has played a central role in racial ghettoization.

The Fair Housing Act was intended to break down historic patterns of segregation. But it was undercut from the start by federal officials, including presidents who believed that segregation was the natural order of things. . . . The new rule . . . provides a clear, forceful definition of the law. It explains that affirmatively furthering fair housing means "replacing segregated living patterns with truly integrated and balanced living patterns, transforming racially and ethnically concentrated areas of poverty into areas of opportunity, and fostering and maintaining compliance with civil rights and fair housing laws. (*New York Times* 2015, paras. 4–5, 8)

The AFFH provision of the Fair Housing Act is separate from the act's anti-discrimination sections, which were interpreted in the *ICP v. Texas* case.[6] The core anti-discrimination provisions provide a basis for establishing the liability of public or private defendants for discriminatory or segregative actions or policy, in response to a lawsuit or HUD administrative complaint. The AFFH provision of the act, in contrast, applies to governmental agencies engaged in housing and urban development. It requires the agencies to not only avoid discriminatory actions but also take affirmative steps to promote fair housing. This provision has been consistently interpreted as the act's pro-integration clause, requiring affirmative action by HUD and its grantees to promote residential integration. This understanding was developed in a series of desegregation cases brought against HUD beginning in the early 1970s.[7] It was extended to state and local grantees by case law and statute.[8] In 1994, HUD affirmed the responsibility of grantees to plan and report on their fair housing progress, implementing a new regulatory and reporting procedure known as the Analysis of Impediments to Fair Housing. But clear metrics and accountability standards were absent. By the beginning of the Obama administration, the Analysis of Impediments process had become an empty bureaucratic ritual for many jurisdictions. This was exemplified by major litigation against Westchester County, New York, in a 2005 suit alleging that the county had falsely certified its compliance with its AFFH obligations.[9] Partly as a result of the Westchester litigation, HUD announced in 2009 its plans to develop a more substantial AFFH regulation, which would standardize the reporting expectations across jurisdictions, explicitly incorporating race and poverty assessments, and would expand the scope of the planning obligation to include public housing agencies.

The development and implementation of the AFFH rule spanned 8 years and the tenure of two HUD secretaries during the Obama administration. The department began conducting "listening sessions" in 2009, and these continued for 2 years. In 2010, the US Government Accountability Office released *HUD*

Needs to Enhance Its Requirements and Oversight of Jurisdictions' Fair Housing Plans, a report that heightened the perceived urgency of reform by explicitly stating what was already well known: many local jurisdictions did not take their fair housing planning and reporting obligations seriously, and the lack of compliance was traceable to the lack of clear requirements on the content of the plans, the absence of requirements for updating or submission of plans, and the lack of oversight by HUD.

Following the report's release, HUD embarked on a series of extended consultations with cities and counties that would be affected by a new rule. Two more years passed before HUD released its proposed AFFH rule in July 2013, and the proposal prompted a record number of public comments.[10] It would take HUD another 2 full years to release the final rule and even longer to release the reporting forms, guidebook, and data tools that accompanied the report.

The final AFFH rule, issued in July 2015,[11] requires thousands of jurisdictions and public housing agencies that receive HUD funds, and all 50 states, to go through a structured planning process every 5 years. That process is intended to explore the extent of racial and economic segregation in the community and region, and it examines in detail the disparities in neighborhoods' access to opportunity. Accompanied by a robust community engagement effort, the process is to lead to the development of concrete goals and strategies in the jurisdiction's Consolidated Plan, Public Housing Agency Plan, and other, related planning documents.

The "Balanced Approach": Fair Housing and Neighborhood Reinvestment

The inclusion of neighborhood revitalization in the final AFFH rule represents a major shift in HUD's interpretation of the Fair Housing Act's AFFH provision. That shift entails support for a "balanced approach,"[12] with investment inside and outside of racially segregated areas. A major part of the delay and controversy in the development of the rule can be traced to concerns from low-income jurisdictions and housing-industry groups that the new rule might prevent the continued development of low-income housing in high-poverty, segregated neighborhoods. In the preamble to the final rule, HUD noted the following:

> A substantial number of commenters who expressed support for the rule stated that the proposed rule did not provide a balanced approach to investment of Federal resources. Commenters stated that the proposed rule appeared to solely emphasize mobility as the means to affirmatively further fair housing and, by such emphasis, the rule devalued the strategy of

making investments in neighborhoods with racially/ethnically concentrated areas of poverty (RCAPs/ECAPs). They stated that the proposed rule could be read to prohibit the use of resources in neighborhoods with such concentrations. Commenters stated that the proposed rule, if implemented without change, would have the unintentional effect of shifting resources away from low-income communities of color, and threaten targeted revitalization and stabilization investments in such neighborhoods if jurisdictions misinterpreted the goals of deconcentration and reducing disparities in access to assets, and focused only on mobility at the expense of existing neighborhood assets. Commenters stated that the final rule must clarify that program participants are expected to employ both strategies—(1) to stabilize and revitalize neighborhoods that constitute RCAPs/ECAPs, and (2) enhance mobility and expand access to existing community assets. Commenters stated that these should not be competing priorities.[13]

In response, HUD agreed to support "a balanced approach to affirmatively furthering fair housing by revising the 'Purpose' section of the rule and the definition of 'affirmatively furthering fair housing.'"[14] Thus, in its revised definition of AFFH, HUD allows for housing investments that preserve existing low-income housing, even where such investments have the effect of perpetuating segregation. But, consistent with prior case law interpreting the Fair Housing Act, the rule pointedly does *not* authorize as a "fair housing" strategy the new construction of low-income housing in segregated areas. The new definition of AFFH indicates the following:

> [AFFH] may include various activities, such as developing affordable housing, and removing barriers to the development of such housing, in areas of high opportunity; *strategically enhancing access to opportunity, including through: targeted investment in neighborhood revitalization or stabilization; preservation or rehabilitation of existing affordable housing;* promoting greater housing choice *within or* outside of areas of concentrated poverty and greater access to areas of high opportunity; *and improving community assets such as quality schools, employment, and transportation.*[15]

What is unspoken in many of the comments, and finessed in HUD's response, is that the primary HUD resources available to low-income communities are low-income housing resources, which have historically been the drivers of racial and economic segregation in these neighborhoods. In our siloed system of government spending, HUD has little direct control over "community assets such as quality schools, employment, and transportation," although local jurisdictions may have flexibility to invest such funds more equitably, and the federal government is beginning to recognize the importance of alignment of its grant programs' goals across agencies (e.g., Castro, King, and Foxx 2016). Also, HUD has never specified precisely what constitutes a reasonable balance between housing mobility and community reinvestment, though it does note that a gross *imbalance* would not satisfy the rule:

> There could be issues, however, with strategies that rely *solely* on investment in areas with high racial or ethnic concentrations of low-income residents to the exclusion of providing access to affordable housing outside of those areas. For example, in areas with a history of segregation, if a program participant has the ability to create opportunities outside of the segregated, low-income areas but declines to do so in favor of place-based strategies, there could be a legitimate claim that HUD and its program participants were acting to preclude a choice of neighborhoods to historically segregated groups, as well as failing to affirmatively further fair housing as required by the Fair Housing Act.[16]

HUD's broad concessions in continuing to permit some significant degree of low-income housing investment in highly segregated communities are contradicted by most of the federal case law cited in the AFFH rule's preamble. Those cases focused on ending the perpetuation of segregation and redirecting federal low-income housing investment away from segregated neighborhoods. However, an important strand of fair housing case law also focuses on the importance of reinvestment to improve and equalize existing housing and neighborhood conditions, particularly in the context of public housing desegregation. An example is the court-ordered remedy in the landmark case of *Walker v. HUD*, a 1985 class action challenging both segregation and unequal conditions for public housing residents in Dallas, Texas. That remedy included both an ambitious housing mobility program and a community revitalization plan to begin to equalize housing and neighborhood conditions for the existing residents.[17] Attorneys for the plaintiffs in that seminal case explained:

> When we address the problems caused by deliberate racial discrimination in public housing programs, the application of traditional dual system liability and remedy principles developed in the school desegregation cases should be considered. Such an approach offers the opportunity both to equalize African-American projects with white-occupied assisted housing and to provide effective access for African-American families to a wide choice of housing opportunities (Julian and Daniel 1989, 667).

Consistent with the aspirations represented by the *Walker* case, most fair housing and civil rights groups supported the final rule's balanced approach to fair housing even while recognizing that it does not specify the extent of balance between mobility and revitalization. They also recognized that the rule does not provide leverage to obtain the resources that poor communities most need (in education, transportation, employment, and public health). Defining what "balance" means in specific local contexts, and using the AFFH rule to leverage nonhousing resources for struggling communities, will be part of the challenge for advocates as the new rule is implemented at the state and local level.

"Racially Concentrated Areas of Poverty"

The final AFFH rule requires grantees to identify and prioritize "racially concentrated areas of poverty" in their jurisdictions,[18] to consider remedial steps to deconcentrate racial and poverty concentration in these areas, and to direct enhanced resources into these neighborhoods. This focus on *poverty* as an element of fair housing analysis is not new, but it has never before been as explicitly set out as it is in the new rule. Notably, poverty is not mentioned in the 1968 Fair Housing Act, though the segregation of low-income families of color by government policy was a fundamental context for congressional consideration of the act (Roisman 2007). Similarly, poverty is not a protected class under the Fair Housing Act, but disparate impact cases, especially those challenging exclusion of low-income housing, rely heavily on the disproportionately high representation of people of color among low-income populations and the disproportionate housing needs faced by low-income families.[19] Both the case law and academic research on the harms of segregation have focused on concentrated poverty's particular harms to low-income families of color and the durability of racial and poverty concentration over time. As the Supreme Court noted in *Texas v. ICP*, "*De jure* residential segregation by race was declared unconstitutional almost a century ago, but its vestiges remain today, intertwined with the country's economic and social life."[20] The 2005 district court opinion in *Thompson v. HUD* is a good example of this line of analysis:

> Baltimore City should not be viewed as an island reservation for use as a container for all of the poor of a contiguous region including Anne Arundel, Baltimore, Carroll, Harford and Howard Counties. Baltimore City contains only approximately 30% of the Baltimore Region's households. In 1940, 19 percent of the population of Baltimore City was African-American. By 2000, the population of Baltimore City was 64 percent African-American, while the population of the rest of the Baltimore Region was 15 percent Black.[21]

Regulatory comments criticizing the inclusion of "racially concentrated areas of poverty" as a particular focus of the new rule prompted the following response from HUD:

> HUD agrees with the comment that the Fair Housing Act does not prohibit discrimination on the basis of income or other characteristics not specified in the Act, and it is not HUD's intent to use the AFFH rule to expand the characteristics protected by the Act. HUD would note that the

majority of its programs are meant to assist low-income households to obtain decent, safe, and affordable housing and such actions entail an examination of income. . . . Accordingly, it is entirely consistent with the Fair Housing Act's duty to affirmatively further fair housing to counteract past policies and decisions that account for today's racially or ethnically concentrated areas of poverty or housing cost burdens and housing needs that are disproportionately high for certain groups of persons based on characteristics protected by the Fair Housing Act. Preparation of an [Assessment of Fair Housing] could be an important step in reducing poverty among groups of persons who share characteristics protected by the Fair Housing Act. . . . In addition, a large body of research has consistently found that the problems associated with segregation are greatly exacerbated when combined with concentrated poverty. That is the legal basis and context for the examination of RCAPs/ECAPs, as required by the rule.[22]

In this light, the focus on poverty concentration in the AFFH rule is not so much a departure from prior practice as it is a recognition of the reality of segregation and of the impact of federal programs and policy on low-income families of color.

The Recognition of Housing's Role as a Platform

Sociologists have long recognized the relation of housing segregation to racial disparities in health, education, and employment. This recognition began with Gunnar Myrdal in 1944: "Housing segregation necessarily involves discrimination . . . [it] permits any prejudice on the part of public officials to be freely vented on Negroes without hurting whites" (618).

Douglas Massey and Nancy Denton elaborated on this insight in 1993: "Residential segregation is the institutional apparatus that supports other racially discriminatory processes and binds them together into a coherent and uniquely effective system of racial subordination" (8).

And Patrick Sharkey expanded this analysis in 2013 by focusing on the intergenerational impacts of living in high-poverty segregated neighborhoods, concluding that "African Americans have been attached to places where discrimination has remained prevalent despite the advances in civil rights made in the 1960s; where political decisions and social policies have led to severe disinvestment and persistent, rigid segregation" (5). He notes that "the effect of living within severely disadvantaged communities accumulates over generations" (7).

Congress also recognized the role of housing as a platform when it enacted the Fair Housing Act in 1968. The HUD preamble to the final AFFH rule quoted the Congressional Record: "The Act recognized that 'where a family lives, where it is allowed to live, is inextricably bound up with better education, better jobs, economic motivation, and good living conditions.'"[23]

The role of housing as a platform for access to opportunity in other areas has been a consistent theme of housing desegregation litigation, from *Gautreaux* (1974) to *Walker* (1989) to *Thompson* (1995) and to *ICP* (2015).[24] For example, the *Walker* district court opinion approving the class settlement includes crime, exposure to environmental toxins, and access to utilities as aspects of fair housing[25]; the *ICP* district court opinion cites school quality[26]; and *Gautreaux's* 1974 court of appeals decision focuses on access to employment:

> [The trial judge's] warning that "By 1984 it may be too late to heal racial divisions," rather than a cliché, is a solemn warning as to the interaction of "White flight" and "black concentration." It is the most serious domestic problem facing America today. As Assistant Secretary Simmons further advises: "As Whites have left the cities, jobs have left with them. After 1960, three-fifths of all new industrial plants constructed in this country were outside of central cities. In some cases as much as 85% of all new industrial plants located outside central cities were inaccessible to Blacks and other minorities who swelled ghetto populations." These words also convey a solemn warning, i.e., we must not sentence our poor, our underprivileged, our minorities to the jobless slums of the ghettos and thereby forever trap them in the vicious cycle of poverty which can only lead them to lives of crime and violence.[27]

The AFFH rule *operationalizes* these fair housing principles as part of the fair housing planning process, requiring an explicit analysis of access to opportunity by geographic area. The rule defines "significant disparities in access to opportunity" as "substantial and measurable differences in access to educational, transportation, economic, and other important opportunities in a community, based on protected class related to housing."[28] It also provides detailed analytical tools for assessing these disparities. The new Assessment of Fair Housing tool supplies index scores for school proficiency, labor market engagement, jobs proximity, transportation costs, transit trips, and environmental health. Scores are arrayed by geographic area, with concurrent demographic analysis of neighborhood race and poverty rates.

In the area of environmental health, for example, the Assessment of Fair Housing tool requires a review of the "location of environmental health hazards":

> Relevant factors to consider include the type and number of hazards, the degree of concentration or dispersion, and health effects such as asthma, cancer clusters, obesity, etc. Additionally, industrial siting policies and incentives for the location of housing may be relevant to this factor (US Department of Housing and Urban Development 2015*b*, Appendix C, 9).

The inclusion of public health metrics provides an important opening for public health advocates and practitioners, who have increasingly recognized the predominant importance of social determinants for health outcomes but have often been frustrated by the limited "jurisdiction" of public health interventions to affect those determinants (Carey, Crammond, and Keast 2014). The new HUD rule will help the public health community engage more effectively in this arena.

Equitable access to quality public schools is also directly emphasized as a fair housing issue:

> The geographic relationship of proficient schools to housing, and the policies that govern attendance, are important components of fair housing choice. The quality of schools is often a major factor in deciding where to live and school quality is also a key component of economic mobility. Relevant factors to consider include whether proficient schools are clustered in a portion of the jurisdiction or region, the range of housing opportunities close to proficient schools, and whether the jurisdiction has policies that enable students to attend a school of choice regardless of place of residence. Policies to consider include, but are not limited to, inter-district transfer programs, limits on how many students from other areas a particular school will accept, and enrollment lotteries that do not provide access for the majority of children. (US Department of Housing and Urban Development 2015*b*, Appendix C, 9)

This tight connection between housing and school policy, long recognized by advocates and academics, was highlighted in 2016 by a joint guidance letter from the secretaries of Housing, Education, and Transportation. The letter exhorted state and local policymakers to work together across their separate silos in order to foster integrated and inclusive communities and schools (Castro, King, and Foxx 2016).

The Shift in Focus from Private Enforcement to Administrative Oversight and Compliance

Like other civil rights era statutes, the Fair Housing Act relied on the federal courts to enable private enforcement against both private and public acts of discrimination. Although the case law evolved in a positive direction after 1968, it was difficult to pursue a claim without an attorney, and enforcement of the act was sporadic. The Fair Housing Amendments Act of 1988 was intended to strengthen private enforcement by creating an administrative complaint mechanism to supplement court enforcement and by enhancing court-awarded attorneys fees available to prevailing plaintiffs.[29]

The 1988 amendments also added new "protected classes."[30] Through the Fair Housing Initiatives Program, the 1988 act began a funding stream to support private fair housing groups across the country in assisting victims of discrimination. In spite of these added incentives, complaints against private acts of discrimination continued to be only a partial solution to the continuing problem of discrimination and segregation in the housing market (Schwemm 2007).

The new AFFH rule is part of a larger trend to use federal administrative oversight and the federal spending power, as an alternative to private enforcement, in promoting civil rights compliance (Pasachoff 2014). These cross-agency "equality directives" (Johnson 2012, 1343) include a proactive assessment of the racial impacts of government actions (e.g., Tegeler 2016) and require federal grantees to avoid adverse impacts on protected classes. In the case of the AFFH rule, they require grantees to take affirmative steps to promote integration. This kind of civil rights funding oversight has the *potential* to change behavior more profoundly than scattered civil rights lawsuits, but it is also highly dependent on the willingness of the federal agency to actually enforce its own directives—that willingness is in turn dependent on the priorities of the political leadership in Washington.

The more proactive federal stance represented by the AFFH rule is a move away from HUD's passive complaint-driven approach to enforcement. Although the Fair Housing Act calls for enforcement "within constitutional limitations,"[31] HUD has never come close to the limits of its statutory and constitutional power over state and local government in the area of civil rights. The department routinely defers to local zoning, jurisdictional limitations, local residency preferences, local notification and approval requirements for public housing, and so on (Tegeler 1994). The new AFFH rule asserts a much stronger federal oversight role over such local government practice. Indeed, the new rule's expectation that local governments no longer participate in exclusionary housing policies has elicited strong "federalism" objections from conservative media outlets. For example, one commentator protested that "AFFH repudiates the core principles of our constitutional system by allowing the federal government to effectively usurp the zoning powers of local governments" (Kurtz 2015, para. 2).[32]

Notwithstanding these protests, the new rule is fully consistent with the current regulatory relationship between federal authority and local government, which largely bypasses the state governments (Davidson 2007). It is also the latest iteration of repeated federal and state efforts to impose a more regional structure on metropolitan government administration—efforts that have often foundered when affordable housing was brought into the discussion (Dreier, Mollenkopf, and Swanstrom 2014).

Conclusion

HUD has a long and ambiguous history in relation to civil rights, shifting between its roles as chief enforcer of the Fair Housing Act and a chief facilitator of state and local discriminatory practices (Rothstein 2017). It has often been brought to account for its segregated policies by the federal courts and has been required to incorporate fair housing goals throughout its administration of housing programs (Poverty & Race Research Action Council 2017; Ellen and Yager 2015). The 2015 AFFH rule, adopted in the wake of the landmark *ICP v. Texas* decision, is the latest phase in this ongoing saga.

Since this chapter was first written, our country has gone through a seismic shift in presidential leadership, veering sharply to the right, with an administration espousing deregulation for deregulation's sake as a major policy goal.[33] In this spirit, in the 50th anniversary year of the Fair Housing Act, HUD has taken the extraordinary step of suspending compliance with the AFFH rule, effectively exempting almost 1,000 jurisdictions from the rule's requirements for an indefinite period.[34] And HUD has indicated its intention to begin the process of amending the rule itself.[35] Whether or not the suspension is permitted to stand, the AFFH rule has given state and local governments a modernized set of tools to address segregation and its consequences.

Notes

1. 135 S. Ct. 2507 (2015).
2. See Metro Broadcasting, Inc. v. FCC, 497 U.S. 547, 585–86 (1990).
3. ICP, 135 S. Ct. at 2525–26 (citation omitted).
4. Affirmatively Furthering Fair Housing, 80 Fed. Reg. 42,272 (July 16, 2015) (codified at 24 C.F.R. pts. 5, 91, 92, 570, 574, 576, 903 (2016)).
5. Affirmatively Furthering Fair Housing, 80 Fed. Reg. at 42,348.
6. For the AFFH provision, see 42 U.S.C. §3608.
7. For a good summary of these cases, see Roisman (2007).
8. See Otero v. New York City Housing Authority, 484 F.2d 1182 (2d Cir. 1973); Housing and Community Development Act of 1974, 42 U.S.C. § 5304(b)(2) (2016).
9. By 2005, when the Westchester litigation was filed, the Analysis of Impediments process had deteriorated to the point where Westchester County, in its annual filings to receive HUD community development funds, routinely certified its compliance with the AFFH provisions of the act by submitting fair housing plans that included no mention of race, and the annual filings asserted that the construction of subsidized housing in already high-poverty, segregated areas satisfied the county's fair housing obligations.
10. Affirmatively Furthering Fair Housing, 78 Fed. Reg. 43,710 (proposed July 19, 2013).
11. Affirmatively Furthering Fair Housing, 80 Fed. Reg. 42,272 (July 16, 2015).
12. 80 Fed. Reg. at 42,277.

13. 80 Fed. Reg. at 42,278.

14. 80 Fed. Reg. at 42,272.

15. 24 C.F.R. § 5.150 (2016) (italics added for emphasis).

16. 80 Fed. Reg. at 42,279 (italics added for emphasis).

17. Walker v. HUD, CA3 85-1210-R (N.D. Tex. Jan. 20, 1987) (consent decree). See also Julian (2008).

18. 24 C.F.R. § 5.154.

19. See, for example, Huntington Branch, NAACP v. Town of Huntington, 844 F.2d 926 (2d Cir. 1988); aff'd in part, 488 U.S. 15 (1988).

20. ICP v. Texas, 135 S. Ct. at 2515–16.

21. Thompson v. HUD, 348 F. Supp. 2d 398, 408 (D. Md. 2005). See also Massey and Denton (1993); Sharkey (2013).

22. 80 Fed. Reg. at 42,283.

23. 80 Fed Reg. at 42,274 (quoting 114 Cong. Rec. 2276, 2707 (Feb. 8, 1968)).

24. Gautreaux v. Chicago Housing Auth., 503 F.2d 930 (7th Cir. 1974); Walker v. HUD, 734 F. Supp. 1231 (N.D. Tex. 1989); Thompson v. HUD, 348 F. Supp. 2d 398 (D. Md. 2005); Texas Department of Housing and Community Affairs v. Inclusive Communities Project, 135 S. Ct. 2507 (2015).

25. Walker v. HUD, 734 F. Supp. 1231, 1266–1267 (N.D. Tex. 1989) (approving consent decree) (citation omitted).

26. ICP v. Texas, 860 F. Supp. 2d 312, 329–30 (N.D. Texas 2012) (citation omitted).

27. Gautreaux v. Chicago Housing Auth., 503 F.2d 930, 938 (7th Cir. 1974) (citation omitted).

28. 24 C.F.R. § 5.152.

29. Fair Housing Amendments Act of 1988, Pub. L. Mo. 100-430, 102 Stat. 1619 (codified as amended in scattered sections of 28 and 42 U.S.C.).

30. 42 U.S.C. § 3606 (2016).

31. 42 U.S.C. § 3601.

32. Conservative commentators had similar things to say about the Supreme Court's "overreaching" in the *ICP* case. See, for example, Barone (2015, para. 10): "Disparate-impact doctrine [will] overturn local zoning laws and place low-income housing in suburbs across the nation." This concern that HUD might somehow override zoning rules led to an amendment to the 2017 federal budget bill prohibiting HUD from directing local governments to change their zoning laws through the AFFH rule (Consolidated Appropriations Act of 2017, Pub. L. No. 115-131, 131 Stat. 135, 790 (2017)).

33. Executive Order 13771, "Reducing Regulation and Controlling Regulatory Costs," 82 Fed. Reg. 9339 (Feb. 3, 2017); Executive Order 13777, "Enforcing the Regulatory Reform Agenda," 82 Fed. Reg. 12,285 (Mar. 1, 2017); "Reducing Regulatory Burden; Enforcing the Regulatory Reform Agenda Under Executive Order 13777," 82 Fed. Reg. 22,344 (May 15, 2017).

34. Affirmatively Furthering Fair Housing: Extension of Deadline for Submission of Assessment of Fair Housing for Consolidated Plan Participants, 83 Fed. Reg. 683 (Jan. 5, 2018); superceded by three notices, posted on May 23, 2018, which substitute a withdrawal of the Assessment of Fair Housing form for the original suspension of compliance (with the same basic effect). See *Notice: Withdrawal*, 83 Fed. Reg. 23,928 (May 23, 2018); *Affirmatively Furthering Fair Housing: Withdrawal of the Assessment Tool for Local*

Governments, 83 Fed. Reg. 23,922 (May 23, 2018); *Affirmatively Furthering Fair Housing (AFFH): Responsibility to Conduct Analysis of Impediments*, 83 Fed. Reg. 23,927 (May 23, 2018).

The author is co-counsel in the federal litigation filed to challenge the suspension of the rule, *National Fair Housing Alliance et al. v. Carson*, which commenced after this article was originally written.

35. Affirmatively Furthering Fair Housing: Streamlining and Enhancements (Advance notice of proposed rulemaking), 83 Fed. Reg. 40,713 (Aug. 16, 2018).

References

Barone, Michael. 2015. "HUD's 'Disparate Impact' War on Suburban America." *National Review*, July 21. http://www.nationalreview.com/article/421406/hud-disparate-impact-suburban-racism.

Carey, Gemma, Brad Crammond, and Robyn Keast. 2014. "Creating Change in Government to Address the Social Determinants of Health: How Can Efforts Be Improved." *BMC Public Health* 14 (1). doi:10.1186/1471-2458-14-1087.

Castro, Julián, John B. King Jr., and Anthony R, Foxx. 2016. Letter to state and local leaders, June 8. http://www.prrac.org/pdf/Joint_Letter_on_Diverse_Schools_and_Communities_AFFH.pdf.

Davidson, Nestor M. 2007. "Cooperative Localism: Federal-Local Collaboration in an Era of State Sovereignty." *Virginia Law Review* 93 (4): 959–1034.

Dreier, Peter, John Mollenkopf, and Todd Swanstrom. 2014. *Place Matters: Metropolitics for the Twenty-First Century*, 3rd rev. ed. Topeka: University Press of Kansas.

Ellen, Ingrid Gould, and Jessica Yager. 2015. "Race, Poverty, and Federal Rental Housing Policy." In *HUD at 50: Creating Pathways to Opportunity*, 103–31. Washington, DC: US Department of Housing and Urban Development, Office of Policy Development and Research. http://www.huduser.gov/portal//hud50th/HUDat50Book.pdf.

Johnson, Olatunde C. A. 2012. "Beyond the Private Attorney General: Equality Directives in American Law." *New York University Law Review* 87 (5): 1339–1413.

Julian, Elizabeth K. 2008. "Fair Housing and Community Development: Time to Come Together." *Indiana Law Review* 41 (3): 555–74.

Julian, Elizabeth K., and Michael M. Daniel. 1989. "Separate and Unequal—The Root and Branch of Public Housing Segregation." *Clearinghouse Review* 23 (6): 666–76.

Kurtz, Stanley. 2015. "Affirmatively Furthering Fair Housing: Sleeper Presidential Campaign Issue." *National Review*, June 10. http://www.nationalreview.com/corner/419560/affirmatively-furthering-fair-housing-sleeper-presidential-campaign-issue-stanley.

Massey, Douglas S., and Nancy A. Denton. 1993. *American Apartheid: Segregation and the Making of the Underclass*. Cambridge, MA: Harvard University Press.

Myrdal, Gunnar. 1944. *An American Dilemma: The Negro Problem and Modern Democracy*. New York: Harper.

National Advisory Commission on Civil Disorders. 1968. *Report of the National Advisory Commission on Civil Disorders*. Report. Washington, DC: US Department of Justice, National Criminal Justice Reference Service.

New York Times. 2015. "The End of Federally Financed Ghettos." July 11. https://www.nytimes.com/2015/07/12/opinion/the-end-of-federally-financed-ghettos.html.

Pasachoff, Eloise. 2014. "Agency Enforcement of Spending Clause Statutes: A Defense of the Funding Cut-Off." *Yale Law Journal* 124 (2): 248–335.

Poverty & Race Research Action Council. 2017. *Fifty Years of "The People v. HUD": A HUD 50th Anniversary Timeline of Significant Civil Rights Lawsuits and HUD Fair Housing Advances.* Washington, DC: Poverty & Race Research Action Council. http://www.prrac.org/pdf/HUD50th-CivilRightsTimeline.pdf.

Roisman, Florence Wagman. 2007. "Affirmatively Furthering Fair Housing in Regional Housing Markets: The Baltimore Public Housing Desegregation Litigation." *Wake Forest Law Review* 42 (2): 333–91.

Rothstein, Richard. 2017. *The Color of Law: A Forgotten History of How Our Government Segregated America.* New York: Liveright.

Schwemm, Robert G. 2007. "Why Do Landlords Still Discriminate (and What Can Be Done about It)?" *John Marshall Law Review* 40 (2): 455–511.

Sharkey, Patrick. 2013. *Stuck in Place: Urban Neighborhoods and the End of Progress toward Racial Equality.* Chicago: University of Chicago Press.

Tegeler, Philip D. 1994. "Housing Segregation and Local Discretion." *Journal of Law and Policy* 3 (1): 209–36.

Tegeler, Philip D. 2016. "Predicting School Diversity Impacts of State and Local Education Policy: The Role of Title VI." In *School Integration Matters: Research-Based Strategies to Advance Equity*, edited by Erica Frankenberg, Liliana M. Garces, and Megan Hopkins, 145–54. New York: Teachers College Press.

US Department of Housing and Urban Development. 2015a. *AFFH Rule Guidebook.* Version 1, December 31. Washington, DC: US Department of Housing and Urban Development. https://www.hudexchange.info/resources/documents/AFFH-Rule-Guidebook.pdf.

US Department of Housing and Urban Development. 2015b. "Assessment of Fair Housing Tool." Washington, DC: US Department of Housing and Urban Development. https://www.hudexchange.info/resource/4865/assessment-of-fair-housing-tool/.

US Government Accountability Office. 2010. *Housing and Community Grants: HUD Needs to Enhance Its Requirements and Oversight of Jurisdictions' Fair Housing Plans.* Report GAO-10-905. Washington, DC: Government Accountability Office. http://www.gao.gov/assets/320/311065.pdf.

6

Enabling More Families with Housing Vouchers to Access Higher-Opportunity Neighborhoods

Barbara Sard

Where families live largely determines the quality of schools that children attend, whether it is safe for the children to play outside, and the ease with which they can obtain basic goods and services such as fresh, reasonably priced food. Location also can affect adults' access to jobs, the cost of getting to work, and the feasibility of balancing childcare responsibilities with work schedules (Briggs 2005a). A large body of evidence shows that, beyond these common-sense impacts of place, growing up in high-poverty neighborhoods diminishes children's long-term chances of success, impairs adults' health, and contributes to intergenerational poverty (for syntheses, see Sard and Rice 2014, 2016; Sharkey et al. 2014). Two recent groundbreaking studies underscore the benefits of providing housing vouchers that enable families to move to better neighborhoods. These studies, by Harvard University economists Raj Chetty, Nathaniel Hendren, and Lawrence Katz, show that children whose families move to better neighborhoods experience lower teenage birth rates, higher college-attendance and marriage rates, and larger earnings gains as adults, relative to children who remain in less advantageous neighborhoods (Chetty and Hendren 2015; Chetty, Hendren, and Katz 2015).

In recent decades, policymakers have adopted various measures to reduce the extent to which federal rental assistance programs leave poor families in distressed neighborhoods. They also have sought to expand access to safe neighborhoods with good schools, recreational opportunities, and nearby jobs. In pursuing these goals, they have relied increasingly on housing vouchers to provide rental assistance, so that families may choose where to live rather than being limited to government-funded projects, which often have been situated in poor, racially concentrated neighborhoods.[1]

Created in the 1970s, the federally funded Housing Choice Voucher (HCV) program now helps over two million low-income households pay for modestly priced, decent-quality homes in the private market. Most vouchers are "tenant based," meaning that families can use them to rent a modestly priced unit of their choice in the private market with the agreement of the landlord. A network of more than 2,100 state and local housing agencies administers the program. Their efforts are subject to oversight by the US Department of Housing and Urban Development (HUD; Center on Budget and Policy Priorities 2017).

Nearly half of the households that use the vouchers include minor children (Mazzara, Sard, and Rice 2016). More families with children are served by the HCV program than by public housing and Project-Based Rental Assistance, the two other major rental-assistance programs, combined (Mazzara, Sard, and Rice 2016). The assistance not only helps these families to afford decent, stable housing and make ends meet but also has the potential to enable the children to grow up in better neighborhoods and thereby to enhance their chances of long-term health and success.

Among HCV families with children during 2014, about one in eight (12.9 percent) used their vouchers to live in a low-poverty area, where fewer than 10 percent of residents were poor (Sard and Rice 2016).[2] Overall, families used vouchers to live in neighborhoods with a median poverty rate of 23.3 percent in 2014. In comparison, the typical poor child lived in a census tract where 24.3 percent of the residents were poor.[3] Research suggests that vouchers—rather than something about the families receiving HCV assistance—have a modest but positive effect in enabling families with children to live in neighborhoods with poverty rates lower than those of the neighborhoods where similarly poor, nonrecipient families reside.[4]

The HCV program has reduced families' housing-cost burdens and homelessness, increasing housing stability (Fischer 2015*b*). In enabling low-income families with children to relocate to lower-poverty neighborhoods—particularly low-income African American and Latino families—it has performed much better than HUD's Project-Based Rental Assistance programs (Sard and Rice 2014). Having a housing voucher also substantially reduces the likelihood of living in an extreme-poverty neighborhood, where 40 percent or more of residents are poor. The chances are considerably lower for voucher families than for similar families that include children and either receive Project-Based Rental Assistance or no housing assistance (Sard and Rice 2016).

But the HCV program does not adequately deliver on its potential to expand children's access to good schools in safe neighborhoods. Some 343,000 children in the HCV program lived in extreme-poverty neighborhoods in 2014 despite the better options that a voucher should make available to them (Sard and Rice 2016). The program can do better.

That more families do not use their vouchers to reside in low-poverty neighborhoods reflects, at least in part, the constraints faced in using them to access neighborhoods with greater opportunities (DeLuca, Garboden, and Rosenblatt 2013; Galster 2013). Some families want the stability of remaining in their current neighborhoods or close to support networks and current jobs, but many are largely unaware of opportunities in unfamiliar neighborhoods and might make different choices if given more information (Darrah and DeLuca 2014). Others require assistance to identify landlords willing to accept vouchers in communities where vouchers are infrequently used and rental vacancies are low. In addition, voucher subsidy caps are often so low that families cannot afford to use the vouchers for units in high-opportunity areas, and other program policies can limit voucher holders' available choices.

Current federal policy essentially assumes that having a housing voucher functions like added income in that both increase rental options. It also assumes that poor families are aware of the housing options available with a voucher. But as Stefanie DeLuca, Philip Garboden, and Peter Rosenblatt (2013, 271) concluded, "The 'free market choice' assumptions behind the HCV program do not hold in reality." Administering agencies decide whether and how to address families' needs for assistance in the search process.[5] Agencies that ignore the need for housing-search assistance or have ineffective or counterproductive policies are at virtually no risk of HUD sanction.

A limited supply of moderately priced rental units in low-poverty, non–racially concentrated neighborhoods is a significant constraint in some cities and counties (Briggs, Comey, and Weismann 2010; McClure 2013).[6] But the supply of rental units in most metropolitan areas is sufficient to enable a much larger share of families to use their vouchers in areas that would likely be better for their children. In those areas, knowledge and access are potentially surmountable barriers. One third of all metropolitan rental units—and more than a quarter of all metropolitan units with rental charges below HUD's Fair Market Rents (FMRs)—are located in neighborhoods with a poverty rate of less than 10 percent (McClure 2013, 216).

Under current federal requirements, public housing agencies (PHAs) have flexibility to implement strategies for improving location outcomes in their HCV programs. State and local governments could facilitate these efforts (Scott et al. 2013). But without federal changes that modify counterproductive policies and encourage housing agencies to take such steps—as well as reliable funding to maintain the number of families receiving HCV assistance and to administer the program effectively—there is little reason to expect better results.

Housing location's effects on low-income families, particularly children, and the location-related performance of federal rental assistance suggest two important and closely related near-term goals: (1) federal rental assistance programs should increase opportunities for families to choose affordable housing outside of extreme-poverty neighborhoods; and (2) the programs should improve families' access to safe low-poverty communities with well-performing schools.

We can make substantial progress toward both goals in the next few years, even amid the fiscal constraints of the current environment and even without congressional action or more federal funding. Specifically, federal, state, and local agencies can make progress toward both goals by adopting four sets of interrelated policy changes:

1. Create strong incentives for local and state housing agencies to achieve better location outcomes.
2. Modify policies that discourage families from living in lower-poverty communities.
3. Minimize jurisdictional barriers that impede relocation to high-opportunity communities.
4. Assist families in using vouchers to live in high-opportunity areas.

This focus on enhancing families' ability to move to areas with more opportunities for their children (or to remain in affordable housing in lower-poverty, high-opportunity neighborhoods) does not imply that policymakers should not pursue broader strategies to increase incomes, enhance safety, and improve educational performance in very poor areas. But the unfortunate reality is that we know relatively little about what types of interventions are effective on a substantial scale at transforming extremely poor, disadvantaged neighborhoods (Bostic 2014; US Government Accountability Office 2012; Abravanel, Pindus, and Theodos 2010; DeLuca and Rosenblatt 2013; Kubisch 2010). Moreover, broader economic development and revitalization strategies often take many years to implement and can be costly (Turner, Popkin, and Rawlings 2009*a*; Popkin and Cunningham 2009).

Create Strong Incentives for Housing Agencies to Achieve Better Location Outcomes

By creating strong incentives for local and state housing agencies to reduce the share of families using vouchers in extreme-poverty areas and to increase the share living in high-opportunity areas, the department can encourage the development of local policies and strategies that respond best to varying local conditions.

GIVE INCREASED WEIGHT TO LOCATION OUTCOMES IN MEASURING AGENCY PERFORMANCE

HUD's most powerful tool to induce changes in the administrative practices of state and local housing agencies is the measure it uses to assess agency effectiveness in managing the HCV program. HUD should revise its performance rating tool to give more significant weight to the types of neighborhoods in which voucher holders live.[7] In addition, HUD should refine its location measures.[8]

To persuade more landlords in higher-opportunity areas to do business with them, agencies must administer their voucher programs competently. They must make prompt payments to owners and conduct efficient inspections (O'Neil 2009). Therefore, performance ratings based in significant part on agency success in enabling families to live in these areas also should encourage improvements in program management.

REINFORCE PERFORMANCE MEASURES BY EFFECTIVELY IMPLEMENTING THE NEW FAIR HOUSING RULE

HUD and all housing agencies administering the HCV program have an obligation to further the purposes of the Fair Housing Act. This obligation to provide support in affirmatively furthering fair housing (AFFH) is commonly known as the AFFH duty. It is specified in Section 3608 of the Fair Housing Act.[9] In 2015, some 47 years after Congress established this duty, HUD finally issued a rule to indicate the steps agencies must take to meet the obligation.[10] The rule requires each grantee (PHAs as well as states and localities that receive HUD funds, individually or in combination) to conduct an Assessment of Fair Housing in which it identifies the factors that primarily contribute to segregation and restriction of housing choice in its region and programs. Through the assessment, agencies are to establish priorities and goals that will guide their planning and investment decisions. The final rule includes important changes that clarify the rule's applicability to the HCV program, highlighting that agencies' assessments should include "enhancing mobility strategies" and encouraging regional strategies.[11] This is particularly important because black and Hispanic families make up most of the assisted families in extreme-poverty areas, and they are less likely than white assisted families to live in low-poverty areas.[12] Grantees' initial assessments are due over the 5 to 7 years following the rule's promulgation.[13] Effective implementation of the AFFH rule would complement a revised and strengthened performance measurement system that emphasizes increasing access to higher-opportunity areas, and effective implementation could also help PHAs receive assistance from other agencies in achieving these goals (on this point, see further discussion elsewhere in the chapter).

PAY AGENCIES ADDITIONAL ADMINISTRATIVE FEES WHEN FAMILIES USE THEIR VOUCHERS IN HIGH-OPPORTUNITY AREAS

A federal policy that financially rewards agencies when families use their vouchers in high-opportunity areas is particularly important in the cases of families for which such moves are especially challenging—families coming from communities that are highly segregated by income and race or ethnicity, for example. The fees earned by PHAs are primarily based on the number of vouchers in use. Leasing units in high-opportunity areas typically takes longer than leasing in neighborhoods where vouchers are commonly accepted. A fee incentive would provide a helpful counterbalance to PHAs' current financial interest in having families locate units as quickly as possible. HUD recently completed a major analysis of the costs of running a well-administered voucher program (US Department of Housing and Urban Development 2015). If HUD adopts a new policy for determining how to allocate administrative fees to agencies, it should incorporate location-based payments as a component of the new formula or as a bonus. Without a change in regulation, HUD could make supplemental disbursements to help agencies offset these costs.[14]

Modify Policies That Discourage Families from Living in Lower-Poverty Communities

Many HCV program policies at both the federal and local levels unintentionally encourage families to use their vouchers in poor and racially concentrated neighborhoods. For example, federal policy has historically capped voucher subsidies on the basis of housing costs for a metropolitan area, ignoring variation in such costs across neighborhoods. Another policy revokes the voucher issued to a family if that family does not find a rental unit within a specified time frame. Implementing locally based payment standards, adopting more flexible search-time policies, and ensuring that agencies provide diverse landlord lists would help families move to higher-opportunity areas.

SET SUBSIDY CAPS FOR SMALLER GEOGRAPHIC AREAS

HCV rental subsidies are capped by a payment standard that the local housing agency sets, and the standard generally can vary by only 10 percent from the FMR figure, which is specified by HUD. Typically, HUD has based FMRs on the cost of modest housing over an entire metropolitan area, but payment standards based on metro-wide FMRs are often too low to cover rent for units in neighborhoods with low poverty, low crime, and strong schools.[15] To access units in those neighborhoods, families must pay out of pocket the amount not covered by the payment standard. The burden is difficult for many families, and the HCV program already requires recipients to pay 30 percent of the family income for rent.[16]

Setting FMRs at the metropolitan level also can result in payment standards that are higher than necessary in areas of concentrated poverty. Such standards can prompt families to choose larger units in those neighborhoods over smaller ones in high-opportunity areas. They may enable owners to charge above-market rents (unless agencies strictly enforce rules requiring that rents be reasonable in the local market).[17] As a result, metropolitan-wide FMRs likely encourage the use of vouchers—and their acceptance by owners—in poor, unsafe neighborhoods with low-quality schools (Edin, DeLuca, and Owens 2012; Collinson and Ganong 2016; Khadduri 2013a).

Through a limited number of local housing agencies, HUD has tested Small Area Fair Market Rents (SAFMRs), which are based on market rents in *individual zip codes* rather than on rents over an entire metro area. Interim results indicate that the use of SAFMRs made more units potentially available to HCV holders in high-rent zip codes and fewer units available at rents under the SAFMR in low-rent zip codes (Finkel et al. 2017). As anticipated, the high-rent zip codes offered higher opportunity: lower poverty and crime rates as well as higher school proficiency, job proximity, and environmental quality. Based on rent cost alone (without considering landlord willingness to rent to voucher holders), SAFMRs created relatively equal numbers of affordable units in different types of neighborhoods, rather than favoring low-rent areas, as metro-wide FMRs do. However, jurisdictions with a substantially larger share of rental units in lower-priced areas had a net loss of potentially available units. About 2 to 4 years after the implementation of SAFMRs in the seven study areas, HCV households were slightly more likely to live in higher-rent, higher-opportunity zip codes with lower shares of minorities, though there were considerable differences among the study areas.[18] Subsidy costs *declined* in the study PHAs by 8 percentage points more than in comparison agencies (Finkel et al. 2017).

In November 2016, HUD issued a new regulation on PHAs in 24 metro areas where vouchers are heavily concentrated in low-income neighborhoods and the rental market is not too tight. The regulation required the agencies to begin basing voucher subsidies on SAFMRs in fiscal year 2018.[19] Sensibly, the policy allows PHAs in other areas to use SAFMRs but does not require them in low-vacancy areas like New York City, where the intense competition for the small number of vacant units could make it difficult for voucher holders to find units in high-rent zip codes. The criteria in the final rule also exclude areas such as Long Beach, California, the demonstration site with negative overall results. There, a small share of rental units is in high-rent zip codes.[20] On August 11, 2017, HUD notified PHAs in 23 of the 24 metro areas (all except Dallas, Texas) that it was suspending the mandatory use of SAFMRs for 2 years. A federal district court found HUD's action to be unlawful and ordered compliance with the mandatory SAFMR policy.[21] HUD directed the approximately 180 PHAs in the affected metro areas to implement SAFMR-based subsidies by April 1, 2018 (US Department of Housing and Urban Development 2018).

PROVIDE VOUCHER HOLDERS WITH INFORMATION ON UNITS IN HIGH-OPPORTUNITY NEIGHBORHOODS

Many housing agencies influence families' neighborhood choices through their lists of landlords willing to rent to voucher holders. HUD requires agencies to provide the list or other resources, such as online search tools, in the information packet offered when families are issued vouchers. But unless the agency makes an intentional and potentially time-consuming effort to solicit listings from landlords in lower-poverty areas, the list will include only the landlords who reach out to the agency. It is likely that landlords turn to agencies when they have difficulty renting units, particularly units located in very poor neighborhoods where families struggle to pay monthly rent unless they have a rental subsidy (DeLuca, Garboden, and Rosenblatt 2013, 280–81; Poverty & Race Research Action Council 2015).[22] Thus, the lists that could facilitate relocation into higher-opportunity areas may effectively reinforce racial and economic segregation.

In 2016, HUD modified its rules to require housing agencies to ensure that such lists or other resources include units in areas "outside of poverty or minority concentration."[23] This is a positive step. Achieving compliance may depend on aggressive monitoring by HUD as well as on efforts to get the major online search tools to meet the new standard. In addition, the department's guidance should encourage agencies to include units in low-poverty areas that do not have a high concentration of voucher holders or other assisted housing.[24] To help "change the default" for families that come from segregated, high-poverty areas, HUD could require agencies to list most prominently the available units in high-opportunity areas.[25]

EXTEND SEARCH PERIODS WHEN FAMILIES NEED MORE TIME TO FIND UNITS IN HIGH-OPPORTUNITY NEIGHBORHOODS

Although federal rules require agencies to give households 60 days to lease a unit with their voucher, they permit (but do not require) agencies to allow additional time.[26] Such a brief period can discourage families from searching for housing in neighborhoods that are harder for them to get to and/or where fewer landlords accept vouchers (DeLuca, Garboden, and Rosenblatt 2013, 275–80).[27] HUD could provide more guidance or could modify its rule on the amount of additional time that families have to search with a voucher. The department could require PHAs to extend the search time if a family requests an extension to find a unit in a low-poverty area. HUD should also consider requiring such extensions when minority families seek to move to an area where they would not be members of the predominant race. In these cases, extensions would affirmatively further fair housing.

Minimize Jurisdictional Barriers That Impede Relocation to High-Opportunity Communities

HUD should modify the administrative geography of the HCV program to substantially reduce the extent to which agencies' service areas (or "jurisdictions") impede the program's ability to promote access to higher-opportunity neighborhoods. In most metropolitan areas, one agency administers the HCV program in the central city and one or more different agencies serve suburban cities and towns. This is the pattern in 97 of the 100 largest metro areas, where 71 percent of households in the HCV program lived in 2015. In 35 of the 100 largest metro areas, voucher administration is divided among 10 or more agencies. This is the case even in midsized metropolitan areas such as Providence, Rhode Island, and Albany, New York, each of which has 35 agencies administering the HCV program (Sard and Thrope 2016).

Rental units in safe neighborhoods with good schools are more plentiful in some suburban areas than in the central cities or older suburbs, which are more likely to have high-poverty neighborhoods with lower-performing schools (Theodos, Coulton, and Budde 2014). But the balkanization of metro-area HCV programs among numerous agencies often impedes greater use of vouchers in the higher-opportunity areas.[28] Agency staff may be unfamiliar with housing opportunities outside of their jurisdiction and are unlikely to assist families in making such moves. Some landlords may be reluctant to do business with an unfamiliar housing agency.

Overcoming these administrative divisions is challenging, and the difficulties are exacerbated by cumbersome federal policies that make it more difficult for families coming from the central city or poor suburban areas to use their vouchers in low-poverty suburban areas with better schools. The problems also are worsened by financial disincentives that make it difficult for housing agencies to encourage such moves. HUD could substantially lessen these barriers by encouraging (or, in limited circumstances, requiring) agencies administering the HCV program in the same metro area to unify their voucher program operations. The department also could reduce the financial disincentives that discourage agencies from promoting the option to use vouchers in another agency's jurisdiction.

ENCOURAGE AGENCIES TO FORM CONSORTIA OR CONSOLIDATE

If PHAs in a metro area were permitted to form a consortium in which each retained its local board but all together had a single voucher-funding contract with HUD, families would be able to use their vouchers to move seamlessly within the cities and towns under the consortium's jurisdiction.[29] Under

HUD's current rules, agencies have little incentive to form consortia,[30] and when they are formed, the agencies operate through separate funding contracts from HUD.[31] In 2014, HUD proposed a revision of its consortia rule to allow all agencies in a consortium to have a single voucher-funding contract with HUD.[32] HUD should finalize this policy change promptly, and its budget should include funds to assist agencies in forming consortia.

REDUCE FINANCIAL DISINCENTIVES FOR AGENCIES TO PROMOTE PORTABILITY MOVES

When a family uses a voucher in a jurisdiction other than that in which it was issued, both agencies—the one with jurisdiction where it was issued and the one with jurisdiction where it is used—typically receive lower fees because they are required to split the administrative payments, yet the agencies typically incur higher costs because of the transfer of paperwork and funds between the agencies.[33] Although HUD's recent procedural changes may reduce some of portability's costs for PHAs, agencies likely will continue to incur financial losses when families move to other jurisdictions. Those losses are disincentives that deter agencies from encouraging such moves (Basolo 2003). HUD could revise its administrative-fee policy to remove the financial disincentives that discourage agencies from continual efforts to inform families of their right to use their vouchers in another agency's jurisdiction (Sard and Thrope 2016).

Assist Families in Using Vouchers in High-Opportunity Areas

The various policy changes described here are within the authority of HUD and the state and local housing agencies that administer the HCV program. If implemented, the changes would significantly expand families' ability to use vouchers to access safer neighborhoods that provide better opportunities. But additional help may be needed from state and local governments and private funding sources to overcome some of the most serious barriers that impede families in their efforts to use vouchers in high-opportunity neighborhoods.[34] This assistance is most likely necessary if efforts to recruit landlords have been unsuccessful or if too few rental options exist in such areas. In addition, experience from a number of local housing-mobility programs indicates that more black and Hispanic families will succeed in moving from low-income, racially segregated areas to high-opportunity, predominantly white neighborhoods if they receive intensive assistance (e.g., O'Neil 2009).[35] Three strategies are key.

STATE AND LOCAL GOVERNMENTS SHOULD ADOPT POLICIES TO ENCOURAGE LANDLORDS IN LOW-POVERTY AREAS TO ACCEPT HOUSING VOUCHERS

State and local policies can influence location outcomes by encouraging landlords in low-poverty areas to accept vouchers. For example, Illinois enacted a property tax abatement for landlords accepting vouchers for rental units in low-poverty areas within prosperous communities.[36] States also could encourage developers to build units in high-opportunity communities where moderately priced rental housing is scarce and to rent a share of the units to voucher holders. Although some of the state agencies that allocate Low-Income Housing Tax Credits (LIHTCs) encourage development in high-opportunity areas, states could do substantially more. For example, in the highly competitive process to receive LIHTC awards, states could give extra points to projects in low-poverty areas or near high-performing schools and could limit preferences for high-poverty areas to those where a comprehensive revitalization effort is under way. States could also eliminate barriers to using LIHTCs in high-opportunity areas. They could remove rigid cost caps that block projects when land costs are high and drop requirements that local officials or state legislators approve the award of credits to build a property in a particular location (Khadduri 2013*b*). Box 6.1 offers examples of how federal LIHTC policy could increase the availability of high-opportunity housing choices for voucher holders.

ENACT STATE OR LOCAL LAWS PROHIBITING DISCRIMINATION AGAINST VOUCHER HOLDERS

Laws that prohibit discrimination against voucher holders could increase the number of rental units available in areas with relatively low levels of poverty and racial segregation. Thirteen states, numerous cities, and many counties have enacted such laws, usually as part of legislation that also prohibits landlords from discriminating against people who rely on benefits from Temporary Assistance for Needy Families or Supplemental Security Income benefits to pay the rent. Recent studies found that such laws increased the percentage of people who successfully lease a unit with a voucher by between 5 and 12 percentage points. Jurisdictions where such a law was enacted made a modest improvement in location outcomes relative to the outcomes in adjacent jurisdictions where there was no anti-discrimination law (Freeman 2012; Freeman and Li 2014).[37]

PROVIDE MOBILITY COUNSELING TO HELP FAMILIES MOVE TO AND REMAIN IN HIGH-OPPORTUNITY NEIGHBORHOODS

There have been efforts in some metro areas to provide intensive mobility counseling to families that want to move to lower-poverty neighborhoods

BOX 6.1
The Low-Income Housing Tax Credit Could Do More to Provide Access to High-Opportunity Areas

The Low-Income Housing Tax Credit (LIHTC), the nation's main policy for developing affordable housing, is a potentially powerful tool to provide poor families access to high-opportunity areas. But LIHTC has performed inadequately in this respect. On average, LIHTC units large enough for families with children are near schools that score at the 31st percentile on standardized tests (Ellen and Horn 2012). This is better than the average for schools near the homes of poor families or voucher holders with children but leaves much room for improvement, given that the majority of LIHTC residents in states with available data have incomes above the poverty line (Hollar 2014). Families are eligible for LIHTC units if their income is below 60 percent of the median income for the area. Area median incomes vary, but the LIHTC income limit is about 200 percent of the federal poverty line (Sard and Rice 2016).

The federal government should ensure that nondiscrimination requirements—including the obligation of federal funding recipients to affirmatively further fair housing and the obligation of LIHTC properties not to discriminate against families with Housing Choice Vouchers (HCVs)—are applied to LIHTC and strictly enforced. HUD can also influence the location of LIHTC developments through its authority to designate Difficult Development Areas, which are areas with high land and construction costs. Projects in such areas are eligible for added credits. In 2016, HUD began setting Difficult Development Areas at the zip code level. This promising change provides additional funding for credits in high-cost, lower-poverty neighborhoods within most major metropolitan areas (Usowski 2016).

Policymakers and the public can better assess LIHTC's effectiveness in furthering key goals, including providing poor families access to high-opportunity neighborhoods, if HUD and state agencies make data available on the income, race, and family composition of tenants in each LIHTC development. No comprehensive national data are available on the families assisted by LIHTC. That is a striking omission for a low-income program that has operated for 27 years and helps develop about 100,000 units each year. In 2008, Congress directed state agencies to submit data on LIHTC tenants and required HUD to publish the data annually.[a] HUD and state agencies have worked to develop a data collection system but have only released partial data (US Department of Housing and Urban Development 2016).

Box 6.1 is adapted from *Realizing the Housing Voucher Program's Potential to Enable Families to Move to Better Neighborhoods,* by Barbara Sard and Douglas Rice (Washington, DC: Center on Budget and Policy Priorities, 2016), 18.

[a] Housing and Economic Recovery Act of 2008, Pub. L. No. 110-289, 122 Stat. 2654, 2874 (2008) (codified at 42 U.S.C. § 1437z–8 (2012)).

(Cunningham et al. 2010). (Some of these programs originated from fair housing lawsuits, and the terms require that destination neighborhoods be predominantly white.) Programs in the Baltimore and Dallas areas have reported significant success in moving substantial numbers of families to predominantly nonminority communities with much lower levels of poverty.

These initiatives provide families with assistance in locating available units, higher rental subsidy levels, payments for security deposits and other moving costs, and counseling to help them adjust to the new neighborhoods. They offer similar services for at least one subsequent move to help families remain in designated opportunity areas.[38] Participation is voluntary, and the programs operate on a regional basis, covering at least the central city and many suburban areas. This enables them to avoid the barriers created by separate agency service areas.[39]

It appears that the share of families moving to and remaining in high-opportunity, lower-poverty, racially integrated neighborhoods was greater among participants in these initiatives than among counterparts participating in HUD's Moving to Opportunity (MTO) demonstration. A Baltimore program with mobility counseling provides an example. The average poverty rate was 10.4 percent in neighborhoods where participating families lived an average of 4 years (and as much as 10 years) following their initial move, and the rate was 30.3 percent in the neighborhood where they lived before that move. In contrast, the average poverty rate in the neighborhoods where MTO families lived at a similar point after their initial MTO moves to low-poverty neighborhoods was 20 percent (DeLuca and Rosenblatt 2017). The Baltimore participants also lived in more racially mixed neighborhoods (37 percent black on average at the 4-year point versus 75 percent minority for MTO families).[40]

Qualitative research on a sample of families that moved to suburban areas through the Baltimore program highlighted the change in families' location-related priorities after they moved, noting that they place a higher value on high-quality schools (Darrah and DeLuca 2014; see also Wogan 2014).[41] The duration of stays in low-poverty neighborhoods is positively associated with improvements in educational results for children, employment results for mothers, and outcomes for adults who moved to low-poverty neighborhoods as young children (Turner, Nichols, and Comey 2012; Chetty, Hendren, and Katz 2015).

Unfortunately, there have been few attempts to rigorously evaluate mobility-promoting programs or the costs and benefits of particular features (Cunningham et al. 2010; Galvez 2010; Rosenbaum and Zuberi 2010). One study in the Chicago area tested the impact of "light-touch" mobility counseling coupled with a $500 incentive paid if a family moved to a designated opportunity area (Schwartz, Mihaly, and Gala 2017, 231). It found that the effects of combining counseling and the incentive did not differ significantly from the effect of the incentive payment alone or from the effect of the usual services PHAs provide (i.e., neither intensive services nor an incentive). It is important to learn more about what types of incentives, services, and policy parameters have the greatest effect under varying local conditions. HUD should encourage such knowledge building. A bill that would direct HUD to conduct a Housing Choice Voucher mobility demonstration recently passed the House of Representatives, and may receive funding beginning in 2019.[42]

In addition, if recent federal underfunding continues and outlays fall short of the costs housing agencies incur to administer the HCV program, agencies will likely need supplemental funds to provide meaningful mobility counseling services. Some HUD funding to states and localities could be used for this purpose. Examples include Community Development Block Grant funds as well as federal housing counseling and fair housing resources that are available on a competitive basis to nonprofit agencies (Scott et al. 2013, 64–68). States and localities also could use other funds they control to assist housing agencies in providing these services. Philanthropy (through such mechanisms as community foundations) could play a significant role in providing initial funding for mobility programs and in supporting the research necessary to build knowledge about the most cost-effective strategies. The results of such research might help agencies obtain subsequent funding from state or local governments by providing a base of knowledge on what works and is most cost efficient.

EXPAND ACCESS TO CARS TO HELP FAMILIES USE VOUCHERS IN LOW-POVERTY AREAS

Both initially and over longer periods of time, access to a functional car or having a driver's license appears to help families use vouchers in low-poverty, safer neighborhoods. Cars make the search for housing easier, particularly in neighborhoods not well served by efficient public transit. Having a car also facilitates access to jobs—either in the old neighborhood or near the new one—and makes it easier to maintain connections to social networks in families' former neighborhoods. For all of these reasons, families with reliable access to cars may be more willing and able to use housing vouchers to move to and remain in low-poverty neighborhoods. Programs to help families own cars or use short-term rental cars could be a useful adjunct to the housing-focused policies discussed in this chapter (Pendall et al. 2014).[43]

Conclusion

An expanding body of evidence suggests that children benefit from living in safe, low-poverty neighborhoods with good schools. It also has shown that growing up in extremely poor neighborhoods with low-performing schools and high levels of crime and violence can undermine their development and well-being over the short and long terms. Yet, the HCV program—the largest federal rental assistance program—does not fulfill its potential to help low-income families avoid high-poverty neighborhoods and access healthier communities with better opportunities.

By making four interrelated sets of policy changes, policymakers and program administrators at the federal, state, and local levels can make substantial progress in the next few years toward the goal of improving opportunities for assisted families. These changes will help more families in the HCV program to live in better locations. In the long run, federal policymakers must provide funding for a significant increase in the number of available housing vouchers if the HCV program is to enable far more low-income families to live in neighborhoods that will provide better opportunities for their children.

Notes

1. Since the early 1980s, the large majority of new units of federal rental assistance funded by Congress have been for tenant-based rental-assistance units (Weicher 2012, 108, Table 4-2).

2. For data on the poverty levels of neighborhoods where families used HCVs in 2014, see Barbara Sard and Douglas Rice (2016); for complete 2010 data, see Sard and Rice (2014, sec. 2). Across the 50 largest metropolitan areas and all family types, 23.1 percent of voucher households lived in low-poverty areas in 2010 (McClure, Schwartz, and Taghavi 2014, Table 4). Kirk McClure, Alex Schwartz, and Lydia Taghavi (2014) analyzed 2010 HUD microdata and census data similar to those used in this analysis. Molly Metzger (2014) also analyzed data on voucher holders (from 2008) in the 50 most populous metropolitan areas but used a different comparison group: households with income below 30 percent of the area median income or $15,000, whichever was lower. (In contrast, this chapter examines voucher data on all families with children by census tract and poverty rate.) She found that the neighborhoods of those voucher households were more segregated by race and income. She noted that the differences in the racial and ethnic composition of the two groups were unlikely to explain the differences in segregation.

3. This was the median poverty rate in tracts for all poor children. The rate comes from American Community Survey data for the 2010–14 period. We used the 2010–14 estimates from Table S1701, "Poverty Status in the Last 12 Months," available from http://factfinder2.census.gov.

4. Research into the effect of housing vouchers on families receiving (or eligible for) Temporary Assistance for Needy Families benefits found that, 4 years after they initially rented housing with a voucher (without any special assistance in their housing search), the families lived in neighborhoods with average poverty rates that were about 2 percentage points lower than the rates in the neighborhoods of counterparts that received no housing assistance (Abt Associates et al. 2006). The neighborhoods of voucher recipients also had a higher average employment rate, a lower average rate of welfare receipt, a lower concentration of minority residents, and a lower rate of female-headed families. The large majority of families that initially used vouchers were still receiving voucher assistance at the 4-year point. Examining vouchers and neighborhood quality, Daniel Gubits, Jill Khadduri, and Jennifer Turnham (2009) compared the poverty rates in census tracts where families lived before receiving vouchers with the rates in the tracts where they lived 4 years after receiving the vouchers. They found that families starting in tracts with poverty rates over 30 percent were, at the 4-year point, living in tracts where the poverty rate was 5.8 percentage points lower on average. These figures stem from a comparison of treatment-group families that initially leased with a voucher (received as part of the demonstration or independently) to control-group families that received no voucher assistance during the study period. The estimates were adjusted for both treatment-group nonparticipation and control-group

"crossover" (i.e., receiving a voucher apart from the demonstration; Gubits, Khadduri, and Turnham 2009, 20).

5. HUD rules require agencies to provide information about housing choices when a family first receives a voucher, including information on the advantages of living in an area that does not have a high concentration of low-income families (24 C.F.R. § 982.301 (2016)). Agencies are not required to assist families in finding a suitable unit, though HUD's *Housing Choice Voucher Program Guidebook* details benefits of offering such assistance (US Department of Housing and Urban Development 2001).

6. Metropolitan areas differ greatly in the share of vouchers used in the suburbs relative to the share of suburban units renting below the Fair Market Rent (FMR; Covington, Freeman, and Stoll 2011).

7. HUD's policy for evaluating agencies' performance in administering the HCV program is called the Section 8 Management Assessment Program (SEMAP). First issued in 1998, the measured performance areas remain largely unchanged. SEMAP scores can affect whether agencies qualify for additional HUD funds or administrative flexibility, and some local agencies take these scores into account in managers' performance reviews and pay determinations. Agencies that perform particularly poorly on any single indicator or overall are subject to corrective action procedures and can lose their HCV contract with HUD if they do not remedy the problems. Less than 4 percent of the total points available under SEMAP's rating system—5 out of a total of 135 points that agencies in metropolitan areas typically are eligible to receive—are based on agencies' use of administrative practices that "expand housing opportunities" (US Department of Housing and Urban Development 2013, 2). Federal regulation defines "expanding housing opportunities" as encouraging participation by landlords whose units are "located outside areas of poverty or minority concentration" and providing information to voucher holders about such opportunities (24 C.F.R. § 985.3(g) (2016)). A similar percentage of *bonus* points is available to agencies in metropolitan areas if half or more of the HCV families with children live in "low poverty" census tracts or the share of families living in such areas increases by 2 percent or more. The regulation defines "low poverty" as a poverty rate of 10 percent or less, or the average poverty rate in the agency's primary service area, whichever is *higher* (24 C.F.R. § 985.3(h) (2016)). As of 2012, only 166 of the 1,403 agencies operating in metropolitan areas claimed these additional 5 points (Center on Budget and Policy Priorities calculation based on HUD SEMAP data).

8. The SEMAP location measures focus on the poverty rates in the neighborhoods where vouchers are used, but the Moving to Opportunity (MTO) demonstration results indicate that measuring location performance solely on that basis does not account for reliable access to well-performing schools. Margery Austin Turner, Susan Popkin, and Lynette Rawlings (2009b, 85–86) documented challenges in objectively defining opportunity areas. The Bipartisan Policy Center's Housing Commission (2013, 99) recently recommended that HUD adopt outcome-based performance measures, including measures that promote access to neighborhoods of opportunity and the deconcentration of poverty.

9. Fair Housing Act of 1968, 42 U.S.C. §§ 3601–3619 (2012).

10. Affirmatively Furthering Fair Housing, 80 Fed. Reg. 42,272 (July 16, 2015) (codified at 24 C.F.R. pts. 5, 91, 92, 570, 574, 576, 903 (2016)).

11. 24 C.F.R. § 5.154(d) (2016).

12. To assist grantees in implementing the final AFFH rule and assessing levels of opportunity in particular neighborhoods, HUD provides agencies with neighborhood-level data on the location of assisted housing, education quality, transit access, levels of poverty and employment, exposure to environmental health hazards, and the availability of other community assets (US Department of Housing and Urban Development 2017a).

13. 24 C.F.R. § 5.154(d) (2016). The deadline for submission of a grantee's Assessment of Fair Housing (AFH) is generally pegged to the due date for the grantee's next 5-year plan. The first deadlines for cities and counties (with exceptions for smaller entities), as well as for PHAs that join with them, began in 2016 and will extend over a 5-year period. By notice published January 5, 2018, HUD delayed all further submissions by local governments to their next AFH submission date that falls after October 31, 2020 (Affirmatively Furthering Fair Housing: Extension of Deadline for Submission of Assessment of Fair Housing for Consolidated Plan Participants, 83 Fed. Reg. 683 (Jan. 5, 2018)). In response to litigation, HUD withdrew this notice (Affirmatively Furthering Fair Housing: Withdrawal of Notice Extending the Deadline for Submission of Assessment of Fair Housing for Consolidated Plan Participants, 83 Fed. Reg. 23,928 (May 23, 2018)). At the same time, however, HUD issued a notice suspending the use of the form that local governments would have to use to submit their AFHs (Affirmatively Furthering Fair Housing: Withdrawal of the Assessment Tool for Local Governments, 83 Fed. Reg. 23,922 (May 23, 2018)), which has the effect of suspending deadlines to submit fair housing assessments. As of this writing, a federal court is considering whether HUD's suspension of the requisite form is unlawful (National Fair Housing Alliance v. Carson, Civil Action No. 1:18-cv-01076 (D.D.C. filed May 29, 2018)). Deadlines for the assessments by PHAs that administer more than 550 vouchers and public housing units and that submit their own assessments (or join only with other PHAs or the state) were supposed to begin in 2017 and to extend over 5 years (US Department of Housing and Urban Development 2017b). The deadlines have not commenced as of this writing because HUD did not finalize certain data that it had to make available to PHAs to trigger their planning obligation.

14. The Obama administration proposed a new HCV administrative-fee policy in the summer of 2016 (Housing Choice Voucher Program—New Administrative Fee Formula, 81 Fed. Reg. 44,100 (July 6, 2016)) but did not take steps to implement these or other changes before leaving office. It appears unlikely that the Trump administration will continue the rule-making process. Even without a new policy, HUD has authority to provide supplemental fees for "extraordinary costs" (24 C.F.R. § 982.152(a)(iii)(C) (2016)), and the department pays $200 to a housing agency for each family that buys a home while participating in the HCV program. HUD could also use this authority to provide additional fees to agencies that assist voucher families in moving to high-opportunity areas.

15. Establishing a More Effective Fair Market Rent System; Using Small Area Fair Market Rents in the Housing Choice Voucher Program Instead of the Current 50th Percentile FMRs, 81 Fed. Reg. 80,567 (Nov. 16, 2016) (codified at 24 C.F.R. pts. 888, 982, 983, 985). See also Fischer (2015a) and Collinson and Ganong (2015).

16. Generally, families pay at least 30 percent of their adjusted income for their housing costs, including rent to landlords and any tenant-paid utilities. The HCV subsidy covers the rest of the cost up to the agency-set payment standard, which varies by family size. If the cost of rent and utilities is above the payment standard, the family pays 100 percent of the additional cost. Families are not permitted to move into units that cost more

than 40 percent of their income. Agencies may vary their payment standards for different neighborhoods, but few do so, and generally they must obtain HUD approval in order to set a payment standard outside of the basic range of 90 to 110 percent of the FMR (Center on Budget and Policy Priorities 2017).

17. Families in higher-poverty census tracts are more likely to rent larger units—that is, units with more bedrooms than their subsidy is based on—compared to voucher holders in lower-poverty tracts (Fischer 2015a). In a study based on ethnographic research in Baltimore, Maryland, Eva Rosen (2014) described the motivations of landlords renting to families with HCVs and the considerations that lead families to rent larger (or nicer) units in racially concentrated, very poor, rough neighborhoods.

18. Over the seven study sites, 20 percent of HCV households lived in high-rent zip codes in 2015. In comparison, 17 percent lived in such zip codes before implementation. This average result masks different impacts in different areas as well as differences between new and existing voucher households. Households with new HCVs were much more likely to rent units in high-rent areas in Laredo, Texas (where the rate quadrupled from 5 to 22 percent), and Chattanooga, Tennessee (where it doubled from 5 to 10 percent). Overall, existing voucher households that moved to new zip codes were much more likely to move to high-rent, high-opportunity areas in 2015 (28 percent) than before the implementation of SAFMRs (18 percent; Finkel et al. 2017).

19. 81 Fed. Reg. at 80,567.

20. The policy includes protections to prevent SAFMRs from causing unintended hardship for low-income families living in low-rent neighborhoods. For example, in areas where the SAFMR is much lower than the metropolitan FMR, HUD will phase in the decline so the amount of rent that vouchers cover does not drop too abruptly. Also, housing agencies can exempt a family from a drop in its subsidy if the family remains in a unit it now rents with a voucher. And agencies can continue using metro-level FMRs for "project-based" vouchers, which are tied to particular housing projects, often to support development and preservation of affordable housing.

21. For an example of the August 11 letter, see Blom (2017). A formal notice of suspension appeared on December 12. See Notice for Suspension of Small Area Fair Market Rent (Small Area FMR) Designations; Solicitation of Comment, 82 Fed. Reg. 58,439 (Dec. 12, 2017). For the injunction, see Open Communities Alliance v. Carson, Civil Action No. 17-2192 (D.D.C. Dec. 23, 2017) (order granting preliminary injunction). HUD did not appeal the court decision.

22. Several studies found that families relied most heavily on the agency-provided list of units in relocating from public housing that was being demolished or rehabilitated (see, e.g., Galvez 2010, 11). Rosen (2014) described similar problems arising when a housing agency relied on a privately compiled website (e.g., http://www.GoSection8.com).

23. 24 C.F.R. § 982.301(b)(11) (2016).

24. David Varady and Reinout Kleinhans (2013) emphasized the potential importance of avoiding the concentration of voucher holders in neighborhoods that are becoming increasingly poor. They argued that this is necessary to prevent negative "spillover" effects from housing assistance programs. They also emphasized the role of targeted landlord outreach and post-move counseling in achieving broader dispersal (outreach and counseling are discussed elsewhere in the chapter).

25. Xavier Briggs, Susan Popkin, and John Goering (2010, 233) emphasized the importance of strategies that would "change the default" of families staying in familiar neighborhoods, citing Richard Thaler and Cass Sunstein (2008).

26. 24 C.F.R. § 982.303 (2016).

27. If families use portability procedures, HUD's 2015 portability rule requires agencies to give a maximum of 30 days of additional time to use a voucher in another jurisdiction (Housing Choice Voucher Program: Streamlining the Portability Process, 80 Fed. Reg. 50,564, 50574 (Aug. 20, 2015) (codified at 24 C.F.R. § 982.355(c)(13) (2016)), effective Sept. 21, 2015). Search time extensions are required as a reasonable accommodation to people with disabilities. In most areas of the country, landlords may legally refuse to accept HCVs unless that refusal can be proven to be a proxy for discrimination based on race, national origin, disability, or family status; such discrimination is prohibited by the Fair Housing Act (42 U.S.C. § 3604 (2012)).

28. For a discussion of school quality's relationships with low-income and racially segregated neighborhoods in central cities and some older suburbs, see Briggs (2005*b*) and Mickelson (2011, 5).

29. Consolidation of separate housing agencies to form a single metro-wide PHA could have even greater benefits. Bruce Katz and Margery Turner (2013) recently recommended regional voucher administration. But for many PHAs, the ability to retain an independent identity is a paramount concern. Thus, PHAs are more likely to pursue administrative economies of scale through consortia than through formal consolidations with other agencies (*Evidence Matters* 2015). HUD has the authority to require consolidation when an agency is not administering the HCV program effectively, even if a state or local law limits the geographic area of agency operation.

30. In 2014, HUD indicated that there were only eight consortia (comprising 35 PHAs) involved in administering the HCV program (Streamlining Requirements Applicable to Formation of Consortia by Public Housing Agencies, 79 Fed. Reg. 40,019 (July 11, 2014)).

31. 24 C.F.R. § 943.100 et seq. (2016).

32. 79 Fed. Reg. at 40,019.

33. Even after a family rents a unit with a voucher, fee-splitting, funds transfers, and records exchanges are required to continue between the issuing and receiving agencies unless the receiving agency absorbs the family relocating into its own HCV program by giving the family a voucher instead of issuing it to a family on the waiting list.

34. In their analysis of how philanthropic investments can help tackle poverty in distressed urban neighborhoods, Turner and colleagues (2014) discussed assisted housing-mobility strategies and support for car access as two promising initiatives to expand residents' choices.

35. Many of the efforts to help voucher holders move to higher-opportunity communities have focused on former public housing residents because the efforts were the result of litigation concerning public housing segregation. The MTO demonstration also involved public housing residents. Jennifer O'Neil (2009) pointed out the greater barriers such families may face relative to the barriers for families that have a history of renting in the private market and familiarity with the workings of the HCV program. Whether families need direct assistance and how much assistance they require will depend on their background as well as on local market characteristics.

36. The Housing Opportunity Area Abatement Program is limited to townships with relatively high real estate evaluations in counties with at least 200,000 residents (P.A. 93-316, 2003 Ill. Laws 2630 (codified as amended at 35 Ill. Comp. Stat. 200/18-173) (2014)). The law defines a "housing opportunity area" as a census tract in which less than 10 percent of residents are poor; in municipalities with 1,000,000 or more inhabitants (i.e., the city of Chicago), it is a tract in which less than 12 percent are poor (§ 18-173(b)). PHAs are responsible for much of the program's administration.

37. The Poverty & Race Research Action Council (2017) maintains a list of laws prohibiting housing discrimination based on source of income, but it is important to note that rigorous enforcement of voucher anti-discrimination laws is rare. Except for requirements concerning properties that receive particular types of federal assistance or tax credits, no federal prohibition prevents discrimination against voucher holders. As mentioned, the Fair Housing Act prohibits discrimination against protected classes of people, and the prohibition includes refusal to accept housing vouchers if refusal is a pretext for discriminating against those classes (42 U.S.C. § 3604 (2012)).

38. Qualitative research with families that moved to low-poverty areas as part of the MTO demonstration indicated that they had difficulty finding new landlords who would accept vouchers in the same or similar communities. Respondents identified the difficulty as a major reason that many families moved back to higher-poverty neighborhoods when their initial lease terminated (Comey, Briggs, and Weismann 2008; Edin, DeLuca, and Owens 2012).

39. In Baltimore, vouchers issued as part of the consent decree in *Thompson v. HUD* must be used initially in a census tract where less than 10 percent of residents are poor, no more than 30 percent are African American, and less than 5 percent receive subsidized housing benefits. Initially, families were required to live in such a tract for 1 year; later the program extended the restriction on where a *Thompson* voucher could be used to 2 years. The program is administered by a nonprofit organization that operates throughout the Baltimore area. In Dallas, the Inclusive Communities Project provides mobility counseling to families with special vouchers issued as part of the settlement in *Walker v. HUD* (Civil Action 3:85-CV-121—R (N.D. Texas)). Since 2011, the counseling has been offered to any family issued a regular voucher by the Dallas Housing Authority and interested in living in a high-opportunity area. The *Walker* vouchers must be used first in an area with no public housing units; the share of area residents who are black and the area's poverty rate must be lower than the averages in the city of Dallas. Under the *Walker* decree, the Dallas Housing Authority can administer all of the vouchers it issues, not just the special vouchers, in any of the seven counties covered by the decree. Both the Baltimore and Dallas programs allow families more than the federally specified period of time to find a rental unit. Both provide additional financial assistance to help with moving costs for families leasing in areas that meet these restrictions or otherwise qualify as high-opportunity destinations. In addition, vouchers used in such areas can pay a higher subsidy than HUD rules usually allow. For Baltimore, see DeLuca and Rosenblatt (2017); Engdahl (2009); Darrah and DeLuca (2014); consent decree, Thompson v. HUD, No. MJG 95-309 (D. Md., Aug. 24, 2012). For Dallas, see Inclusive Communities Project (2013) and the court orders relevant to the settlement vouchers gathered at https://static1.squarespace.com/static/58b9e76e17bffc3590518d43/t/58bdcd4c1b10e3957cde0061/1488833870147/settlement+voucher+documents.pdf.

40. Baltimore mobility program participants also moved to, and remained in, neighborhoods with lower-poverty, high-performing neighborhood schools. Comparable data on duration of stay in low-poverty areas were not available for the Dallas program, though administrative data indicated that the 2,087 families with *Walker* vouchers have lived in their current home in an area that meets program requirements for an average of 4 years (Elizabeth Julian, president of the Inclusive Communities Project, personal communication). For a similar analysis of MTO families, see Ludwig (2012).

41. The Baltimore program's mobility counseling has an education component to help parents better understand what different schools offer and to help students adjust to their new schools (DeLuca et al. 2012). Other research has suggested that the extent of family members' social integration with new neighbors influences the family's values and interest in remaining in a different type of neighborhood (e.g., Varady and Kleinhans 2013).

42. On July 10, 2018, the US House of Representatives approved H.R. 5793, the Housing Choice Voucher Mobility Demonstration Act of 2018, by a strong bipartisan vote of 368 to 19 (115 Cong., https://www.congress.gov/bill/115th-congress/house-bill/5793). Concerning the status of funding for the demonstration, see Bell (2018).

43. Rolf Pendall and colleagues (2014) used data from the MTO demonstration and the Welfare to Work Voucher program. The study found that the share of the study period spent living in a neighborhood with a poverty rate of less than 10 percent was larger among families with access to a car than among families without such access, regardless of what group they were assigned to as part of either demonstration (the proportion of the study period was 4.9 percentage points larger for MTO participants with access and 5.7 points larger for Welfare to Work participants with access). Vehicle access mattered almost as much as receiving a geographically restricted voucher for lengthening the duration of MTO families' stay in a low-poverty neighborhood, and such access significantly lowered their rate of re-entry into higher-poverty neighborhoods. Pendall and colleagues acknowledge, however, that families with cars may have differed in unobserved ways from families without them, as car access was not a factor in either study's selection of treatment and control groups (see also Pendall et al. 2015). According to the National Consumer Law Center (2017), more than 120 nonprofit organizations across the country help low-wage working families obtain cars.

References

Abravanel, Martin D., Nancy M. Pindus, and Brett Theodos. 2010. *Evaluating Community and Economic Development Programs*. Research Report, September. Washington, DC: Urban Institute. http://www.urban.org/UploadedPDF/412271-New-Markets-Tax-Credit-Program.pdf.

Abt Associates, Gregory Mills, Daniel Gubits, Larry Orr, David Long, Judie Feins, Bulbul Kaul, Michelle Wood, Amy Jones and Associates, Cloudburst Consulting, and the QED Group. 2006. *Effects of Housing Vouchers on Welfare Families*. Report, September. Washington, DC: US Department of Housing and Urban Development, Office of Policy Development and Research.

Basolo, Victoria. 2003. "Local Response to Federal Changes in the Housing Voucher Program: A Case Study of Intraregional Cooperation." *Housing Policy Debate* 14 (1): 143–68. doi:10.1080/10511482.2003.9521471.

Bell, Alison. 2018. "House Approval of Housing Voucher Mobility Demonstration Is Encouraging." *Off the Charts* (blog), Center on Budget and Policy Priorities, July 12, 2018. https://www.cbpp.org/blog/house-approval-of-housing-voucher-mobility-demonstration-is-encouraging.

Bipartisan Policy Center. 2013. *Housing America's Future: New Directions for National Policy*. Housing Policy Commission Report, February. Washington, DC: Bipartisan Policy Center. http://bipartisanpolicy.org/sites/default/files/BPC_Housing%20Report_web_0.pdf.

Blom, Dominique. 2017. Letter from the assistant secretary for public and Indian housing to public housing agency executive director, August 11. Accessed February 12, 2018. http://prrac.org/pdf/Small_FMR_Letter_A_8-11-2017.pdf.

Bostic, Raphael W. 2014. "CDBG at 40: Opportunities and Obstacles." *Housing Policy Debate* 24 (1): 297–302. doi:10.1080/10511482.2013.866973.

Briggs, Xavier de Souza, ed. 2005a. *The Geography of Opportunity: Race and Housing Choice in Metropolitan America*. Washington, DC: Brookings Institution Press.

Briggs, Xavier de Souza. 2005b. "More Pluribus, Less Unum? The Changing Geography of Race and Opportunity." In *The Geography of Opportunity: Race and Housing Choice in Metropolitan America*, edited by Xavier de Souza Briggs, 63–87. Washington, DC: Brookings Institution Press.

Briggs, Xavier de Souza, Jennifer Comey, and Gretchen Weismann. 2010. "Struggling to Stay out of High-Poverty Neighborhoods: Housing Choice and Locations in Moving to Opportunity's First Decade." *Housing Policy Debate* 20 (3): 383–427. doi:10.1080/10511481003788745.

Briggs, Xavier de Souza, Susan J. Popkin, and John Goering. 2010. *Moving to Opportunity: The Story of an American Experiment to Fight Ghetto Poverty*. New York: Oxford University Press.

Center on Budget and Policy Priorities. 2017. "Policy Basics: The Housing Choice Voucher Program." Report, May 3 revision. Washington, DC: Center on Budget and Policy Priorities. https://www.cbpp.org/research/housing/policy-basics-the-housing-choice-voucher-program.

Chetty, Raj, and Nathaniel Hendren. 2015. "The Impacts of Neighborhoods on Intergenerational Mobility: Childhood Exposure Effects and County-Level Estimates." Working Paper 21156, revised September. Cambridge, MA: National Bureau of Economic Research. doi:10.3386/w21156.

Chetty, Raj, Nathaniel Hendren, and Lawrence F. Katz. 2015. "The Effects of Exposure to Better Neighborhoods on Children: New Evidence from the Moving to Opportunity Experiment." Working Paper 21156, revised September. Cambridge, MA: National Bureau of Economic Research. doi:10.3386/w21156.

Collinson, Robert A., and Peter Ganong. 2015. "The Incidence of Housing Voucher Generosity." Social Science Research Network Paper 2255799. http://papers.ssrn.com/sol3/Papers.cfm?abstract_id=2255799.

Collinson, Robert A., and Peter Ganong. 2016. "Incidence and Price Discrimination: Evidence from Housing Vouchers." Working Paper 13-7, Revised April 2016. Cambridge,

MA: Harvard University, Joint Center for Housing Studies. http://www.jchs.harvard
.edu/sites/jchs.harvard.edu/files/w13-7_ganong_revised2016.pdf.

Comey, Jennifer, Xavier de Souza Briggs, and Gretchen Weismann. 2008. "Struggling to Stay out of High-Poverty Neighborhoods: Lessons from the Moving to Opportunity Experiment." Three-City Study of Moving to Opportunity, Brief 6, March. Washington, DC: Urban Institute. http://www.urban.org/UploadedPDF/411635_high-poverty_neighborhoods.pdf.

Covington, Kenya, Lance Freeman, and Michael A. Stoll. 2011. "The Suburbanization of Housing Choice Voucher Recipients." Metropolitan Opportunity Series paper, October. Washington, DC: Brookings Institution. http://www.brookings.edu/~/media/research/files/papers/2011/10/11-housing-suburbs-covington-freeman-stoll/1011_housing_suburbs_covington_freeman_stoll.pdf.

Cunningham, Mary K., Molly M. Scott, Chris Narducci, Sam Hall, and Alexandra Stanczyk. 2010. "Improving Neighborhood Location Outcomes in the Housing Choice Voucher Program: A Scan of the Mobility Assistance Programs." Brief, September. Washington, DC: What Works Collaborative. http://www.urban.org/UploadedPDF/412230-Improving-Neighborhood-Location.pdf.

Darrah, Jennifer, and Stefanie DeLuca. 2014. "'Living Here Has Changed My Whole Perspective': How Escaping Inner-City Poverty Shapes Neighborhood and Housing Choice." *Journal of Policy Analysis and Management* 33 (2): 350–84. doi:10.1002/pam.21758.

DeLuca, Stefanie, Greg J. Duncan, Micere Keels, and Ruby Mendenhall. 2012. "The Notable and the Null: Using Mixed Methods to Understand the Diverse Impacts of Residential Mobility Programs." In *Neighbourhood Effects Research: New Perspectives*, edited by Maarten van Ham, David Manley, Nick Bailey, Ludi Simpson, and Duncan Maclennan, 195–223. Dordrecht, Netherlands: Springer.

DeLuca, Stefanie, Philip M. E. Garboden, and Peter Rosenblatt. 2013. "Segregating Shelter: How Housing Policies Shape the Residential Locations of Low-Income Minority Families." *Annals of the American Academy of Political and Social Science* 647 (1): 268–99. doi:10.1177/0002716213479310.

DeLuca, Stefanie, and Peter Rosenblatt. 2013. "Sandtown-Winchester—Baltimore's Daring Experiment in Urban Renewal: 20 Years Later, What Are the Lessons Learned?" *Abell Report* 26 (8): 1–12. http://www.abell.org/sites/default/files/publications/arn1113.pdf.

DeLuca, Stefanie, and Peter Rosenblatt. 2017. "Walking away from *The Wire*: Housing Mobility and Neighborhood Opportunity in Baltimore." *Housing Policy Debate* 27 (4): 519–46. doi:10.1080/10511482.2017.1282884.

Edin, Kathryn, Stefanie DeLuca, and Ann Owens. 2012. "Constrained Compliance: Solving the Puzzle of MTO's Lease-Up Rates and Why Mobility Matters." *Cityscape* 14 (2): 181–94. https://www.huduser.gov/portal/periodicals/cityscpe/vol14num2/Cityscape_July2012_constrained_compliance.pdf.

Ellen, Ingrid Gould, and Keren Mertens Horn. 2012. *Do Federally Assisted Households Have Access to High Performing Public Schools?* Civil Rights Research, November. Washington, DC: Poverty & Race Research Action Council. http://files.eric.ed.gov/fulltext/ED538399.pdf.

Engdahl, Lora. 2009. *New Homes, New Neighborhoods, New Schools: A Progress Report on the Baltimore Housing Mobility Program*. Report, October. Washington, DC: Poverty

& Race Research Action Council and Baltimore Regional Housing Campaign. http://www.prrac.org/pdf/BaltimoreMobilityReport.pdf.

Evidence Matters. 2015. "Strategies for Regional Collaboration," Summer/Fall, 13–17. https://www.huduser.gov/portal/periodicals/em/fall15/highlight2.html.

Finkel, Meryl, Samuel Dastrup, Kimberly Burnett, Thyria Alvarez, Carissa Climaco, and Tanya de Sousa. 2017. *Small Area Fair Market Rent Demonstration Evaluation: Interim Report*. Washington, DC: US Department of Housing and Urban Development, Office of Policy Development and Research. https://www.huduser.gov/portal/sites/default/files/pdf/SAFMR-Interim-Report.pdf.

Fischer, Will. 2015a. *Neighborhood-Based Subsidy Caps Can Make Housing Vouchers More Efficient and Effective*. Report, June 10. Washington, DC: Center on Budget and Policy Priorities. http://www.cbpp.org/sites/default/files/atoms/files/6-10-15hous.pdf.

Fischer, Will. 2015b. *Research Shows Housing Vouchers Reduce Hardship and Provide Platform for Long-Term Gains among Children*. Report, October 7. Washington, DC: Center on Budget and Policy Priorities. http://www.cbpp.org/files/3-10-14hous.pdf.

Freeman, Lance. 2012. "The Impact of Source of Income Laws on Voucher Utilization." *Housing Policy Debate* 22 (2): 297–318. doi:10.1080/10511482.2011.648210.

Freeman, Lance, and Yunjing Li. 2014. "Do Source of Income Anti-Discrimination Laws Facilitate Access to Less Disadvantaged Neighborhoods?" *Housing Studies* 29 (1): 88–107. doi:10.1080/02673037.2013.824559.

Galster, George C. 2013. "U.S. Assisted Housing Programs and Poverty Deconcentration: A Critical Geographic Review." In *Neighbourhood Effects or Neighbourhood Based Problems? A Policy Context*, edited by David Manley, Maarten van Ham, Nick Bailey, Ludi Simpson, and Duncan Maclennan, 215–49. Dordrecht, Netherlands: Springer.

Galvez, Martha M. 2010. "What Do We Know about Housing Choice Voucher Program Location Outcomes? A Review of Recent Literature." What Works Collaborative Brief, August. Washington, DC: Urban Institute. http://www.urban.org/UploadedPDF/412218-housing-choice-voucher.pdf.

Gubits, Daniel B., Jill Khadduri, and Jennifer Turnham. 2009. "Housing Patterns of Low Income Families with Children: Further Analysis of Data from the Study of the Effects of Housing Vouchers on Welfare Families." Working Paper W09-7, September. Cambridge, MA: Harvard University, Joint Center for Housing Studies. http://www.jchs.harvard.edu/sites/jchs.harvard.edu/files/w09-7.pdf.

Hollar, Michael K. 2014. *Understanding Whom the LIHTC Program Serves: Tenants in LIHTC Units as of December 31, 2012*. Report, December. Washington, DC: US Department of Housing and Urban Development, Office of Policy Development and Research. http://www.huduser.org/portal/publications/hsgfin/understanding_LIHTC.html.

Inclusive Communities Project. 2013. "Mobility Works." Report, April. Dallas, TX: Inclusive Communities Project. http://www.inclusivecommunities.net/MobilityWorks.pdf.

Katz, Bruce, and Margery Austin Turner. 2013. "Invest but Reform: Streamline Administration of Housing Choice Voucher Program." Remaking Federalism Renewing the Economy Paper, January. Washington, DC: Brookings Institution. http://www.brookings.edu/research/papers/2013/09/30-housing-choice-voucher-katz-turner.

Khadduri, Jill. 2013a. "Commentary: Crime as a Dimension of Neighborhood Quality." *Cityscape* 15 (3): 159–63. http://www.huduser.gov/portal/periodicals/cityscpe/vol15num3/ch8.pdf.

Khadduri, Jill. 2013b. *Creating Balance in the Locations of LIHTC Developments: The Role of Qualified Allocation Plans*. Report, February. Washington, DC: Poverty & Race Research Action Council and Abt Associates. http://www.prrac.org/pdf/Balance_in_the_Locations_of_LIHTC_Developments.pdf.

Kubisch, Anne C. 2010. "Structures, Strategies, Actions, and Results of Community Change Efforts." In *Voices from the Field III: Lessons and Challenges from Two Decades of Community Change Efforts*, edited by Anne C. Kubisch, Patricia Auspos, Prudence Brown, and Tom Dewar, 15–50. Washington, DC: Aspen Institute. http://www.aspeninstitute.org/sites/default/files/content/docs/pubs/VoicesIII_FINAL_0.pdf.

Ludwig, Jens. 2012. "Guest Editor's Introduction." *Cityscape* 14 (2): 1–28. http://www.huduser.org/portal/periodicals/cityscpe/vol14num2/Cityscape_July2012_guest_introduction.pdf.

Mazzara, Alicia, Barbara Sard, and Douglas Rice. 2016. *Rental Assistance to Families with Children at Lowest Point in Decade*. Report, October 18. Washington, DC: Center on Budget and Policy Priorities. https://www.cbpp.org/research/housing/rental-assistance-to-families-with-children-at-lowest-point-in-decade.

McClure, Kirk. 2013. "Which Metropolitan Areas Work Best for Poverty Deconcentration with Housing Choice Vouchers?" *Cityscape* 15 (3): 209–36. http://www.huduser.gov/portal/periodicals/cityscpe/vol15num3/ch15.pdf.

McClure, Kirk, Alex F. Schwartz, and Lydia B. Taghavi. 2014. "Housing Choice Voucher Location Patterns a Decade Later." *Housing Policy Debate* 25 (2): 215–33. doi:10.1080/10511482.2014.921223.

Metzger, Molly W. 2014. "The Reconcentration of Poverty: Patterns of Housing Voucher Use, 2000 to 2008." *Housing Policy Debate* 24 (3): 544–67. doi:10.1080/10511482.2013.876437.

Mickelson, Roslyn Arlin. (2011). "Exploring the School-Housing Nexus: A Synthesis of Social Science Evidence." In *Finding Common Ground: Coordinating Housing and Education Policy to Promote Integration*, edited by Philip Tegeler, 5–8. Washington, DC: Poverty & Race Research Action Council. http://prrac.org/pdf/HousingEducationReport-October2011.pdf.

National Consumer Law Center. 2017. "Find a Program." Working Cars for Working Families program summary. Accessed July 3. http://www.workingcarsforworkingfamilies.org/find-a-program.

O'Neil, Jennifer Lee. 2009. "Housing Mobility Counseling: What's Missing?" In *Public Housing and the Legacy of Segregation*, edited by Margery Austin Turner, Susan J. Popkin, and Lynette Rawlings, 115–25. Washington, DC: Urban Institute Press.

Pendall, Rolf, Christopher Hayes, Arthur George, Casey Dawkins, Jae Sik Jeon, Elijah Knapp, Evelyn Blumenberg, Gregory Pierce, and Michael Smart. 2015. "Driving to Opportunities: Voucher Users, Cars, and Movement to Sustainable Neighborhoods." *Cityscape* 17 (2): 57–87. http://www.huduser.gov/periodicals/cityscpe/vol17num2/ch2.pdf.

Pendall, Rolf, Christopher Hayes, Arthur George, Zach McDade, Casey Dawkins, Jae Sik Jeon, Elijah Knapp, Evelyn Blumenberg, Gregory Pierce, and Michael Smart.

2014. *Driving to Opportunity: Understanding the Links among Transportation Access, Residential Outcomes, and Economic Opportunity for Housing Voucher Recipients*. Report, March. Washington, DC: Urban Institute. http://www.urban.org/UploadedPDF/413078-Driving-to-Opportunity.pdf.

Popkin, Susan J., and Mary K. Cunningham. 2009. "Has HOPE VI Transformed Residents' Lives?" In *From Despair to Hope: HOPE VI and the New Promise of Public Housing in America's Cities*, edited by Henry G. Cisneros and Lora Engdahl, 191–204. Washington, DC: Brookings Institution Press.

Poverty & Race Research Action Council. 2015. *Constraining Choice: The Role of Online Apartment Listing Services in the Housing Choice Voucher Program*. Civil Rights Research, June. Washington, DC: Poverty & Race Research Action Council. http://prrac.org/pdf/ConstrainingChoice.pdf.

Poverty & Race Research Action Council. 2017. "Expanding Choice: Practical Strategies for Building a Successful Housing Mobility Program; Appendix B: State, Local, and Federal Laws Barring Source-of-Income Discrimination." May revision. Washington, DC: Poverty & Race Research Action Council. http://www.prrac.org/pdf/AppendixB.pdf.

Rosen, Eva. 2014. "Selection, matching, and the Rules of the Game: Landlords and the Geographic Sorting of Low-Income Renters." Working Paper W14-11, June. Cambridge, MA: Harvard University, Joint Center for Housing Studies. http://www.jchs.harvard.edu/sites/jchs.harvard.edu/files/w14-11_rosen_0.pdf.

Rosenbaum, James E., and Anita Zuberi. 2010. "Comparing Residential Mobility Programs: Design Elements, Neighborhood Placements, and Outcomes in MTO and Gautreaux." *Housing Policy Debate* 20 (1): 27–41. doi:10.1080/10511481003599845.

Sard, Barbara, and Douglas Rice. 2014. *Creating Opportunity for Children: How Housing Location Can Make a Difference*. Report, October 15. Washington, DC: Center on Budget and Policy Priorities. http://www.cbpp.org/research/creating-opportunity-for-children.

Sard, Barbara, and Douglas Rice. 2016. *Realizing the Housing Voucher Program's Potential to Enable Families to Move to Better Neighborhoods*. Policy Futures Report. Washington, DC: Center on Budget and Policy Priorities.

Sard, Barbara, and Deborah Thrope. 2016. *Consolidating Rental Assistance Administration Would Increase Efficiency and Expand Opportunity*. Policy Futures Report, April 11. Washington, DC: Center on Budget and Policy Priorities. https://www.cbpp.org/sites/default/files/atoms/files/4-11-16hous.pdf.

Schwartz, Heather L., Kata Mihaly, and Breann Gala. 2017. "Encouraging Residential Moves to Opportunity Neighborhoods: An Experiment Testing Incentives Offered to Housing Voucher Recipients." *Housing Policy Debate* 27 (2): 230–60. doi:10.1080/10511482.2016.1212247.

Scott, Molly M., Mary K. Cunningham, Jennifer Biess, Jennifer Lee O'Neil, Philip Tegeler, Ebony Gayles, and Barbara Sard. 2013. *Expanding Choice: Practical Strategies for Building a Successful Housing Mobility Program*. Report. Washington, DC: Urban Institute and Poverty & Race Research Action Council. http://www.urban.org/UploadedPDF/412745-Expanding-Choice.pdf.

Sharkey, Patrick, Amy Ellen Schwartz, Ingrid Gould Ellen, and Johanna Lacoe. 2014. "High Stakes in the Classroom, High Stakes on the Street: The Effects of Community

Violence on Students' Standardized Test Performance." *Sociological Science* 1: 199–220. doi:10.15195/v1.a14.

Thaler, Richard H., and Cass R. Sunstein. 2008. *Nudge: Improving Decisions about Health, Wealth, and Happiness.* New Haven, CT: Yale University Press.

Theodos, Brett, Claudia Coulton, and Amos Budde. 2014. "Getting to Better Performing Schools: The Role of Residential Mobility in School Attainment in Low-Income Neighborhoods." *Cityscape* 16 (1): 61–84. http://www.huduser.gov/portal/periodicals/cityscpe/vol16num1/ch3.pdf.

Turner, Margery Austin, Peter Edelman, Erika Poethig, and Laudan Aron. 2014. *Tackling Persistent Poverty in Distressed Urban Neighborhoods: History, Principles, and Strategies for Philanthropic Investment.* Research Report, July. Washington, DC: Urban Institute. http://www.urban.org/UploadedPDF/413179-Tackling-Persistent-Poverty-in-Distressed-Urban-Neighborhoods.pdf.

Turner, Margery Austin, Austin Nichols, and Jennifer Comey. 2012. *Benefits of Living in High-Opportunity Neighborhoods: Insights from the Moving to Opportunity Demonstration.* Report, September. Washington, DC: Urban Institute. http://www.urban.org/UploadedPDF/412648-Benefits-of-Living-in-High-Opportunity-Neighborhoods.pdf.

Turner, Margery Austin, Susan J. Popkin, and Lynette Rawlings. 2009a. "Building Healthy Mixed-Income Developments: Barriers to Neighborhood Health and Sustainability." In *Public Housing and the Legacy of Segregation*, edited by Margery Austin Turner, Susan J. Popkin, and Lynette Rawlings, 13–30. Washington, DC: Urban Institute Press.

Turner, Margery Austin, Susan J. Popkin, and Lynette Rawlings. 2009b. "Moving to Neighborhoods of Opportunity: Overcoming Segregation and Discrimination in Today's Housing Markets." In *Public Housing and the Legacy of Segregation*, edited by Margery Austin Turner, Susan J. Popkin, and Lynette Rawlings, 79–98. Washington, DC: Urban Institute Press.

US Department of Housing and Urban Development. 2001. *Housing Choice Voucher Program Guidebook.* Handbook 7420.10G. Washington, DC: US Department of Housing and Urban Development, Office of Public and Indian Housing.

US Department of Housing and Urban Development. 2013. "Section 8 Management Assessment Program (SEMAP) Certification." Form HUD-52648. Washington, DC: US Department of Housing and Urban Development, Office of Public and Indian Housing.

US Department of Housing and Urban Development. 2015. *Housing Choice Voucher Program Administrative Fee Study: Final Report.* Washington, DC: US Department of Housing and Urban Development. https://www.huduser.gov/portal/publications/pdf/AdminFeeStudy_2015.pdf.

US Department of Housing and Urban Development. 2016. *Understanding Whom the LIHTC Program Serves: Data on Tenants in LIHTC Units as of December 31, 2014.* Report, December. Washington, DC: US Department of Housing and Urban Development, Office of Policy Development and Research. https://www.huduser.gov/portal/sites/default/files/pdf/LIHTC-TenantReport-2014.pdf.

US Department of Housing and Urban Development. 2017a. "AFFH Data and Mapping Tool." Accessed August 31. https://www.hudexchange.info/resource/4867/affh-data-and-mapping-tool/.

US Department of Housing and Urban Development. 2017b. "Interim Guidance for Program Participants on Status of Assessment Tools and Submission Options." Program guidance, January 18. Washington, DC: US Department of Housing and Urban Development. https://www.hudexchange.info/resources/documents/Interim-Guidance-for-Program-Participants-on-Status-of-Assessment-Tools-and-Submission-Options.pdf.

US Department of Housing and Urban Development. 2018. "Guidance on Recent Changes in Fair Market Rent (FMR), Payment Standard, and Rent Reasonableness Requirements in the Housing Choice Voucher Program." Notice PIH 2018-01 (HA), January 17. Washington, DC: US Department of Housing and Urban Development, Office of Public and Indian Housing. https://www.hud.gov/sites/dfiles/PIH/documents/PIH-2018-01.pdf.

US Government Accountability Office. 2012. *Limited Information on the Use and Effectiveness of Tax Expenditures Could Be Mitigated through Congressional Attention.* Report GAO-12-262, February. Washington, DC: US Government Accountability Office. http://www.gao.gov/assets/590/588978.pdf.

Usowski, Kurt. 2016. "HUD Advances Opportunity and Fair Housing for Low-Income Renters With Small Difficult Development Areas." Message from PD&R Senior Leadership. *PD&R Edge*, January 25. https://www.huduser.gov/portal/pdredge/pdr-edge-frm-asst-sec-012516.html.

Varady, David, and Reinout Kleinhans. 2013. "Relocation Counselling and Supportive Services as Tools to Prevent Negative Spillover Effects: A Review." *Housing Studies* 28 (2): 317–37. doi:10.1080/02673037.2013.767882.

Weicher, John C. 2012. *Housing Policy at a Crossroads: The Why, How, and Who of Assistance Programs.* Washington, DC: AEI Press.

Wogan, J. B. 2014. "Is There a Better Model for Housing Vouchers?" *Governing*, March 25. http://www.governing.com/topics/health-human-services/better-model-affordable-housing-vouchers.html.

7

The Community Reinvestment Act as a Catalyst for Integration and an Antidote to Concentrated Poverty*

John Taylor and Josh Silver

Policymakers tend to focus on federal programs as the primary remedies for alleviating poverty; however, it is the market that truly dictates one's ability to rise. Having a decent-paying job and an investment in a home that increases in value helps far more people out of poverty than a government program.

Enacted in 1977, the Community Reinvestment Act (CRA) redirects the market toward combating poverty.[1] Specifically, it creates an affirmative obligation for the market, through banks, to create jobs in low- and moderate-income (LMI) communities. It does this by encouraging investments in businesses and home mortgages for LMI borrowers. The act also requires banks to serve the credit needs of LMI communities in ways that are consistent with safety and soundness.

Federally administered CRA performance evaluations rate banks on their efforts to meet the act's requirements, and these exams are based on the loans, investments, and services that evaluated banks provide in LMI neighborhoods. By promoting responsible lending, the CRA has increased homeownership and small-business ownership in such neighborhoods. Indeed, from 1996 through 2015, CRA-covered banks issued more than 24 million small-business loans in LMI tracts, and these loans were worth over $973 billion. In the same time period, CRA-covered banks made community development loans of more than $883 billion.[2] Such loans support affordable housing and economic development projects benefiting LMI communities.

---

*Portions of this chapter have been adapted with permission from *The Community Reinvestment Act: How CRA Can Promote Integration and Prevent Displacement in Gentrifying Neighborhoods*, by the National Community Reinvestment Coalition (2016).

As originally conceived, the CRA was not intended to promote desegregation. Its focus was not on encouraging whites to move into minority neighborhoods or on helping the poor to move into affluent areas. Rather, the act was geared toward channeling private-sector capital, specifically bank financing, to revitalize LMI neighborhoods. The results have been impressive, and the focus on revitalizing distressed neighborhoods may have been necessary, but that focus and the scale of bank lending have not been sufficient to effect a significant reduction in the number of impoverished neighborhoods. What is needed perhaps is not only more financing for distressed neighborhoods but also efforts to encourage integration—that is, efforts that generate opportunities for middle- and upper-income people to move into poor neighborhoods and opportunities for lower-income people to move into middle- and upper-income neighborhoods.

The CRA can be helpful in desegregating neighborhoods. Over the years, the federal agencies implementing the act have developed guidance encouraging banks to pursue mixed-income housing opportunities and also to finance developments that are located in gentrifying neighborhoods but that do not displace LMI residents. However, the guidance has not been effectively reflected in CRA exams. This chapter explores how improved examination procedures can make the act more effective in promoting integration within gentrifying and distressed neighborhoods. It also explores how the CRA, in combination with the recent fair housing rule issued by the US Department of Housing and Urban Development (HUD),[3] can combat concentrations of poverty.

As part of this exploration, the chapter first summarizes trends in the concentration of poverty and gentrification. It then discusses how the CRA operates and how regulatory initiatives use the act to address segregation. The chapter also identifies financing tools and programmatic approaches that can aid desegregation. Finally, the chapter presents results from a survey of CRA exams. The chapter reveals the state of the art in the use of the CRA to encourage desegregation. Recommendations form the concluding part of the chapter.

Trends of Concentrated Poverty

Unfortunately, concentrated poverty, as defined by census tracts with large percentages of impoverished residents, has increased in the United States since 2000. Paul Jargowsky (2013) reported that it surged from 1970 to 1990, decreased in the 1990s, and rose again in the 2000s. Despite the common perception that poverty touches only a small portion of the population, the reality is that, because of its magnitude, poverty affects all of us directly or indirectly. Jargowsky noted that 71 million people, or one fourth of the US population, resided in neighborhoods with poverty rates of at least 20 percent.

The booming economy of the 1990s likely contributed to the decrease in concentrated poverty, just as the ensuing Great Recession's high unemployment and foreclosures undoubtedly contributed to its increase at the new century's beginning. The recession led to substantial declines in home mortgage and small-business lending within LMI neighborhoods (Silver, Pradhan, and Cowan 2013; Bhutta and Ringo 2016). The decreased lending, in turn, drove up poverty, in part because residents were not able to maintain employment through small-business creation or to acquire equity through homeownership. Conversely, a strengthened CRA might have promoted increases in lending that encouraged integration as well as additional investment in poor census tracts.

According to the Brookings Institution's Elizabeth Kneebone (2014), the share of poor people living in distressed census tracts (tracts in which more than 40 percent of the residents were impoverished) increased from 9.1 percent in 2000 to 12.2 percent for the period from 2008 through 2012. During this time, the number of distressed tracts and the population in these tracts both grew by 75 percent.

The same study highlighted that distressed tracts are no longer an urban phenomenon: of residents dwelling in distressed neighborhoods within the 100 largest metropolitan areas, 26 percent lived in the suburbs, and that represents a spike from the 18 percent in 2000. In addition, the number of high-poverty tracts (those in which 20–40 percent of residents are poor) increased significantly in the suburbs. Almost half (46 percent) of all residents dwelling in high-poverty tracts in large metropolitan areas lived in the suburbs (Kneebone 2014). The suburbanization of poverty has implications for CRA compliance and policy: In which areas should banks and other stakeholders pursue desegregation lending strategies? In particular, which high-poverty tracts should be targeted for investment to prevent them from turning into distressed tracts?

Minorities are disproportionately represented among residents in distressed census tracts, but these tracts are becoming more racially diverse (Jargowsky 2013). Almost 40 percent of the residents of distressed tracts are African American. However, between 2000 and 2011, the share of white residents living in impoverished neighborhoods increased from 20 to 26 percent, and the share of Hispanics remained constant at about 30 percent. A strategy for meeting CRA obligations through desegregationist lending would further diversify distressed tracts.

The well-documented impacts of concentrated poverty include inferior schools as well as unemployment and vulnerability to crime. Raj Chetty, Nathaniel Hendren, and Lawrence Katz's seminal research has documented how moving to nonpoor neighborhoods improves the life chances and earnings of low-income children, showing that the improvements are tied to attending schools with more affluent classmates (Chetty and Hendren 2015; Chetty, Hendren, and Katz 2015; Harvard University 2015).

Trends in Gentrification

An increase in concentrated poverty is not the only factor intensifying segregation by race and income. Neighborhood gentrification can also exacerbate segregation if the process is not managed in a manner that minimizes displacement. Studies show that gentrification has expanded in US metropolitan areas.

Ingrid Gould Ellen (2016) has documented this expansion over, as of this writing, the last 15 years. Fourteen percent of low-income census tracts across the country experienced an increase in income from 2000 through 2014, but income grew in just 9 percent of these tracts from 1980 through 1990. Ellen also showed that 35 percent of low-income tracts experienced an increase in college-educated residents from 2000 through 2014; in contrast, 25 percent of these tracts saw an increase from 1990 through 2000 (Ellen 2016; see also Ellen and Ding 2016).

Victor Couture and Jessie Handbury (2016) found that gentrification has been most prevalent in the 50 largest metropolitan areas of the country. From 2000 to 2010, a majority of those areas saw rapid growth in the number of young professionals, and more of the growth occurred in urban neighborhoods than in suburban ones. That trend stands in marked contrast to the one observed from 1970 through 2000. Between 2000 and 2010, the numbers of college-educated professionals aged 25 to 34 grew by 44 percent in the downtown urban neighborhoods of large cities. That rate was 3.2 times faster than the 14 percent growth in the suburbs. Couture and Handbury attributed the downtown migration to the proximity of amenities such as theaters and restaurants.

It would be logical to assume that displacement of lower-income residents from gentrifying neighborhoods accompanies housing price increases and a significant in-migration of middle- and upper-income young professionals. However, Miriam Zuk and colleagues' (2015) review of the literature revealed mixed results among studies probing for displacement. Even studies using the same data came to different conclusions. Zuk and colleagues (2015, 33–35) offered a number of methodological reasons for the inconsistencies, including the lack of a common definition for gentrification as well as differences in sources of data, time periods studied, and control and comparison groups.

In a recent study in Philadelphia, Lei Ding, Jackelyn Hwang, and Eileen Divringi (2015) found that lower-income residents with lower credit scores were no more likely to move from gentrifying neighborhoods than from non-gentrifying ones. However, the disaggregated results revealed that renters in gentrifying neighborhoods were more likely to experience displacement. In addition, residents who had low credit scores and moved out of gentrifying neighborhoods were more likely to move into neighborhoods with lower incomes, higher crime rates, lower-performing schools, and higher unemployment.

Low–credit score residents moving out of gentrifying neighborhoods were more likely than those who remained to experience declines in credit scores; those who remained in the neighborhoods experienced an increase in credit scores.

One reason that the data have not shown widespread displacement from gentrification is that many lower-income residents strive to remain in gentrifying neighborhoods so that their families can benefit from improving neighborhood amenities, schools, and job prospects (Zuk et al. 2015, 33). However, increases in housing cost burden pose a potential problem.[4] Tenants in gentrifying neighborhoods face rent increases when the local market heats up, and homeowners' effective monthly costs grow with rising property taxes, which also increase escrow costs. Few studies have examined the housing cost burdens of lower-income households in gentrifying neighborhoods, but this issue is likely a significant one in hot markets.

Another rarely examined subject is the equity accumulation of lower-income homeowners in neighborhoods experiencing gentrification. One of the few studies on this issue focused on homeowners affiliated with Manna Inc., a nonprofit housing developer and counseling agency in Washington, DC. A significant concentration of these homeowners resided in the district's Shaw neighborhood, which has experienced gentrification during the last two decades. The study found that the median amount of equity built by Manna homeowners was more than $170,000. The two quintiles with greatest gains had median equity gains of $576,000 and $316,000, respectively (Silver et al. 2014; see also Oh et al. 2015, 3).

In addition to considering gentrification's impacts on renters and homeowners, researchers must also assess the impacts on small businesses. Many neighborhood-based small businesses pay rent for their physical space. Rents in gentrifying neighborhoods can increase significantly and become unaffordable. In one of the few studies on the subject, Rachel Meltzer (2016) found that the departure and stay rates of small businesses in New York City did not vary significantly by whether a neighborhood was gentrifying. However, her case studies in East Harlem and Sunset Park documented departures of local businesses and increases in chain stores.

Lastly, little research has considered whether gentrification is associated with increases in concentration of poverty. Data limitations have prevented definitive conclusions, but Claire Zippel's (2016) preliminary examination for the DC Fiscal Policy Institute suggests a possible relationship such that gentrification in neighborhoods of the northwest part of the District of Columbia may have been associated with the migration of lower-income and minority households to impoverished neighborhoods east of the Anacostia River.

In sum, research has suggested that gentrification imposes costs on lower-income households and small businesses but also offers benefits.

Costs
- Displacement of renters and homeowners
- Increases in housing cost burden due to increases in rents and property taxes
- Declines in credit scores for lower-income residents leaving neighborhoods
- Possible displacement of neighborhood-based small businesses
- Increased rent burdens for neighborhood-based small businesses
- Possible increases in concentrated poverty as lower-income residents move from gentrifying neighborhoods to lower-income neighborhoods

Benefits
- Equity increases for homeowners
- Improvements in the credit scores of lower-income residents
- Access to improving schools
- More local businesses and grocery stores for shopping
- Increased access to jobs
- More customers for long-standing neighborhood businesses
- Increases in race and income integration

The review suggests that gentrification does not retain the negative connotations it has acquired in some circles; it is needed in a number of distressed communities. The policy and programmatic approaches to economic development should not reflexively move to stop gentrification. A more sensible approach to economic development involves managing gentrification and promoting integration. The trend toward rising gentrification provides policymakers and practitioners with opportunities to better manage it. The challenge is to do so in ways that minimize displacement and other costs while maximizing the benefits. The CRA can play a role in those tasks.

How the CRA Can Combat Segregation

One of three bank regulatory agencies conducts each CRA evaluation: the Federal Reserve Board, the Federal Deposit Insurance Corporation, and the Office of the Comptroller of the Currency (OCC). Banks with assets over $1 billion receive the most comprehensive exam, which evaluates lending, investments, and services. The lending test scrutinizes the number and percentage of loans to LMI people and neighborhoods. The investment test examines equity investments in LMI neighborhoods and grants to nonprofits serving LMI people and neighborhoods. The service test evaluates the bank branches and basic bank services available for LMI consumers and neighborhoods. Banks with less than $1 billion in assets are subject to a streamlined exam that mostly focuses on retail lending activities. CRA exams produce one of four ratings: passing ratings are Outstanding and Satisfactory; failing ratings are Needs to Improve and Substantial Noncompliance. Examiners employ quantitative and qualitative criteria to determine the ratings for banks' lending, investments, and services. Qualitative criteria include the degree to which examiners provide favorable consideration for activities depending on the extent to which they benefit low- and moderate-income people and/or neighborhoods.

Banks do not face immediate sanctions or monetary penalties if they fail the exam, but poor ratings can result in delays or denials of merger applications and damage a bank's reputation. Although lending and service to minorities are not explicit criteria on CRA exams, the exam is accompanied by a fair lending review. If the evaluating agency determines that a bank discriminated or violated consumer protection laws, it may downgrade the bank's rating.

As the CRA has been implemented through the bank exams, the act's main approach to combating poverty and the concentration of poverty has been to facilitate bank lending, investing, and services in LMI neighborhoods. Indeed, moving success stories have documented the role of CRA-motivated affordable housing and economic development initiatives in helping to revitalize neighborhoods.[5] But efforts under the CRA have not focused on combating concentration of poverty by lending in a pro-integrative manner—for example, by lending in ways that help poor people move into middle-income neighborhoods or that help middle-income people move into poor neighborhoods. The CRA could powerfully complement the objectives of Affirmatively Furthering Fair Housing (AFFH), a federal requirement for local jurisdictions to promote integration, if the relevant federal agencies encouraged bank programs that lend in a pro-integrative manner (additional information on AFFH is provided elsewhere in the chapter).

The federal agencies that regulate banks have taken initial steps to promote desegregation. They developed a question and answer (Q&A) document with items on mixed-income housing and gentrifying neighborhoods.[6] The document guides federal CRA examiners, banks, community organizations, and others in the interpretation and use of the CRA.

The evaluation criteria in the lending, investment, and service tests assess the extent to which bank activities are innovative and responsive to community needs. These criteria could be applied more explicitly in the Q&A about mixed-income housing and gentrification to indicate that activities that desegregate neighborhoods are innovative and responsive to community needs.

The Q&A document also encourages favorable consideration for mixed-income housing developments but should be changed to encourage mixed-income housing in distressed neighborhoods and in neighborhoods transitioning out of distressed status. One item from the Q&A document (quoted subsequently) discusses a situation in which an activity was not primarily consistent with the CRA regulation's definition of "community development."[7] Under that definition, community development included the development of affordable housing for LMI households. According to the Q&A item, pro rata consideration is available for mixed-income housing that includes units set aside for LMI people:

> *What is meant by the term "primary purpose" as that term is used to define what constitutes a community development loan, a qualified investment, or a community development service?*
>
> ... Generally, a loan, investment ... will be determined to have a "primary purpose" of community development only if it meets the criteria described above. However, an activity involving the provision of affordable housing also may be deemed to have a "primary purpose" of community development in certain other limited circumstances. ... Activities related to the provision of mixed-income housing, such as in connection with a development that has a mixed-income housing component or an affordable housing set-aside required by Federal, state, or local government, also would be eligible for consideration as an activity that has a "primary purpose" of community development at the election of the institution. In such cases, an institution may receive pro rata consideration for the portion of such activities that helps to provide affordable housing to low- or moderate-income individuals. For example, if an institution makes a $10 million loan to finance a mixed-income housing development in which 10 percent of the units will be set aside as affordable housing for low- and moderate-income individuals, the institution may elect to treat $1 million of such loan as a community development loan. In other words, the pro rata dollar amount of the total activity will be based on the percentage of units set aside for affordable housing for low- or moderate-income individuals.[8]

The quoted item presents an example in which 10 percent of the units were set aside for LMI people, the total financing was $10 million, and the bank could count $1 million as a community development loan. The difficulty, however, is that this guidance could discourage development of mixed-income housing. A bank might legitimately decide to devote the entire $10 million loan to housing for LMI people in a distressed neighborhood and have the whole sum considered on its CRA exam rather than just the $1 million. This guidance could very well be counterproductive because, in a number of circumstances, promoting income mixes in distressed neighborhoods may be necessary to desegregate them. A fix for this potentially perverse incentive is to expand the Q&A item, adding guidance that, in evaluating compliance with CRA lending requirements, the exam will consider the entire amount of a loan for development of mixed-income housing intended to help desegregate the surrounding neighborhood, not just the amount of the loan that finances units for LMI households.

A related question concerns what constitutes mixed-income housing. The CRA regulations and Q&A offer no explicit definition, but a 40 percent threshold is mentioned in a Q&A as an illustrative example.[9] In the Q&A, 40 percent of the units are for LMI families. In general, it would seem that less than 40 percent of the units for either LMI or middle- and upper-income families does not represent a development that is substantially mixed income. If the Q&A were changed to specify that 40 percent of the units for either LMI or middle and upper income are generally regarded as mixed-income housing, the guidance would be more helpful in promoting the desegregation of impoverished neighborhoods because it would influence CRA examiners considering mixed-income housing in distressed neighborhoods. (A lower percentage of the units being for LMI or non-LMI families could still garner favorable consideration, but not as much as a development that hit the 40 percent target.)

The Q&A document also specifically addresses how bank financing in gentrifying neighborhoods should be considered on CRA exams:

Under the lending test applicable to small, intermediate small, or large institutions, how will examiners evaluate home mortgage loans to middle- or upper-income individuals in a low- or moderate-income geography?

A5. Examiners will consider these home mortgage loans under the performance criteria of the lending test. . . . Examiners could view home mortgage loans to middle-income individuals in a low-income geography very differently. For example, if the loans are for homes or multifamily housing located in an area for which the local, state, tribal, or Federal government or a community-based development organization has developed a revitalization or stabilization plan (such as a Federal enterprise community or empowerment zone) that includes attracting mixed-income residents to establish a stabilized, economically diverse neighborhood, examiners may give more consideration to such loans, which may be viewed as serving the low- or moderate-income community's needs as well as serving those of the middle- or upper-income borrowers. If, on the other hand, no such plan exists and there is no other evidence of governmental support for a revitalization or stabilization project in the area and the loans to middle- or upper-income borrowers significantly disadvantage or primarily have the effect of displacing low- or moderate-income residents, examiners may view these loans simply as home mortgage loans to middle- or upper-income borrowers who happen to reside in a low- or moderate-income geography and weigh them accordingly in their evaluation of the institution.[10]

Item A5 suggests that CRA examiners would not give favorable consideration to lenders financing large-scale middle- and upper-income developments in overheated markets if such developments would result in the displacement of the LMI residents of gentrifying neighborhoods. In contrast, the guidance offers favorable consideration to banks if financing promoted mixed-income housing in such neighborhoods. It also indicates that favorable consideration would be given if the bank's financing and activities were part of a neighborhood plan developed by the government or a nonprofit or were consistent with such a plan. However, item A2 adds the point that development of middle- and upper-income housing would receive little weight in the CRA exam if the neighborhood needed LMI housing and the bank was not financing such housing:

> *Will activities that provide housing for middle-income and upper-income persons qualify for favorable consideration as community development activities when they help to revitalize or stabilize a distressed or underserved nonmetropolitan middle-income geography or designated disaster areas?*
>
> A2. An activity that provides housing for middle- or upper-income individuals qualifies as an activity that revitalizes or stabilizes a *distressed* nonmetropolitan middle-income geography . . . if the housing directly helps to revitalize or stabilize the community by attracting new, or retaining existing, businesses or residents. . . . The Agencies generally will consider all activities that revitalize or stabilize a *distressed* nonmetropolitan middle-income geography . . . but will give greater weight to those activities that are most responsive to community needs, including needs of low- or moderate-income individuals or neighborhoods. Thus, for example, a loan solely to develop middle- or upper-income housing in a community in need of low- and moderate-income housing would be given very little weight if there is only a short-term benefit to low- and moderate-income individuals in the community through the creation of temporary construction jobs.[11]

This Q&A item needs more nuance. Almost all neighborhoods could be considered to be in need of LMI housing. The item should be revised to state that an analysis of performance context (local economic conditions and demographic composition) will be used to determine whether the neighborhood is one in which prices and rents are increasing rapidly; middle- and upper-income developments in such neighborhoods are likely to intensify unaffordable housing cost burdens for LMI residents. The guidance in this item should not discourage banks from providing financing for middle- and upper-income housing in neighborhoods that can benefit from it but should instead caution against an exclusive focus on middle- and upper-income housing (as opposed to mixed-income housing) in overheated markets. (Such a focus is revealed in an analysis similar to that described by Mallach, whose work is described in the next section.)

Financing Tools and Programmatic Approaches That Could Garner CRA Credit

The Q&A items just discussed could be powerful instruments for promoting integration, but other tools and approaches are also particularly effective in fostering sustainable, affordable housing for LMI families within integrated neighborhoods.

Mallach (2008, 3) asserted that an assessment of neighborhood housing markets is the first step for stakeholders in promoting neighborhood integration. He contended that jurisdictions and localities should conduct data analysis to develop indicators for the state of housing markets in their neighborhoods. The jurisdiction could then choose the appropriate community revitalization or stabilization strategy for the analyzed neighborhoods.

Mallach (2008) developed a typology of neighborhood housing markets and identified six market types. Neighborhoods with the first, second, and third market types are in various stages of economic distress. Those markets are characterized by housing supply that exceeds demand, by the number of absentee owners exceeding that of owner occupants, and by high rates of abandoned and vacant housing. For these neighborhoods, the objective is to jump-start the housing market and reverse the cycle of disinvestment by engaging in large-scale housing and economic development projects (Mallach 2008).

The National Community Reinvestment Coalition (NCRC) believes that development efforts in neighborhoods with one of these three types of markets could also focus on mixed-income housing because desegregating these neighborhoods is of utmost importance (Mallach 2008). Some markets have amenities that make them attractive to non-LMI households (e.g., ready access to transit or a major entertainment district). If a market has those prospects, introducing mixed-income housing there would make more sense than concentrating the poor further by developing additional housing solely for LMI households. Using the CRA to encourage mixed-income developments in neighborhoods with one of the first three market types would be a novel use of the act and could significantly help to break up the cycle of concentrated poverty in some communities.

In the neighborhood markets that Mallach (2008) assigned to the fourth, fifth, and sixth types, housing demand exceeds supply, abandoned and vacant housing stock is relatively rare or absent, and the number of owner-occupants surpasses the number of absentee owners. Gentrification accelerates in markets 5 and 6. Mallach (2008, 5) suggests that community development and stabilization initiatives focus not on large-scale redevelopment projects but on scattered-site rehabilitation and preservation of affordable housing. In gentrifying neighborhoods within markets 5 and 6, NCRC suggests that using the CRA to finance LMI housing is likely more important than using it to finance mixed-income housing. The markets in those neighborhoods are already effective in attracting non-LMI households.

Several other tools and approaches can be useful for preserving affordable housing. We discuss several in the succeeding sections.

COLLABORATIONS BETWEEN COMMUNITY-BASED ORGANIZATIONS AND BANKS

Community-based organizations, such as nonprofit housing developers, have missions that focus on empowering communities of color and/or LMI neighborhoods. They also have an unmatched commitment to underserved populations and will work assiduously to promote the long-term welfare of those populations. When banks partner with community-based organizations and finance their housing developments, the organizations can create enduring developments for underserved populations.

LOW-INCOME HOUSING TAX CREDITS

Investors receive Low-Income Housing Tax Credits (LIHTCs) for investing in rental housing units that serve tenants with low income, typically those with income between 50 and 60 percent of the median income for the area where the housing is located. Rent for the units is also based on a percentage of the area median income, and the units are set aside for lower-income tenants for periods of 15 years or more. LIHTC projects can be sited in integrating neighborhoods, and financial incentives encourage investors to locate the projects in census tracts with high construction or land costs (Office of the Comptroller of the Currency [OCC] 2014).

LIMITED-EQUITY CO-OPS

In a limited-equity co-op, residents share ownership of a multifamily building. They have rights commonly associated with homeownership, such as the right to pass their property to their heirs, but when they sell their units, they do not receive the full market price; residents agree to cap the prices of units in order to keep them affordable for future buyers (Levy, Comey, and Padilla 2006).

COMMUNITY LAND TRUSTS

A community land trust is run by a nonprofit organization that owns the land and provides 99-year leases to lower-income homeowners, who receive loans to buy homes on the land: homeowners own their home but lease the land. They also agree to limits on equity appreciation, accepting only a portion of the equity when they sell so that the homes remain affordable for other lower-income homeowners (Community-Wealth.org n.d.; Levy, Comey, and Padilla 2006).

RIGHT OF FIRST REFUSAL AND THE TENANT OPPORTUNITY TO PURCHASE ACT

The District of Columbia serves as an example of a city that established protections against displacement of low-income tenants. The district's Tenant Opportunity to Purchase Act requires landlords to offer tenants a right of first refusal if the landlord is interested in selling the building.[12] During a specified time period, a tenant association has the right to match the terms of any contract for sale between the landlord and a third party, either buying the building itself or arranging for the building to be purchased by a nonprofit organization that will maintain it as affordable housing. To facilitate bank financing of purchases by the tenants or the tenants' designee, the law extends time periods further if a lender indicates in writing that it will attempt to arrange financing.[13]

LOCAL HOUSING PROGRAMS FOR FIRST-TIME AND LOWER-INCOME HOMEOWNERSHIP

Local jurisdictions use HUD programs, including the HOME Investment Partnerships Program and Community Development Block Grants, to develop homeownership initiatives for lower-income residents. These local efforts can include grants and low-interest second-lien loans that are forgivable after a specified time period. They enable purchases in neighborhoods where gentrification is beginning and home prices are still affordable so that the lower-income homeowners can benefit from the gentrification.

INCLUSIONARY ZONING

Cities have enacted inclusionary zoning policies in hot-market neighborhoods (categories 5 and 6 in the typology by Mallach 2008). Under those policies, developers can receive a density bonus that allows them to build more units than zoning usually permits. In return, developers make a certain percentage of the units affordable for lower-income households (Levy, Comey, and Padilla 2006, 5).

In addition to working with jurisdictions implementing inclusionary zoning, banks can participate in efforts to promote integration by financing LIHTC projects, limited-equity co-ops, and community land trusts. They can offer first-lien loans for homebuyers through local housing programs. Large-scale and mixed-income developments are appropriate for neighborhoods with markets in categories 1 through 3. Banks can also be involved in planning efforts by local jurisdictions that have implemented initiatives such as inclusionary zoning and have targeted neighborhood markets with the features of categories 5 and 6 in Mallach's (2008) typology.

How the CRA Can Complement Fair Housing Law

The federal AFFH rule implemented during the Obama administration requires state and local jurisdictions receiving HUD funding to develop plans to affirmatively further fair housing. This requirement can also include development of plans to promote integration in gentrifying or distressed neighborhoods. The rule defines "affirmatively furthering fair housing" as "taking meaningful actions, in addition to combating discrimination, that overcome patterns of segregation and foster inclusive communities free from barriers that restrict access to opportunity based on protected characteristics" (US Department of Housing and Urban Development 2015, 5).[14]

The AFFH rule requires each jurisdiction receiving HUD funding to develop an Assessment of Fair Housing (AFH), which is a planning and strategy document intended to ensure compliance with civil rights and fair housing laws. The assessment involves a data analysis to identify patterns of segregation, concentrated areas of poverty, and significant disparities in access to opportunity for protected classes. In completing the assessment, the jurisdiction also identifies contributing factors that perpetuate segregation, fair housing goals, and strategies that are designed to overcome the contributing factors. In 2018, during the Trump administration, HUD first suspended and then rescinded the AFFH rule that the department promulgated during the Obama administration. HUD then reinstated the prior rule and requirement called Analysis of Impediments (AI). Local jurisdictions preparing an AI can still consider integration initiatives in both gentrifying and distressed neighborhoods in a manner similar to that as if they were preparing an AFH (US Department of Housing and Urban Development 2018). The remainder of this chapter generically refers to the AI (formerly AFH) requirement as the fair housing requirement.

Gentrifying neighborhoods can be regarded as areas of opportunity in which jurisdictions seek to preserve housing affordability for people of color who are long-term residents. In fact, HUD's previous AFFH rule discusses a strategy for promoting integration by preventing displacement of people of color from areas "experiencing economic improvement."[15] In addition, jurisdictions can partially meet the fair housing requirements by promoting income diversity in neighborhoods with significant concentrations of poverty.

In its AI, a jurisdiction could highlight the efforts of banks to meet CRA obligations by preserving affordable housing and providing opportunities for lower-income people of color to remain in gentrifying neighborhoods.

The AI could also discuss mixed-income housing initiatives in distressed neighborhoods. By marrying the fair housing requirement and the CRA, federal public policy can provide powerful inducements for leveraging substantial bank financing to promote desegregation.

Surveys of CRA Exams

To develop a deeper understanding of the ways in which CRA exams rate bank activities and of the role played by the Q&A guidance, the NCRC conducted two surveys of recent evaluations. In the first, NCRC reviewed the exams of large banks engaged in large metropolitan areas undergoing gentrification. In the second, the coalition reviewed the exams of banks engaged in mixed-income housing efforts within areas of concentrated poverty. (Details on the selection of banks and metropolitan areas may be found in the appendix to this chapter.) The surveys also highlight tools and approaches that examiners think are innovative and responsive to the need to desegregate neighborhoods.

CRA EXAMS AND GENTRIFYING NEIGHBORHOODS

The first survey investigated the frequency with which the CRA Q&A guidance on gentrification is employed in CRA exams. In identifying the banks whose exams would be included, NCRC assumed that the CRA exams of the largest banks would have the most detailed descriptions of community development activities. In addition, NCRC assumed that the largest metro areas with neighborhoods experiencing gentrification would offer the most examples of efforts to promote integration in gentrifying neighborhoods. Accordingly, NCRC identified 10 of the largest banks (by asset size) with recent CRA exams and 14 large metropolitan areas experiencing gentrification.

Since not all of the banks operated in each metropolitan area selected by NCRC, the survey ended up with a sample of 63 metropolitan areas (this was out of 140 possible combinations of banks and metropolitan areas; some of the metropolitan areas in the sample appear more than once since more than one of the sampled banks engaged in activities in those areas). The survey of exams identified just three projects involving investments or community development lending in gentrifying neighborhoods: a housing investment by HSBC Bank USA, N.A., in Manhattan, an economic development investment by U.S. Bank National Association in Seattle, and a Capital One National Association construction loan for low-income housing in a gentrifying area of Northern Virginia (OCC 2011, 2012*a*, 2012*b*).

The CRA exams for those banks did not adequately describe the context of two of the three projects for which banks received favorable consideration. HSBC Bank USA, N.A.'s investment was laudable in that it preserved 1,688 units of affordable housing, but the CRA exam's description offered little detail on the project's scope: "One example of the bank's investment responsiveness is a $50 million investment in Manhattan Plaza. This investment helped to preserve 1,688 units of affordable housing in the Hell's Kitchen area of Manhattan. Tenants' rents are subsidized by HUD's Section 8 and New York's Mitchell-Lama programs" (OCC 2012a, 18). The full scope of the bank's effort and of its responsiveness to a need—preserving affordable housing and integration—would have been more clearly indicated if the CRA exam had fully described the gentrification occurring in the neighborhood. That process was detailed in an article retrieved by NCRC (Schulz 2015).

The description of U.S. Bank National Association's Seattle investment was even less detailed: "four NMTC [New Market Tax Credit] investments totaling more than $50 million to renovate a nine-acre historic district in downtown Seattle, which is home to 250 small owner-operated businesses, 100 seasonal farmers, and 200 arts and craft vendors" (OCC 2012b, 68). The project involved helping smaller businesses remain and thrive in an area near Seattle's downtown. The location led NCRC to classify the area as a site of gentrification. As described earlier, the most intense gentrification pressures often occur in neighborhoods near downtown areas.

The Capital One, National Association CRA exam provided the most detailed of the three descriptions:

> In June 2010, CONA [Capital One, National Association] provided a $7.6 million loan to fund the construction and permanent financing for a 90-unit affordable housing property in Arlington, VA. All of the units will be affordable to low- and moderate-income families earning up to 60% of area median income. . . . The construction of this housing development addresses an important community need, as it will replace 24 apartments lost through a land trade and add 66 new apartments to Arlington's supply of affordable rental housing. In addition, the development is located in the growing Ballston corridor, which has seen the loss of many affordable units to rapid urbanization and conversion of rental units to high-end, for-sale condominiums. The development's location provides ready access to everyday community services, as it is located within walking distance of bus lines and Metro lines providing access to employment centers. (OCC 2011, 27–28)

Despite the detail, the discussion does not explain the activity's full significance in terms of promoting integration within a changing neighborhood. Contrary to the guidance in the CRA Q&A document, it also does not describe whether Capital One, National Association's investment was part of a government or nonprofit plan for the area.

In general, it is not clear why the CRA exams for three large banks offer so little detail on financing of pro-integrative projects in gentrifying neighborhoods. The descriptions of complex projects tend to be sparse, and exams for large banks often are hundreds of pages long. Nevertheless, the exams should highlight responsive, innovative, and complex financing projects in gentrifying neighborhoods. In addition, the exams should identify the relevant CRA Q&A items in cases that involve such projects.

Another explanation for the meager coverage devoted to these projects in CRA exams may be that the financing for pro-integrative projects is low because banks seek the safest ways to gain favorable CRA consideration. Financing projects in LMI neighborhoods is the surest means to gain favorable CRA consideration, and guidance in the CRA Q&As sanctions mixed-income projects in gentrifying neighborhoods, but banks may be hesitant to commit substantial resources. In part, the reluctance may be due to the lack of regular communication between banks and CRA examiners, who could provide guidance on how projects will be considered in exams. It would seem that an imbalance—financing channeled solely to economically distressed neighborhoods or to gentrifying ones—would be less favorably received than a balanced approach. If evaluators examined performance context, the analysis would identify gentrification and indicate a need for pro-integrative financing. Also, given the AFFH rule, CRA examiners should promote a mix of financing that encourages economic revitalization in distressed neighborhoods and integration in gentrifying ones.

In sum, are banks financing pro-integrative projects but these projects are not regularly noted by CRA exam narrative, or are banks hesitating to finance pro-integrative projects because CRA examiners regard this financing in an inconsistent and unpredictable manner? The NCRC survey cannot determine the precise cause for the relative paucity of pro-integrative projects. However, the financing for these projects would increase if federal bank agencies promoted the projects and implemented the Q&As in a clearer manner. Financing for the projects would also increase if CRA examiners were more consistent in acknowledging them.

CRA EXAMS, CONCENTRATED POVERTY, AND MIXED-INCOME HOUSING

NCRC's second survey assessed the consideration given in CRA exams to banks for mixed-income housing developed as part of efforts to desegregate neighborhoods and reduce concentrated poverty. As the appendix details, NCRC selected 10 large banks, accessed their recent CRA exams, and reviewed the descriptions of their activities in 20 metropolitan areas with large concentrations of poverty (the metropolitan areas with the highest percentage of poor people living in census tracts where more than 40 percent of residents were in poverty). For each bank, NCRC reviewed the CRA exam to identify which of the 20 metropolitan areas were in the exam. Using this process for each bank, NCRC identified 56 bank–metropolitan area combinations (some of the metropolitan areas are duplicated because banks often served the same metropolitan area).

The survey identified a few instances in which CRA exams gave favorable consideration to banks for mixed-income housing. Only 2 of 56 surveyed metropolitan areas, or just 3.6 percent, featured affordable housing projects with mixed-income housing. In some of the projects, a small percentage of units was set aside for middle- or upper-income households. For example, a Citibank, N.A. CRA exam conducted by the OCC in 2010 described an affordable housing project in Philadelphia. The project consisted of 73 units, and 71 of those were reserved for LMI households. Although the percentage of units reserved for non-LMI households was very small, it was included because the examiner appeared to be probing for mixed-income housing.

The same exam for Citibank, N.A. noted a project in Los Angeles. Although the city is not one of the 56 identified metro areas, the project is worthy of mention: "The Rosslyn Lofts are located in a low-income census tract in downtown Los Angeles in a former hotel built in 1913 known originally as the 'Rosslyn Million Dollar Fireproof Hotel'. The architecturally beautiful property will provide much needed affordable housing and help in the revitalization of one of Los Angeles' most important historical and cultural centers. The four percent LIHTC qualified rehabilitation will feature 259 studio apartments restricted to individuals earning at 35 percent and 60 percent of average median income (AMI) as well as 38 market rate apartments" (OCC 2010, 22).

The second case in the survey is from the 2012 CRA exam of U.S. Bank National Association. The exam describes an affordable housing project in Milwaukee: "A $20.5 million construction loan to finance the development of a 140-unit mixed income housing project, located in in [sic] a moderate-income census tract. Of the 140 units, 121 will be restricted to families with incomes at varying levels (30–60 percent) of the area median income" (OCC 2012*b*, 75).

Mixed-income housing projects are rarely noted in CRA exams. When they are cited, the descriptions are cursory. They do not indicate the importance of the projects in terms of reducing concentrations of poverty, desegregating neighborhoods, or making projects more financially feasible by using the rents of non-LMI households to cross-subsidize the rents of LMI households. If CRA examiners were intent on promoting integration in gentrifying neighborhoods or distressed ones, they would provide more robust descriptions of pro-integrative housing projects. The goals of such projects are not only consistent with guidance in the Q&A items discussed earlier but also innovative and responsive to community needs.

Recommendations

The preceding analysis and NCRC's work around projects associated with CRA enable us to offer a series of recommendations for various stakeholders. If the stakeholders collaborate, efforts can reach a larger scale and succeed at promoting integration in both gentrifying and distressed neighborhoods.

COMMUNITY GROUPS

Community groups should participate in HUD's fair housing process and ensure that jurisdictions have plans for integrating gentrifying neighborhoods as well as distressed ones. They should also ensure that banks are involved in these plans. Community groups should review CRA exams to determine whether banks are promoting integration in their lending products and programs. The groups should engage in regular dialogue with bank CRA officers regarding integrative efforts in those projects and programs.

Open and honest dialogue is needed in communities. Instead of "fighting" gentrification, community groups and other stakeholders need to manage gentrification and fight segregation, which retards efforts to lessen inequality and poverty. In order to successfully integrate neighborhoods, we must collectively combat the notion that African American residents do not want to live near white people. People of color must be open to whites in their community, and lower-income people must be tolerant of people who are financially well-off moving into their communities. In suburbs, whites and people who are financially well-off must be tolerant of people of color and people of modest income moving into their neighborhoods. To create openness toward integration, community organizations and local agencies need to promote dialogue through community events, facilitated sessions, and other venues.

LOCAL PUBLIC AGENCIES

When developing their AI plans, local jurisdictions must implement community input and public-meeting requirements rigorously. Jurisdictions should solicit the participation of community organizations and banks in efforts to promote integration. Banks should be asked to develop products and participate in local agency programs that help maintain affordable rental and homeowner units in gentrifying and distressed neighborhoods.

BANKS

Banks should incorporate the goal of maintaining integration as an explicit part of their CRA strategy. With community groups, they should discuss and consider developing mixed-income housing as well as low down payment loans for lower-income homeowners. They should work to preserve housing for low-income tenants through processes such as those covered by the Tenant Opportunity to Purchase Act. Finally, banks should work with community groups and local public agencies in developing fair housing plans that promote integration.

REGULATORS

Examiners should improve performance context analyses conducted for CRA exams so that those efforts identify cities and neighborhoods experiencing significant amounts of gentrification and concentrated levels of poverty (CRA examiners and researchers at the agencies can draw on the resources described in this chapter to identify gentrifying and distressed areas). CRA examiners should then view pro-integrative bank financing in gentrifying and distressed neighborhoods as responsive to needs and eligible for favorable CRA consideration. When CRA examiners identify community development investments or loans that promote integration, they should explicitly discuss this on CRA exams as well as cite the Q&A that supports their findings. The agencies should also generate case studies in which findings from CRA exams illustrate successful integration programs. Finally, the agencies should rephrase some of the Q&A guidance regarding gentrification and mixed-income housing to remove the disincentives that these items may inadvertently impose on desegregation initiatives.

Conclusion

Despite increases in the rates of gentrification and concentrated poverty, there are few examples in CRA exams of bank financing that promotes integration. This chapter is designed to clarify how banks can receive favorable consideration on CRA exams for desegregation. It reviews policy approaches and programs through which banks can promote integration. It advocates for joining the CRA and HUD fair housing requirements to promote integration. If stakeholders, including banks, do not take advantage of opportunities to use and mold market forces to promote integration, we will miss significant opportunities to respond to community needs and improve the quality of life for lower-income individuals and people of color—populations that are too often left behind.

Notes

1. Community Reinvestment Act of 1977, 12 U.S.C. §§ 2901–2908 (2015).

2. These estimates are based on calculations made by the National Community Reinvestment Coalition (NCRC) using data from the Federal Financial Institutions Examination Council web page: https://www.ffiec.gov/cra/default.htm.

3. Affirmatively Furthering Fair Housing, 80 Fed. Reg. 42,272 (July 16, 2015) (to be codified at 24 C.F.R. pts. 5, 91, 92, 570, 574, 576, 903 (2016)).

4. *Housing cost burden* is the monthly housing cost (either rent or mortgage payment) divided by income. If housing cost exceeds 30 percent of monthly income, the household is considered to have a cost burden. If housing cost exceeds 50 percent of monthly income, the household is considered to have a severe housing cost burden, which makes it difficult to afford other basic necessities.

5. The Office of the Comptroller of the Currency (OCC) produces a publication called *Community Developments*. This publication covers a variety of topics and CRA success stories. The March 2017 issue was devoted to affordable housing (see particularly Black 2017). For links to several of the office's community affairs publications, see https://www.occ.gov/publications/publications-by-topic/community-affairs/index-ca-publications.html#cdi.

6. Community Reinvestment Act; Interagency Questions and Answers Regarding Community Reinvestment, 81 Fed. Reg., 48,506, 48,553–54 (July 25, 2016) (to be codified at 12 C.F.R. pts. 25, 195, 228, 345).

7. The definition of *community development* may be found at 12 C.F.R. § 25.12(g) (2016).

8. 81 Fed. Reg. at 48,530.

9. See item A3, 81 Fed. Reg. at 48,553–4.

10. 81 Fed. Reg. at 48,538.

11. 81 Fed. Reg. at 48,526–7.

12. Tenant Opportunity to Purchase Act of 1980, D.C. Code § 42-3404 (2016).

13. For a description of how the act works, see the website for the District of Columbia's Office of the Tenant Advocate: http://ota.dc.gov/page/tenant-opportunity-purchase-act-topa.

14. See also 80 Fed. Reg. at 42,289 (codified at 24 C.F.R. § 5.152).

15. 80 Fed. Reg. at 42,279.

16. For a list of bank holding companies by asset size, see http://www.ffiec.gov/nicpubweb/nicweb/HCSGreaterThan10B.aspx.

17. See https://www.ffiec.gov/nicpubweb/nicweb/HCSGreaterThan10B.aspx.

References

Bhutta, Neil, and Daniel R. Ringo. 2016. "Residential Mortgage Lending from 2004 to 2015: Evidence from the Home Mortgage Disclosure Act Data." *Federal Reserve Bulletin* 102, no. 6 (February). https://www.federalreserve.gov/pubs/bulletin/2016/pdf/2015_HMDA.pdf.

Black, David. 2017. "Preservation of LIHTC Properties: Year 15 Considerations." *Community Developments*, March, 13–16. https://www.occ.gov/publications/publications-by-type/other-publications-reports/cdi-newsletter/affordable-housing-march-2017/article-05-black.html.

Chetty, Raj, and Nathaniel Hendren. 2015. "The Impacts of Neighborhoods on Intergenerational Mobility: Childhood Exposure Effects and County-Level Estimates." Working paper, May. Cambridge, MA: Harvard University Department of Economics. http://www.equality-of-opportunity.org/images/nbhds_paper.pdf.

Chetty, Raj, Nathaniel Hendren, and Lawrence F. Katz. 2015. "The Effects of Exposure to Better Neighborhoods on Children: New Evidence from the Moving to Opportunity Experiment." Working paper, August. Cambridge, MA: Harvard University Department of Economics. http://www.equality-of-opportunity.org/images/mto_paper.pdf.

Community-Wealth.org. n.d. "Overview of Community Land Trusts." Accessed February 9, 2017. http://community-wealth.org/strategies/panel/clts/index.html.

Couture, Victor, and Jessie Handbury. 2016. "Urban Revival in America, 2000 to 2010." Paper presented at the Federal Reserve Bank of Philadelphia Research Symposium on Gentrification and Neighborhood Change, Philadelphia, May 25. https://www.philadelphiafed.org/community-development/events/2016/research-symposium-on-gentrification.

Ding, Lei, Jackelyn Hwang, Eileen Divringi. 2015. "A Practitioner's Summary: Gentrification and Residential Mobility in Philadelphia." Discussion Paper. Philadelphia: Federal Reserve Bank of Philadelphia. https://www.philadelphiafed.org/-/media/community-development/publications/discussion-papers/discussion-paper_a-practitioners-summary.pdf?la=en.

Ellen, Ingrid Gould. 2016. "Gentrification in the 21st Century: Potential Threats and Opportunities." Presentation at the annual conference of the National Community Reinvestment Coalition, Washington, DC, March 17.

Ellen, Ingrid Gould, and Lei Ding. 2016. "Advancing Our Understanding of Gentrification." *Cityscape* 18 (3): 3–8. https://www.huduser.gov/portal/periodicals/cityscpe/vol18num3/guest.pdf.

Harvard University, Department of Economics. 2015. "New Research on Mobility: Studies by Profs. Chetty, Hendren, and Katz." News release, May 4. http://economics.harvard.edu/news/new-research-mobility-studies-profs-chetty-hendren-and-katz.

Jargowsky, Paul A. 2013. *Concentration of Poverty in the New Millennium: Changes in Prevalence, Composition, and Location of High-Poverty Neighborhoods*. Report. New York: Century Foundation and Rutgers University Center for Urban Research and Education. https://tcf.org/assets/downloads/Concentration_of_Poverty_in_the_New_Millennium.pdf.

Kneebone, Elizabeth. 2014. "The Growth and Spread of Concentrated Poverty, 2000 to 2008–2012." Metropolitan Opportunity Series Report. Washington, DC: Brookings Institution. https://www.brookings.edu/interactives/the-growth-and-spread-of-concentrated-poverty-2000-to-2008-2012/.

Levy, Diane K., Jennifer Comey, and Sandra Padilla. 2006. *Keeping the Neighborhood Affordable: A Handbook of Housing Strategies for Gentrifying Areas*. Washington, DC: Urban Institute. http://www.urban.org/sites/default/files/alfresco/publication-pdfs/411295-Keeping-the-Neighborhood-Affordable.PDF.

Maciag, Mike. 2015. "Gentrification in America Report." *Governing*, February. http://www.governing.com/gov-data/gentrification-in-cities-governing-report.html.

Mallach, Alan. 2008. *Managing Neighborhood Change: A Framework for Sustainable and Equitable Revitalization*. Report. Montclair, NJ: National Housing Institute. http://www.nhi.org/research/521/managing_neighborhood_change/.

Meltzer, Rachel. 2016. "Gentrification and Small Business: Threat or Opportunity?" *Cityscape* 18 (3): 57–85. https://www.huduser.gov/portal/periodicals/cityscpe/vol18num3/ch3.pdf.

Office of the Comptroller of the Currency (OCC). 2010. "Community Reinvestment Act Performance Evaluation." Evaluation of Citibank, N.A., July 26. Washington, DC: OCC. https://www.occ.gov/static/cra/craeval/jul10/1461.pdf.

Office of the Comptroller of the Currency (OCC). 2011. "Community Reinvestment Act Performance Evaluation." Evaluation of Capital One, National Association, April 4. Washington, DC: OCC. http://www.occ.gov/static/cra/craeval/feb12/13688.pdf.

Office of the Comptroller of the Currency (OCC). 2012a. "Community Reinvestment Act Performance Evaluation." Evaluation of HSBC Bank USA, N.A., September 30. Washington, DC: OCC. http://www.occ.gov/static/cra/craeval/nov13/24522.pdf.

Office of the Comptroller of the Currency (OCC). 2012b. "Community Reinvestment Act Performance Evaluation." Evaluation of U.S. Bank National Association, March 31. Washington, DC: OCC. https://www.occ.gov/static/cra/craeval/jul16/24.pdf.

Office of the Comptroller of the Currency (OCC). 2014. *Low-Income Housing Tax Credits: Affordable Housing Investment Opportunities for Banks*. Insights Report, April. Washington, DC: OCC. http://www.occ.gov/topics/community-affairs/publications/insights/insights-low-income-housing-tax-credits.pdf.

Oh, Seunghoon, Josh Silver, Annelise Osterberg, and Jaclyn Tules. 2015. *Does Nonprofit Housing Development Preserve Neighborhood Diversity? An Investigation into the Interaction between Affordable Housing Development and Neighborhood Change*. Report. Washington, DC: Manna. http://www.mannadc.org/wp-content/uploads/2015/07/Final_Neighborhood_Impact_Analysis_7_1.pdf.

Schulz, Dana. 2015. "Hell's Kitchen, Once the 'Wild West', Now Undergoing Rapid Gentrification." *6sqft*, April 30. https://www.6sqft.com/hells-kitchen-once-the-wild-west-now-undergoing-rapid-gentrification/.

Silver, Josh, Seunghoon Oh, Annelise Osterberg, Jaclyn Tules. 2014. *The Financial Benefits of Homeownership: An Evaluation of a Nonprofit Housing Development Model*. Report. Washington, DC: Manna. http://www.mannadc.org/wp-content/uploads/2015/06/The-Benefits-of-Homeownership-An-evaluation-of-Nonprofit-Development.pdf.

Silver, Josh, Archana Pradhan, and Spencer M. Cowan. 2013. *Access to Capital and Credit in Appalachia and the Impact of Financial Crisis and Recession on Commercial Lending and Finance in the Region*. Report, July. Washington, DC: Appalachian Regional Commission and National Community Reinvestment Coalition. https://www.arc.gov/research/researchreportdetails.asp?REPORT_ID=104.

US Department of Housing and Urban Development. 2015. *AFFH Rule Guidebook*. Vers. 1, December 31. Washington, DC: Department of Housing and Urban Development. https://www.hudexchange.info/resources/documents/AFFH-Rule-Guidebook.pdf.

US Department of Housing and Urban Development. 2018. "HUD Withdraws Fair Housing Assessment Tool." Press release HUD No. 18-044, May 18. https://www.hud.gov/press/press_releases_media_advisories/HUD_No_18_044.

Wikipedia. 2018. "List of United States Cities by Population." Last modified February 9, 2018. https://en.wikipedia.org/wiki/List_of_United_States_cities_by_population.

Zippel, Claire. 2016. "DC Black Residents Increasingly Live East of the Anacostia River." *The District's Dime* (blog), September 28. https://www.dcfpi.org/all/dcs-black-residents-increasingly-live-east-of-the-anacostia-river/.

Zuk, Miriam, Ariel H. Bierbaum, Karen Chapple, Karolina Gorska, Anastasia Loukaitou-Sideris, Paul Ong, and Trevor Thomas. 2015. "Gentrification, Displacement, and the Role of Public Investment: A Literature Review." Working Paper 2015-05. San Francisco: Federal Reserve Bank of San Francisco. http://www.frbsf.org/community-development/files/wp2015-05.pdf.

APPENDIX

METHODOLOGY FOR SURVEYS

This appendix details the methods used by the National Community Reinvestment Coalition (NCRC) to conduct two surveys of recent Community Reinvestment Act (CRA) evaluations completed for large banks. The first survey of CRA exams focused on the consideration given by evaluators to CRA-related bank activities in gentrifying neighborhoods and on the extent to which the exams incorporated question and answer (Q&A) guidance on gentrification. The second survey examined the consideration given to banks for engagement in mixed-income housing projects located within areas of concentrated poverty.

CRA Exams from Large Banks Engaged in Neighborhoods Experiencing Gentrification

The NCRC used the Federal Financial Institutions Examination Council's web page to identify the 10 large banks whose CRA exams are described in the discussion of results from the first survey.[16] Banks with the largest assets (by dollar amount) were selected on the assumption that they would have the most sophisticated methods for extending pro-integrative financing in gentrifying neighborhoods, and a recent CRA exam was available for each bank. The selection also assumed that these banks would likely cover the largest number of large metropolitan areas and cities experiencing considerable gentrification. The selected institutions included JPMorgan Chase, N.A.; Bank of America, N.A.; Wells Fargo Bank, National Association; U.S. Bank National Association; PNC Bank, N.A.; Capital One, National Association; HSBC Bank USA, N.A.; TD Bank, NA; SunTrust Bank; and Fifth Third Bank.

The largest banks by asset size are reported by the Federal Financial Institutions Examination Council (FFIEC) in an online table.[17] The survey used retail banks and discarded investment banks that were among the largest banks by asset size. The FFIEC table lists two banks in the top 10 that are not retail banks and thus not used for the survey. The survey used retail banks because they have a lending and investment test on their CRA exams, which were used to cull information on the banks' community development lending and investment activity. Moreover, retail banks tend to be more familiar with the needs of the metropolitan areas they serve because they have more extensive branch networks than those of investment banks. The survey of banks serving metropolitan areas experiencing high levels of gentrification was conducted in the winter of 2016. CRA exams more than 10 years old or conducted by the defunct Office of Thrift Supervision were not used; this criterion disqualified two banks in the top 10 at the time of this survey. The survey then selected only retail banks that were the next largest by asset size on the table.

Metropolitan Areas Experiencing Gentrification

From Mike Maciag's (2015) list of cities experiencing the greatest levels of gentrification, NCRC selected the 14 cities with the largest populations: Washington, DC, Seattle, Denver, Austin, New York, Philadelphia, San Diego, Fort Worth, Nashville, Boston, San Francisco, Houston, Chicago, and Jacksonville (Wikipedia 2018). The literature reviewed earlier indicated that gentrification was most intense in the largest cities.

CRA Exams from Large Banks Funding Mixed-Income Housing in Areas of Concentrated Poverty

As indicated, NCRC conducted a second survey in the winter of 2017. This survey of CRA exams was to investigate bank involvement in mixed-income housing projects located within areas of concentrated poverty. Given the availability of current CRA exams (NCRC found more current exams for Citibank, N.A., and Branch Banking and Trust than we were able to find for the first survey), some of the banks whose CRA exams were selected for this second survey differed from those selected as part of the survey on gentrifying metropolitan areas. The banks represented in the second survey included JPMorgan Chase Bank, N.A.; Wells Fargo Bank, National Association; Bank of America, N.A.; Citibank, N.A.; U.S. Bank National Association; PNC Bank, N.A.; Capital One, National Association; TD Bank, NA; Branch Banking and Trust Company; and HSBC Bank USA, N.A.

Metropolitan Areas with High Concentrations of Poverty

To conduct the second survey, NCRC required a standard for measuring poverty concentration. The analyses reported in this chapter used Kneebone's (2014) measure of distressed census tracts. In such tracts, 40 percent or more of the residents live below the poverty line. Consulting that study's analysis of American Community Survey data on concentrated poverty for the period from 2008 through 2012 (Kneebone 2014), NCRC identified the 20 metropolitan areas with the largest percentages of poor residents living in distressed census tracts: McAllen, Texas; Fresno, California; Toledo, Ohio; Milwaukee, Wisconsin; Memphis, Tennessee; Springfield, Massachusetts; Detroit-Warren, Michigan; Cleveland, Ohio; Youngstown, Ohio; Bakersfield, California; Syracuse, New York; El Paso, Texas; Jackson, Mississippi; Rochester, New York; Hartford, Connecticut; Dayton, Ohio; Philadelphia, Pennsylvania; Buffalo, New York; Tucson, Arizona; and Louisville, Kentucky. Of these 20 metropolitan areas, McAllen had the highest percentage (50 percent) of poor residents living in distressed census tracts, and Louisville had the lowest (19 percent; Kneebone 2014).

8

Promoting Poverty Deconcentration and Racial Desegregation through Mixed-Income Development[*]

Mark L. Joseph

Overview

This chapter examines the achievements, limitations, and outlook of mixed-income development as a strategy for poverty deconcentration and racial desegregation. There have been two major approaches to deconcentrating high-poverty public housing developments in the United States: dispersal and mixed-income development. The dispersal strategy relies largely on the Housing Choice Voucher program, discussed by Barbara Sard in Chapter 6 (see also Goetz 2003a, 2003b). As Sard indicates in that chapter, and as has been well documented elsewhere, the dispersal strategy is the larger of the two approaches in terms of numbers of households relocated, but it has some significant downsides (see, e.g., Fraser, Oakley, and Levy 2013). Chief among these are the fact that most voucher holders relocate to high-poverty, racially segregated neighborhoods, thereby undermining the policy's deconcentration and desegregation goals (see Chapter 6, this volume; Basolo 2013; Varady and Walker 2003). Furthermore, voucher holders can become isolated from the vital supports, services, and social networks they count on in their public housing developments (Skobba and Goetz 2013). They also often endure stigma and alienation in their new neighborhoods.

In contrast, mixed-income development is a targeted, place-based approach to deconcentration and desegregation (Chaskin and Joseph 2015). Rather than mixing low-income families into other neighborhoods, such redevelopment

---

[*] This chapter expands on themes and insights summarized in Joseph and Yoon (forthcoming).

draws high-income families into the original public housing site. The basic approach involves the relocation of all residents from a site (or the phased relocation around areas of a site), the demolition of the original housing, and the construction of a brand-new development. Within the new development, some units are set aside for public housing residents, some are priced "affordably" through the use of subsidies, and some are available at market rates. Where there is a market for homeownership, the developments can incorporate for-sale units as well as rentals. Many developments incorporate other amenities such as pools, recreation centers, and technology centers. There is often attention to associated improvements to the local schools, parks, and retail centers (Cisneros and Engdahl 2009).

Relative to the dispersal approach, the mixed-income approach is considerably more expensive and much more visible. It directly benefits significantly fewer public housing households and can be even more politically controversial. However, it facilitates far more intentionality and control over the processes of desegregation and reintegration, thus enabling the *potential* that low-income families will receive more effective long-term support. Furthermore, through the complete transformation of the public housing site and its rebirth as an attractive, well-designed and well-maintained housing complex, cities are able to catalyze the revitalization of long-marginalized neighborhoods and advance the turnaround of swaths of the urban core.

Much of the contention around the mixed-income approach stems from the fact that it leverages market processes and private actors to implement public housing redevelopment. Private real estate developers are directly engaged in public–private partnerships to build new rental and for-sale housing on land owned by housing authorities. In most cases, private developers take the lead on design, planning, construction, marketing, property management, and social services provided for all residents. In relinquishing the lead redevelopment role to the private sector, housing authorities reinforce fears about gentrification and displacement as well as questions about the capacity of real estate developers to manage a comprehensive social-change effort aimed at reintegrating low-income households into mainstream society.

Cities clearly stand to benefit by reclaiming the inner core for upscale, market-rate development, but the rhetoric of policymakers usually focuses on the presumptive benefits to the low-income residents of deteriorating, crime-ridden public housing developments. Additional, theorized benefits of mixed-income housing fall into four broad categories: social capital, informal social control, social learning, and the political economy of place (Chaskin and Joseph 2015; Joseph 2006; Joseph, Chaskin, and Webber 2007). First, the *social capital* argument holds that integrating public housing residents into economically diverse developments may connect them to the relational networks of their higher-income neighbors (Putnam 2000; Coleman 1988). Second, the presence of higher-income residents may promote more effective *informal social control* and thus greater safety and order (Chaskin and Joseph 2013; Sampson and Groves 1989). Third, higher-income residents may serve as role models and, through a process of *social learning*, contribute to the modification of aspirations and behavior among those who have been segregated in high-poverty neighborhoods (Bandura 1977; Wilson 1987). Finally, the presence of higher-income residents may activate the *political economy of place*, attracting greater local investment as well as more responsive services from public- and private-sector sources (Logan and Molotch 1987).

One of the underlying themes in this volume is the question of how explicitly race must be addressed in housing policy design and implementation in order to effectively combat racial segregation. As described in other chapters, early public housing desegregation efforts had defined goals around racial desegregation, but by the 1990s, federal and local policy had shifted to focus explicitly on income mixing and implicitly on racial integration. This was most evident in the evolution from the Gautreaux desegregation program in Chicago to the federal Moving to Opportunity demonstration (Briggs, Popkin, and Goering 2010; Polikoff 2006). The mixed-income approach exemplifies this shift away from explicit goals around race, even though there is often an implicit intention that the new mixed-income developments will be racially and economically integrated. Thus, mixed-income development is most often conceptualized as a poverty deconcentration policy. Depending on the local city and neighborhood context, it often can promote some degree of racial desegregation as well.

Mixed-income development has proven to be an effective way to harness private-sector interest in urban revitalization in order to generate the production of high-quality affordable housing. Almost 85,000 subsidized units have been created through the federal HOPE VI program (Gress, Cho, and Joseph 2016). Beyond physical redevelopment and residential integration, there is evidence of additional benefits: the promotion of safer, more stable communities and broader neighborhood revitalization (Bair and Fitzgerald 2005; Levy and Gallagher 2006; Turbov and Piper 2005; Zielenbach 2003). Despite these positive achievements, significant questions remain. How can we increase the benefits to low-income households through this approach, and how can we avoid producing what Robert Chaskin and I have called *incorporated exclusion*: physical integration in these new mixed-income contexts reproduces marginalization and leads more to withdrawal and alienation than to engagement and inclusion (Chaskin and Joseph 2015, 21). In a recent article, my coauthors and I examined in some detail the enduring significance of race as a factor in the perceptions of residents and development professionals associated with the new developments and as a relevant factor in intergroup tensions (Khare, Joseph, and Chaskin 2015). This significance raises important questions and cautions as local municipalities devise plans to affirmatively further fair housing and consider mixed-income development as a key component of local strategies to promote integration.

In this chapter, I briefly review the history of mixed-income housing implementation in the United States before summarizing evidence on the benefits and shortcomings of mixed-income development. I then propose an array of strategies that can strengthen the effectiveness of the mixed-income approach as a tool for poverty deconcentration and desegregation.

A Brief History of Mixed-Income Housing Policy in the United States

Early precursors to the mixed-income development approach date back to the 1970s, when the Massachusetts Housing Finance Agency encouraged local housing authorities to create mixed-income, multifamily housing (Ryan and Massachusetts Housing Finance Agency 1974). In the 1980s and early 1990s, the government in Montgomery County, Maryland, used inclusionary zoning laws to promote the development of several mixed-income housing sites (Barnett 2003; Brophy and Smith 1997; Schubert and Thesher 1996). Also in the 1980s, private developers began to partner with housing authorities to undertake some high-profile physical transformations of public housing into mixed-income developments. The George L. Vaughn public housing development in St. Louis, Missouri, was redeveloped by McCormack Baron into Murphy Park, a community with 413 mixed-income units (Baron 2009). Boston's Columbia Point public housing complex was redeveloped into Harbor Point by Corcoran Jennison and included 1,283 mixed-income units (Breitbart and Pader 1995; Pader and Breitbart 1993; Roessner 2000).

In 1989, the US Congress established the National Commission on Severely Distressed Public Housing to investigate the condition of the nation's public housing and to recommend a plan of action. The commission found that 86,000 units, about 6 percent of the total public housing stock at the time, were "severely distressed" in terms of physical deterioration, household conditions, crime rates, vacancy rates, and low rent collection (National Commission on Severely Distressed Public Housing 1992, 15; Wexler 2001). Among other policy changes, the commission recommended income mixing within the developments to decrease the high concentrations of extremely poor households. In 1990, the US Department of Housing and Urban Development launched the Mixed-Income New Communities Strategy demonstration to pilot a mixed-income transformation approach. Ultimately, the only demonstration site funded through the program was Lake Parc Place, in Chicago. At that site, 282 rental units were developed; 50 percent were allocated for public housing and 50 percent were allocated for units deemed affordable for the working poor (Ceraso 1995; Rosenbaum, Stroh, and Flynn 1998; Schill 1997).

In 1992, Congress passed the Housing and Community Development Act,[1] which allocated $300 million to fund the planning and early implementation of what came to be known as HOPE VI. Although the program was initially intended to rehabilitate developments exclusively as public housing, the priorities shifted by 1995 to promoting mixed-income development.[2] The shift to poverty deconcentration through mixed-income development was made explicit in the 1996 congressional appropriations bill, which stated that HOPE VI funds should be used to build or provide replacement housing, "which will avoid or lessen concentrations of very low-income families."[3] Several federal policy changes channeled federal funds to leverage private-sector funding in order to produce what came to be termed *mixed-finance* projects (Katz 2009; Turbov 2006).

THE HOPE VI PROGRAM

Over the course of the HOPE VI program, 261 revitalization grants were awarded, totaling approximately $6 billion. In the funded developments, 75,896 households have been relocated, 98,639 public housing units have been demolished, and 74,223 subsidized rental units have been rehabilitated or newly constructed (Gress, Cho, and Joseph 2016). By the end of 2014, only 19,993 HOPE VI households (or 26 percent of all affected households) had returned to revitalized units in their original developments (Gress, Cho, and Joseph 2016). Although the program has been commended for the successful physical transformation of public housing sites and for evidence of improvements to the broader neighborhoods—lower crime and increased investment—HOPE VI has been widely criticized for reducing the number of affordable housing units, its problems in relocating families and delays in constructing new units, and the low rates at which the original public housing residents have returned to the new developments (Buron et al. 2002; Popkin et al. 2004, Turbov and Piper 2005).[4]

CHOICE NEIGHBORHOODS INITIATIVE

In 2010, the Obama administration phased out new funding for HOPE VI and replaced it with the Choice Neighborhoods Initiative. A more comprehensive approach to mixed-income public housing transformation, the initiative was designed to address some of the shortcomings of the HOPE VI program. Whereas HOPE VI redevelopment plans focused mainly on the public housing site itself, the Choice Neighborhoods Initiative promotes redevelopment of the site and the surrounding neighborhood. There is also an increased focus on preparing residents for successful relocation and a one-for-one replacement requirement: each unit demolished for redevelopment must be replaced by a unit at the same site or in the surrounding area. Each recipient of a grant from the initiative develops a Transformation Plan, which includes assessments and strategies in three areas: people, housing, and neighborhood. Public–private partnerships are urged to address issues of workforce development, education, and transportation in these plans (Urban Institute and MDRC 2015; Khare 2015). As of 2015, the US Department of Housing and Urban Development had allocated 63 Choice Planning grants of up to $500,000 and 18 Choice Implementation grants of up to $30 million (US Department of Housing and Urban Development 2017).

LARGE-SCALE, MIXED-INCOME, PUBLIC HOUSING TRANSFORMATIONS BY CITIES

In addition to the two major federal mixed-income development programs, a few cities have implemented large-scale efforts to desegregate their public housing stock through mixed-income development. Atlanta was the first to launch such an effort, in 1994. In what has turned out to be the most complete mixed-income transformation in the United States, the city demolished the entire stock of family public housing (Boston 2005; Oakley, Ruel, and Reid 2013a, 2013b; Ruel et al. 2013; Tester et al. 2011; Vale 2013). As of 2015, 3,900 public housing replacement units had been created in Atlanta's 16 mixed-income developments, which contain about 10,000 mixed-income units (Atlanta Housing Authority 2016).

In 1999, Chicago launched its Plan for Transformation, which aimed to demolish all high-rise public housing in the city, replacing a total of 49,000 units with 25,000 new or renovated units (Chicago Housing Authority 2000). About 7,700 of those would be in 10 new major mixed-income developments with a total of about 17,000 mixed-income units. Unlike Atlanta, Chicago planned to retain a substantial portion of its low-rise public housing, leaving about 14 family public housing developments. As of 2014, 3,415 public housing units had been created in Chicago's mixed-income developments (Chaskin and Joseph 2015).

San Francisco launched HOPE SF in 2006, a mixed-income transformation in eight public housing sites, four of which have become the focus of the first phase of the initiative (Joseph et al. 2015). The initiative's objective is to build a total of 4,700 mixed-income units at these sites, including 1,900 replacement public housing units. The first units were occupied at one of the sites in 2012, and there are now just over 100 units occupied at that site.

In Washington, DC, the New Communities Initiative launched in 2005 with the intention of creating 6,000 public housing replacement units in four public- and assisted-housing developments. The initiative has encountered extensive delays due to multiple turnovers in mayoral administrations; although 1,041 off-site units have been constructed and occupied, no on-site housing had been built as of mid-2016 (New Communities Initiative 2015).

Besides these four cities with formal transformation initiatives, Memphis, Tennessee, New Orleans, Louisiana, Seattle, Washington, and other cities have completed mixed-income transformations of multiple public housing developments, and most cities now have major mixed-income developments. The National Initiative on Mixed-Income Communities has cataloged information on over 300 mixed-income developments located in 146 cities and involving over 100 private developers (National Initiative on Mixed-Income Communities Database 2016).

What Do We Know? Summarizing the Evidence

At sites across the United States, mixed-income development has achieved some remarkable accomplishments, particularly in the areas of physical transformation, safety, security, and neighborhood revitalization. Yet there is mounting evidence that the approach has failed to achieve the intended results for the most vulnerable individuals and has marginalized residents of deteriorated public housing developments—the very residents who were, according to the policy rhetoric, intended to be the primary beneficiaries of these multimillion dollar investments.

PHYSICAL TRANSFORMATION

Mixed-income development is perhaps at its most impressive when one compares before-and-after photos of the housing complexes. In order to market the developments to a mixed-income population, developers have generally made good on the commitment to create a high-quality appearance for both the market-rate and subsidized units, which have similar designs and architectural features. The units are largely indistinguishable from the outside. Large, foreboding superblocks have been broken up and street grids re-established. Much care has been taken to create attractive, well-landscaped environments. Often central to the design are New Urbanist planning principles and the recognition that well-designed environments can promote social interaction as well as social control (Barnett 2003; Bohl 2000; Calthorpe 1993; Katz 1993; Talen 2002). Many mixed-income developments have won urban design and architectural awards. Residents of market-rate units tell stories about being impressed to find such nicely designed, conveniently located housing on a side of town they previously avoided. Low-income residents give tours of their units with great pride and say they never imagined they would live in such high-quality housing and surroundings (Chaskin and Joseph 2015; Joseph and Chaskin 2010; Levy, McDade, and Bertumen 2013).

SAFETY AND SECURITY

Another major success of mixed-income development is the marked decrease in crime that accompanies the physical transformation. Of course, some of this decrease is likely driven by the depopulation of the old public housing developments and their surrounding areas, a depopulation effected through eviction, relocation, or displacement. But the fact remains that crime rates in and around the development areas have demonstrably decreased after redevelopment (Cahill, Lowry, and Downey 2011; Chaskin and Joseph 2015; Zielenbach 2003; Zielenbach and Voith 2010).

BROADER NEIGHBORHOOD REVITALIZATION

The other important positive impact of mixed-income development is the catalyzing or acceleration of physical and economic revitalization in the surrounding neighborhood (Chaskin and Joseph 2015; Turbov and Piper 2005, Zielenbach 2003; Zielenbach and Voith 2010). Entire areas of a city end up turning around because of the demolition of public housing and its replacement. In its place are new market-rate homes and other amenities such as parks, recreation centers, and retail establishments. In some cases, mixed-income transformation was the catalyst for a broader revitalization. In others, gentrification had already begun to take hold in an area but stalled at the edge of the old public housing development. In both scenarios, mixed-income development generates an effective platform for further housing and business investments. It should also be noted that revitalization can vary greatly in pace and robustness, depending on the strength of the market in the area of the city and in the broader metropolitan area.

Thus, on some of its key goals, particularly those that involve the transformation of place and the rekindling of market forces, mixed-income development has been an overwhelming success. But for whom and at what opportunity cost? I turn now to the many ways in which mixed-income development has fallen short of its stated policy aims. The shortcomings can be grouped into three areas: the small number of beneficiaries relative to the number of eligible households, problems with implementation, and challenges in the post-development communities.

EXCLUSION AT MULTIPLE STAGES

One of the most prominent critiques of mixed-income development has centered on the loss of affordable housing units for the most vulnerable households (Bennett, Smith, and Wright 2006). In Chicago, for example, an initial housing stock of 49,000 units (of which 24,000 were vacant at the launch of the Plan for Transformation) is being reduced to 25,000 units. Only about 7,700 of those units are to be replaced by the new mixed-income developments, and only about 3,400 units had been completed in the first 15 years of the initiative (Chaskin and Joseph 2015). As noted previously, 98,639 subsidized rental units were demolished nationally over the 18 years of the HOPE VI program and the lost stock was replaced by only 74,223 rental units (Gress, Cho, and Joseph 2016).

A second form of exclusion is effected through the screening and other factors that have led to the extremely low rates at which original public housing residents have returned to the new developments. Studies report average return rates of 5 to 20 percent across developments (Buron et al. 2002; Comey 2007). As of 2014, the reoccupancy rate across HOPE VI developments was 26 percent (Gress, Cho, and Joseph 2016), and the Atlanta Housing Authority estimated that 8 percent returned there. The rate was approximately the same in Chicago, though almost 90 percent of original residents initially elected to retain their right to return to the new developments (Chaskin and Joseph 2015; Chaskin et al. 2012).

Many factors contribute to these low return rates, including the length of time between relocation and reoccupancy, resident preferences to move to the private market with housing choice vouchers, the small sizes of units in the new developments, resident uncertainty about whether the new environment will be welcoming, and relocation decisions made with limited time or information (Joseph and Chaskin 2012). Key among these are the eligibility requirements and screening procedures put in place by housing authorities and private developers. Chicago, for instance, has some of the most stringent return criteria. Eligibility to return is contingent upon lease compliance, a criminal background check, a credit check, a household visit, employment for at least 30 hours a week (or search for employment), and, in most developments, a drug test.

In the discussion of post-development challenges (see next section), I touch upon a third form of exclusion: the incorporated exclusion that emerges for relocated public housing residents who move back to the redeveloped communities.

IMPLEMENTATION CHALLENGES

Mixed-income development is exceedingly complex. It is difficult to plan, design, finance, execute, and sustain. Although a growing number of housing authority executives, private developers, and other key institutional partners possess extensive experience and expertise in successfully navigating the challenges of mixed-income development, there are enough examples of bankruptcies, broken contracts, and multiyear delays to show that extreme caution is warranted in considering this approach. Given the constraints of this chapter, I will briefly highlight five dimensions of complexity: political, market, financing, collaboration, and operational.

Political Complexity

The political complexity of mixed-income transformation stems from the substantial political will required on the part of mayors. They must initiate and sustain a commitment to dedicating the necessary resources. And while executing the large-scale venture, they must galvanize public, civic, and private support. Bureaucratic inertia poses additional challenges, as do the deep distrust and dysfunction that have shaped many public housing authorities for decades. Affordable housing activists and other public housing advocates are often highly skeptical of the motives for privatizing the production and management of public housing. Many put up strong political and legal resistance.

Market Complexity

As a market-driven approach to achieving social goals, mixed-income development generates particular tensions. How are market goals and social goals balanced? For example, how can one catalyze private investment and attract market-rate homebuyers and renters to previously marginalized areas while producing units for low-income renters and integrating those renters fully into the new communities? The Great Recession exposed the vulnerabilities of a social housing approach that is so dependent on the private market. The housing crisis as well as subsequent retrenchment of the banks and lenders prevented many homebuyers from qualifying for mortgages, existing homebuyers and renters fell behind on monthly payments, and the value of market-rate properties dropped. These events made homeowners even more sensitive to and less tolerant of adverse behavior in the new developments. The production of for-sale units in mixed-income developments stalled while rental development continued, creating a misalignment in the planned tenure mix.

Complex Financial Structures

The complex layering of public and private financing is essential to generate the tens of millions of dollars required for each phase of mixed-income development. These projects require extremely high levels of resources. The process of negotiating mixed-income deals is highly complex, time consuming, and cost intensive. Each of the funding streams comes with its own regulations and requirements, and the Low-Income Housing Tax Credit financing, so crucial for the layer of subsidized rental housing, has particularly stringent and restrictive compliance requirements.

Complex Collaborations

Managing the public–private collaborations among the multiple actors in a mixed-income development is another key dimension of complexity. Actors must collaborate at two main levels: the level of the initiative and that of the site. The initiative level involves collaborations among representatives from multiple city, county, and state governments; private development companies; the developers' property-management and service-provision partners; civic actors; housing advocates; resident representatives; and other nonprofit organizations. At the level of the site, a similar array of actors must reach consensus on the master plan for redevelopment. They collaborate over multiple years through the design, financing, relocation, demolition, construction, reoccupancy, and community-building phases of the redevelopment.

Operational Complexity

Finally, initiative- and site-level collaborations must contend with numerous operational complexities. Some physical design decisions are relatively easy: reestablishing the street grid with lower-rise housing whose market-rate units are indistinguishable from the subsidized ones. Other consequential decisions have to be made with little evidence about the trade-offs. For example, decisions must be made about the relative proportions of housing type and income mix as well as about the extent to which the public spaces near market-rate units will be physically integrated with the spaces near subsidized units. Despite general knowledge of the poor public housing conditions that necessitated the mixed-income transformation, housing authorities and their partners have not anticipated the extreme deprivation and isolation among most of the resident households. These factors have been deeply challenging to address. A substantial expansion of case management resources and social services has been necessary to stabilize and advance household well-being.

CONTINUED ECONOMIC AND SOCIAL EXCLUSION AMONG THE POOR

This brings us to a third major shortcoming of mixed-income developments: the disappointing results of efforts to effectively reintegrate low-income residents into the economic and social mainstream. Central to the rationale for mixed-income development is the expectation that integrating the poor into housing complexes with higher-income residents will extend greater economic and social opportunity to previously isolated households. Instead, numerous studies have revealed that former public housing residents, despite residing in mixed-income environments, still live in a state of personal deprivation (Chaskin and Joseph 2015; Chaskin et al. 2012; Levy, McDade, and Bertumen 2013). While there are certainly instances of success for individual households, residents on the whole are living in higher-quality housing and enjoying more stable, peaceful surroundings but not on a trajectory for upward mobility.

Adding to the detrimental nature of this shortcoming is the fact that social realities in the new mixed-income developments have tended to reproduce incorporated exclusion—the marginalization and stigmatization by race and class—rather than to generate more inclusive environments of social connection and mutual exchange (Chaskin and Joseph 2015, 21; see also Graves 2010; Khare, Joseph, and Chaskin 2015; Kleit 2005; Kleit and Carnegie 2011; McCormick, Joseph, and Chaskin 2012; Tach 2009). Numerous obstacles stand in the way of building cross-race and cross-class ties: lifestyles, behavioral and cultural differences, segregated physical designs, and life-stage differences, such as whether children are in the household (Chaskin and Joseph 2011, 2015; Fraser, Chaskin, and Bazuin 2013; Levy, McDade, and

Bertumen 2013). Moreover, resident associations and other participatory mechanisms were intended to serve as instruments of inclusion in mixed-income developments and their surrounding neighborhoods but instead tend to be exclusionary (Chaskin, Khare, and Joseph 2012). Stigmatized, unequal treatment from other residents and development staff has also impeded inclusion, as has a predilection for formal control methods (security cameras and zero-tolerance policing) instead of informal community control (August 2016; Chaskin and Joseph 2013; Graves 2010; Joseph and Chaskin 2010; Tach 2009).

These social challenges are complicated by racial dynamics and by the enduring salience of an urban underclass narrative in which African Americans are viewed as the undeserving poor, victims of their own behavioral shortcomings and content with their dependence on handouts from the state. Many African American residents view such redevelopment through a racialized frame, perceiving whites to be the true intended beneficiaries of revitalization, and the inclusion and tolerance for blacks as only temporary. The economic diversity *within* the African American population in mixed-income developments and prevailing intraracial tensions around accepted norms of behavior add further complexity. In a process of "secondary marginalization," some low-income blacks feel judged by and alienated from whites and from more affluent blacks (Khare, Joseph, and Chaskin 2015, 480; Cohen 1999).

A Reality Check Regarding Mixed-Income Assumptions

From the emerging state of knowledge, it appears we can refute several assumptions that undergird the mixed-income approach (see Chaskin and Joseph [2015] and Levy, McDade, and Bertumen [2013] for a more in-depth treatment of some of these issues).

ADDRESSING HOUSEHOLD POVERTY REQUIRES MORE THAN MIXED-INCOME HOUSING

Improving housing conditions and social mix will not fundamentally change educational opportunities or labor-market access. There are limits to what spatial strategies can do in terms of reshaping the social, economic, and political processes required to address unequal access and opportunity (DeFillipis 2013). The mixed-income approach must be accompanied by structural reforms in education, employment, criminal justice, and health care.

PHYSICAL INTEGRATION ALONE WILL NOT BUILD SOCIAL TIES ACROSS INCOME AND RACE

Cross-race and cross-class exchanges have been limited. They have been extremely casual, failing to yield instrumental benefits for the poor, or they have been contentious, contributing to conflict between low- and higher-income residents (Chaskin and Joseph 2015). Population diversity, rather than functioning as a catalyst for bridges of opportunity, has led to more surveillance, stricter regulations on the behavior of low-income neighbors, and more stringent rule enforcement (Chaskin and Joseph 2013; Graves 2010; Tach 2009).

THE PRIMARY IMPACTS OF SOCIAL MIXING MAY OR MAY NOT BE BENEFICIAL TO LOW-INCOME AFRICAN AMERICANS

For the poor, the benefits of living in mixed-income communities include the resultant improvements in safety and the built environment, not engagement with and learning from their higher-income neighbors (Chaskin and Joseph 2011, 2015; Joseph and Chaskin 2010). Those neighbors bring political and economic power to a community. Despite its potential benefits, that power can also result in zero-tolerance policing and perceptions that there are double standards in the application of rules and sanctions. The market power of newcomers can trigger the development of local amenities that make the community unaffordable for low-income households, thereby compromising the benefits of social mixing.

MAJOR CHALLENGES IMPEDE THE HARNESSING OF MARKET FORCES TO PROMOTE INCLUSION OF THE MOST VULNERABLE

Privatization and market forces are limited in their potential to generate opportunity and pathways out of poverty. The pervasive market orientation of mixed-income development requires engagement with profit-seeking private actors and indoctrination of low-income households in "market norms," but the context also hinders efforts to prioritize social goals.

MIXED-INCOME DEVELOPMENT DOES NOT NECESSARILY GENERATE "CHOICE" THAT LEADS TO IMPROVEMENTS IN THE LIVES OF THE POOR

Although mixed-income development certainly creates a housing option that did not exist previously, several factors limit the extent to which such an option can empower low-income households. Insufficient time to make residential decisions, limited access to information, and family exigencies such as health challenges, household debt, and criminal history are fundamental constraints that shape the choices available to residents relocating from public housing developments (Joseph and Chaskin 2012). Other limitations are imposed by eligibility criteria, screening processes, and the constrained supply of replacement public housing units in mixed-income developments.

Strengthening Mixed-Income Development Practice and Policy

Much has been learned about the possibilities and limitations of mixed-income development as an approach to poverty deconcentration and racial desegregation. The absence of a more promising alternative, the potential of mixed-income housing as a platform if better implemented, and the imperative of leveraging urban revitalization to promote socioeconomic integration lead me to conclude that the mixed-income approach should be pursued with even more vigor, commitment, and skill as one of multiple policy approaches to poverty deconcentration and racial desegregation. Residence in a mixed-income development is not a good fit for every low-income household, nor is the approach appropriate for every development partnership. But with better execution, this approach can be an important tool in our urban equity and inclusion arsenal.

I now turn to recommendations for strengthening this approach. Although I share a range of ideas below, their operationalization will come down to a few key policy and practice mechanisms. It will be critical to maintain and, more importantly, to increase the flow of resources to programs like Choice Neighborhoods and the Low-Income Housing Tax Credit program, which fund mixed-income development. But it is also vital to focus on guiding *how* these resources are spent. The processes by which federal, state, and local governments define the criteria for selecting funding recipients—criteria specified in such documents as notices of funding availability, requests for proposals, and Qualified Allocation Plans—provide key opportunities to influence how implementers think about and execute their mixed-income strategies. Many of the recommendations that follow could be written explicitly into these funding criteria. Furthermore, technical assistance and consultation are critically important, underfunded, and underconceived components of mixed-income development. They can guide design and implementation. Despite the complexity of these endeavors and the increasing number of new actors getting into mixed-income development, technical assistance, if it is available, often consists of large-scale convenings and webinars. There is a need for well-timed, context-specific, hands-on assistance that is relevant to the current priorities, opportunities, and challenges of the local effort.

STRENGTHENING RESOURCES, FINANCING, AND LONG-TERM SUSTAINABILITY

As noted earlier, mixed-income projects are also referred to as "mixed finance" because of the variety of public and private funding that must be secured in order to implement them. This results in a complex layering of public funds, private investments and loans, philanthropic grants, and developer fees. There is a significant opportunity cost associated with dedicating public infrastructure and affordable housing funds to these mixed-income projects. Given the loss of affordable units, low rates of return, and social challenges that have resulted from these projects, cities and housing authorities are under great pressure to demonstrate that the public expenditures achieve social goals, such as successful economic and racial integration, in addition to physical redevelopment and market revitalization. An important and somewhat counterintuitive reality is that the public subsidy is a critical component not only because it ensures that projects include affordable housing units, but also because it makes the *entire* mixed-income project possible. Renting and selling market-rate units in a revitalizing neighborhood often means setting rents or sales prices that would be impossible without major discounts. Those discounts are enabled by the public transfer of land, the public investment in infrastructure, and the Low-Income Housing Tax Credit subsidy that helps in constructing the buildings and equipping the systems.

Another point for consideration by policymakers is that the layering of public and private financing also generates a thicket of regulation and protocols that can greatly complicate and delay a project. Policy reforms that streamline and coordinate these requirements will save valuable time, energy, and funds that can be dedicated to project implementation and success.

Finally, there is the matter of ensuring long-term financial sustainability of these housing complexes as mixed-income sites. Policies and strategies must be put in place to help the developments weather changes in local market trends, to ensure a flow of public operating dollars for the below–market rate units, and to sustain sufficient demand for the market-rate units at a price point that enables high-quality management and maintenance of the entire property (Abravanel, Levy, and McFarland 2009).

STRATEGIC CLARITY ABOUT GOALS AND APPROACHES

In any new mixed-income project, a crucial first step is to devote sufficient time and energy to securing consensus among the myriad stakeholders, who must come to accord about the goals and strategies to be deployed. Several critical questions should be considered collectively. What are the social goals for the redevelopment? Do they include rates of return, upward economic mobility, and social inclusion in the housing and surrounding neighborhood? What are the market goals? Do they include profitability, financial sustainability, growth of the tax base, and private investment in the neighborhood? Given the particular neighborhood, city, and institutional context, where is there alignment in these goals, where is there conflict, and how will those conflicts be reconciled? What are the roles and responsibilities of various actors in pursuing these goals? What additional resources and capacity are necessary?

Achieving consensus around goals, strategies, and roles, and then establishing a strong, multiyear, local public–private collaboration, requires extremely effective local leadership and management. The experience and capacity of the private developer, its management, and resident services partners are critical, as are the stability and competence at the public housing authority. Just as essential is a municipal point person who has direct access to top policymakers, is responsible for leading the initiative, and coordinates the various public agencies and private entities. Also essential is a local organization that can serve as a base for community engagement and strategy implementation efforts that must be sustained over time.

DESIGN ENHANCEMENTS THAT FACILITATE GREATER INCLUSION

A key design consideration for new developments is the mix of housing types, including replacement public housing, tax credit–financed housing, market-rate rental units, and for-sale units. This mix will be shaped by many factors. Common examples include expectations regarding the return of relocated residents, constraints on unit density and building height, and the development team's philosophy on social mix. There is no one-size-fits-all prescription for social mix. The optimal proportions will vary depending on the size of the development and available financing streams, as well as on the market conditions and socioeconomic mix in the community. Social mix is also shaped by the skills and commitment that developers and the property management team bring to the task of managing inclusion. One last aspect of the proportional-mix consideration is the need to mitigate the effects of the extreme socioeconomic distance often present between residents in market-rate units and counterparts in subsidized ones. This can be accomplished by incorporating units and housing types along a continuum of income levels. Ideally, these various social-mix decisions should be driven less by financing stipulations or relocation negotiations than by strategic choices to establish conditions for a well-functioning community.

Spatial arrangements in the new development also require consideration. Will units for residents of different income levels be integrated or segregated within the buildings of a complex? The fullest integration would be preferable in order to maximize the potential for repeated interaction and engagement, but blending market-rate and subsidized units in the same building can be financially complex, and increased integration of neighbors from different socioeconomic backgrounds requires highly effective property management. Spatial-arrangement considerations extend beyond the residential configuration; "third places" are also important within a development (Oldenburg 1999, xvii). These are lobby areas, meeting rooms, parks, recreation centers, technology centers, commercial establishments, and schools—places where residents can encounter one another in routine, comfortable ways (Oldenburg 1999). The more that communal, public space is limited in favor of private spaces, the more likely that some residents, especially youth, will appropriate available areas—front steps, street corners, and parking lots—for social activities that others find objectionable (Chaskin, Sichling, and Joseph 2013).

PROMOTING SUCCESSFUL RELOCATION AND HIGHER RATES OF RETURN

Far greater mixed-income success is possible if a much greater proportion of households is able to move from public housing into quality alternatives within less segregated, lower-poverty neighborhoods. That approach requires a policy focused more on relocation than on place-based undertakings. Policy recommendations for improving the Housing Choice Voucher program are fully relevant here, and several are elaborated in the chapter by Barbara Sard (Chapter 6). These recommendations involve increasing the number of units available in low-poverty neighborhoods, strengthening relocation counseling, improving information, extending time for decision-making, bolstering quality control on units, and broadening access to post-relocation supportive services. But we must also find ways to increase the return rates so that more of the original public housing residents can benefit from the multimillion-dollar investments in mixed-income communities. Units in new developments should accommodate public housing relocatees: they should be of adequate size and have enough bedrooms to match the needs of the relocated population. Phased relocation on site is a proven means of enabling public housing residents to remain in the community instead of dispersing to other areas of the city. A strong resident relocation-rights agreement should specify the parameters for return, including protections against overly stringent or arbitrary screening procedures and a clear and transparent process for appeals. Early and consistent engagement, combined with targeted support, is critical to help relocating households address issues that could prevent them from returning to the development. Common examples of these barriers include unpaid rent, nonleaseholders residing in the units, criminal background, substance abuse, and other issues that cause instability in households.

HIGH-INTENSITY CASE MANAGEMENT AND SUPPORTIVE SERVICES

Development teams and their social-service partners must be prepared for the severe personal and family issues that significant proportions of public housing residents struggle with. Social services should range from less intensive but ongoing support (e.g., employment readiness, job placement, and financial management) to more intensive case management, counseling, and wrap-around services. The Housing Opportunities and Services Together initiative, implemented in both mixed-income and traditional public housing developments within several US cities by Susan Popkin and her colleagues at the Urban Institute, is a leading example of an effort to fully integrate services for high-need households into public housing redevelopment (Popkin et al. 2012).

GREATER DIRECT FOCUS ON UPWARD MOBILITY

Although some investments must be directed at household stabilization, there should also be long-term investments to promote self-sufficiency and economic mobility among public housing residents and other low-income renters. In addition to investments in educational advancement, vocational training, and soft-skills training, these should include more intensive workforce-engagement strategies such as transitional employment initiatives with local employers. Community benefits agreements with companies involved in the redevelopment should include provisions for training programs geared to the jobs that will be created. Asset-building strategies, such as financial counseling services and Individual Development Accounts, should also be adapted to mixed-income developments. The federal Family Self-Sufficiency program and the Jobs Plus Initiative have both demonstrated success in increasing earnings and assets among public housing residents, but neither has been targeted in mixed-income developments (Bloom, Riccio, and Verma 2005; Riccio 2010; Sard 2001).

MORE PROACTIVE, INTENTIONAL COMMUNITY BUILDING
AND "EFFECTIVE NEIGHBORING"

Preventing the emergence of challenging social dynamics among residents with different socioeconomic backgrounds requires early and consistent attention as well as a deliberate strategy. First and foremost, the marketing and recruitment process must be highly transparent about the socioeconomic mix, community engagement, and neighboring that will be required to make the community successful. A clear and inclusive process should be implemented for establishing norms and expectations among residents. The objective is to collectively establish community norms that protect order, safety, and the upkeep of the housing complex. Those norms should not overly restrict individual freedom and access to public space or disproportionately direct punitive responses on the poor. Given the key role of property managers in monitoring residents' behavior, they should receive intensive training and technical assistance. Although many residents will not be interested in forming deep social bonds with their neighbors, most will likely see the value of working toward "effective neighboring," such that residents know their neighbors by name, keep an eye on each other's homes, and establish enough familiarity and comfort to be able to constructively work through any conflicts that emerge (Joseph and Gress 2013, 9; Joseph 2016). Above all, the goal is to ensure that all residents feel welcome and respected as a full members of the new mixed-income community. Youth from the low-income households are a key subpopulation that would benefit from a proactive effort at positive and constructive engagement, given that they have often generated conflict and complaints among mixed-income neighbors. Positive youth engagement would include more intentional mentoring and outreach by adult members of the community as well as more opportunities for constructive activities, particularly opportunities for youth to be positioned as leaders in intergenerational and youth-focused activities (Chaskin, Sichling, and Joseph 2013).

MORE INCLUSION IN GOVERNANCE AND DECISION-MAKING

One dimension of the incorporated exclusion experienced by low-income households in mixed-income developments is the lack of voice in local governance bodies such as condominium, homeowners, and neighborhood-resident associations. Attention should be directed toward promoting opportunities for engagement and deliberation among residents across incomes and housing tenures. New mechanisms might be created for this kind of dialogue, and existing forums could be encouraged to become more inclusive. Promoting inclusion requires ensuring that marginalized groups have meaningful representation and participate actively in such forums. But it also requires building capacity to help low-income residents advocate for themselves and to help development professionals and higher-income residents engage effectively where there is significant income and racial diversity.

APPLYING INSIGHTS FROM MIXED-INCOME DEVELOPMENT TO OTHER INTEGRATION APPROACHES

Besides directly enhancing mixed-income development practice and policy, the insights and strategies derived from the approach could be applied in other place-based efforts to effect residential integration. In particular, insights from mixed-income development could inform efforts that include inclusionary zoning, project-based vouchers, and housing choice vouchers. Those efforts currently have little intentionality and devote little attention to social goals beyond the production of affordable housing. They might have a greater effect on social mobility if combined with strong employment and asset-building programs. The impact on social mobility might also be improved if those efforts devoted more attention to leveraging socioeconomic integration as a way to generate greater social capital and access to opportunity.

THE IMPERATIVE OF BROADER STRUCTURAL CHANGE

An overarching implication of existing research is that mixed-income development is far from a silver bullet and must complement other anti-poverty strategies to facilitate a path toward self-sufficiency and social and economic mobility for low-income residents. Even an enhanced mixed-income approach cannot overcome the broad structural factors that create and reproduce urban poverty: inequalities in access to quality education, the absence of living-wage employment for persons with limited education and skills, and disproportionate incarceration rates. Mixed-income housing should be seen as a necessary but insufficient platform upon which other self-sufficiency efforts must be built.

Conclusion

Despite its limited impact on the majority of urban poor households and its shortcomings in terms of social cohesion and economic mobility, mixed-income development is burgeoning in cities across the United States, and for good reason. The mixed-income approach represents a win-win-win proposition: it offers city governments a way to build their tax base and reduce the social costs of high-poverty communities; it offers private real estate developers a way to cash in on the renaissance of demand for urban living; and it offers advocates a means to secure more affordable housing for the poor. Although mixed-income development is complex and expensive, there is no question that public housing developments can be physically transformed, the approach can drastically reduce the concentration of poverty, and the resulting communities can spark broader neighborhood and city revitalization. But as I've argued here, poverty deconcentration is not the same as true integration and the production of mixed-income housing; it is the first step in promoting equity and inclusion for public housing residents. Furthermore, poverty deconcentration is not necessarily racial desegregation. I urge a dual focus on income *and* racial integration to more fully address the social realities that encumber some of the most marginalized members of our society. While policymakers should continue to pursue mixed-income development as one element of a comprehensive approach to poverty deconcentration and racial desegregation, it is imperative that the strategy be strengthened to yield far more benefit for low-income households, whose isolation and deprivation are usually cited as the motivations for this complex and expensive endeavor.

Notes

1. Housing and Community Development Act of 1992, Pub. L. No. 102-550, 106 Stat. 3672.

2. For more on the design and implementation of the HOPE VI program, see Cisneros and Engdahl (2009); Popkin (2010); Popkin et al. (2004); Popkin, Levy, and Buron (2009);

Sard and Staub (2008); HOPE VI Improvement and Reauthorization Act of 2007, H.R. 3524, 110th Cong. (2007); S. 829.

3. Omnibus Consolidated Rescissions and Appropriations Act of 1996, Pub. L. No. 104-134, 110 Stat. 1321, 1321-269.

4. See also Reauthorization of the Hope VI Program: Hearing Before the Senate Committee on Banking, Housing, and Urban Affairs, 110th Cong. (2007).

References

Abravanel, Martin D., Diane K. Levy, and Margaret McFarland. 2009. *The Uncharted, Uncertain Future of HOPE VI Redevelopments: The Case for Assessing Project Sustainability*. Report, July. Washington, DC: Urban Institute. http://www.urban.org/sites/default/files/alfresco/publication-pdfs/411935-The-Uncharted-Uncertain-Future-Of-HOPE-VI-Redevelopments.PDF.

Atlanta Housing Authority. 2016. "AHA-Sponsored Mixed-Use, Mixed-Income Communities." Accessed March 1, 2016. http://atlantahousing.org/docs/sponsored-communities.pdf.

August, Martine. 2016. "Revitalisation Gone Wrong: Mixed-Income Public Housing Redevelopment in Toronto's Don Mount Court." *Urban Studies* 53 (16): 3405–22. doi:10.1177/0042098015613207.

Bair, Edward, and John M. Fitzgerald. 2005. "Hedonic Estimation and Policy Significance of the Impact of HOPE VI on Neighborhood Property Values." *Review of Policy Research* 22 (6): 771–86. doi:10.1111/j.1541-1338.2005.00175.x.

Bandura, Albert. 1977. *Social Learning Theory*. Englewood Cliffs, NJ: Prentice Hall.

Barnett, Jonathan. 2003. *Redesigning Cities: Principles, Practice, Implementation*. Chicago: Planners Press.

Baron, Richard D. 2009. "The Evolution of HOPE VI as a Development Program." In *From Despair to Hope: HOPE VI and the New Promise of Public Housing in America's Cities*, edited by Henry G. Cisneros and Lora Engdahl, 31–47. Washington, DC: Brookings Institution Press.

Basolo, Victoria. 2013. "Examining Mobility Outcomes in the Housing Choice Voucher Program: Neighborhood Poverty, Employment, and Public School Quality." *Cityscape* 15 (2): 135–54.

Bennett, Larry, Janet L. Smith, and Patricia A. Wright, eds. 2006. *Where Are Poor People to Live? Transforming Public Housing Communities*. Armonk, NY: M. E. Sharpe.

Bloom, Howard S., James A Riccio, and Nandita Verma. 2005. *Promoting Work in Public Housing: The Effectiveness of Jobs-Plus; Final Report*. New York: MDRC. http://files.eric.ed.gov/fulltext/ED484619.pdf.

Bohl, Charles C. 2000. "New Urbanism and the City: Potential Applications and Implications for Distressed Inner-City Neighborhoods." *Housing Policy Debate* 11 (4): 761–801. doi:10.1080/10511482.2000.9521387.

Boston, Thomas D. 2005. "The Effects of Revitalization on Public Housing Residents: A Case Study of the Atlanta Housing Authority." *Journal of the American Planning Association* 71 (4): 393–407. doi:10.1080/01944360508976710.

Breitbart, Myrna Margulies, and Ellen J. Pader. 1995. "Establishing Ground: Representing Gender and Race in a Mixed Housing Development." *Gender, Place and Culture* 2 (1): 5–20. doi:10.1080/09663699550022053.

Briggs, Xavier de Souza, Susan J. Popkin, and John M. Goering. 2010. *Moving to Opportunity: The Story of an American Experiment to Fight Ghetto Poverty*. New York: Oxford University Press.

Brophy, Paul C., and Rhonda N. Smith. 1997. "Mixed-Income Housing: Factors for Success." *Cityscape: A Journal of Policy and Development Research* 3 (2): 3–31.

Buron, Larry, Susan J. Popkin, Diane K. Levy, Laura E. Harris, and Jill Khadduri. 2002. *The HOPE VI Resident Tracking Study: A Snapshot of the Current Living Situation of Original Residents from Eight Sites*. Report. Washington, DC: US Department of Housing and Urban Development.

Cahill, Meagan, Samantha Lowry, and P. Mitchell Downey. 2011. *Movin' Out: Crime Displacement and HUD's HOPE VI Initiative*. Research Report, August. Washington, DC: Urban Institute. http://www.urban.org/sites/default/files/alfresco/publication-pdfs/412385-Movin-Out-Crime-and-HUD-s-HOPE-VI-Initiative.PDF.

Calthorpe, Peter. 1993. *The Next American Metropolis: Ecology, Community, and the American Dream*. New York: Princeton Architectural Press.

Ceraso, Karen. 1995. "Is Mixed-Income Housing the Key?" *Shelterforce*, March/April, 21–25. https://shelterforce.org/1995/03/01/is-mixed-income-housing-the-key/.

Chaskin, Robert J., and Mark L. Joseph. 2011. "Social Interaction in Mixed-Income Developments: Relational Expectations and Emerging Reality." *Journal of Urban Affairs* 33 (2): 209–37. doi:10.1111/j.1467-9906.2010.00537.x.

Chaskin, Robert J., and Mark L. Joseph. 2013. "'Positive' Gentrification, Social Control and the 'Right to the City' in Mixed-Income Communities: Uses and Expectations of Space and Place." *International Journal of Urban and Regional Research* 37 (2): 480–502. doi:10.1111/j.1468-2427.2012.01158.x.

Chaskin, Robert J., and Mark L. Joseph. 2015. *Integrating the Inner City: The Promise and Perils of Mixed-Income Public Housing Transformation*. Chicago: University of Chicago Press.

Chaskin, Robert J., Mark L. Joseph, Sara Voelker, and Amy Dworsky. 2012. "Public Housing Transformation and Resident Relocation: Comparing Destinations and Household Characteristics in Chicago." *Cityscape* 14 (1): 183–214.

Chaskin, Robert J., Amy T. Khare, and Mark L. Joseph. 2012. "Participation, Deliberation, and Decision Making: The Dynamics of Inclusion and Exclusion in Mixed-Income Developments." *Urban Affairs Review* 48 (6): 863–906. doi:10.1177/1078087412450151.

Chaskin, Robert J., Florian Sichling, and Mark L. Joseph. 2013. "Youth in Mixed-Income Communities Replacing Public Housing Complexes: Context, Dynamics and Response." *Cities* 35:423–31. doi:10.1016/j.cities.2013.03.009.

Chicago Housing Authority. 2000. *Chicago Housing Authority: Plan for Transformation; Improving Public Housing in Chicago and the Quality of Life*. Chicago: Chicago Housing Authority. https://www.hud.gov/sites/documents/CHAFY2000-ANNUAL-PLAN.PDF.

Cisneros, Henry G., and Lora Engdahl, eds. 2009. *From Despair to Hope: HOPE VI and the New Promise of Public Housing in America's Cities*. Washington, DC: Brookings Institution Press.

Cohen, Cathy J. 1999. *The Boundaries of Blackness: AIDS and the Breakdown of Black Politics*. Chicago: University of Chicago Press.

Coleman, James S. 1988. "Social Capital in the Creation of Human Capital." *American Journal of Sociology* 94 (Suppl.): S95–S120. doi:10.1086/228943.

Comey, Jennifer. 2007. "HOPE VI'd and On the Move." HOPE VI: Where Do We Go from Here Brief 1, June. Washington, DC: Urban Institute. http://www.urban.org/sites/default/files/alfresco/publication-pdfs/311485-HOPE-VI-d-and-On-the-Move.PDF.

DeFilippis, James. 2013. "On Spatial Solutions to Social Problems." *Cityscape* 15 (2): 69–72.

Fraser, James C., Robert J. Chaskin, and Joshua Theodore Bazuin. 2013. "Making Mixed-Income Neighborhoods Work for Low-Income Households." *Cityscape* 15 (2): 83–100.

Fraser, James, C., Deirdre Oakley, and Diane K. Levy, eds. 2013. "Mixed Messages on Mixed Income." Special issue, *Cityscape* 15 (2).

Goetz, Edward G. 2003a. *Clearing the Way: Deconcentrating the Poor in Urban America*. Washington, DC: Urban Institute Press.

Goetz, Edward G. 2003b. "Housing Dispersal Programs." *Journal of Planning Literature* 18 (1): 3–16. doi:10.1177/0885412203251339.

Graves, Erin M. 2010. "The Structuring of Urban Life in a Mixed-Income Housing 'Community'." *City and Community* 9 (1): 109–31. doi:10.1111/j.1540-6040.2009.01305.x.

Gress, Taryn H., Seungjong Cho, and Mark L. Joseph. 2016. *HOPE VI Data Compilation and Analysis*. Report, National Initiative on Mixed-Income Communities. Washington, DC: US Department of Housing and Urban Development, Office of Policy Development and Research.

Joseph, Mark L. 2006. "Is Mixed-Income Development an Antidote to Urban Poverty?" *Housing Policy Debate* 17 (2): 209–34. doi:10.1080/10511482.2006.9521567.

Joseph, Mark L. 2016. "A Critical Piece of the Mixed Income Puzzle." *Shelterforce*, February 19. https://shelterforce.org/2016/02/20/a_critical_piece_of_the_mixed_income_puzzle/.

Joseph, Mark L., and Robert J. Chaskin. 2010. "Living in a Mixed-Income Development: Resident Perceptions of the Benefits and Disadvantages of Two Developments in Chicago." *Urban Studies* 47 (11): 2347–66. doi:10.1177/0042098009357959.

Joseph, Mark L., and Robert J. Chaskin. 2012. "Mixed-Income Developments and Low Rates of Return: Insights from Relocated Public Housing Residents in Chicago." *Housing Policy Debate* 22 (3): 377–405. doi:10.1080/10511482.2012.680479.

Joseph, Mark L., Robert J. Chaskin, and Henry S. Webber. 2007. "The Theoretical Basis for Addressing Poverty through Mixed-Income Development." *Urban Affairs Review* 42 (3): 369–409. doi:10.1177/1078087406294043.

Joseph, Mark L., and Taryn H. Gress. 2013. *State of the Field Scan #1: Social Dynamics in Mixed-Income Developments*. Report, November. Cleveland, OH: Case Western Reserve University, Mandel School of Applied Social Sciences, National Initiative on Mixed-Income Communities. http://nimc.case.edu/wp-content/uploads/2015/08/State-of-the-Field-Scan-1_Social-Dynamics-in-Mixed-Income-Developments1.pdf.

Joseph, Mark L., Nancy Latham, Rachel Garshick Kleit, and Steven LaFrance. 2015. "Can San Francisco Get Mixed-Income Public Housing Redevelopment Right?"

Shelterforce, December 8. http://www.shelterforce.org/article/4329/can_san_francisco_get_mixed-income_public_housing_redevelopment_right/.

Joseph, Mark L. and Miyoung Yoon. Forthcoming. "Mixed-Income Development." In *The Wiley-Blackwell Encyclopedia of Urban and Regional Studies*, edited by Anthony M. Orum. West Sussex, United Kingdom: Wiley.

Katz, Bruce. 2009. "The Origins of HOPE VI." In *From Despair to Hope: HOPE VI and the New Promise of Public Housing in America's Cities*, edited by Henry G. Cisneros and Lora Engdahl, 15–29. Washington, DC: Brookings Institution Press.

Katz, Michael B., ed. 1993. *The "Underclass" Debate: Views from History*. Princeton, NJ: Princeton University Press.

Khare, Amy T. 2015. "Putting People Back into Place-Based Public Policies." In "Urban Policy in the Time of Obama," ed. James DeFilippis, special issue, *Journal of Urban Affairs* 37 (1): 47–52. doi:10.1111/juaf.12161.

Khare, Amy T., Mark L. Joseph, and Robert J. Chaskin. 2015. "The Enduring Significance of Race in Mixed-income Developments." *Urban Affairs Review* 51 (4): 474–503. doi:10.1177/1078087414537608.

Kleit, Rachel Garshick. 2005. "HOPE VI New Communities: Neighborhood Relationships in Mixed-Income Housing." *Environment and Planning A* 37 (8): 1413–41. doi:10.1068/a3796.

Kleit, Rachel Garshick, and Nicole Bohme Carnegie. 2011. "Integrated or Isolated? The Impact of Public Housing Redevelopment on Social Network Homophily." *Social Networks* 33 (2): 152–65. doi:10.1016/j.socnet.2011.01.001.

Levy, Diane K., and Megan Gallagher. 2006. *HOPE VI and Neighborhood Revitalization: Final Report*. Washington, DC: Urban Institute.

Levy, Diane K., Zach McDade, and Kassie Bertumen. 2013. "Mixed-Income Living: Anticipated and Realized Benefits for Low-Income Households." *Cityscape* 15 (2): 15–28.

Logan, John R., and Harvey L. Molotch. 1987. *Urban Fortunes: The Political Economy of Place*. Berkeley: University of California Press.

McCormick, Naomi J., Mark L. Joseph, and Robert J. Chaskin. 2012. "The New Stigma of Relocated Public Housing Residents: Challenges to Social Identity in Mixed-Income Developments." *City and Community* 11 (3): 285–308. doi:10.1111/j.1540-6040.2012.01411.x.

National Commission on Severely Distressed Public Housing. 1992. *The Final Report of the National Commission on Severely Distressed Public Housing*. Washington, DC: National Commission of Severely Distressed Public Housing.

National Initiative on Mixed-Income Communities. 2016. Database. Accessed March 27, 2016. http://nimc.case.edu/database/.

New Communities Initiative. 2015. *2015 Annual Report*. Washington, DC: New Communities Initiative. http://dcnewcommunities.org/wp-content/uploads/2016/04/NCI-AnnualReport1.19-WebReady.pdf.

Oakley, Deirdre, Erin Ruel, and Lesley Reid. 2013a. "Atlanta's Last Demolitions and Relocations: The Relationship between Neighborhood Characteristics and Resident Satisfaction." *Housing Studies* 28 (2): 205–34. doi:10.1080/02673037.2013.767887.

Oakley, Deirdre, Erin Ruel, and Lesley Reid. 2013*b*. "'It was really hard. . . . It was alright. . . . It was easy.' Public Housing Relocation Experiences and Destination Satisfaction in Atlanta." *Cityscape* 15 (2): 173–92.

Oldenburg, Ray. 1999. *The Great Good Place: Cafés, Coffee Shops, Bookstores, Bars, Hair Salons, and Other Hangouts at the Heart of a Community*. New York: Marlowe.

Pader, Ellen J., and Myrna Margulies Breitbart. 1993. "Transforming Public Housing: Conflicting Visions for Harbor Point." *Places* 8 (4): 34–41.

Polikoff, Alexander. 2006. *Waiting for Gautreaux: A Story of Segregation, Housing, and the Black Ghetto*. Evanston, IL: Northwestern University Press.

Popkin, Susan J. 2010. "A Glass Half-Empty? New Evidence from the HOPE VI Panel Study." *Housing Policy Debate* 20 (1): 43–63. doi:10.1080/10511481003599852.

Popkin, Susan J., Bruce Katz, Mary K. Cunningham, Karen D. Brown, Jeremy Gustafson, and Margery A. Turner. 2004. *A Decade of HOPE VI: Research Findings and Policy Challenges*. Washington, DC: Urban Institute.

Popkin, Susan J., Diane K. Levy, and Larry Buron. 2009. "Has Hope VI Transformed Residents' Lives? New Evidence from the Hope VI Panel Study." *Housing Studies* 24 (4): 477–502. doi:10.1080/02673030902938371.

Popkin, Susan J., Molly M. Scott, Joe Parilla, Elsa Falkenburger, Marla McDaniel, and Shinwon Kyung. 2012. "Planning the Housing Opportunity and Services Together Demonstration: Challenges and Lessons Learned." Housing and Opportunity Services Together Brief 1, February. Washington, DC: Urban Institute. http://www.urban.org/sites/default/files/alfresco/publication-pdfs/412516-Planning-the-Housing-Opportunity-and-Services-Together-Demonstration.PDF.

Putnam, Robert D. 2000. *Bowling Alone: The Collapse and Revival of American Community*. New York: Simon and Schuster.

Riccio, James A. 2010. "Sustained Earnings Gains for Residents in a Public Housing Jobs Program: Seven-Year Findings from the Jobs-Plus Demonstration." Policy Brief, January. New York: MDRC. http://files.eric.ed.gov/fulltext/ED514703.pdf.

Roessner, Jane. 2000. *A Decent Place to Live: From Columbia Point to Harbor Point—A Community History*. Boston: Northeastern University Press.

Rosenbaum, James E., Linda K. Stroh, and Cathy A. Flynn. 1998. "Lake Parc Place: A Study of Mixed-Income Housing." *Housing Policy Debate* 9 (4): 703–40. doi:10.1080/10511482.1998.9521314.

Ruel, Erin, Deirdre A. Oakley, Chandra Ward, Reneé Alston, and Lesley W. Reid. 2013. "Public Housing Relocations in Atlanta: Documenting Residents' Attitudes, Concerns and Experiences." *Cities* 35:349–58. doi:10.1016/j.cities.2012.07.010.

Ryan, William, and Massachusetts Housing Finance Agency. 1974. *All in Together: An Evaluation of Mixed-Income Multi-Family Housing*. Boston: Massachusetts Housing Finance Agency.

Sampson, Robert J., and W. Byron Groves. 1989. "Community Structure and Crime: Testing Social-Disorganization Theory." *American Journal of Sociology* 94 (4): 774–802. doi:10.1086/229068.

Sard, Barbara. 2001. *The Family Self-Sufficiency Program: HUD's Best Kept Secret for Promoting Employment and Asset Growth*. Report, April. Washington, DC: Center on Budget and Policy Priorities. http://files.eric.ed.gov/fulltext/ED452327.pdf.

Sard, Barbara, and Leah Staub. 2008. *House Bill Makes Significant Improvement in "HOPE VI" Public Housing Revitalization Program: Provisions to Overcome Employment Barriers Need Strengthening.* Washington, DC: Center on Budget and Policy Priorities.

Schill, Michael H. 1997. "Chicago's Mixed-Income New Communities Strategy: The Future Face of Public Housing?" In *Affordable Housing and Urban Redevelopment in the United States*, edited by Willem van Vliet, 135–57. Thousand Oaks, CA: Sage.

Schubert, Michael F., and Alison Thresher. 1996. "Lessons from the Field: Three Case Studies of Mixed-Income Housing Development." Great Cities Institute Working Paper, April. Chicago: University of Illinois at Chicago.

Skobba, Kimberly, and Edward G. Goetz. 2013. "Mobility Decisions of Very Low-Income Households." *Cityscape* 15 (2): 155–72.

Tach, Laura M. 2009. "More Than Bricks and Mortar: Neighborhood Frames, Social Processes, and the Mixed-Income Redevelopment of a Public Housing Project." *City and Community* 8 (3): 269–99. doi:10.1111/j.1540-6040.2009.01289.x.

Talen, Emily. 2002. "The Social Goals of New Urbanism." *Housing Policy Debate* 13 (1): 165–88. doi:10.1080/10511482.2002.9521438.

Tester, Griff, Erin Ruel, Angela Anderson, Donald C. Reitzes, Deirdre Oakley. 2011. "Sense of Place among Atlanta Public Housing Residents." *Journal of Urban Health* 88 (3): 436–53. doi:10.1007/s11524-011-9579-0.

Turbov, Mindy. 2006. "Public Housing Redevelopment as a Tool for Revitalizing Neighborhoods: How and Why Did It Happen and What Have We Learned?" *Northwestern Journal of Law and Social Policy* 1 (1): 167–201.

Turbov, Mindy, and Valerie Piper. 2005. "HOPE VI and Mixed-Finance Redevelopments: A Catalyst for Neighborhood Renewal—A Discussion Paper Prepared for The Brookings Institution Metropolitan Program." *Journal of Affordable Housing & Community Development Law* 15 (1): 27–103. http://www.jstor.org/stable/25782773.

Urban Institute and MDRC. 2015. *Choice Neighborhoods: Baseline Conditions and Early Progress.* Report to the US Department of Housing and Urban Development. Washington, DC: Urban Institute.

US Department of Housing and Urban Development. 2017. "Choice Neighborhoods." Accessed October 10, 2017. https://www.hud.gov/program_offices/public_indian_housing/programs/ph/cn.

Vale, Lawrence J. 2013. *Purging the Poorest: Public Housing and the Design Politics of Twice-Cleared Communities.* Chicago: University of Chicago Press.

Varady, David P., and Carole C. Walker. 2003. "Housing Vouchers and Residential Mobility." *Journal of Planning Literature* 18 (1): 17–30. doi:10.1177/0885412203254333.

Wexler, Harry J. 2001. "HOPE VI: Market Means/Public Ends—The Goals, Strategies, and Midterm Lessons of HUD's Urban Revitalization Demonstration Program." *Journal of Affordable Housing and Community Development Law* 10 (3): 195–233.

Wilson, William J. 1987. *The Truly Disadvantaged: The Inner City, the Underclass, and Public Policy.* Chicago: University of Chicago Press.

Zielenbach, Sean. 2003. "Assessing Economic Change in HOPE VI Neighborhoods." *Housing Policy Debate* 14 (4): 621–56. doi:10.1080/10511482.2003.9521489.

Zielenbach, Sean, and Richard Voith. 2010. "HOPE VI and Neighborhood Economic Development: The Importance of Local Market Dynamics." *Cityscape* 12 (1): 99–132.

9

Market-Savvy Housing and Community Development Policy

GRAPPLING WITH THE EQUITY-EFFICIENCY TRADE-OFF

Todd Swanstrom

The American healthcare system often avoids tough choices under the illusion that everyone should receive the best medical care possible, even if that means spending hundreds of thousands of dollars to keep someone alive for a few weeks.[1] To ration healthcare on the basis of cost-effectiveness, many believe, would be irresponsible; so-called government death panels should not be able to "pull the plug on grandma." Of course, we do ration healthcare; we just do it unintentionally. Those with health insurance generally receive whatever health services risk-averse doctors recommend; those without coverage often cannot afford even basic services. We spend billions on end-of-life care but lack funding for preventive medicine and public health measures that research shows would result in many more life-years saved per dollar spent. Based on market principles and fee-for-service insurance, our healthcare system obscures the trade-off we have implicitly made: huge investments in end-of-life care at the expense of primary care and disease prevention, especially for those at the bottom of the socioeconomic ladder.

Similarly, our housing and community development policies avoid tough choices, ultimately harming the neediest households. Ironically, this harm is caused by policies that give highest priority to producing affordable housing for the poorest families. The nub of the problem is that we do not sufficiently consider market conditions when allocating scarce resources. Market strength varies tremendously within and across metropolitan areas, but our model for housing and community development policies is based on one type of metropolitan area: a strong-market metro on one of the two coasts. A model designed to maximize the production of affordable housing makes sense in tight housing markets but can actually worsen housing conditions when applied to weak-market regions and neighborhoods. Like our medical system, our housing policy paradigm directs resources to the most distressed neighborhoods—places where the near-term chance of market recovery is negligible—but underinvests in healthy neighborhoods that are threatened by blight and contagious abandonment.

Our reluctance to ration housing and community development funding on the basis of market imperatives is rooted in the belief that such an approach will widen inequalities. Policy deliberations are haunted by what Arthur Okun (1975) called "the big trade-off" between equality and efficiency. In housing and community development, this trade-off implies a stark choice: policies can focus resources on the neighborhoods and households that have the greatest needs but offer little possibility of leveraging private investment, or they can focus them on areas and households that have the fewest needs but greatest potential to leverage private investment. In short, housing and community development policy that pursues housing equity generally does so at the expense of efficiency in development; policy that focuses on efficient development generally surrenders the ability to improve housing equity.

This chapter grapples with the equity-efficiency trade-off and recommends ways to reconcile these conflicting objectives. The goal of housing and community development policy is to increase the number of stable, integrated communities that provide individuals with platforms to succeed in life. By mixing and matching place-based policies with people-based ones, by taking into account neighborhood trends, and by understanding neighborhoods within a broader regional context, policymakers can diminish, if not eliminate, the trade-off between equity and efficiency.

I begin by developing a typology of housing market strength and show how market strength is rooted in social as well as economic processes. To maximize efficiency and equity, I argue, we need different approaches for three types of different neighborhood housing markets—weak, middle, and strong. I illustrate my argument with examples from the St. Louis, Missouri, metropolitan area. Even though we can reduce the steepness of the equity-efficiency trade-off, we still are faced with unavoidable trade-offs. There will always be winners and losers. In allocating scarce resources, decision makers must consider community cohesion, institutional capacity, and social justice. Adaptation to market realities is necessary for fair and effective housing and community development policies, but such adaptation alone is not sufficient to secure just housing outcomes. Deep-seated historical inequities, especially those grounded in past racist practices, present additional challenges.

The Nature of Strong and Weak Housing Markets

According to free market economics, supply and demand are in dynamic equilibrium. If demand exceeds supply, prices rise, reducing the number of customers and attracting more investors to the task of supplying the product. If supply exceeds demand, the opposite will happen. Supply and demand are, thereby, brought back into balance. At root, strong and weak housing markets have an imbalance of supply and demand: a strong market is one in which demand outstrips supply, and a weak market is one in which demand lags behind supply. Strong and weak housing markets are characterized by reinforcing boom-and-bust cycles that short-circuit the processes of market equilibrium. These processes raise challenging issues for policymakers.

Housing market strength can be measured at different geographic scales, from the neighborhood to the city to the region. One indicator of market strength is the ratio of the median home price to median income. Compared to other large metro areas, the St. Louis region has a relatively weak housing market. In 2014, St. Louis had a ratio of 2.85, ranking 20th out of the 25 largest metros. With a ratio of 7.82, Los Angeles ranked first.[2] The strength or weakness of regional housing markets can also be evaluated by examining the relationship between wages and rents. The "housing wage" is defined as the full-time hourly wage needed to afford a typical two-bedroom apartment (National Low Income Housing Coalition 2015, 1); it was $15.69 an hour in 2014 in the St. Louis metropolitan area.[3] That was well below the national average ($19.35 an hour) and almost half the Los Angeles housing wage ($27.38; National Low Income Housing Coalition 2015).

Housing market strength varies more *within* metropolitan areas than across them. Every metropolitan area has relatively hot and cold housing submarkets. The old adage that the three most important characteristics of real estate are location, location, location is a testament to the varying strength of local real estate markets. The contrasts in St. Louis housing submarkets are sharp and dramatic. In large swaths of North St. Louis, the housing market has collapsed and many owners have walked away from their properties. Only a few miles away in the St. Louis County suburbs of Ladue and Frontenac, many homes sell for over a million dollars and nice homes are being torn down to make way for fancier ones.[4]

Weak housing submarkets are not just characterized by low demand and prices; they suffer from systematic market failures that prevent the market from recovering without outside intervention. In theory, markets are supposed to operate like a thermostat, bringing supply and demand into dynamic equilibrium and insuring that every property put up for sale finds a willing buyer. When buyers and sellers make decisions independently of each other, the equilibrating process should work. Housing markets, however, are notoriously social in nature: we care who purchases the property near us—we care about their income, their race, and their lifestyle. In a neighborhood where land values are declining, there is a tipping point. Beyond it, reinforcing causal loops can drive prices down further until the market can no longer sustain itself.[5]

Figure 9.1 depicts three types of neighborhoods. What I call *middle market neighborhoods* have a balance of supply and demand. They are relatively stable. I reserve the terms *strong market* and *weak market* for housing submarkets characterized by reinforcing causal loops that drive prices either up or down. In Max Weber's (1947, 89) terminology, these market categories are "ideal types"; no neighborhood is characterized purely by reinforcing or balancing loops; every neighborhood is a mixture. Broadly speaking, however, neighborhoods fit into one of these three categories.

Weak markets can be identified using a wide array of empirical indicators.[6] In a weak market, there are not enough willing buyers to replace those who move out in the normal turnover of a neighborhood. As a result, vacancy rates soar to dangerously high levels (20 percent or more) and vacant homes blight the community. In weak markets, housing prices fall below replacement value (how much it would cost to rebuild the structure at current construction costs). As a result, developers cannot make a profit building new housing. Also, landlords are not able to charge high enough rents to cover their costs and some walk away from their properties. Homeowners defer maintenance because they will not recoup the cost of repairs upon sale. In weak markets, homeowners are replaced by absentee owners and speculators, who rent to households at the

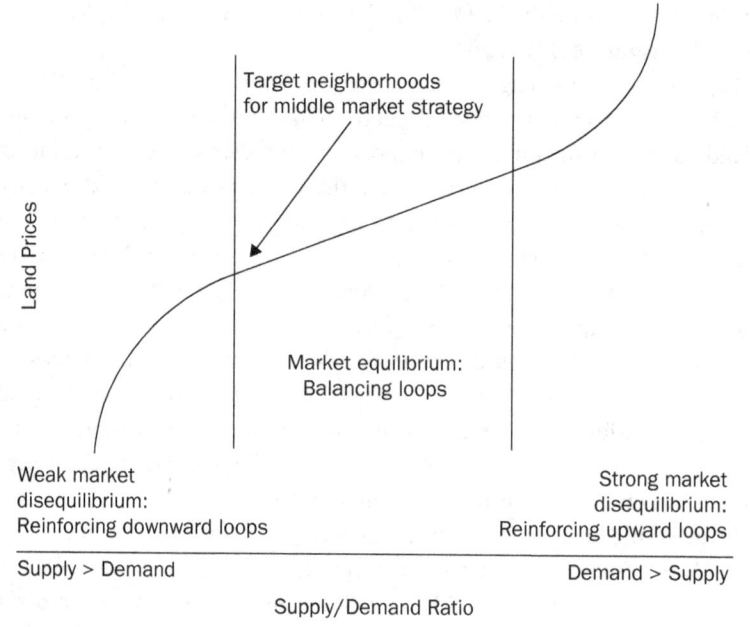

FIGURE 9.1 A typology of market strength.

bottom of the rental market. Compared with homeowners, renters tend to be more transient and less involved in the community.[7]

Neighborhood decline would be a slow, smooth process if housing demand were autonomous and each household made decisions independently of the others. But decline occurs very rapidly when processes of social contagion are set in motion. Racial transition can lead to panic selling by some households, resulting in falling home prices that encourage others to sell before prices fall even further. The shift from homeowners to renters frays the social fabric, and rising crime can further weaken the market. These reinforcing causal loops are difficult to reverse.

In strong markets, causal loops operate in the opposite direction. When rental vacancies occur or houses are put up for sale, they are snapped up quickly by an ample supply of eager customers. Strong markets have a stable base of responsible homeowners and landlords. Attracted by rising prices, new residents and property owners continually invest in the housing stock. Such markets are perceived as having bright futures. Like weak markets, strong markets are characterized by feedback loops, but the reinforcing causal loops in strong markets drive prices up, not down. Exclusionary land use policies, such as minimum-lot zoning or the prohibition of multifamily housing, can prevent the housing supply from keeping pace with demand, causing prices to soar. Rising prices can set in motion a speculative fever that causes investors to flood a hot neighborhood, creating geographically confined housing bubbles that can undermine community cohesion and displace long-time residents. *Gentrification* is the term commonly used to describe housing price bubbles in older urban neighborhoods.

Policy Approaches to Weak, Middle, and Strong Markets

I have briefly noted the trade-off policymakers face in allocating housing and community development dollars toward different types of neighborhood markets: if policies target weak market neighborhoods, the funds will go to the neediest areas but will not leverage much additional market investment. The result will be affordable housing in neighborhoods where no one wants to live and new infrastructure in areas where no new business wants to open. Due to low land prices, the cost of such weak-market policies is lower, but they offer little potential for stimulating sustainable development. Conversely, if policymakers target strong markets, the likelihood of leveraging additional market investment will be higher but the neediest areas will see little benefit (Figure 9.2). This trade-off between targeting those in need and leveraging the market, however, is not as steep as policymakers commonly assume.

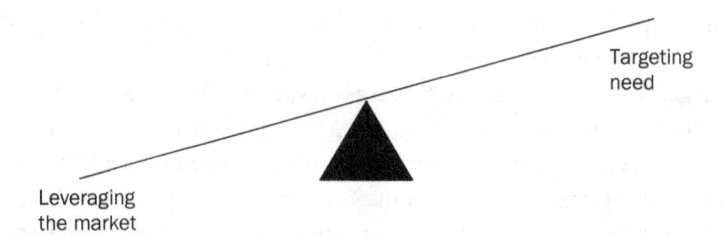

FIGURE 9.2 The equity-efficiency trade-off: targeting need or leveraging private investment.

STRATEGIES FOR WEAK MARKET NEIGHBORHOODS

Not only does it make sense from an equity perspective to concentrate housing subsidies in the worst-off neighborhoods but there are other forces pushing in this direction. NIMBYism in middle- and strong-market communities funnels subsidized-housing production programs into weak market areas, and many policies incentivize a supply-side strategy in those neighborhoods. The Low-Income Housing Tax Credit (LIHTC) program, for example, subsidizes housing production, and state housing agencies often give extra points for applications targeting development in areas of impacted poverty (Orfield et al. 2015, 594–99). Community development corporations can become dependent on the developer fees from LIHTC projects, and the number of new affordable housing units produced is a criterion that funders often use to evaluate projects. For similar reasons, too often, people with housing choice vouchers end up in high-poverty neighborhoods (McClure, Schwartz, and Taghavi 2015; Metzger 2014).

A quick look at the facts, however, suggests the flaw in concentrating housing subsidies in weak market communities. Hackworth has estimated the generalized replacement value for a home in 2010 at roughly $122,565 (Hackworth 2014, 25).[8] Replacement costs vary with construction costs in the area, the type of housing, and other factors, but Hackworth's estimate is a good starting point. It is probably impossible to build an average-sized home anywhere for much less than $100,000. In many distressed urban neighborhoods of North St. Louis, homes sell for less than $50,000. Given the replacement cost estimate, each new unit of housing would require a subsidy of at least $50,000 in order to find a willing buyer. If the housing subsidies were used to build low-income apartments, the cost per unit would be low because of low land prices, but it makes no sense to incentivize families to move into neighborhoods with few job opportunities and many burdens, including high crime and low-performing schools.

More importantly, subsidizing housing in weak market neighborhoods can actually weaken the market further. Those areas already suffer from a surplus of housing, and building new units will only further widen the gap between supply and demand. And it will likely lead to more vacancies as people move from nearby neighborhoods into the subsidized new housing. In the weakest areas, the housing market does not function properly. Lacking sales on comparable properties in the area, lenders are unable to establish a fair price and they are unwilling to issue mortgages. By itself, subsidized housing production in weak market neighborhoods benefits neither the people involved (other than temporarily giving them a physically bettter unit) nor the places.

Many community development practitioners embrace a supply approach over a strategy for generating demand, assuming that the "task at hand is to make the market more affordable to low-income families" (Buki and Schilling 2010a). In weak markets, however, the main reason housing is unaffordable is not an inadequate supply of affordable housing. Rather, the problem is that many households lack sufficient incomes to afford *decent* housing. Direct income or demand-side subsidies (vouchers) would address the problem. Rent and income trends in the St. Louis metropolitan area provide evidence for this assessment. From 1990 to 2014, the area's median rent increased by 10.9 percent in constant dollars, rising to only $632 a month by 2014. During this same period, median income fell by 3 percent.[9]

Data for the region as a whole, however, do not do justice to the low housing demand in weak market neighborhoods. Economic inequity has widened in St. Louis (Holmes and Berube 2016), and it is reflected in the neighborhood landscape. In 2010, 98,953 people lived in census tracts that, since 1970, had transitioned from low poverty (less than 15 percent) to high poverty (30 percent plus) (Swanstrom, Webber, and Metzger 2017). It is not just that neighborhoods have more poor individuals. Research has consistently shown that people in areas in which more than 20 percent of households have incomes below the poverty line consistently have poorer life outcomes, even after controlling for individual poverty and other factors.[10] Concentrated poverty weakens housing demand through a number of pathways, including increased crime, but the most direct link is probably through low-performing schools.

Housing demand in older neighborhoods has also been subject to the powerful depressive effect of housing overproduction on the suburban fringe. For many decades, the production of new housing units in the St. Louis region has consistently outpaced the growth of new households. Between 1990 and 2014, the St. Louis metropolitan area built 277,493 units of housing but the number of new households increased by only 136,262. During this period, *the region overproduced housing by 141,231 units.*[11]

With the massive overproduction of housing, the question for the St. Louis metropolitan area is not *whether* there will be vacant housing but *where* that vacant housing will be located. Despite the demolition of tens of thousands of homes by the city of St. Louis, vacancy rates have soared to dangerously high levels—over 20 percent in most neighborhoods of North St. Louis, in pockets on the south side, and even across the city border in the suburbs of north St. Louis County. Vacant housing is not just an *effect* of weak housing markets; it is also a *cause* of weak markets. Housing vacancies have been associated with higher crime and risk of fires, and they negatively affect the perception of neighborhoods (Research for Democracy 2001). Once abandonment begins, it can be difficult to stop. Vacancies cause more vacancies in a process of contagious abandonment (Dear 1975, 67). They also depress property values. A study of blight in Philadelphia found that homes within 150 feet of a vacant property experienced an average loss of $7,627 in sales value, and the estimate was robust after the inclusion of controls for other factors. The negative spillover effect of vacancies fell to $3,542 at a distance of 300 to 449 feet; beyond that, the effect of vacancy was not statistically significant (Research for Democracy 2001).

In sum, large swaths of the St. Louis region have extraordinarily weak housing markets caused by deep-seated trends in the regional housing market. Housing demand is constantly being siphoned from older urban neighborhoods out to the suburban periphery. In effect, the older neighborhoods in St. Louis are running up the down escalator, and their ability to compete in the marketplace is further weakened by the reinforcing causal loops discussed earlier.

Race, a final factor causing weak housing markets, cannot be overlooked. The weakest markets in the St. Louis region are predominantly African American. Indeed, among census tracts in the St. Louis region that were predominantly African American in 1970 and surrounded by other predominantly African American census tracts, not a single one rebounded from urban decline (Swanstrom, Webber, and Metzger 2017). The neighborhoods north of the city's infamous "Delmar divide" are stigmatized by race. Because of the mix of powerful regional and local forces weakening housing demand, a mix that includes racial prejudice, bringing weak market neighborhoods back into market equilibrium is extremely challenging.

The strategy for weak markets, and the first job for policymakers in those areas, must be to build housing demand so that the market can function again. Only after the market has been re-established should new housing be built. Housing demand in weak market neighborhoods can be boosted but most of the necessary policies are politically unrealistic. Portland, Oregon, has an urban growth boundary that pushes housing demand back toward the center, but an urban growth boundary in the St. Louis region is highly unlikely, especially at this late stage of suburban sprawl.[12] Increasing the incomes of residents in weak market neighborhoods should be a high priority, but local governments and nonprofits generally lack the policy levers to do this. Housing policy, by itself, is rarely an effective instrument for boosting housing demand in such neighborhoods. Demand-side subsidies, such as housing choice vouchers, can boost demand, but such subsidies are almost never powerful enough to jump-start weak housing markets. Indeed, if voucher holders saturate a weak market community, their presence can stigmatize the area as a dumping ground for subsidized housing, weakening its attractiveness for working- and middle-class homeowners.[13] Mixed-income housing makes the most sense, but it is difficult to attract middle-income families to disadvantaged neighborhoods.

Rebuilding weak markets requires a comprehensive approach with enough power to stop or reverse the reinforcing causal loops that undermine market confidence. If only one factor, such as high-quality housing, is addressed, the effort will be overwhelmed by the effects of other factors, such as high crime, low-performing schools, and poor job access. Policymakers must address all, or most, of these factors simultaneously.

The track record of efforts to rebuild weak markets is not encouraging. An evaluation of 48 comprehensive community initiatives over a 20-year period came to the conclusion that individuals who participated in the programs benefited, but "those programs did not produce population-level changes," such as reductions in poverty rates or increases in rates of homeownership (Kubisch et al. 2010, vii). Despite those results, weak market communities have been turned around. The South Bronx is a good example. In that case, however, the city of New York invested billions of dollars and public transit gave the community ready access to the booming Manhattan job market.

The great difficulty of turning around weak markets does not mean that we should abandon them. Indeed, it would be irresponsible to pull out of neighborhoods because their markets are weak. In 1966, Roger Starr advocated *planned shrinkage*—pulling public services out of the weak market areas. In 1976, as New York City's housing commissioner, Starr advocated closing subway stations, firehouses, and schools in the weakest market areas of the South Bronx. But cities cannot pull out of weak market neighborhoods the way doctors on the battlefield withdraw care from patients who have no chance to live. On the battlefield, it makes sense to invest limited medical services in patients who have at least a chance to survive. The analogy between medical triage and planned neighborhood shrinkage breaks down, however, because neighborhoods do not die. Even the weakest neighborhoods have people living in them; the poorest households have few choices of where to live. Politicians, especially in ward-based systems of representation, are under constant pressure not to abandon the neediest neighborhoods.

Given the moral and political imperatives to invest in weak market neighborhoods, how should we approach this task? It is wildly unrealistic to expect all weak market neighborhoods to come back. Between 1950 and 2010, the population of the city of St. Louis fell by 62.7 percent, or 537,502 people (Wikipedia 2017). This population is not coming back. For good reasons, many policy analysts have recommended rightsizing, which requires facing up to the fact that housing demand has permanently shrunk, and therefore targeting resources to a much smaller footprint in order to rebuild the market (Dewar and Thomas 2012). City services are maintained in weak market neighborhoods, but scarce housing and community development dollars are reserved for clusters of strength. Realistically, this means connecting these nodes of strength in weak market neighborhoods to middle and strong markets.

Cities have generally shunned a rightsizing strategy for weak market areas. Politicians and the public have difficulty facing up to the reality that not all neighborhoods can prosper (Thomson 2013). They cling to an "urban growth paradigm" which assumes expanding resources that can be spread across all weak market areas, but the "peanut butter" approach has little prospect of jump-starting the market (Silverman, Yin, and Patterson 2015).

Politicians have attacked rightsizing efforts as conspiracies to abandon black neighborhoods. In 1975, Team Four, a kind of rightsizing strategy, was proposed for St. Louis. It called for concentrating scarce development subsidies on areas that still had substantial strengths that could be leveraged for growth.[14] At the same time, Team Four insisted that basic services should be maintained in the weakest market areas. After the *St. Louis Post-Dispatch* published an article mistakenly stating that Team Four planned to withdraw services from the predominantly black North Side (Sutin 1975), a coalition formed to oppose it. The African American newspaper characterized Team Four as a proposal to "let the near-North side of St. Louis die" (*St. Louis Argus* 1975, quoted in Cooper-McCann 2013, 29).

Although Team Four was never implemented, many believe that it has guided city policy ever since. The North Side has continued to decline even as the central corridor has thrived. More than 30 years after Team Four was proposed, a congressional field hearing was held in St. Louis to air grievances against it (Subcommittee on Housing and Community Opportunity 2008). Yet there is little evidence that city policies intentionally starved the North Side. There are many reasons for the North Side's decline and the central corridor's prosperity, including the fact that nearly all of the region's major urban amenities are located in the central corridor. The misguided attack on Team Four has made it more difficult to implement a rightsizing strategy in the weak market neighborhoods of St. Louis.

In conclusion, investments in weak market communities need to be carefully thought out. The most valuable asset many weak market communities have is vacant land (Mallach 2012, 103–6). Urban agriculture serving niche markets can be profitable, and sewer utilities are often willing to pay communities to convert vacant land for storm water retention. However, given the powerful regional and local forces driving down these communities, the chances of reviving the weakest housing markets are very slim. A better strategy would be to help households trapped in weak market communities move to stronger communities.[15]

STRATEGIES FOR MIDDLE MARKET NEIGHBORHOODS

As just discussed, subsidizing housing in weak market areas will generally not jump-start the market and in fact could weaken it. Conversely, investments in the strongest market areas will leverage little additional investment; they may end up gilding the lily or simply boosting developers' profits for projects that would have happened anyway. If the goal is to leverage the market, middle market neighborhoods should receive the greatest attention. The sweet spot for leveraging lies in the middle.

The key to maximizing market leverage is to identify underleveraged assets. Other things being equal, housing subsidies should target neighborhoods that are "undervalued"—that is, areas where the underlying assets and amenities are not fully capitalized in land values. Examples of such assets include historic housing stock, parks, museums, high-performing schools, quality public transit (especially light rail), and pedestrian-friendly mixed-use districts. Identifying undervalued neighborhoods is difficult because markets are generally efficient: local amenities usually are capitalized in land prices. Distorted perceptions, however, can interfere with market efficiency. Such distortions find impetus in racial bias, an exaggerated fear of crime, and graffiti or broken windows, which foster perceptions of disorder.

Investing in middle market neighborhoods is like taking a public health approach to community development. Instead of trying to turn around neighborhoods that are already blighted, a better approach would be to invest in basically healthy neighborhoods before they tip down into mutually reinforcing processes of contagious abandonment and decline.[16] Neighborhoods best suited to a middle market strategy are those on the temporal and spatial edges between stability and decline, strength and weakness. Figure 9.1 illustrates this perspective: the targets for a middle market strategy are neighborhoods whose prices have dropped to the point where the neighborhood could tip over into reinforcing cycles of decline. Geographically, middle market neighborhoods are located between areas of strength and weakness. A number of cities have used market value analysis as developed by The Reinvestment Fund to identify middle market neighborhoods (Goldstein 2014). However, even with sophisticated quantitative techniques, it is difficult to identify the perfect candidates for a middle market strategy. After all, it is almost impossible to identify the counterfactual: had we not intervened in neighborhood X, it would have fallen into contagious abandonment and decline. Nevertheless, the concept is clear: the best candidates are those that, while still healthy today, could tumble down in the near future.

One goal of a middle market strategy is to inoculate neighborhoods against contagious decline. The Healthy Neighborhoods approach has a number of different components, including the following:

- Lifting up and promoting the amenities of the area
- Concentrating on appearances through neighborhood cleanups and small but visible capital improvements

- Focusing not on affordable housing for those with the lowest incomes but on homeownership for stable families

Many federal housing programs cannot be used in a middle market strategy because they have individual income cutoffs or are limited to low- and moderate-income census tracts. Baltimore's Healthy Neighborhoods program was able to access funds without those constraints. Participating banks, which in some cases receive credit on Community Reinvestment Act evaluations, offer mortgages up to 110 percent of value and at favorable interest rates. The extra funds above what is used to pay for the house are used to pay for visible repairs to the exterior of the home.

A middle market strategy is designed to boost market confidence. Confidence is social in nature. Homeowners will be much more likely to invest if their neighbors are also investing. Social capital and civic bonds should be taken into account when choosing neighborhoods for a middle market strategy. Neighborhoods with high-capacity community development corporations and strong social capital tend to be more effective at implementing a middle market strategy. Research has shown that strong social capital is associated with neighborhood stability (Temkin and Rohe 1998) and "active community-based organizations and social institutions" promote stable integrated neighborhoods (Nyden, Maly, and Lukehart 1997, 508; see also Ferman, Singleton, and DeMarco 1998).

Middle market strategies can be controversial because they do not focus resources on the neighborhoods and families that most need help. Proposals to target subsidies based on market strengths have been attacked as exemplifying the worst excesses of neoliberalism, and critics have asserted that they allow the market to dictate policy in a kind of neo–social Darwinism.[17] The implication is that such an approach, like rationing end-of-life medical care, is immoral—the equivalent of playing God by deciding which neighborhoods will be helped to revitalize and which will be allowed to languish. In fact, it is irresponsible not to make the tough decisions to recenter development. Policymakers who avoid such decisions may, in effect, consign every neighborhood to decline.

If implemented correctly, middle market strategies can promote equity. Equity planning is a movement within the planning profession to "provide a wider range of choices for those individuals and groups who have few, if any, choices" (Cleveland City Planning Commission 1975, 7). One of the founding documents of equity planning, the 1975 *Cleveland Policy Planning Report*, recommended against building subsidized housing in Cleveland's most deteriorated areas and gave highest priority to reinvestment in middle neighborhoods (Cleveland City Planning Commission 1975).[18] The recommendations were justified on equity and efficiency grounds (Cooper-McCann 2013, 36). Equity is best served by encouraging poor families to move out of the most deteriorated neighborhoods into high-opportunity areas, and it is a more efficient use of scarce public funds to invest in neighborhoods on the brink of decline than to embark on the usually futile task of trying to revitalize severely distressed communities. Investing in neighborhoods that are still healthy but are on the edge of decline, both temporally and geographically, can be a highly effective use of scarce funds. Once neighborhoods regain market confidence, homeowners, even those with modest incomes, will invest in housing (Buki and Schilling 2010b). Public investments will leverage private investment, eventually benefiting not just the owners but everyone in the area.

Middle market strategies raise issues similar to those associated with racial-integration maintenance programs (Keating 1994). In effect, middle market strategies are economic integration programs. Subsidizing homeownership in middle market neighborhoods is similar to subsidizing home purchases by whites in communities threatened by a racial tipping point. From the viewpoint of individual equity, neither approach makes sense. Programs to maintain a racial balance have been successfully sued on the ground that they violate the 1968 Fair Housing Act by discriminating against individual black households.[19] Such programs are defensible, however, from the viewpoint of spatial equity and community stability. Moreover, economic class is not a suspect classification, and economic integration programs would therefore surely survive judicial challenge. Suburbs have been discriminating on economic grounds for decades. If preserving viable mixed-income (and mixed-race) communities is a goal of public policy, then focusing scarce resources on more prosperous households is a defensible way to stabilize communities that would otherwise tumble into urban decline. The payoff for relatively modest investments could be significant.

STRATEGIES IN STRONG MARKET NEIGHBORHOODS

Policymakers need to take into account the dynamic relationship between people-based policies and place-based ones in order to develop smart strategies for strong markets. In a strong market, demand has outstripped supply, driving up housing prices. Strong markets can be viewed as the mirror image of weak markets: market disequilibrium occurs because reinforcing cycles promote rapid price increases and supply does not keep pace with demand. Affordable housing advocates have decried the forces of re-urbanization, or gentrification. As young professionals move into select older neighborhoods, rising rents displace long-time, low-income and minority residents. Instead of being a threat, however, strong markets can open up opportunities to build stable, integrated communities. Sufficient political will, however, is necessary to seize that opportunity, which must be viewed dynamically, in regional context, and from the viewpoint of people as well as places.

From the viewpoint of equity and efficiency, it makes no sense to invest in strong market communities. They are already doing well and do not need help. Subsidizing such markets will generally not leverage much additional investment because high demand and rising prices already give owners and developers strong incentives to invest. Indeed, housing subsidies in strong markets may only widen inequalities by benefiting high-income homeowners and lining the pockets of developers.

On the other hand, if we shift our equity perspective from places to people, a strong case can be made for using housing subsidies to build and maintain affordable housing in strong market communities. Housing is more than a physical container; it provides access to a bundle of housing services. Strong market communities generally have low crime, good schools, access to job opportunities, and valuable amenities, such as parks and public transit. Research has shown that relocating low-income families to strong market communities improves their life chances.[20]

People-based subsidies in strong markets advance equity, but land prices are high, and the price per unit is higher than in weaker markets. Public policies often discourage the construction of affordable housing in strong market communities. For example, the Fair Market Rent (FMR) used for Section 8 vouchers is based on rents in the entire metropolitan area. Apartments in strong markets tend to charge rents above the FMR and therefore few housing choice voucher holders are able to use them to access high-opportunity neighborhoods (US Department of Housing and Urban Development 2017).[21]

The steep trade-off between equity and efficiency in strong markets is not written in stone. With sufficient political will, cities can leverage market strength to create affordable housing at little cost to the taxpayers. Just as exclusionary zoning can bottle up the benefits of strong markets for the affluent, inclusionary zoning can spread the benefits of those markets to low- and moderate-income households. Simply allowing higher densities can help to bring supply closer to balance with demand and reduce the burden that high land prices impose on lower-income renters.

Cities can go further. With demand so far ahead of supply in strong markets, governments can require developers to create affordable housing without killing the market. Inclusionary zoning has been used by hundreds of strong market cities and counties to create affordable housing. In exchange for density bonuses, the government requires developers to set aside a certain percentage of the units for affordable housing. Under New York City's mandatory inclusionary zoning ordinance, in exchange for selective rezoning that loosens rules on density, height, and parking, developers are required to set aside up to 30 percent of all units for permanently affordable housing. According to one estimate, the ordinance will generate up to 32,000 affordable housing units at little or no cost to taxpayers (Association for Neighborhood and Housing Development 2014; Madar and Willis 2015).

Instead of being a bête noire, strong urban markets should be embraced by progressives concerned about inequity. Such markets create centripetal economic forces that enable local governments to use their taxing powers for redistributive purposes. But, as stated earlier, the embrace of strong market strategies requires political will. In 1995, New York, the quintessential strong market city, spent 830 percent more per capita on housing than the average for 32 other large cities with populations over 250,000 (cited in Schwartz 1999, 841).[22] Between 1987 and 2013, the city spent billions of dollars, much of it out of general-fund revenues, to construct, rehabilitate, and preserve 318,000 units of affordable housing (Schwartz 2015, 292). There is little evidence that New York City's inclusionary zoning or its taxes, among the highest in the nation, damaged the real estate market.

The strategy toward strong submarkets in weaker market metropolitan areas like St. Louis needs to be more nuanced, but even in these contexts the market can be leveraged to promote equity and inclusion. Regulatory barriers to affordable housing in strong submarkets should be removed. There are over 300 general-purpose governments in the St. Louis metropolitan area with land use authority. Unfortunately, these governments have few incentives to build affordable housing. Homeowners in strong market suburbs have little incentive to permit, let alone require, the construction of housing for households that will consume more in public and educational services than they contribute back in taxes. Fiscal zoning, policies designed to zone in taxable resources while zoning out service responsibilities, is rampant in St. Louis (Gordon 2008). The political constituencies that would want to move into these suburbs do not have voting rights within them. Without action by the Missouri legislature or the courts (as happened with *Mount Laurel* in New Jersey), it is difficult to imagine any significant progress in opening up the suburbs to significant amounts of affordable housing.

Strong submarkets in the city of St. Louis are another story. A study of neighborhood change in St. Louis classified 16 percent of the census tracts in the older parts of the region as "rebound" tracts, which are defined as tracts that have shown significant improvement in incomes, rents, and housing prices (Swanstrom, Webber, and Metzger 2017, 332). Almost all are located in the city's central corridor. The borders of the city of St. Louis encompass most of these emerging strong markets, and advocates of affordable housing vote in city elections. With sufficient political will, city government can implement policies to produce and preserve affordable housing in these strong submarkets.

First, the city should invest resources to enable low-income and minority households to live in strong market areas. Rebound neighborhoods in St. Louis are the most economically and racially diverse neighborhoods in the region. Low-Income Housing Tax Credit and Section 8 units in those neighborhoods have contributed to this diversity (Swanstrom, Webber, and Metzger 2017, 345). Housing subsidies have time limits, however, and they are expensive. The key to ensuring long-term affordability is control over land costs. The market is probably not strong enough yet in most rebound neighborhoods to support inclusionary zoning. Indeed, it is only in recent years that developers have built new housing without subsidies. Policy approaches in weak market metros like St. Louis need to take into account not just current conditions but neighborhood trends as well. Rents are still relatively affordable in the rebound neighborhoods of St. Louis; in 2010, the average median monthly rent in rebound tracts was only $563; after taking into account average utility costs, the median apartment in these neighborhoods would be affordable to a family making only about half of the median income for the metropolitan area. Rents are going up, however. In rebound tracts, they rose by a hefty 20.4 percent between 2000 and 2010 (Swanstrom, Webber, and Metzger 2017, 339). The increases are primarily due to rising land costs. To ensure long-term affordability, nonprofit-owned housing and community land trusts should be given high priority. In this sense, weak market cities like St. Louis can learn from hot market cities on the two coasts. If land can be purchased before prices have peaked, alternative forms of ownership can lock in affordable housing, achieving a bigger bang with scarce public bucks.

In addition to expanding the supply of affordable housing within strong market neighborhoods, policies are needed to extend market strength into weak market neighborhoods. In St. Louis, this requires spreading the wealth of the central corridor into weak market neighborhoods, especially into the overwhelmingly black neighborhoods north of the infamous Delmar divide. Special taxing districts or tax increment financing districts can span strong and weak markets along major north–south thoroughfares. Funds generated in the more prosperous parts can be used to improve the infrastructure and to jumpstart the market in weaker areas. More importantly, ways must be found to link residents of North St. Louis to the expanding job base in the central corridor (Mallach 2016). Building the north–south extension of MetroLink, the light rail system, would be one way to do this.

Conclusion: Building on Strength and the Dilemma of Race

The goal of housing and community development policies should be to develop housing markets that are neither too hot nor too cold. Supply and demand should be balanced. Ideally, the neighborhood should include a mix of housing types and incomes in order to encourage racial and ethnic diversity. Table 9.1 sums up the main lessons of market-savvy housing and community development policies. The two empty cells mark where, other things being equal, scarce housing and community development dollars should not be invested. We should not provide housing subsidies for low-income families to live in weak market settings. Place-based initiatives in weak market communities must be done in

TABLE 9.1
Market-savvy housing and community development policies

	Weak Market	Middle Market	Strong Market
Invest in People		Stable Homeowners	Permanently Affordable Housing
Invest in Places	Comprehensive Community Initiatives	Visible Improvements, Marketing of Assets	

a comprehensive but targeted manner with sufficient scale to move the market. We should not invest scarce development dollars in strong market areas. If we invest in strong market areas—in suburbs or gentrified urban neighborhoods—policies should give highest priority to attracting and retaining low-income households. Highest priority should be given to neighborhoods on the temporal and spatial edges—neighborhoods that are located between strong- and weak-market areas and still have functioning housing markets but could tip over into reinforcing cycles of decline. Those areas have the greatest potential to promote both equity and efficiency.

Public policies should always build on strengths, and it is always better to have strong markets than weak ones. Strong markets provide opportunities to multiply public investments to the benefit of those most in need. They also provide "sticky" capital that can be taxed or regulated without fear that it will flee. Instead of deriding the movement of millennials and young professionals into older urban neighborhoods, legacy cities should embrace this trend as a political opportunity to leverage emerging market strength for the public good.

The assertion that policy interventions should take market strength into account requires acknowledging other community strengths that can also be leveraged to promote efficient and equitable outcomes. Strong civic institutions in a neighborhood can compensate, at least in part, for market weaknesses. Strong social capital has been correlated with neighborhood stability (Temkin and Rohe 1998). Collective efficacy, or the willingness of neighbors to intervene to achieve social order in their neighborhood, is correlated with lower crime, independent of the socioeconomic position of the community (Sampson 2012). In Cleveland, Neighborhood Progress Inc. has targeted nine communities that are not classic middle market neighborhoods but that have strong community development corporations and civic assets. Those attributes heighten their likelihood of succeeding at neighborhood stabilization. The goal of community development is not just to build strong markets but to nurture strong communities where attachments to place transcend purely economic calculations.

The argument that we should build on strength is persuasive, but a troubling injustice still hangs over our policy deliberations. As Richard Rothstein documents in his chapter for this volume (Chapter 2), public policies in St. Louis and other metropolitan areas have forcibly consigned African Americans to weak market communities. In 2013, weak market neighborhoods in St. Louis were 88.9 percent nonwhite (the city as whole is about 53 percent nonwhite). Middle market neighborhoods were not lily white; in fact, they were 36.8 percent nonwhite but still less than the city as whole.[23] A middle market strategy can provide substantial benefits for African Americans. Largely as a result of stagnant housing values, in 2013, African American median household wealth was only 8.2 percent of white household wealth (Jones 2017). A middle market strategy would help many blacks preserve and expand their household wealth, but it would not address the underlying structural inequalities that consign so many African American families to weak market neighborhoods. To correct this injustice, Rothstein suggests having the government purchase homes from whites in strong market suburbs and sell them back to blacks at the same price (controlling for inflation) their grandparents would have paid if they had been permitted to buy them many years ago. A program of real estate reparations would be just, but it is a political nonstarter.

The build-on-strength approach advocated here is much more politically realistic but it inherently disadvantages African Americans trapped in weak market neighborhoods. If the pattern of racial segregation in St. Louis resembled a checkerboard, then it would be easier to build out from strength into weak market black communities. However, weak market black neighborhoods in North St. Louis form one continuous enclave north from Delmar Boulevard into the suburbs of St. Louis County.[24] In the absence of a massive affirmative action program for places like North St. Louis, policymakers confront a daunting dilemma. As Herbert Rubin (2000, 273) put it, "Renewal is about compensating for past inequities but doing so in ways that make financial sense for the present." Tough choices remain.

Notes

1. The case for rationing healthcare services is made by Leonhardt (2009), Singer (2009), and Porter (2012).

2. Charles Buki and Elizabeth Schilling (2010*b*, para. 6) write: "We regard a market with housing cost to income ratios of between 2.7–3.3 to be stable and balanced. Much north of 4 and housing cost burdens for working families are a real problem. Much less than 2.5 and there will be vacancy, creeping abandonment, and other signs of real trouble."

3. The typical apartment is defined as one offered at or below the Fair Market Rent (FMR), which is set by the US Department of Housing and Urban Development. To be deemed affordable, the cost of housing and utilities must come to no more than 30 percent of household income.

4. The sales price approximation is based on the author's review of listings on the Zillow website: https://www.zillow.com. Weak housing submarkets are well known in older industrial cities like St. Louis and Detroit. They are less well known in hot market cities like San Francisco, where the average price of a home now exceeds $1 million, yet many

neighborhoods in strong market cities are plagued by weak markets and falling home prices (Florida and Bendix 2015).

5. A "causal loop" is a circular process where cause and effect reinforce one another in reinforcing cycles of cumulative causation. For an early explanation of the principle of cumulative causation and how it contradicts economic theory, see Gunnar Myrdal (1964, Appendix 3).

6. Methods of gauging market strength are drawn from Alan Mallach (2012) and Jason Hackworth (2014).

7. Empirical research has consistently linked homeownership with higher levels of social capital and community cohesion. For a review of the evidence, see William Rohe and Mark Lindblad (2013).

8. Hackworth's estimate is based on work by Edward Glaeser and James Gyourko (2005).

9. Author's calculations based on data from the US Census Bureau's 1990 decennial census and the American Community Survey 5-year estimates. Data were accessed via American FactFinder: https://factfinder.census.gov.

10. The assertion that 20 percent is the tipping point for the negative effects of concentrated poverty finds support in Galster (2010). For a synthesis of the research on the negative contextual effects of concentrated poverty, see Peter Dreier, John Mollenkopf, and Todd Swanstrom (2014, Chapter 3).

11. Author's calculations based on US Census Bureau (2016a, 2016b, 2016c, 2016d). St. Louis is not alone in overproducing housing (Bier and Post 2006; Bier 2017).

12. St. Louis is one of the most sprawled-out metropolitan areas in the country. Between 1982 and 1997, for example, the population of the metropolitan area increased by 6.0 percent, but the built-up urbanized land area increased by 25.1 percent (Fulton et al. 2001).

13. Scholarly reviews of research have found that subsidized housing often has no effect on surrounding property values and may, in fact, increase them. However, studies also have found that large concentrations of subsidized housing in weak market communities can have negative effects on surrounding property values. For a succinct synthesis of four literature reviews on this issue, see Center for Housing Policy (2009).

14. My account of Team Four is based on work by Patrick Cooper-McCann (2013).

15. Myron Orfield and colleagues (2015) argue that a dispersal strategy makes more sense than investing housing subsidies in racially segregated areas of concentrated poverty. Edward Goetz (2015) criticizes the dispersal strategy and defends place-based community development. In effect, I argue that dispersal and development strategies are both correct strategies when applied to the appropriate context that is largely determined by market strength.

16. My discussion of middle market strategy draws heavily on the work of Charles Buki and Elizabeth Schilling (2010a, 2010b) and David Boehlke (2012). The middle market strategy has been implemented most successfully in Baltimore's Healthy Neighborhoods initiative. For an insightful overview of the middle neighborhoods approach, see Paul Brophy (2016).

17. For a critique of using market value analysis to target subsidies to middle market neighborhoods in Baltimore, see Kate Davidoff (2015).

18. At the same time, the equity planners in Cleveland clearly asserted the duty of the city to help neighborhoods that received no concentrated housing and community development

assistance. In an implicit rejection of "planned shrinkage," Norman Krumholz, Cleveland's planning director, recommended maintaining basic city services in the weakest market areas (Cooper-McCann 2013, 36).

19. For the constitutional arguments against racial-integration maintenance programs, see Rodney Smolla (1981). The federal government successfully sued a private housing developer that received federal subsidies. The suit sought to prevent the development from implementing racial quotas in an effort to maintain racial integration (*United States v. Starrett City Associates*, 840 F.2d 1096 (2d Cir. 1988)).

20. Two experiments, one mandated by the courts (Gautreaux) and one mandated by Congress (Moving to Opportunity), provide evidence for the positive effects on families and individuals of moving from a high-poverty to a low-poverty community. For a synthesis of the research on these policy experiments and on place effects more generally, see Dreier, Mollenkopf, and Swanstrom 2014, Chapter 3.

21. During the Obama administration, the US Department of Housing and Urban Development (HUD) established a pilot program to calculate FMRs for smaller areas and, thereby, to give voucher holders access to higher-opportunity areas. In August of 2017, under the Trump administration, HUD announced a 2-year suspension of the Small Area Fair Market Rents demonstration program. Because of a legal settlement, the program will still apply in the Dallas metropolitan area (US Department of Housing and Urban Development 2017).

22. The original survey was by Victoria Basolo. Schwartz cites a personal communication with Basolo as the source for his numbers.

23. Data on middle and low market neighborhoods are from Ira Goldstein, William Schrecker, and Jason Rosch (2016, 38). Citywide data are from US Census Bureau (2017).

24. Douglas Massey and Nancy Denton (1993, 74) identify such a pattern as one of the five characteristics of "hypersegregation."

References

Association for Neighborhood and Housing Development. 2014. "Mandatory Inclusionary Zoning: Ensuring Affordability as a Part of New York City's Future." White Paper, April. New York: Association for Neighborhood and Housing Development. https://www.anhd.org/wp-content/uploads/2011/07/ANHD-2014-White-paper-Mandatory-IZ-How-many-units-MIZ-could-create.pdf.

Bier, Thomas E. 2017. *Housing Dynamics in Northeast Ohio: Setting the Stage for Resurgence*. Cleveland, OH: MSL Academic Endeavors eBooks. https://engagedscholarship.csuohio.edu/msl_ae_ebooks/4.

Bier, Thomas, and Charlie Post. 2006. "Vacating the City: An Analysis of New Homes vs. Household Growth." In *Redefining Urban and Suburban America: Evidence from Census 2000*, Vol. 3. Edited by Alan Berube, Bruce Katz, and Robert D. Lang, 167–89. Washington, DC: Brookings Institution Press.

Boehlke, David. 2012. "Preserving Healthy Neighborhoods: Market-Based Strategies for Housing and Neighborhood Revitalization." In *Rebuilding America's Legacy Cities: New Directions for the Industrial Heartland*, edited by Alan Mallach, 143–62. New York: American Assembly.

Brophy, Paul C., ed. 2016. *On the Edge: America's Middle Neighborhoods.* New York: American Assembly.
Buki, Charles, and Elizabeth Humphrey Schilling. 2010a. "Notes on Structural Change: Redefining the Problem of Weak Markets." *Planetizen*, January 28. http://www.planetizen.com/node/42691.
Buki, Charles, and Elizabeth Humphrey Schilling. 2010b. "The Right Interventions to Restore Confidence in Weak Markets." *Planetizen.* February 4. http://www.planetizen.com/node/42768.
Center for Housing Policy. 2009. *"'Don't Put It Here!' Does Affordable Housing Cause Nearby Property Values to Decline?"* Insights from Housing Policy Research Policy Brief. Washington, DC: Center for Housing Policy.
Cleveland City Planning Commission. 1975. *Cleveland Policy Planning Report*, Vol. 1. Cleveland, OH: Cleveland City Planning Commission. eCommons, Cornell University Library. https://ecommons.cornell.edu/handle/1813/40857.
Cooper-McCann, Patrick D. 2013. "Urban Triage in Cleveland and St. Louis." Master's thesis, Urban and Regional Planning, University of Michigan.
Davidoff, Kate. 2015. "From Protest Politics to Granite Countertops: The Shifts in Community Development in Baltimore, Maryland from 1950-2010." PhD diss., Graduate Program in Planning and Public Policy, Rutgers University.
Dear, Michael J. 1975. "Abandoned Housing." In *Urban Policymaking and Metropolitan Dynamics: A Comparative Geographical Analysis*, edited by John S. Adams, 59–99. Cambridge, MA: Ballinger.
Dewar, Margaret, and June Manning Thomas, eds. 2012. *The City after Abandonment.* Philadelphia: University of Pennsylvania Press.
Dreier, Peter, John Mollenkopf, and Todd Swanstrom. 2014. *Place Matters: Metropolitics for the Twenty-First Century*, 3rd ed. Lawrence: University Press of Kansas.
Ferman, Barbara, Theresa Singleton, and Don DeMarco. 1998. "West Mount Airy, Philadelphia." *Cityscape* 4 (2): 29–59.
Florida, Richard, and Aria Bendix. 2015. "Mapping the Great Housing Divide in New York and San Francisco." *CityLab*, October 12. https://www.citylab.com/equity/2015/10/mapping-the-great-housing-divide-in-new-york-and-san-francisco/405022/.
Fulton, William, Rolf Pendall, Mai Nguyen, and Alicia Harrison. 2001. *Who Sprawls the Most? How Growth Patterns Differ across the U.S.* Survey Series Report. Washington, DC: Brookings Institution, Center on Urban and Metropolitan Policy.
Galster, George C. 2010. "The Mechanism(s) of Neighborhood Effects: Theory, Evidence, and Policy Implications." Paper presented at the ESRC Seminar Neighbourhood Effects: Theory and Evidence, St. Andrews University, Scotland, February 4–5.
Glaeser, Edward L., and James Gyourko. 2005. "Urban Decline and Durable Housing." *Journal of Political Economy* 113 (2): 345–75. doi:10.1086/427465.
Goetz, Edward. 2015. "Poverty-Pimping CDCs: The Search for Dispersal's Next Bogeyman." *Housing Policy Debate* 25 (3): 608–18. doi:10.1080/10511482.2015.1035012.
Goldstein, Ira. 2014. "Making Sense of Markets: Using Data to Guide Reinvestment Strategies." In *What Counts: Harnessing Data for America's Communities*, edited by the Federal Reserve Bank of San Francisco and Urban Institute, 75–87. San Francisco: Federal Reserve Bank of San Francisco.

Goldstein, Ira, William Schrecker, and Jason L. Rosch. 2016. "Demographics and Characteristics of Middle Neighborhoods in Select Legacy Cities." In *On the Edge: America's Middle Neighborhoods*, edited by Paul C. Brophy, 21–48. New York: American Assembly.

Gordon, Colin. 2008. *Mapping Decline: St. Louis and the Fate of the American City*. Philadelphia: University of Pennsylvania Press.

Hackworth, Jason. 2014. "The Limits to Market-Based Strategies for Addressing Land Abandonment in Shrinking American Cities." *Progress in Planning* 90: 1–37. doi:10.1016/j.progress.2013.03.004.

Holmes, Natalie, and Alan Berube. 2016. *City and Metropolitan Inequity on the Rise, Driven by Declining Incomes*. Washington, DC: Brookings Institution.

Jones, Janelle. 2017. "The Racial Wealth Gap: How African-Americans Have Been Shortchanged out of the Materials to Build Wealth." Working Economics Blog, Economic Policy Institute, February 13. https://www.epi.org/blog/the-racial-wealth-gap-how-african-americans-have-been-shortchanged-out-of-the-materials-to-build-wealth/.

Keating, W. Dennis. 1994. *The Suburban Racial Dilemma: Housing and Neighborhoods*. Philadelphia: Temple University Press.

Kubisch, Anne C., Patricia Auspos, Prudence Brown, and Tom Dewar, eds. 2010. *Voices from the Field III: Lessons and Challenges from Two Decades of Community Change Efforts*. Washington, DC: Aspen Institute.

Leonhardt, David. 2009. "Health Care Rationing Rhetoric Overlooks Reality." *New York Times*, June 17. http://www.nytimes.com/2009/06/17/business/economy/17leonhardt.html.

Madar, Josiah, and Mark Willis. 2015. "Creating Affordable Housing out of Thin Air: The Economics of Mandatory Inclusionary Zoning in New York City." Research Brief, March. New York: NYU Furman Center.

Mallach, Alan. 2012. "Depopulation, Market Collapse, and Property Abandonment: Surplus Land and Buildings in Legacy Cities." In *Rebuilding America's Legacy Cities: New Directions for the Industrial Heartland*, edited by Alan Mallach, 85–110. New York: American Assembly.

Mallach, Alan. 2016. "The Uncoupling of the Economic City: Increasing Spatial and Economic Polarization in American Older Industrial Cities." *Urban Affairs Review* 51 (4): 443–73. doi:10.1177/1078087414537609.

Massey, Douglas S., and Nancy A. Denton. 1993. *American Apartheid: Segregation and the Making of the Underclass*. Cambridge, MA: Harvard University Press.

McClure, Kirk, Alex F. Schwartz, and Lydia B. Taghavi. 2015. "Housing Choice Voucher Location Patterns a Decade Later." *Housing Policy Debate* 25 (2): 215–33. doi:10.1080/10511482.2014.921223.

Metzger, Molly W. 2014. "The Reconcentration of Poverty: Patterns of Housing Voucher Use, 2000 to 2008." *Housing Policy Debate* 24 (3): 544–67. doi:10.1080/10511482.2013.876437.

Myrdal, Gunnar. 1964. *An American Dilemma*, Vol. 2. New York: McGraw-Hill.

National Low Income Housing Coalition. 2015. *Out of Reach 2015: Low Wages and High Rents Lock Renters Out*. Washington, DC: National Low Income Housing Coalition.

Nyden, Philip, Michael Maly, and John Lukehart. 1997. "The Emergence of Stable Racially and Ethnically Diverse Urban Communities: A Case Study of Nine U.S. Cities." *Housing Policy Debate* 8 (2): 491–534. doi:10.1080/10511482.1997.9521262.

Okun, Arthur M. 1975. *Equality and Efficiency: The Big Tradeoff*. Washington, DC: Brookings Institution.

Orfield, Myron, Will Stancil, Thomas Luce, and Eric Myott. 2015. "High Costs and Segregation in Subsidized Housing Policy." *Housing Policy Debate* 25 (3): 574–607. doi:10.1080/10511482.2014.963641.

Porter, Eduardo. 2012. "Rationing Health Care More Fairly." *New York Times*, August 21. http://www.nytimes.com/2012/08/22/business/economy/rationing-health-care-more-fairly.html.

Research for Democracy. 2001. *Blight Free Philadelphia: A Public-Private Strategy to Create and Enhance Neighborhood Value*. Report. Philadelphia, PA: Research for Democracy.

Rohe, William M., and Mark Lindblad. 2013. "Reexamining the Social Benefits of Homeownership after the Housing Crisis." Paper originally presented at the symposium on Homeownership Built to Last: Lessons of the Housing Crisis on Sustaining Homeownership for Low-Income and Minority Families, Harvard University, Boston, MA, April.

Rubin, Herbert J. 2000. *Renewing Hope within Neighborhoods of Despair: The Community-Based Development Model*. Albany: State University of New York Press.

Sampson, Robert J. 2012. *Great American City: Chicago and the Enduring Neighborhood Effect*. Chicago: University of Chicago Press.

Schwartz, Alex F. 1999. "New York City and Subsidized Housing: Impacts and Lessons of the City's $5 Billion Capital Budget Housing Plan." *Housing Policy Debate* 10 (4): 839–77.

Schwartz, Alex F. 2015 *Housing Policy in the United States*, 3rd ed. New York: Routledge.

Silverman, Robert Mark, Li Yin, and Kelly L. Patterson. 2015. "Municipal Property Acquisition Patterns in a Shrinking City: Evidence for the Persistence of an Urban Growth Paradigm in Buffalo, NY." *Cogent Social Sciences* 1 (1): article 1012973. doi:10.1080/23311886.2015.1012973.

Singer, Peter. 2009. "Why We Must Ration Health Care," *New York Times Magazine*, July 15. http://www.nytimes.com/2009/07/19/magazine/19healthcare-t.html?pagewanted=all.

Smolla, Rodney A. 1981. "Integration Maintenance: The Unconstitutionality of Benign Programs That Discourage Black Entry to Prevent White Flight," *Duke Law Journal*, December (no. 6): 891–939.

Starr, Roger. 1966. *Urban Choices: The City and Its Critics*. London: Pelican.

St. Louis Argus. 1975. "Block Units Strongly Oppose Plan Four." June 19, 16B.

Subcommittee on Housing and Community Opportunity of the Committee on Financial Oversight. 2008. *The Use of Federal Housing and Economic Development Funds in St. Louis: From "Team 4" Into the Future*. Serial 110-96. Washington, DC: US. Government Printing Office. https://www.gpo.gov/fdsys/pkg/CHRG-110hhrg41727/pdf/CHRG-110hhrg41727.pdf.

Sutin, Philip. 1975. "Plan Said to Hurt Black Area in City." *St. Louis Post-Dispatch*, May 19, 1B.

Swanstrom, Todd, Henry S. Webber, and Molly W. Metzger. 2017. "Rebound Neighborhoods in Older Industrial Cities: The Case of St. Louis." In *Economic*

Mobility: Research and Ideas on Strengthening Families, Communities, and the Economy, edited by the Federal Reserve Bank of St. Louis and the Board of Governors of the Federal Reserve System, 325–51. St. Louis, MO: Federal Reserve Bank of St. Louis.

Temkin, Kenneth, and William M. Rohe. 1998. "Social Capital and Neighborhood Stability: An Empirical Investigation." *Housing Policy Debate* 9 (1): 61–88. doi:10.1080/10511482.1998.9521286.

Thomson, Dale E. 2013. "Targeting Neighborhoods, Stimulating Markets: The Role of Political, Institutional, and Technical Factors in Three Cities." in *The City after Abandonment*, edited by Margaret Dewar and June Manning Thomas, 104–32. Philadelphia: University of Pennsylvania Press.

US Census Bureau. 2016a. "Building Permits: Permits by County or Place." Accessed February 6. http://www.census.gov/construction/bps/.

US Census Bureau. 2016b. "General Housing Characteristics: 2000." Census 2000, Table QT-H1. Accessed February 8. http://factfinder2.census.gov.

US Census Bureau. 2016c. "Population and Housing Units." 1990 Census of Population and Housing, Table 30. Accessed February 8. https://www.census.gov/history/www/reference/publications/demographic_programs_1.html.

US Census Bureau. 2016d. "Selected Housing Characteristics." 2010–2014 American Community Survey 5-Year Estimates, Table DP04. Accessed February 8. http://factfinder2.census.gov.

US Census Bureau. 2017. "St. Louis city, Missouri (County); St. Louis city, Missouri; St. Louis County, Missouri." American Community Survey. Accessed January 4, 2018. https://www.census.gov/quickfacts/fact/table/stlouiscitymissouricounty,stlouiscitymissouri,stlouiscountymissouri/PST045217.

US Department of Housing and Urban Development, Office of Policy Development & Research. 2017. "Small Area Fair Market Rents." Accessed December 13. https://www.huduser.gov/portal/datasets/fmr/smallarea/index.html.

Weber, Max. 1947. *The Theory of Social and Economic Organization*. New York: Free Press.

Wikipedia. 2017. "List of Shrinking Cities in the United States." Last modified December 31, 2017. Accessed January 2, 2017. https://en.wikipedia.org/wiki/List_of_shrinking_cities_in_the_United_States.

10

Financing Affordability
TAX INCREMENT FINANCING AND THE POTENTIAL FOR CONCENTRATED REINVESTMENT

Sarah L. Coffin

Central cities and distressed communities across the United States struggle to create economic development that stimulates investment without burdening taxpayers. Taxpayers, on the other hand, place increasing pressure on elected officials to develop tools that will reap near-term returns on investment and not just windfall profits for wealthy developers. Tax increment financing (TIF) has become a tool of choice among local governments for attracting local economic development in the face of these challenges. Municipalities use TIF to fund spatially targeted infrastructure needs and to meet development costs. The tool has become increasingly important as municipal budgets have shrunk and federal spending has devolved to state and local governments (Sagalyn 1990; Clarke and Gaile 1992; Squires and Hutchison 2014). Developers are also attracted to the tool for its flexibility. In some cases, it can be used to preempt the blighted conditions it was intended to address (Greenbaum and Landers 2014). The challenge is to craft TIF strategies that begin to address growing metropolitan inequality and segregation by promoting broad economic and community development goals.

This chapter lays out the intuition behind TIF and the mechanics of how it works, focusing on how it has affected and might be used to address economic isolation. A brief history of TIF is presented as well as some major critiques of how this tool has been implemented. Next, a case study of TIF use in St. Louis County, Missouri, is given. The chapter closes with a proposed series of measures that local and state governments can take to ensure that TIF financing is more equitable. These include a reconsideration of how TIF investment decisions are made and of ways to include the voices of affected residents in both the process and outcomes of projects. Concentrated reinvestment can be more inclusive as well as profitable.

The Reasoning for TIF

A municipality has two primary ways to raise revenue: increasing jobs and increasing taxes. Attracting new jobs is difficult in an aging city that faces low to no economic growth, crumbling infrastructure, and spreading blight.[1] These communities struggle to attract investors, and residents seldom support tax increases to fund development efforts. They often challenge municipal attempts to extract additional revenue for critical infrastructure projects that do not have a clear and immediate payoff. Thus, municipalities are forced to find creative ways to attract new investment with existing revenue.

From the public sector's standpoint, the place-based nature of TIF is attractive. Typically targeted toward a specific geographic location, TIF enables the municipality to lock down the investment to a place, extending the public benefit of tax dollars by attaching these resources to the improvements and the location rather than allowing the subsidy to become absorbed into developer profits once the project is completed. Traditional economic development tools like tax abatement direct subsidy to the property owner by lowering tax payments, and that property owner can choose to invest the savings in the property, or not; because the owner is not obligated to reinvest the tax savings, the local government may or may not see added investment from the subsidy, and the tax incentive's effect on public revenue is deferred. Therefore, TIF is politically appealing: local elected officials recognize the potential for "costless" growth, and developers receive direct assistance with development costs.

The challenge comes when a struggling municipality diverts precious resources away from present needs to fund a TIF project that provides only localized benefits. These kinds of projects typically yield low-wage, low-skilled employment opportunities, new infrastructure for the immediate location, and blight clearance, but the projects often are not connected to the rest of the municipality or region and do not generate a net gain (Lester 2014).

Further, the diversion of funds from other taxing entities (e.g., school and fire districts) forces those entities to manage the service demands stimulated by development without the revenue that the development generates (Weber 2010; Tomme 2005). In most states, the enabling legislation permits municipalities to establish TIF districts and specifies the purposes for which captured funds may be used. The incremental revenue from all of the taxing jurisdictions is captured to support the project's infrastructure and development needs. For example, a school district's enrollment may increase with the opening of a TIF-funded housing project, but the district will receive no revenue from the new arrivals until the TIF expires (Weber 2003, 2010). Thus, as one might expect, school districts and their supporters generate much of the opposition to TIF projects. For all of these reasons, the public may rightfully question the benefits of diverting local resources via TIF.

TIF is as an attractive approach also because it is perceived to be budget neutral and to provide resources without increasing taxes. Rather, TIF funds projects by diverting resources from the general revenue pool with the expectation that the project's completion will stimulate new investment, create jobs, increase property values, and enlarge the tax base (LeRoy 2008).

As TIF has become a primary economic development tool (49 states now have TIF-enabling legislation[2]), additional questions have arisen about the tool's use (Briffault 2010). Are the communities most in need of redevelopment benefiting from TIF, or are the bulk of TIF's benefits being realized in more affluent communities that are already in a strong position to attract developers' dollars? In many cases, TIF has become a *de facto* proxy for planning. That has equity implications for housing and other development activities. Is TIF a viable instrument for targeting concentrated reinvestment that promotes equity? Can TIF become a tool that helps existing residents participate in emerging economic opportunities associated with large-scale urban reinvestment?

How TIF Works

The mechanics of the TIF process differ across cities, and particulars depend on the structure of the state legislation enabling TIF. In all cases, the process begins with a municipality designating an area for TIF (i.e., a TIF district) and "freezing" the area's property taxes at a baseline valuation. The clock then starts on the project (which typically extends for 20 to 30 years), and any appreciation in property taxes over and above the baseline is assigned to the project as payments-in-lieu-of-taxes (PILOTs). These PILOTs are used to pay for approved project costs.[3] The next step can involve (1) issuing bonds or (2) implementing a "pay as you go" structure. If the municipality chooses to issue bonds based on the estimated PILOTs to be generated by the project, the resulting revenue is used to make the initial payment for infrastructure improvements in the designated area. The municipality then allows private developers to use the TIF district's bond money to pay for project-specific infrastructure improvements (e.g., parking lots, roads, and landscaping improvements), and those investments offset private development costs for the proposed project. When the new development is completed, any tax revenue above the original baseline is captured by the municipality and used to repay the bonds.

In a "pay as you go" structure, the project does not receive up-front public investment in public infrastructure for the designated area. Instead, as the project begins to accrue in value, the developers receive the accrued PILOTs, which are then used to cover development costs and infrastructure improvements for approved projects within the designated area.

A key challenge to this process lies in how the community justifies the diversion of tax revenues to pay for project costs. Ideally, the community would conduct an analysis of the existing conditions, and this analysis would demonstrate that the proposed development would not be viable *but for* the use of TIF. Much depends upon this "but for" clause: whether the project would be viable without TIF depends on a determination that the area within the project's footprint is blighted—that its condition limits the area's real estate potential—and on how blight is defined. The definition is specified in state TIF statutes, and certain physical conditions must be present (e.g., aging infrastructure, obsolete street grids and buildings) to justify public expenditure on an area deemed blighted. However, those definitions have expanded over the years to include "future blight." Some critics argue that such expansions are nothing more than a tool for municipal tax grabs (e.g., Gordon 2003, 327).

The History of TIF

The impact of TIF on local government has increased in recent decades but the origins of TIF's use as an economic development tool are in the early postwar era. First implemented in California in 1952, TIF permitted cities to avoid the difficulties associated with obtaining electoral support for the revenue increases required to garner the federal government's matching funds for urban renewal (Johnson 1999; Kriz 2001; Weber and O'Neill-Kohl 2013). However, TIF use did not become widespread in the United States until the 1970s. Because of the recession early in that decade and the subsequent fiscal stress, states and cities turned to local economic development programs, particularly but not exclusively TIF (Kelmanski 1990). The turn to TIF was also fueled by the tax revolt that swept through the United States in the late 1970s. In California, for instance, TIF popularity rose in reaction to the passage of Proposition 13, which set a ceiling on local property taxes (Klacik and Nunn 2001).

In the late 1970s and 1980s, TIF became an increasingly attractive redevelopment technique as federal funding for urban renewal projects and other public-financing opportunities dried up (Klacik and Nunn 2001).[4] Since the Reagan administration, cuts to federal spending for local programs have prompted state and local governments to search for alternative sources of local revenue to fund economic development strategies.

Widening inequality gaps between municipalities have been another, complicating part of TIF's history, particularly gaps in the revenue municipalities received and in the capacity for making investments in public infrastructure to support local economic development activity. Those gaps continue to widen as some municipalities struggle to meet the increasing needs of low-income residents in the face of shrinking economic activity. In municipalities where expenses are rising and revenue is dwindling, efficiency often wins out over equity: the ease of diverting existing funds to targeted private investment wins out over the equity concerns such as the reduction in resources from municipal institutions like schools. As a result, TIF now funds sports stadiums, golf courses, shopping malls, and mixed-use commercial retail and office projects—projects typically not focused on equity concerns (Weber and O'Neill-Kohl 2013).

TIF Critiques

Despite the tool's broad appeal, TIF is not without its detractors. Criticism has touched upon many aspects of TIF's use and the associated outcomes. Particularly noteworthy are criticisms that have focused on process issues, such as lack of transparency and accountability, as well as on outcome challenges like the disconnect between project impacts and public goals. For example, the public seldom has the opportunity to comment on the financing aspects of TIF projects. Public input is generally sought at the end of the project planning phase, and those solicitations focus on the physical aspects of the site plan. Moreover, the TIF process lacks accountability when a project fails to generate promised benefits. Although reporting during the project assists localities in accounting for project expenditures per job created, follow-up reporting on project goals and forecasted growth outcomes is rare. The lack of transparency and accountability fosters public distrust in the process (U.S. PIRG Education Fund 2011). Detractors have also expressed substantial concerns about mismatched revenue streams, resident displacement, and lack of public awareness concerning the tool (U.S. PIRG Education Fund 2011; Weber 2010; Tomme 2005; Dye, Merriman, and Goulde 2014; LeRoy 2008).

Additional critiques call into question the reallocation of resources for TIF projects (Weber, Bhatta, and Merriman 2007; Lester 2014; Lefcoe 2011). If the underlying purpose of economic development is to achieve equitable economic growth in a market or local economy and the purpose of incentive-based economic development programs like TIF is to correct local market failure, thereby stimulating a more equitable economic growth, TIF *can* stimulate private investments that increase the value of the district's tax base, but new revenues do not flow to the municipality or to any of the other overlapping jurisdictions (e.g., school districts and counties that share in the property tax base) until after the designated project period ends. Rather, the new revenues are used to pay off the debt or to invest in further improvements for the district, and the capture of revenue may continue for as long as 30 years (Weber 2010).

The capacity question—whether a municipality can afford to divert limited resources for development for an extended period of time—is a key consideration for cash-strapped communities. The potential costs of reallocation call into question the benefits of TIF and its effects on overall growth within the community.

Opposition has also come from property owners within proposed TIF districts. Existing stakeholders become increasingly burdened as improvements are completed, property values increase, and gentrification pressures grow. To be sure, the investment is generally welcomed in neglected neighborhoods, but little attention is paid during the development process to potential displacement of the economically disadvantaged. As Weber, Bhatta, and Merriman (2007) point out, mixed-use TIF districts are likely to increase surrounding housing values, but those increases also threaten the tenure of low-income (often longtime) residents. Residents priced out of the area's emerging economy lose the chance to participate in the positive changes effected by development.

Finally, the literature has questioned whether TIF is as effective as traditional economic development strategies. A study of TIF use in the Chicago metropolitan area found that municipalities adopting TIF grew more slowly after adoption than those that did not adopt it (Dye and Merriman 2000). Between the years 1980 and 1984, all municipalities that would later adopt TIF had a mean growth rate that was roughly equal to those of municipalities that did not adopt TIF. And between the years 1992 and 1995, the growth rate was substantially lower among TIF communities than among municipalities that did not adopt TIF. In particular, municipalities that adopted TIF saw employment and revenue growth in TIF districts, but growth remained flat in both categories for the rest of the community. The findings suggest that TIF may stimulate growth within the TIF district but that lower growth often results elsewhere in the community.

The Case of TIF in St. Louis County

Missouri often stands out as a prominent TIF state because of the prevalence of the tool's use. The state's TIF law provides flexibility and broad authority to capture multiple tax streams.[5] These attributes make TIF a popular option for supporting development around the state (Mason and Thomas 2010). In fact, Missouri's statute permits communities using TIF to capture economic activity taxes (e.g., sales tax) in addition to traditional property and utility taxes. Thus, the tool provides a large potential pool from which to fund project costs. The ability to capture sales tax revenue can generate retail opportunity as well as considerable competition among municipalities for retail dollars. Some argue that this ability distorts the market for retail jobs and leads to increasingly unsustainable outcomes (e.g., Luce 2003).

St. Louis County is located immediately to the west of the city of St. Louis and is one of the largest TIF users in the St. Louis metro. As of 2012, St. Louis

County's commitment to TIF projects (that for the county and municipalities combined) was approximately $1.05 billion. That sum amounted to more than 43 percent of the TIF-related tax commitments in the St. Louis region (East-West Gateway Council of Governments 2012). In a 2012 review of St. Louis County TIF activity, the regional council of governments reported that TIF-using jurisdictions added an additional $73.8 million between 2010 and 2012 (East-West Gateway Council of Governments 2012). This level of local public investment has drawn attention to TIF's role in promoting economic development within St. Louis County and throughout the region. It also has prompted questions about whether the tool remedies the situations it was originally designed to address.

Supporters over the years have argued that TIF projects preempt blight, allowing project areas and their communities to stay one step ahead of the market (City of Richmond Heights 2003). Others claim that the tool has created a retail shell-game in which sales receipts simply move around the region (e.g., Gordon 2008). For example, a neighboring municipality might try to attract an existing big-box retailer with TIF incentives in an effort to capture their existing revenue and jobs, resulting in a net zero gain for the region and a net negative impact on the affected residents. A 2009 study suggested that the claim is not unfounded. The East-West Gateway Council of Governments (2009) examined TIF use across the St. Louis region, finding that its use in St. Louis County has been characterized by an overdependence on retail. Single-use retail was the most common type of TIF project, accounting for 55 percent of all TIF projects in the county (East-West Gateway Council of Governments 2009). The Council also found that this overreliance has widened the inequality gap among municipalities. Those communities with a solid tax base have the capacity to draw in new, often higher-end retail, while poorer municipalities struggle to attract any retail at all. What remains clear is that municipalities have few tools to support local economic development goals, and the paucity of alternatives often leads them to chase projects instead of establishing sound, long-term development plans (East-West Gateway Council of Governments 2012).

The case study involved an analysis of TIF use by the municipalities in St. Louis County. Because of TIF's popularity and the broad economic disparities across the county's municipalities, focus was placed on the relationship between use of the tool and patterns of distress. The indicators used for this analysis parallel the state's criteria for a blight designation. Those criteria are specified in the TIF-enabling statute. Of the 90 municipalities in St. Louis County, 42 have at least one TIF district. Most (55 percent, or 23) approved their first TIF project between 1995 and 2004. Among the remaining TIF-using communities, 14 percent (6) approved the first project between 1985 and 1994, and 31 percent approved their first project after 2005.

Most of the municipalities not engaged in TIF activity are sixth-tier cities, meaning that they are not typically organized as full-time municipalities. A full-time municipality has the capacity to hire a professional staff to manage the business of government (e.g., planning and zoning, economic development, and public works). Thus, these smaller communities are not commonly engaged in any kind of direct economic development activity. Among the remaining 42 TIF communities, most had launched their first TIF projects by 2004. The 2008 recession likely slowed later TIF activity.

To examine whether patterns of TIF use overlap with socioeconomic trends in the county, a distress index was constructed for an analysis of patterns of neighborhood decline.[6] As Figure 10.1 shows, TIF is used in some municipalities with moderate-to-severe levels of distress and in others with an average level of stability. These patterns support claims that TIF is being used both to preempt blight in stable areas and to fund large-scale reinvestment in distressed communities.

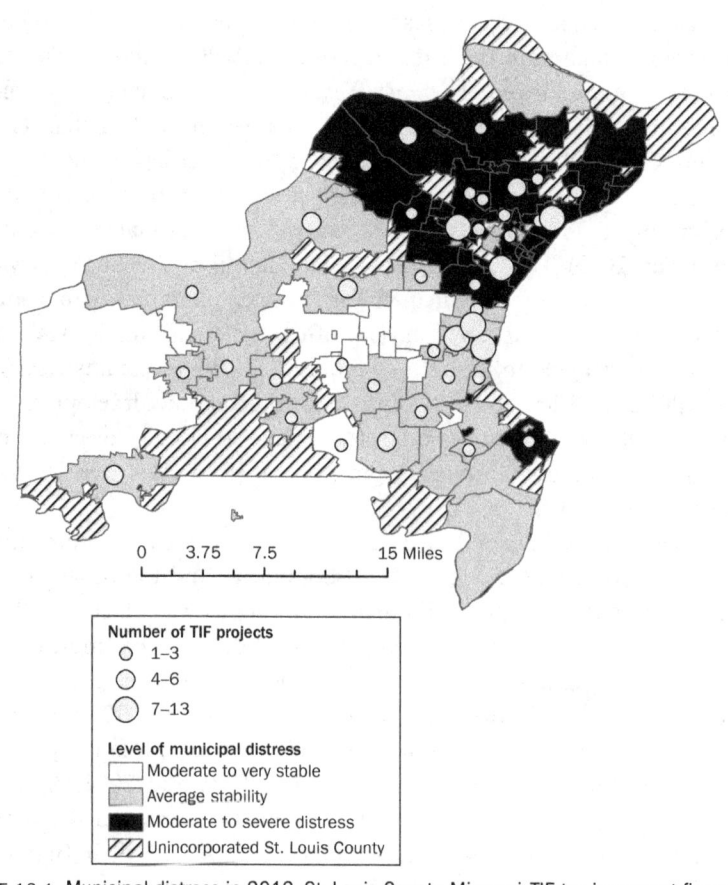

FIGURE 10.1 Municipal distress in 2012, St. Louis County, Missouri. TIF, tax increment financing.

There are good reasons to look at these patterns through a racial lens. The St. Louis region was thrust into the international spotlight after Michael Brown's death in Ferguson, Missouri (a city located on the north side of St. Louis County), and the region is now well known for its segregation. In the aftermath of the protests, surface issues revealed significant problems with the local criminal justice system, yet the underlying patterns of both racial and income separation tell an additional story, which suggests these structural inequalities are deeply rooted and widespread. The St. Louis region is marked by a set of historical spatial inequalities. The products of zoning, land-use patterns, and intentional policy choices, these inequalities remain unaddressed (Smith 2014; see Chapter 2, this volume). As Figure 10.2 illustrates, the racial separation is very apparent.[7] The racial divide occurs along the central corridor, with the

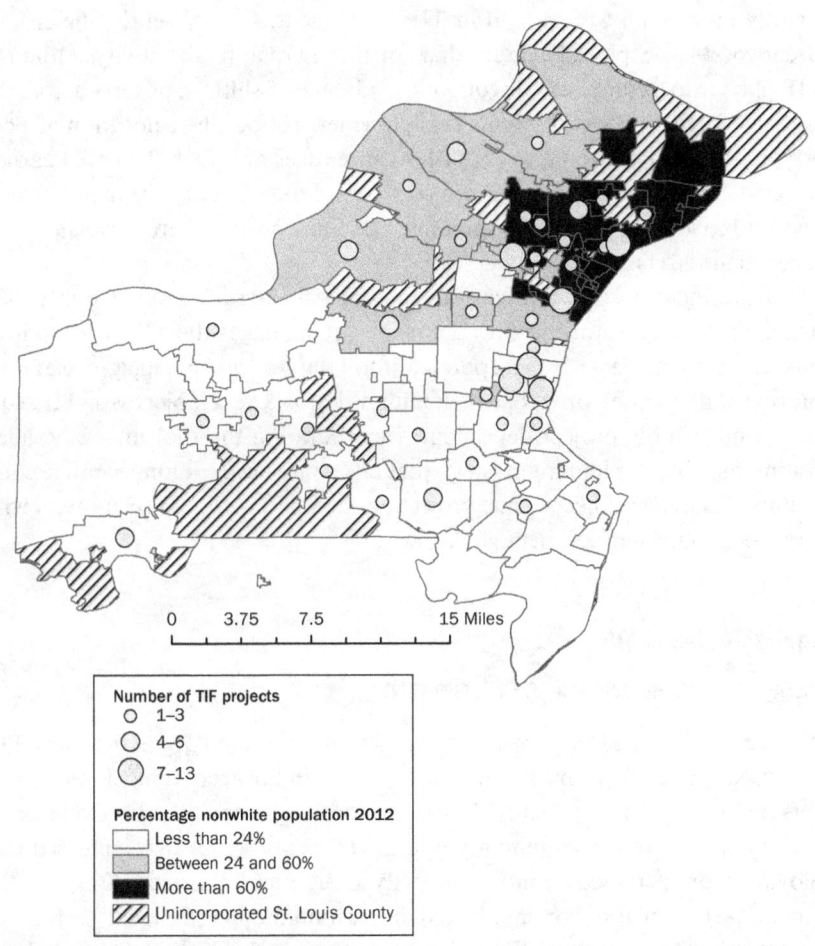

FIGURE 10.2 Percentage of nonwhites in population by municipality in 2012, St. Louis County, Missouri. TIF, tax increment financing.

highest concentrations of nonwhite residents living in Northside communities adjacent to the city of St. Louis.

The Ferguson crisis and the ensuing response have provided a backdrop for this discussion. The notable patterns in TIF investment observed in this analysis suggest that the tool is used in minority and nonminority municipalities alike but that the majority of TIF projects are located in majority-white areas. Likewise, some of the starkest economic contrasts line up through the central corridor of the county. The analysis shows that municipalities with poverty levels below the county mean are making TIF investments in excess of those by municipalities with poverty levels that exceed the county mean by 12 percent or more. The sharpest contrast can be seen between Brentwood, Missouri, and Jennings, Missouri. Brentwood is a wealthy community in the central corridor of the county. TIF investment there stands in excess of $90 million; Jennings, a northern suburb with a poverty level that exceeds the county average, has slightly more than $16 million in TIF investment. Consequently, the city of Brentwood has captured a larger share of the regional retail activity. Although TIF plays into a complicated economic landscape of shifts in poverty across the country, further policy questions begin to emerge about the colocation of poverty and racial isolation and about how incentives are used. As noted earlier, the evidence suggests that most projects in St. Louis County are retail focused and lead to jobs that generally offer low pay. Such positions are correlated with race (Artur 2011).

The kinds of spatial disparities presented in the St. Louis County case heighten the importance of how a community manages the TIF development process and whether it is incorporated into a larger, citizen-engaged planning process that focuses on broader community goals and objectives. TIF success is not simply project dependent. Incorporating the tool into a broader, community-based planning strategy that takes into account longer-range community visioning and economic projections can better align TIF projects with larger economic development goals.

Equitable Use of TIF

REDESIGNING ECONOMIC DEVELOPMENT

At its core, TIF is not the problem. In fact, one can even argue that how TIF gets used is not the problem. The challenge lies in how economic development gets defined by a municipality. Generally speaking, economic development is activity that increases community wealth. This can be through increased employment or increased economic activity (Leigh and Blakeley 2017). In the term's narrowest use, communities define economic development as revenue preservation (e.g., preservation of the tax base), whether that entails preservation of the retail tax base (as is the case with so many of the TIF projects in St. Louis County) or of property value (McLean and Voytek 1992). As a result, economic development programming that focuses on revenue preservation fails to account for those aspects of a community not directly engaged in economic activity. Improving the plight of poorer residents is seldom a motivation. Rather, it is measured as a consequence that must be addressed. Municipalities often have visioning documents that discuss broad themes for their economic development program, but these efforts typically lack an equity focus, instead basing their rationale on several flawed arguments. First, they often adhere to the narrow definition of development mentioned previously, a definition that focuses exclusively on tax base. Municipalities with such a focus ignore their ability to drive development of the sustainable job opportunities needed to draw an educationally diverse workforce. A second common flaw in municipal development plans is the tendency to rely on implementation by the private market. Inclusion often loses out when private markets drive public sector priorities. Municipalities require a diversity of economic development approaches that will lead to diverse and inclusive development, which in turn will lead to robust job opportunities for residents *and* strengthen the revenue base to support community growth into the future. For example, the city of Cleveland has developed an economic inclusion plan that links groups focused on issues such as small-business participation (especially by minorities and women), living wages, and localized production with supports to facilitate business creation and retention, outside investment, and workforce development. The focus on outcomes rather than on tools provides more flexibility in how development occurs. The focus is no longer on figuring out how to make the tool work for the project. The question becomes how well does the project fit the community? (City of Cleveland 2017).

TIF AS A TOOL THAT SUPPORTS INCLUSION

Given that TIF is intended to address a market failure across a broad spectrum of land uses, the tool is well positioned to support inclusion in several sectors of development. In particular, TIF has become a key means to broaden inclusion within a community's economic development program. Attaching "inclusionary zoning" requirements to residential TIF projects—requirements that a specific percentage of units be designated as affordable—is one way of accomplishing this goal. For instance, the city of Chicago passed an ordinance in 2007 that requires a 20 percent affordable housing set-aside as a condition of TIF support. In other words, a project that includes at least 10 units of housing and receives TIF support from the city must set aside 20 percent of the units as affordable for households earning at or below 100 percent of the area median income (AMI) if the housing is to be sold and 50–60 percent of AMI if it is to be rented (City of Chicago 2016). Alternatively, developers can elect to pay $100,000 per required unit to the city's Affordable Housing

Opportunity Fund (City of Chicago 2016). Policies like Chicago's Affordable Requirements Ordinance promote inclusion by embedding affordability within the TIF project.

Exploring how cities use TIF to preserve existing affordable housing and promote new development of such housing, a 2011 report outlined the innovative ways in which municipalities leverage public assets to support community goals (PeopleTrust 2011). In addition to Chicago, the authors point to efforts in cities like Portland, Oregon, and Austin, Texas. Housing set-aside programs in those cities target urban renewal areas in a way that can avoid potential gentrification effects. Several states have similar programs that require developers to include a range of affordability options if they are to receive TIF support. In Maine, the Affordable Housing Tax Increment Financing Program targets rental units, requiring developers to maintain affordability at 120 percent AMI for at least 30 years. In Minnesota, state statute requires developers seeking TIF support for housing to include some form of affordability in the project plan. This innovative approach staggers the set-aside requirements so that the number of units set aside as affordable increases with the intended percentage of AMI. For example, "20 percent of the units must be occupied by households at 50 percent or below AMI," but "40 percent of the units must be occupied by households at 60 percent [or] below AMI" (PeopleTrust 2011, 16). This provides some flexibility for the developer while also allowing a locality to meet affordability goals.

The program in Massachusetts goes even further. The state's Urban Center Housing Tax Increment Financing Program supports the development of affordable housing within commercial centers, encouraging infill projects that facilitate increased density. Municipalities adopting the program for a designated TIF zone are required to set aside 25 percent of the units as affordable to households with income at or below 80 percent of AMI (PeopleTrust 2011).

The case of St. Louis County suggests broader lessons for TIF use. While TIF is generally used to promote retail development, the county could direct those resources in a way that is more inclusive. For example, the community could link TIF use to broader inclusion goals to be outlined in a comprehensive plan. A developer would gain access to more generous incentives by incorporating those goals. The key would be to have a sound planning process in place that supports inclusion goals.

In the absence of meaningful reform at the federal level, local innovation is needed to support more inclusive approaches to development. If federal support programs begin to target larger-scale urban investment, TIF and similar kinds of development tools can become important leverage instruments that lead to a new wave of development programming, one that is inclusive and supports local government initiatives.

Despite TIF's remarkable flexibility and potential to promote more equitable outcomes, changes are needed to help state and local governments harness private market forces in a way that leads to a fairer distribution of resources. At the state level, performance priorities can be used to strengthen development activity's focus on equity. For example, states can require TIF projects to include performance targets for more and better quality affordable housing in areas of opportunity. States also can require more and greater income sharing among those districts (schools, public safety, parks) affected by local TIF projects. A broader revenue-sharing agreement could help offset negative development impacts so that these districts can maintain a consistent level of service quality. Most importantly, states can require projects to report more and better data, including downloadable spatial data, so that the information needed to track TIF performance is publicly accessible.

At the local level, communities can establish affordable housing performance requirements. These are typically paired with a bonus, such as an increased density allowance, a reduced parking allowance, or some other form of permitting allowance that is appealing to the developer. This leveraging is critical to accommodate the market demands associated with more equitable approaches to development. Yet while projects require the promise of profit for success, some sort of performance should be required before an incentive is awarded.

Among local governments, inclusionary zoning is becoming a broadly accepted tool for strategically and equitably implementing performance requirements. Typically developed as a part of a comprehensive planning process whereby community input establishes the zoning and development priorities, inclusionary zoning requires developers to set aside a certain portion of a project for low-income housing. In exchange, developers are promised incentives such as TIF and cost offsets, density bonuses, fee waivers, and relaxed site-plan requirements (e.g., requirements concerning parking and open space). The project is able to maintain acceptable profit margins in exchange for more and better affordable housing units per the targeted area. Such arrangements promote the development of mixed-income communities that provide more access to opportunity. In redevelopment areas, the requirement can include one-for-one replacement of affordable units or take the form of an overlay district,[8] a zoning modification tool that targets areas lacking in affordable housing options. If the regional housing market is not strong enough to support a one-for-one replacement of affordable units, then requirements can consider a predetermined target for the overall number of affordable units and allocate the project incentive proportionately. The key point is that these determinations should be made through a community-centered comprehensive planning process undertaken prior to the launch of the project. Ultimately, states and local governments can attract wanted investment while financing affordability through TIF.

Conclusion

At this writing, it is clear that we can no longer count on federal support for local investment priorities. The Trump administration's budgetary priorities suggest a commitment to severely slashing the very social programs designed to promote a more equitable approach to development. For example, the administration has proposed steep cuts in funding for the Department of Housing and Urban Development and has endorsed the elimination of the Community Development Block Grant Program. The stated reasoning suggests that state and local governments are in a better position to know how to meet the needs of residents (DelReal 2017). How state and local governments will be able to fill in these considerable budget gaps is yet to be determined. The proposals also cut deeply into areas that have no connection to local development or affordable housing production in the United States. State and local governments will need to rely almost exclusively on state and local development activity to support local needs and priorities.

Solving the puzzle of equitable development financing requires an acknowledgment that the neoliberal policies of past decades have perpetuated the inequality gap. A focus on free-market forces does not solve the economic challenges facing middle- and low-income households. When more people are able to participate in an improving economy, overall economic outcomes rise (Leigh and Blakeley 2017). When local governments leverage the private market to create balanced projects, performance requirements pay for themselves. Likewise, local governments that maintain commitments to transparency and local participation can increase community support and improve participation in the development process.

Notes

1. The term *blight* has many meanings and in urban policy circles has a particular, legislative definition. For the purposes of this chapter, blight refers to physical conditions that suggest limited real estate market potential in a neighborhood. Examples of such conditions include obsolete buildings and infrastructure, physical decay in structures, and other indicators that suggest socioeconomic decline (Gordon 2003).

2. Arizona is the only state with no state TIF legislation (Council of Development Finance Agencies 2017).

3. Approved project costs commonly include improvements to infrastructure such as streets and water/sewer systems. Private improvements to parking lots, landscaping, and buildings within a project area can also be included, as can associated administrative costs.

4. Over half of the states that have enacted TIF legislation did so between the years 1974 and 1979 (Kelmanski 1990).

5. Real Property Tax Increment Allocation Redevelopment Act, Mo. Rev. Stat. §§ 99.800–99.865 (2016).

6. A distress index was calculated using US Census data to develop a set of z-values for every municipality. The values were based on the county's mean value and standard deviation for each of seven indicators. The distress index represents the sum of each indicator's z-value, and scores were ranked by quartiles. For reporting purposes, I consider scores within the two quartiles below the mean to indicate very low and low levels of distress, respectively; scores within the two quartiles above the mean indicate moderate and severe levels, respectively. I do not report on communities whose scores are equal to the mean. The index was derived from two sets of indicators. The property use indicators included the percentage of housing units that were renter occupied, the percentage of housing units that were vacant, and the percentage of housing units that were built prior to 1950. The socioeconomic indicators included the percentage of households earning less than half of the median income for the St. Louis metropolitan area, the percentage of the population aged 25 years or over and who had less than a high school education, the percentage of households whose head was unemployed, and the percentage of female-headed households. Evidence indicates that these indicators are associated with neighborhood decline. For example, high levels of renter-occupied housing are predictive of neighborhood decline (Galster et al. 2003) and vacancy rates are an indicator of neighborhood stability (Wilson and Kelling 1982). Additional evidence has suggested that rates of poverty and female-headed households are positively correlated with neighborhood stress (Peake 1997; Wilson and Kelling 1982). The age of housing stock is another indicator of declining neighborhoods (Galster et al. 2003), and the Missouri TIF statue identifies housing stock aged 35 years or older as one of the criteria for determining applicability of TIF development efforts (Mo. Rev. Stat. § 99.805 (2016)). Information about TIF districts was collected by the St. Louis County Department of Planning. These data are reported annually to the Missouri Department of Economic Development.

7. A binary measure of racial groupings is used for Figure 10.2. An estimated 70 percent of St. Louis County's population was white in 2012 (down from 76 percent in 2008), and on average across municipalities within the county, nonwhites comprised 40 percent of the population. A similar measure was not developed for black persons because they make up the vast majority of nonwhite persons in St. Louis County; less than 5 percent of the county's population was neither white nor black in 2012. Areas with high relative proportions of nonwhite persons can generally be assumed to have high relative proportions of black persons. Given the racial makeup of St. Louis County, it is not practical to look at patterns of isolation for other racial groups.

8. An overlay district is a layer of land regulation that modifies existing zoning requirements to meet specified goals for a district. Common uses focus on the preservation of historic character or the promotion of sustainable development practices. Application to affordable housing is a more recent use of the tool.

References

Artur, David. 2011. "The Polarization of Job Opportunities in the U.S. Labor Market: Implications for Employment and Earnings." *Community Investments* 23 (2): 11–16, 40–41.

Briffault, Richard. 2010. "The Most Popular Tool: Tax Increment Financing and the Political Economy of Local Government." *University of Chicago Law Review* 77 (1): 65–95.

City of Chicago. 2016. "Affordable Requirements Ordinance." Accessed April 19, 2016. http://www.cityofchicago.org/city/en/depts/dcd/supp_info/affordable_housingrequirementsordinance.html.

City of Cleveland. 2017. "Economic Inclusion Plan." Accessed November 13, 2017. http://www.rethinkcleveland.org/About-Us/Our-Initiatives/Economic-Inclusion/Economic-Inclusion-Plan.aspx.

City of Richmond Heights, MO. 2003. Minutes of the March 3 city council meeting. Accessed May 15, 2005. http://www.richmondheights.org/RichmondMinutes/6265/images/4-21-03%20council%20minutes.pdf.

Clarke, Susan E., and Gary L. Gaile. 1992. "The Next Wave: Postfederal Local Economic Development Strategies." *Economic Development Quarterly* 6 (2): 187–98. doi:10.1177/089124249200600207.

Council of Development Finance Agencies. 2017. "CDFA Spotlight: Understanding Tax Increment Financing." Accessed April 20, 2017. https://www.cdfa.net/cdfa/cdfaweb.nsf/ordredirect.html?open&id=understandingtif.html.

DelReal, Jose A. 2017. "Trump Budget Asks for $6 Billion in HUD Cuts, Drops Development Grants." *Washington Post*, March 16. https://www.washingtonpost.com/politics/trump-budget-asks-for-6-billion-in-hud-cuts-drops-development-grants/2017/03/15/1b157338-09a0-11e7-b77c-0047d15a24e0_story.html?utm_term=.462202a0a0ff.

Dye, Richard F., and David F. Merriman. 2000. "The Effects of Tax Increment Financing on Economic Development." *Journal of Urban Economics* 47 (2): 306–28. doi:10.1006/juec.1999.2149.

Dye, Richard F., David F. Merriman, and Katherine Goulde. 2014. "Tax Increment Financing and the Great Recession." *National Tax Journal* 67 (3): 697–718. doi:10.17310/ntj.2014.3.08.

East-West Gateway Council of Governments. 2009. *An Assessment of the Effectiveness and Fiscal Impacts of the Use of Local Development Incentives in the St. Louis Region: Interim Report*. St. Louis, MO: East-West Gateway Council of Governments. http://www.ewgateway.org/wp-content/uploads/2017/08/TIFInterimRpt.pdf.

East-West Gateway Council of Governments. 2012. "The Use of Development Incentives in the St. Louis Region—Update August 2012." St. Louis, MO: East-West Gateway Council of Governments. https://www.ewgateway.org/wp-content/uploads/2017/08/DevIncentivesRpt.pdf.

Galster, George C., Roberto G. Quercia, Alvaro Cortes, and Ron Malega. 2003. "The Fortunes of Poor Neighborhoods." *Urban Affairs Review* 39 (2): 205–27. doi:10.1177/1078087403254493.

Gordon, Colin. 2003. "Blighting the Way: Urban Renewal, Economic Development, and the Elusive Definition of Blight." *Fordham Urban Law Journal* 31 (2): 305–37.

Gordon, Colin. 2008. *Mapping Decline: St. Louis and the Fate of the American City*. Philadelphia: University of Pennsylvania Press.

Greenbaum, Robert T., and Jim Landers. 2014. "The Tiff over TIF: A Review of the Literature Examining the Effectiveness of the Tax Increment Financing." *National Tax Journal* 67 (3): 655–74. doi:10.17310/ntj.2014.3.06.

Johnson, Craig L. 1999. "Tax Increment Debt Finance: An Analysis of the Mainstreaming of a Fringe Sector." *Public Budgeting and Finance* 19 (1): 47–67. doi:10.1046/j.0275-1100.1999.01156.x.

Kelmanski, J. S. 1990. "Using Tax Increment Financing for Urban Redevelopment Projects." *Economic Development Quarterly* 4 (1): 23–28. doi:10.1177/089124249000400103.

Klacik, J. Drew, and Samuel Nunn. 2001. "A Primer on Tax Increment Financing." In *Tax Increment Financing and Economic Development: Uses, Structures, and Impact*, edited by Craig L. Johnson and Joyce Y. Man, 15–29. Albany: State University of New York Press.

Kriz, Kenneth A. 2001. "The Effect of Tax Increment Finance on Local Government Financial Condition." *Municipal Finance Journal* 22 (1): 41–64.

Lefcoe, George. 2011 "Competing for the Next Hundred Million Americans: The Uses and Abuses of Tax Increment Financing." *The Urban Lawyer* 43 (2): 427–82.

Leigh, Nancy Green, and Edward J. Blakely. 2017. *Planning Local Economic Development: Theory and Practice*. 6th ed. Thousand Oaks, CA: Sage.

LeRoy, Greg. 2008. "TIF, Greenfields, and Sprawl: How an Incentive Created to Alleviate Slums Has Come to Subsidize Upscale Malls and New Urbanist Developments." *Planning and Environmental Law* 60 (2): 3–11. doi:10.1080/15480750802202991.

Lester, T. William. 2014. "Does Chicago's Tax Increment Financing (TIF) Programme Pass the 'But-for' Test? Job Creation and Economic Development Impacts Using Time-Series Data." *Urban Studies* 51 (4): 655–74. doi:10.1177/0042098013492228.

Luce, Thomas. 2003. "Reclaiming the Intent: Tax Increment Finance in Kansas City and St. Louis Metropolitan Areas." Discussion paper. Washington, DC: Brookings Institution Center on Urban and Metropolitan Policy.

Mason, Susan, and Kenneth P. Thomas. 2010. "Tax Increment Financing in Missouri: An Analysis of Determinants, Competitive Dynamics, Equity, and Path Dependency." *Economic Development Quarterly* 24 (2): 169–79. doi:10.1177/0891242409358080.

McLean, Mary L., and Kenneth P. Voytek. 1992. *Understanding Your Economy: Using Analysis to Guide Local Strategic Planning*. Chicago, IL: Planners Press.

Peake, Linda J. 1997. "Toward a Social Geography of the City: Race and Dimensions of Urban Poverty in Women's Lives." *Journal of Urban Affairs* 19 (3): 335–61. doi:10.1111/j.1467-9906.1997.tb00501.x.

PeopleTrust. 2011. *Tax Increment Financing Case Studies: How Cities and States Use Tax Increment Financing to Develop and Preserve Affordable Housing in Their Communities*. Report, February. Austin, TX: PeopleTrust.

Sagalyn, Lynn B. 1990. "Explaining the Improbable: Local Redevelopment in the Wake of Federal Cutbacks." *Journal of the American Planning Association* 56 (4): 429–41. doi:10.1080/01944369008975447.

Smith, Jeff. 2014. *Ferguson in Black and White*. Kindle Single. Seattle, WA: Amazon Digital Services. https://www.amazon.com/kindle/dp/B00PZCM3HQ/ref=rdr_kindle_ext_eos_detail.

Squires, Graham, and Norman Hutchinson. 2014. "The Death and Life of Tax Increment Financing (TIF): Redevelopment Lessons in Affordable Housing and Implementation." *Property Management* 32(1): 368–77.

Tomme, Alyson. 2005. "Tax Increment Financing: Public Use or Private Abuse?" *Minnesota Law Review* 90 (1): 213–35.

U.S. PIRG [Public Interest Research Group] Education Fund. 2011. *Tax-Increment Financing: The Need for Increased Transparency and Accountability in Local Economic Development Subsidies*. Report. Washington, DC: U.S. PIRG Education Fund. http://www.uspirg.org/sites/pirg/files/reports/Tax-Increment-Financing.pdf.

Weber, Rachel. 2003. "Can Tax Increment Financing (TIF) Reverse Urban Decline?" Working paper WP03RW1. Cambridge, MA: Lincoln Institute for Land Policy.

Weber, Rachel. 2010. "Selling City Futures: The Financialization of Urban Redevelopment Policy." *Economic Geography* 86 (3): 251–74. doi:10.1111/j.1944-8287.2010.01077.x.

Weber, Rachel, Saurav Dev Bhatta, and David Merriman. 2007. "Spillovers from Tax Increment Financing Districts: Implications for Housing Price Appreciation." *Regional Science and Urban Economics* 37 (2): 259–81. doi:10.1016/j.regsciurbeco.2006.11.003.

Weber, Rachel, and Sara O'Neill-Kohl. 2013. "The Historical Roots of Tax Increment Financing, or How Real Estate Consultants Kept Urban Renewal Alive." *Economic Development Quarterly* 27 (3): 193–207. doi:10.1177/089124241348701

Wilson, James Q., and George L. Kelling. 1982. "Broken Windows: The Police and Neighborhood Safety." *Atlantic*, March, 29–38.

11

Beyond Education Triage
BUILDING BRAIN REGIMES IN METROPOLITAN AMERICA
William F. Tate IV

The Brain and Learning

Historically, the aims of public education in the United States have varied. It has been seen as a great equalizer, a path to a literate citizenry, a science and technology pipeline, a venue for morality formation, and a vehicle for patriotism indoctrination (Fuhrman and Lazerson 2005). Despite the changes over time in public education's stated aims, schools and the education system have played a consistent role as interventions for the brain and mind. An important role for families, educational institutions, and other supportive agencies is to nurture the brain and mind from the prenatal stage to late adolescence. Learning in schools involves changes to the brain, including neuronal growth processes (Bransford, Brown, and Cocking 1999). Neuroscience research confirms the significant role that social context plays in the development of the structure of the mind by modifying the structures of the brain (National Research Council and Institute of Medicine 2000). Brain development is context dependent and not solely a formation of predetermined pathways.

Neuroscientists hypothesize that brain development is negatively altered by the environmental conditions associated with poverty (Farah et al. 2006). Economic disadvantage contributes to the overrepresentation of Blacks and Hispanics in toxic residential neighborhoods that lead to exposure to psychological stressors, including crime, violence, material deprivation, joblessness, underemployment, and family conflict (Williams and Purdue-Vaughns 2016). In fact, poverty is tied to numerous disparities, including disparities in school readiness and academic performance. A growing number of researchers have sought to understand the brain mechanisms underlying the influence of poverty on children's learning and achievement. Nicole Hair and colleagues (2015) examined child poverty's relationships with the brain development and academic achievement of children and adolescents aged 4 to 22. Their findings linked poverty to structural differences in several areas of the brain associated with school readiness skills. Poverty's greatest influence was detected among children from the poorest households. In the brains of children with household income below 150 percent of the federal poverty level, regional gray matter volumes were 3 to 4 percentage points below the developmental norm. A larger difference of 8 to 10 percentage points was observed for children with household incomes below the federal poverty level. Differences in brain development were consequential. On average, children living in low-income households scored 4 to 7 points lower on standardized examinations. Maturational lags in the frontal and temporal lobes explained up to 20 percent of the gap in test scores. The import of these influences is expressed in the opening lines of an editorial by Joan Luby (2015, E1): "Because the brain is the organ from which all cognition and emotion originates, healthy human brain development represents the foundation of our civilization. Accordingly, there is perhaps nothing more important that a society must do than foster and protect the brain development of our children."

In the United States, public education is one of our primary brain and mind interventions. By law and folkway, geographically constructed political boundaries determine its distribution. These constructions shape opportunity to learn in metropolitan America, where class and race are powerful predictors of school quality (Tate 2008). Public education, as a brain development strategy, has been and continues to be subject to the legacy of segregation in the United States. Going forward, it will be subject to emerging demographic trends related to metropolitan segregation, school segregation, and school composition.

Metropolitan Segregation

In 1935, W. E. B. DuBois stated: "The Negro needs neither segregated schools nor mixed schools. What he needs is Education. What he must remember is that there is no magic, either in mixed schools or in segregated schools" (335). His insightful remark remains relevant today in light of residential-segregation trends, school district segregation, school composition configurations, and within-school segregation patterns. In the metropolitan ecology of the United States, segregation is, metaphorically speaking, hardwired.

METROPOLITAN RESIDENTIAL SEGREGATION

In the last two decades of the twentieth century, the population of the United States grew by 62 million people (Reardon, Yun, and Chmielewski 2012). Nearly all of this growth occurred in metropolitan areas, and particularly in suburbia. However, the growth was modest in the central cities. Racial composition of metropolitan regions also changed during this time frame. The White metropolitan population increased by over 18 million while the nonwhite metropolitan population grew by 42 million. Whites dropped from 78 percent to 65 percent of the metropolitan population and from 87 percent to 74 percent of the suburban population. In contrast, Black, Hispanic, and Asian populations in metropolitan areas grew by 45, 166, 245 percent, respectively. Most of this growth occurred in the suburbs, with White, Black, Hispanic, and Asian population increases by 24, 104, 229, and 297 percent, respectively.

Despite the demographic change and the passing of four decades since the Fair Housing Act was enacted, the United States continues to experience high levels of racial residential segregation. That segregation has been documented in numerous studies (e.g., Galster 2012; Massey and Denton 1993). William Frey (n.d.) used data from the 2010 census to estimate that the nation's 70 largest metropolitan regions had a score of 50 or higher on the Black–White segregation index.[1] He also reported a score of 50 or higher on the Hispanic–White segregation index for the 24 largest metropolitan regions in the country. By both metrics, the nation's largest metropolitan regions remain segregated.

Residential mobility has not been a solution to residential segregation. In a study of Chicago, Robert Sampson (2012) found that the greater the similarity between the demographic compositions of two neighborhoods, the higher the likelihood that they were connected through residential exchange: mobility reinforced racially segregated residential patterns. Similarly, Kyle Crowder, Jeremy Pais, and Scott South (2012) studied the mobility patterns of Black and White families in 289 metropolitan regions across the country, reporting that families tend to move to other places where members of their race or ethnicity constitute a majority of the population.

Evidence also suggests that residential mobility does not foster greater educational opportunity at scale. Molly Metzger and colleagues (2015) conducted analyses that controlled for major predictors of housing mobility, finding that students experiencing at least one residential move over the period of a year sustained an estimated 50 percent decrease in the likelihood of earning a high school diploma by age 25. In a related study, Brett Theodos, Claudia Coulton, and Amos Budde (2014) examined the dynamic interplay among residential mobility, school mobility, and educational opportunity in 10 low-income neighborhoods. Despite high levels of mobility, children transferring schools in the study did not, on average, enter higher-ranked schools. On the rare occasion when a child upgraded to a better school, the transition was associated with an advantageous residential move.

Too few highly mobile families are upgrading their residential status to improve educational opportunity, and residential mobility is associated with lower educational attainment. Metropolitan regions in the United States are segregated, and for purposes of educational policy, there is no reason to develop school-reform strategies assuming that this part of the ecology will change in the near term.

SCHOOL DISTRICT SEGREGATION

In their analysis of the *Brown v. Board of Education* decision at its 60th anniversary, Gary Orfield and Erica Frankenberg (2014) reported on enrollment trends in the nation's schools between 1968 and 2011. In the years since the decision, White enrollment declined by 28 percent, Black enrollment increased by 19 percent, and Latino enrollment soared by 495 percent. In 1968, White enrollment was nearly four times greater than the combined Black and Latino enrollment, but it was only a fifth greater than the combined enrollment in 2011. Orfield and Frankenberg (2014) argued that, if it were feasible to create a perfectly even distribution of students from all racial groups, contact with White students would decline among students of all races because Whites represent a declining share of the total.

Yet, it should not be surprising that rapid suburbanization has not changed school district–level segregation patterns in metropolitan America. The demographic shifts in enrollment trends are coupled with a consistent finding: segregation along racial and ethnic lines has remained fairly constant (Wells et al. 2012). In an analysis of 337 metropolitan areas with at least two districts serving primarily suburban students, Sean Reardon, John Yun, and Anna Chmielewski (2012) found that minority suburbanization led to increased segregation of Black, Hispanic, and Asian students from White students. A second finding has policy implications: "Racial segregation does not appear to change much in response to socioeconomic segregation patterns. That is, socioeconomic segregation does not appear to serve as a strong proxy for racial segregation. This finding, if supported in other empirical research, casts doubt on the hope that race-neutral strategies (whether housing policies or student assignment policies) can be effective in producing substantial racial desegregation as an inevitable result" (Reardon, Yun, and Chmielewski 2012, 101).

SCHOOL COMPOSITION EFFECTS

In light of the persistent racial segregation in metropolitan America, it is important to ask: How does the persistence of racial segregation in metropolitan America influence the composition of student populations in schools? Further, does school composition affect the development of children and youth? Past research suggests possible answers. A preponderance of social science evidence indicates that racially diverse schools are positively associated with achievement in math, reading, and science, as well as with school completion, critical thinking, and academic engagement of pupils across racial groups (Berands and Penaloza 2010; Borman et al. 2004; Guryan 2004; Hogrebe and Tate 2010).

For example, Mark Berands and Roberto Penaloza's (2010) examination of the relationship between racial isolation and mathematics achievement revealed that, from 1972 to 2004, increases in school segregation corresponded to significant increases in the Latino–White and Black–White test score gaps. School segregation's effects outweighed the positive changes in family background measures for the nonwhite demographic groups. Jonathan Guryan's (2004) analysis of data from the 1970 and 1980 censuses suggested that desegregation plans of the 1970s reduced Black high school dropout rates by 2 to 3 percentage points during the decade. The results were more robust in school districts that had large declines in racial segregation.

A substantial literature indicates that a school's racial composition has direct and independent effects on its students' performance and opportunity to learn (Mickelson 2008). It is tempting to argue for policies that would foster greater racial heterogeneity in the school context. For example, Gerald Grant's (2009) study of metropolitan Raleigh, North Carolina, indicated that improved education outcomes resulted from school district mergers. The school district in the city of Raleigh, which has many areas of concentrated poverty and racial isolation, merged with the more affluent district in Wake County. The study suggested that socioeconomic integration effectively reduced the departure rate of Whites from public education. Racial achievement gaps also narrowed. However, mergers are challenging political endeavors, and the one in the Raleigh area was a tenuous political arrangement ultimately reversed by affluent suburban leadership. Political dynamics aside, the scope and scale of metropolitan mergers required to effect school reform would be nothing short of monumental.

Another strategy to change the racial composition of school districts is to alter school attendance zones. Meredith Richards (2014) examined 15,290 attendance zones in 663 school districts to estimate the effect of attendance-zone gerrymandering on school diversity. The results indicated that such gerrymandering typically increased segregation in attendance-zone districts experiencing rapid racial or ethnic change. This finding is important in light of rapid population shifts in the United States. However, attendance-zone gerrymandering had relatively minor effects on Black–White and Hispanic–White segregation as compared to its effects on segregation between nonwhite groups and on segregation between Whites and Asians. The relatively minor effect on Black–White segregation was likely a product of population distribution: shifting attendance boundaries within a district had little effect on Black–White segregation because much of that segregation occurred along district boundaries rather than within districts. Gerrymandering was associated with reductions in segregation in a significant minority of districts. Most of these districts were under court-ordered desegregation plans, but such plans are expiring and have a very narrow legal foundation. Thus, this legal mechanism is not an option.

Other research suggests that there are fewer opportunities for students of color in racially heterogeneous schools because White students, by way of custom, policy, and practice, are positioned to hoard the best teachers, academic programs, and supports (Darling-Hammond 2010; Ladson-Billings 2006; Lewis and Diamond 2015; Mickelson 2015; Stiff, Johnson, and Akos 2011). The racialized nature of metropolitan housing patterns and the limited effects of mobility on segregation represent formidable barriers to school opportunity. Coupled with the evidence from the school composition literature, racial isolation remains important in discussions of opportunity to learn. However, studies of intraschool racial disparities suggest that Du Bois was prophetic in calling for quality schools rather than integrated ones. The challenge is how to improve school quality.

Triage Regime

Scholars have argued for decades that viewing education reform only in terms of altering classrooms and schools would result in predictable failure (Gordon 1970; Sarason 1990). For example, Seymour Sarason (1990, 43–44) offered the following remark:

> What is there about school systems that prevents them from recognizing a problem before it reaches epidemic proportions? In other words, what is there about a school system that renders it virtually incapable of adopting a preventive stance? I offer the hypothesis that by organization, ideology, and knowledge, school personnel accept the responsibility to deal with the problems of *individuals*. They may not like it, they may feel adequate or inadequate, but they try to deal with the problems of individual children. They feel they have to. . . . This may seem obvious, but precisely because it is so obvious—so right, natural, and proper—we too often fail to ask what the schools are doing to prevent these problems. (Italics in original)

Schools are organized to deal with the short-term problems of individual children. In this era of high-stakes testing and accountability models, there is tremendous pressure to sort schools, classrooms, and students on the basis of their performance on accountability metrics. Thus, education is organized today in a fashion similar to medical triage. Ian Robertson-Steel (2006) described the history of the word *triage*. It is derived from the French word *trier*, which the surgeon-in-chief of Napoleon's Imperial Guard applied in 1792 to the process of sorting the casualties of warfare. The original concepts of triage—the sorting of casualties based on their immediate need for medical care and on their chances of benefitting from the care—remain intact today. Triage is very often applied when limited medical resources must be assigned to optimize the number of survivors. In this chapter, the metaphor of "triage" is used in reference both to students tracked within schools and to schools sorted within high-stakes accountability systems. David Gillborn (2001, 5–6) describes the relationship between medical triage and high-stakes educational reform:

> Some people have such severe injuries that, given the constraints of the situation (where there are insufficient resources to meet all needs) they are judged unlikely to survive even with additional attention: they may receive painkillers but they are not rushed into the operating theatre. In effect, they are allowed to die. These decisions would be unthinkable under normal circumstances, but are made in response to a prioritisation of need in relation to current circumstances and finite resources. . . . Comparable decisions are now being made by teachers as they try to ensure their school's survival within the educational market place. The extraordinary demands of successive reforms, for year-on-year improvements . . . are such that schools are seeking new ways of identifying *suitable cases for treatment*, i.e. pupils who will show the maximum return (in terms of the benchmark) from receipt of additional resources of teacher time and support.

Kendall Paine (2015) reported that schools evaluated on the basis of proficiency categories in statewide tests used these data to track students into green, yellow, and red categories. They then channeled resources toward the yellow group as a strategy to raise the overall percentage of students deemed proficient. Jennifer Booher-Jennings (2005) described a similar triage effort in Texas schools.

Diverting resources away from proficient students or from students viewed as "lost causes" is not fair, and it is antithetical to evidence-based good practice (Cohen, Raudenbush, and Ball 2003; Raudenbush 2012). Educational triage imposes a ceiling above talented students by limiting their access to cognitively demanding experiences. And it simultaneously relegates students in need of greater developmental supports to the mundane world of stopgap strategies focused on filling time rather than building the conceptual bridges required to learn the tested curriculum.

Accountability and high-stakes testing exert additional pressures to adopt triage strategies, and those pressures shape decisions beyond the choices reflected in the behavior of school officials working directly with students. The pressures and consequences of poor school-level performance have been associated with changes in the foundational relationship between the state and school districts. Specifically, metropolitan communities with poor-performing schools have turned to chartering policies as ways to support improvement in school quality and related academic outcomes. Charter schools are public schools granted permission by way of contract with an authorizing agency to provide instruction and other education-related services. The charter is a contract that allows the school to operate in an autonomous fashion in pursuit of educational objectives. In theory, charter schools are subject to market forces such as student demand and demand for quality service. Market forces and chartering contracts align to position the authorizing authority to purge the system of charter schools that perform poorly. The pressure to improve students' assessment results year-to-year creates a quick-fix reform mindset. "Innovation" is triaging in the form of selective investment in charter schools that promote their ability to generate results in short order.

A growing body of research shows that charter schools have had decidedly mixed results. For example, a study published in 2015 by the Center for Research on Education Outcomes at Stanford University found wide variance in charter school performance. The study analyzed student-level data obtained from 41 urban areas in 22 states. The data were collected during the school years from 2006–7 through 2011–12. The outcomes of interest included academic advancement of a typical student in a charter school in 1 year's time, and the study compared that outcome with the same measure for a peer from a traditional public school in the same metropolitan area as the charter school. In aggregate, students enrolled in urban charter schools experienced greater advancement in math by a standard deviation of 0.055 and greater advancement in reading by a standard deviation of 0.039. The study also found that urban charter school students received the equivalent of 40 additional days of learning in math and 28 additional days of learning in reading. Moreover, the learning gains in both math and reading were significantly larger for Black, Hispanic, low-income, and special-education students in charter schools than for their respective counterparts in public schools. Despite identifying positive outcomes in the aggregate, the report indicated that there are urban communities in which the typical student from the matched public school outperformed the typical students from a majority of charter schools, with some charter students lagging behind in distressing fashion. In many urban areas, no charter school achieved better gains than the public school alternative and more than a majority of the charter schools were significantly worse. Other studies have generated similar findings (Lubienski and Lubienski 2013).

As part of the triage regime, it should come as no surprise that evidence suggests that charter schools do little to change the racial composition of school populations. Ron Zimmer and colleagues (2009) tracked charter movers in eight cities before and after they transitioned to a charter school. On average, transferring students moved to charter schools with racial compositions that did not differ dramatically from the compositions of the traditional public schools they left behind. Across cities, the likelihood that an African American student would move to a charter school was positively associated with the percentage of African American students at that school; African American students were more likely than White or Hispanic counterparts to move to a charter school in which members of the student's own race constituted a higher percentage of the student population. Other studies have found that charter school choice has a homogenizing effect on racial diversity; students of all races, most notably traditional racial minorities, leave more heterogeneous public schools to enroll in charter schools with students of the same race (Booker, Zimmer, and Buddin 2005; Garcia, Barber, and Molnar 2009).

The triage regime storyline has mixed results. The regime has narrowed curriculum implementation to the tested curriculum and fostered an unproductive set of educational practices focused on assessment outcomes. Emerging results suggest that the charter innovation is gaining some traction on the academic front. However, the segregative effects of charter schools remain a concern.

Academic Attainment: Intergenerational Investment

Triage strategies do little to address the intergenerational nature of academic attainment.[2] Multiple studies have identified three intertwined concepts related to the intergenerational nature of attainment, concluding that these concepts should be taken into consideration when one attempts to build effective strategies to accelerate the school performance of traditionally underserved groups (Chetty et al. 2014; Katznelson 2005; Miller 1995; Primus 2006; Shapiro 2004; Yeakey and Shepard 2012). All three concepts are relevant to residents of metropolitan communities:

1. Generally, academic achievement patterns among African American and Latino urban dwellers with low socioeconomic status (SES) reflect the fact that the variation in family resources plays a greater role than the variation in school resources (e.g., school funding and local revenue generation). Achievement and resource-allocation patterns indicate that most high-SES students receive several times more resources than most low-SES students do, and much of this resource gap is a function of family resources rather than school resources.
2. Within demographic groups, educational attainment is the result of an intergenerational process: education-related family resources are school resources that have accrued across multiple generations. On average, the current investments in metropolitan America's low-SES African American and Latino students—investments in the form of intergenerationally accrued, education-relevant family resources—are significantly less than comparable investments in White children.
3. Educational attainment is in large measure a function of the quality of the education-relevant opportunity structures of several generations. The pace of educational advancement over generations depends on the pace at which multiple generations of traditionally underresourced metropolitan families obtain resources linked to positive school outcomes.

Many underserved children living in segregated metropolitan regions experience two impactful resource disadvantages—school funding inequities and limited family resources. School funding formulas use local property taxes as part of the resource allocation model. Despite state and federal contributions to education funding, more affluent communities with excellent housing stock experience greater benefit relative to poor, segregated communities in some states (Baker and Corcoran 2012). Discriminatory housing practices that denied African American families access to homeownership or confined homeownership opportunities to specific communities, thereby hampering wealth accruement, represent a form of intergenerational theft in lost financial assets, school funding gaps, and limited access to quality education (Ladson-Billings 2006; Shapiro 2004). Disadvantage accrues across generations in urban communities with a history of segregation (Chetty et al. 2014).

The need for intervention to address intergenerational disadvantage is clear. The triage efforts in education are not aligned with the nature of the challenge. Moreover, the hardwired nature of segregation in metropolitan America suggests that integration strategies, even those that succeed in generating desired education effects, are politically infeasible. There is little evidence to suggest that the social solidarity, altruism, and trust across racial groups is sufficiently robust to change societal norms and values about metropolitan segregation. Putnam (2007) offered evidence from the Social Capital Community Benchmark Survey that indicates residents living in ethnically diverse neighborhoods reported lower trust levels, including with in-group members, than those reported by counterparts residing in ethnically homogenous neighborhoods; altruism and community cooperation were rarer, and friends fewer, in diverse communities. Putnam referred to this phenomenon as "hunkering down," and its effect on community cohesion is a challenge to civic engagement and collective action. There is no easy solution.

Regional Brain Regimes

Urban communities have a long history of building segregation regimes, industrial regimes, and sports regimes (Stone 1989). Regimes are public–private partnerships organized to attain a common goal. For years, these partnerships have engaged in practices and regulatory actions that have fostered residential segregation. There are countless examples of innovation and business clusters (telecommunications, biotechnology, and information technology clusters) developed through the support of regime politics. It is very common to observe regimes organized by communities for the purpose of recruiting or retaining a professional sports team. For example, in 2015, the St. Louis region proposed a plan with over $500 million in investments to retain a losing football team. It is ironic how much the region was willing to spend to retain an industry that destroys the brain.

In pursuit of their aims, regimes are able to generate significant financial resources, land agreements, and cooperation. Regional brain regimes are needed to address the intergenerational problems of low academic achievement and educational attainment in urban America. These regimes must extend beyond typical school district boundaries to include public–private partnerships and nonprofits. Their specific aims must be the prevention of injuries to the brain by way of social conditions as well as the protection and nurture of the brain through young adulthood. Box 11.1 describes examples of interventions, policies, and programs that might be included in such a regime. The intent is not to be exhaustive. Rather, the goal is to begin a process of framing. Local communities should use regional data to design their own brain regime targets.

The strategies included in Box 11.1 have the potential to address the intergenerational challenge of academic performance without being stifled by the realities of the segregation regimes that exist in metropolitan America. I only included strategies with an empirical base that suggests positive effects. Finally, all of the included brain-regime strategies take into consideration the developmental processes in a life-course perspective.

BOX 11.1
Brain Regime Strategies

Strategy Universal Prenatal Care

Goal Remove financial and nonfinancial barriers to prenatal care

Evidentiary Base Evidence indicates that low–birth weight children are at greater risk for cognitive and academic-performance problems than are their normal–birth weight peers, and that the risk for negative outcomes increases as birth weight decreases (Reichman 2005). A reflection of maternal educational attainment, prenatal care predicts a child's future educational opportunity and outcomes. Other research demonstrates that the relationship between low birth weight (less than 2,000 grams, or about 4.5 pounds) and cognitive performance persists through adolescence (Whitaker et al. 2006). The urban community has been especially challenged by low–birth weight trends.

Strategy Public Health Insurance

Goal Expand Medicaid in all states

Evidentiary Base Cohodes and colleagues (2016) found that the expansion of public health care in the form of Medicaid reduced high school dropout rates, increased college attendance, and improved the rate of college degrees earned. Under national healthcare reform, the states have an opportunity to expand Medicaid to provide health insurance for single parents who earn up to 138 percent of the federal poverty level, or about $25,000 for a family of three. Although the evidence suggests that Medicaid expansion should remain an important policy target for health and education reformers, attempts to expand Medicaid coverage have failed in many states.

Strategy Regional Preschool Clearinghouse

Goal Develop a publicly accessible repository of preschools where inclusion indicates that the preschool aligns with evidence-based practice

Box 11.1 (*Continued*)

Box 11.1 *(Continued)*

Evidentiary Base Despite an evidence-based framework to support family decision-making related to preschool placement, this important research has not been promoted or used in a fashion that is consistent with its importance (see, e.g., Hustedt et al. 2010; National Institute of Child Health and Human Development Early Child Care Research Network 2000). Typically, the period from birth to age 4 is one in which language, literacy development, and early mathematical understandings are central concerns. Language and literacy development are foundational readiness areas for overall school success. Regional dissemination of information related to preschool quality can inform parental/caregiver decision-making in support of this development.

Strategy African American Business Development

Goal Create incentives and supports for more African American–owned businesses in metropolitan America

Evidentiary Base Parker (2015) found that the presence of African American businesses contributed to the decline in Black youth violence in the 1990s but that the rate of paid employees in Black firms was unrelated to such violence. She argued that, beyond increasing Blacks on the payroll, Black firms provided role models, value changes, and social buffers.

Strategy Income and Employment of Nonresident Fathers

Goal Provide resources enabling poor men with low educational attainment to support their children

Evidentiary Base Primus (2006) describes local experiments that offer matching payments by the government to lower child support orders so that they are aligned with noncustodial parents' ability to pay.

Metropolitan communities across the United States are struggling with public education, segregation, and the creation of opportunity structures. Too many treat education as triage activity rather than viewing learning as a developmental process that requires organized and sustained intergenerational investment. There is hope, but constructive progress requires a new societal priority: protecting and nurturing the brain from conception to late adolescence. Our metropolitan regimes have fostered segregation and sports. Building brain regimes has the potential for significant advances in learning and life-course outcomes. Ultimately, if brain regimes are to be realized, metropolitan regions need to generate the regime practices and partnerships associated with the intense efforts to attract and retain professional sports teams and other industrial clusters. However, the need for a catalytic agent exists.

Urban Universities as Catalysts

In his 2003 work, Richard Levin (2003, 98) writes the following:

> On our campuses we are devoted to the full development of human potential, and we provide extraordinary support to facilitate such development

in our students and faculty. Outside our walls, many of our neighbors live in conditions that do not provide sufficient opportunity for the realization of their potential. To ensure the health of our democracy, we must help provide those without privilege access to such opportunity and the knowledge to make use of it.

Our responsibility as institutions of higher education thus transcends mere pragmatism. We must help our cities become what we hope our campuses are—places where human potential can be fully realized.

Levin's assessment and plea warrants a response. Urban universities have much to offer to the development of brain regimes. The corpus of knowledge related to understanding, nurturing, and protecting the brain embodies a major contribution of universities toward the advancement of society (Association of American Universities n.d.). However, there remains a need to better understand the relationship between segregation and brain development. Urban universities play key roles in communities experiencing segregation or its intergenerational effects. In addition to targeting community service engagements, they provide the institutional capacity and anchor for research and related civic problem-solving involving education, health, economic development, and environmental protection (Friedman, Perry, and Menendez 2014).

With respect to moving from the segregation regime to the brain regime, research-intensive urban universities are positioned to address many questions and problems that remain unanswered. A few examples of potential contributions include the following:

- Seek to describe the causal pathways through which segregation and impoverished family resources contribute to negative outcomes for individual students and to persistent inequalities across demographic groups in education and developmental outcomes (National Research Council and Institute of Medicine 2000).
- Examine segregation's relationships with its negative effects (e.g., chronic stress) and how brain insults (e.g., lead ingestion, nutrition) disrupt child and adolescent development.
- Investigate the quality, efficacy, and supply of preschool and childcare services.
- Study regional collaboration and partnerships in education, including interdistrict transfer policies.
- Design, develop, and evaluate urban, industrial clusters (e.g., biotechnology hubs) that embody best practices gleaned from research on mixed-income housing, walkable communities, and access to quality schools and healthcare (Tate 2008).
- Initiate collaborative studies that bridge the divides between the fields (e.g., education, brain sciences, sociology, policy studies, and

social work), especially cooperative efforts to better understand the mechanisms causing social disparities, to create intervention strategies, and to evaluate those strategies.

This list is not exhaustive. Moreover, every university offers distinct human capital with varying expertise. A sound strategy for starting is to build on the institutional strengths. For example, the UChicago Consortium on School Research offers technical evaluation studies of policies and programs in the Chicago public schools. The Civil Rights Project at the University of California, Los Angeles, conducts policy studies of local, state, and national issues, with the aim of eliminating disparities associated with segregation. However, there remains a space for other universities to further address the challenges of (1) integrating child development research, brain science, and genetics; (2) linking developmental science and applied science of child and adolescent interventions; (3) generating a learning science and learning analytics that are sufficiently robust to positively influence student outcomes; and (4) formulating policy and programming based on synthesis of discoveries (National Research Council and Institute of Medicine 2000).

It is very rare that universities generate and synthesize knowledge across disparate fields, with an aim to inform policy and practice. Rarer still is the effort to organize a university–community partnership focused on the protecting the brain from the adverse effects of racial segregation and concentrated poverty. Yet, the need is clear.

Notes

1. The segregation index measures the degree to which the minority group is distributed differently across the census tract. The scores range from 0 (completely integrated) to 100 (completely segregated), and the value indicates the percentage of the minority group that would have to move to be distributed exactly like Whites.

2. In this context, *intergenerational* refers to change in academic attainment occurring from one generation to the next.

References

Association of American Universities. n.d. "Researching the Brain, Seeking Cures." Accessed December 22, 2017. https://www.aau.edu/research/featured-research/researching-brain-seeking-cures.

Baker, Bruce D., and Sean P. Corcoran. 2012. *The Stealth Inequities of School Funding: How State and Local School Finance Systems Perpetuate Inequitable Student Spending*. Report. Washington, DC: Center for American Progress.

Berands, Mark, and Roberto V. Penaloza. 2010. "Increasing Racial Isolation and Test Score Gaps in Mathematics: A 30-Year Perspective." *Teachers College Record* 112 (4): 978–1007.

Booher-Jennings, Jennifer. 2005. "Below the Bubble: 'Educational Triage' and the Texas Accountability System." *American Educational Research Journal* 42 (2): 231–68. doi:10.3102/00028312042002231.

Booker, Kevin, Ron Zimmer, and Richard Buddin. 2005. "The Effects of Charter Schools on School Peer Composition." Working paper WR-306-EDU. Santa Monica, CA: RAND. http://www.rand.org/pubs/working_papers/WR306.html?src=mobile.

Borman, Kathryn M., Tamela McNulty Eitle, Deanna Michael, David J. Eitle, Reginald Lee, Larry Johnson, Deirdre Cobb-Roberts, Sherman Dorn, and Barbara Shircliffe. 2004. "Accountability in a Postdesegregation Era: The Continuing Significance of Racial Segregation in Florida's Schools." *American Educational Research Journal* 41 (3): 605–31. doi:10.3102/00028312041003605.

Bransford, John D., Ann L. Brown, and Rodney R. Cocking, eds. 1999. *How People Learn: Brain, Mind, Experience, and School*. Washington, DC: National Academy Press.

Center for Research on Education Outcomes. 2015. *Urban Charter School Study Report on 41 Regions*. Report. Stanford, CA: Stanford University, Center for Research on Education Outcomes.

Chetty, Raj, Nathaniel Hendren, Patrick Kline, and Emmanuel Saez. 2014. "Where Is the Land of Opportunity? The Geography of Intergenerational Mobility in the United States." *Quarterly Journal of Economics* 129 (4): 1553–1623. doi:10.1093/qje/qju022.

Cohen, David K., Stephen W. Raudenbush, and Deborah Loewenberg Ball. 2003. "Resources, Instruction, and Research." *Educational Evaluation and Policy Analysis* 25 (2): 119–42. doi:10.3102/01623737025002119.

Cohodes, Sarah R., Daniel S. Grossman, Samuel A. Kleiner, and Michael F. Lovenheim. 2016. "The Effect of Child Health Insurance Access on Schooling: Evidence from Public Insurance Expansions." *Journal of Human Resources* 51 (3): 727–59. doi:10.3368/jhr.51.3.1014-6688R1.

Crowder, Kyle, Jeremy Pais, and Scott J. South. 2012. "Neighborhood Diversity, Metropolitan Constraints, and Household Migration." *American Sociological Review* 77 (3): 325–53. doi:10.1177/0003122412441791.

Darling-Hammond, Linda. 2010. *The Flat World and Education: How America's Commitment to Equity Will Determine Our Future*. New York: Teachers College Press.

Du Bois, W. E. B. 1935. "Does the Negro Need Separate Schools?" *Journal of Negro Education* 4 (3): 328–35. doi:10.2307/2291871.

Farah, Martha J., David M. Shera, Jessica H. Savage, Laura Betancourt, Joan M. Giannetta, Nancy L. Brodsky, Elsa K. Malmud, and Hallam Hurt. 2006. "Childhood Poverty: Specific Associations with Neurocognitive Development." *Brain Research* 1110 (1): 166–74. doi:10.1016/j.brainres.2006.06.072.

Frey, William H. n.d. "New Racial Segregation Measures for Large Metropolitan Areas: Analysis of the 1990–2010 Decennial Censuses; Race Segregation for Largest Metro Areas (Population over 500,000)." Accessed December 22, 2017. http://www.psc.isr.umich.edu/dis/census/segregation2010.html.

Friedman, Debra, David C. Perry, and Carrie Menendez. 2014. *The Foundational Role of Universities as Anchor Institutions in Urban Development: A Report of National Data and Survey Findings.* Washington, DC: Coalition of Urban Serving Universities and Association of Public Land-Grant Universities.

Fuhrman, Susan, and Marvin Lazerson, eds. 2005. *The Public Schools.* New York: Oxford University Press.

Galster, George C. 2012. "Urban Opportunity Structure and Racial/Ethnic Polarization." In *Research on Schools, Neighborhoods, and Communities: Toward Civic Responsibility*, edited by William F. Tate IV, 47–66. Lanham, MD: Rowman and Littlefield.

Garcia, David R., Rebecca Barber, and Alex Molnar. 2009. "Profiting from Public Education: Education Management Organizations and Student Achievement." *Teachers College Record* 111 (5): 1352–79.

Gillborn, David. 2001. "'Raising Standards' or Rationing Education? Racism and Social Justice in Policy and Practice." Working paper. London: University College London, Institute of Education. http://eprints.ioe.ac.uk/1640/1/gillborn2001raising105text.pdf.

Gordon, Edmund W. 1970. "Introduction." *Review of Educational Research* 35 (1): 1–12. doi:10.3102/00346543040001001.

Grant, Gerald. 2009. *Hope and Despair in the American City: Why There Are No Bad Schools in Raleigh.* Cambridge, MA: Harvard University Press.

Guryan, Jonathan. 2004. "Desegregation and Black Dropout Rates." *American Economic Review* 94 (4): 919–43. doi:10.1257/0002828042002679.

Hair, Nicole L., Jamie L. Hanson, Barbara L. Wolfe, and Seth D. Pollak. 2015. "Association of Child Poverty, Brain Development, and Academic Achievement." *JAMA Pediatrics* 169 (9): 822–29. doi:10.1001/jamapediatrics.2015.1475.

Hogrebe, Mark C., and William F. Tate IV. 2010. "School Composition and Context Factors That Moderate and Predict 10th-Grade Science Proficiency." *Teachers College Record* 112 (4): 1096–1136.

Hustedt, Jason T., W. Steven Barnett, Kwanghee Jung, and Allison H. Friedman. 2010. *The New Mexico PreK Evaluation: Impacts from the Fourth Year (2008–2009) of New Mexico's State-Funded PreK Program.* Research Report, November. New Brunswick, NJ: Rutgers University, National Institute for Early Education Research.

Katznelson, Ira. 2005. *When Affirmative Action Was White: An Untold History of Racial Inequality in Twentieth-Century America.* New York: W.W. Norton.

Ladson-Billings, Gloria. 2006. "From the Achievement Gap to the Education Debt: Understanding Achievement in U.S. Schools." *Educational Researcher* 35 (7): 3–12. doi:10.3102/0013189X035007003.

Levin, Richard, C. 2003. *The Work of the University.* New Haven, CT: Yale University Press.

Lewis, Amanda E., and John B. Diamond. 2015. *Despite the Best Intentions: How Racial Inequality Thrives in Good Schools.* New York: Oxford University Press.

Lubienski, Christopher A., and Sarah Theule Lubienski. 2013. *The Public School Advantage: Why Public Schools Outperform Private Schools.* Chicago: University of Chicago Press.

Luby, Joan L. 2015. "Poverty's Most Insidious Damage: The Developing Brain." *JAMA Pediatrics* 169 (9): 810–11. doi:10.1001/jamapediatrics.2015.1682.

Massey, Douglas S., and Nancy A. Denton. 1993. *American Apartheid: Segregation and the Making of the Underclass.* Cambridge, MA: Harvard University Press.

Metzger, Molly W., Patrick J. Fowler, Courtney Lauren Anderson, and Constance A. Lindsay 2015. "Residential Mobility during Adolescence: Do Even 'Upward' Moves Predict Dropout Risk?" *Social Science Research* 53:218–30. doi:10.1016/j.ssresearch.2015.05.004.

Mickelson, Roslyn Arlin. 2008. "Twenty-First Century Social Science on School Racial Diversity and Educational Outcomes." *Ohio State Law Journal* 69 (6): 1173–1227.

Mickelson, Roslyn Arlin. 2015. "The Cumulative Disadvantages of First- and Second-Generation Segregation for Middle School Achievement." *American Educational Research Journal*, 52(4): 657–92. doi:10.3102/0002831215587933.

Miller, L. Scott. 1995. *An American Imperative: Accelerating Minority Educational Advancement*. New Haven, CT: Yale University Press.

National Institute of Child Health and Human Development (NICHD) Early Child Care Research Network. 2000. "Characteristics and Quality of Child Care for Toddlers and Preschoolers." *Applied Developmental Science* 4 (3): 116–35. doi:10.1207/S1532480XADS0403_2.

National Research Council and Institute of Medicine. 2000. *From Neurons to Neighborhoods: The Science of Early Childhood Development*, edited by Jack P. Shonkoff and Deborah A. Phillips. Washington, DC: National Academy Press.

Orfield, Gary, and Erica Frankenberg. 2014. *Brown at 60: Great Progress, a Long Retreat and an Uncertain Future*. With the assistance of Jongyeon Ee and John Kuscera. Report, May 15 revision. Los Angeles: University of California, Civil Rights Project.

Paine, Kendall K. 2015. "The Harrowing, Narrowing Effects of Data." *Teachers College Record*, October 30. http://www.tcrecord.org/content.asp?contentid=18235.

Parker, Karen F. 2015. "The African-American Entrepreneur–Crime Drop Relationship: Growing African-American Business Ownership and Declining Youth Violence." *Urban Affairs Review* 51 (6): 751–80. doi:10.1177/1078087415571755.

Primus, Wendell. 2006. "Improving Public Policies to Increase the Income and Employment of Low-Income Nonresident Fathers." In *Black Males Left Behind*, edited by Ronald B. Mincy, 211–48. Washington, DC: Urban Institute Press.

Putnam, Robert D. 2007. "*E Pluribus Unum*: Diversity and Community in the Twenty-First Century. The 2007 Johan Skytte Prize Lecture." *Scandinavian Political Studies* 30 (2): 137–74. doi:10.1111/j.1467-9477.2007.00176.x.

Raudenbush, Stephen W. 2012. "Can School Improvement Reduce Racial Inequality." In *Research on Schools, Neighborhoods, and Communities: Toward Civic Responsibility*, edited by William F. Tate IV, 233–48. Lanham, MD: Rowan and Littlefield.

Reardon, Sean F., John T. Yun, and Anna K. Chmielewski. 2012. "Suburbanization and School Segregation." In *Research on Schools, Neighborhoods, and Communities: Toward Civic Responsibility*, edited by William F. Tate IV, 85–102. Lanham, MD: Rowman and Littlefield.

Reichman, Nancy E. 2005. "Low Birth Weight and School Readiness." *Future of Children* 15 (1): 91–116. http://futureofchildren.org/sites/futureofchildren/files/media/school_readiness_15_01_fulljournal.pdf.

Richards, Meredith P. 2014. "The Gerrymandering of School Attendance Zones and the Segregation of Public Schools: A Geospatial Analysis." *American Educational Research Journal* 51 (6): 1119–57. doi:10.3102/0002831214553652.

Robertson-Steele, Iain. 2006. "Evolution of Triage Systems." *Emergency Medicine Journal* 23 (2): 154–55. doi:10.1136/emj.2005.030270.

Sampson, Robert J. 2012. *Great American City: Chicago and the Enduring Neighborhood Effect*. Chicago: University of Chicago Press.

Sarason, Seymour B. 1990. *The Predictable Failure of Educational Reform: Can We Change Course before It's Too Late?* San Francisco: Jossey-Bass.

Shapiro, Thomas M. 2004. *The Hidden Cost of Being African American: How Wealth Perpetuates Inequality*. New York: Oxford University Press.

Stiff, Lee V., Janet L. Johnson, and Patrick Akos. 2011. "Examining What We Know for Sure: Tracking in Middle Grades Mathematics." In *Disrupting Tradition: Research and Practice Pathways in Mathematics Education*, edited by William F. Tate IV, Karen D. King, and Celia Rousseau Anderson, 63–75. Reston, VA: National Council of Teachers of Mathematics.

Stone, Clarence N. 1989. *Regime Politics: Governing Atlanta, 1946–1988*. Lawrence: University Press of Kansas.

Tate, William F., IV. 2008. "Geography of Opportunity: Poverty, Place, and Educational Outcomes." *Educational Researcher* 37 (7): 397–411. doi:10.3102/0013189X08326409.

Theodos, Brett, Claudia Coulton, and Amos Budde. 2014. "Getting to Better Performing Schools: The Role of Residential Mobility in School Attainment in Low-Income Neighborhoods." *Cityscape* 16 (1): 61–84.

Wells, Amy Stuart, Douglas Ready, Jacquelyn Duran, Courtney Grzesikowski, Kathryn Hill, Allison Roda, Miya Warner, and Terrenda White. 2012. "Still Separate, Still Unequal, But Not Always So 'Suburban': The Changing Nature of Suburban School Districts in the New York Metropolitan Area." In *Research on Schools, Neighborhoods, and Communities: Toward Civic Responsibility*, edited by William F. Tate IV, 125–49. Lanham, MD: Rowan and Littlefield.

Whitaker, Agnes H., Judith F. Feldman, John M. Lorenz, Sa Shen, Fiona McNicholas, Marlon Nieto, Dawn McCulloch, Jennifer A. Pinto-Martin, and Nigel Paneth. 2006. "Motor and Cognitive Outcomes in Nondisabled Low-Birth-Weight Adolescents: Early Determinants." *Archives of Pediatric and Adolescent Medicine* 160:1040–46. doi:10.1001/archpedi.160.10.1040.

Williams, David R., and Valerie Purdie-Vaughns. 2016. "Needed Interventions to Reduce Racial/Ethnic Disparities in Health." *Journal of Health Politics, Policy and Law* 41 (4): 627–51. doi:10.1215/03616878-3620857.

Yeakey, Carol Camp, and David L. Shepard. 2012. "The Downward Slope of Upward Mobility in a Global Economy." In *Living on the Boundaries: Urban Marginality in National and International Contexts*, edited by Carol Camp Yeakey, 3–22. Bingley, United Kingdom: Emerald.

Zimmer, Ron, Brian Gill, Kevin Booker, Stephane Lavertu, Tim R. Sass, and John Witte. 2009. *Charter Schools in Eight States: Effects on Achievement, Attainment, Integration, and Competition*. Report. Santa Monica, CA: RAND Corporation.

12

Concluding Thoughts on an Agenda for Solving Segregation

Henry S. Webber and Molly W. Metzger

Throughout the 1950s and 1960s, the United States government declared war on racial segregation. The 1954 Supreme Court decision in *Brown v. Board of Education* unanimously concluded that racial segregation led to adverse consequences for African Americans. "Separate educational facilities are inherently unequal," said the Supreme Court.[1] Dr. Martin Luther King Jr. led a national movement for racial integration—a movement focused in good part on desegregating housing and schools. Government policy, particularly during the Great Society period in the mid-1960s, made racial integration a national priority. The Civil Rights Act of 1964 banned the use of federal funds for segregated programs and schools.[2] The Fair Housing Act of 1968 made race-based discrimination in housing illegal.[3]

In the 50 years since passage of the two acts, we have become a wealthier society. Progress has been made on some fronts. Between 1969 and 2014, the percentage of African American families with incomes over $100,000 has gone from 2.2 percent to 12.6 percent.[4] It is no longer a surprise to see an African American lawyer, doctor, or business executive. In aggregate, though, the pace of progress has been very disappointing. A recent and very detailed study by Sean Reardon and Kendra Bischoff concluded that, from 1970 through 2009, racial segregation decreased only slightly and segregation by social class increased: "As overall income inequality grew in the last four decades, high- and low-income families have become increasingly less likely to live near one another. Mixed income neighborhoods have grown rarer" (2011, i).

This lack of progress is particularly notable in light of the increasingly strong evidence of the negative effects of segregation. Thirty years ago, in *The Truly Disadvantaged: The Inner City, the Underclass, and Public Policy,* William Julius Wilson (1987) hypothesized sharply negative effects of living surrounded by very poor neighbors. Research has confirmed Wilson's hypothesis: neighborhood economic context exerts considerable influence on many life outcomes. Living in a seriously disadvantaged neighborhood, for example, lowers high school graduation rates by as much of 20 percentage points (Wodtke, Harding, and Elwert 2011). High family income conveys advantages to children; low family income conveys disadvantages. Neighborhood differences multiply these family income differentials. Robert Putnam (2015), among others, has documented the strongly negative trends of income segregation and their effects on low-income white children. Increasingly, the poor of all races live in resource-deprived communities with weak schools, high crime, and few neighbors possessing the individual social capital to successfully advocate for neighborhood improvement. As Jason Purnell notes in his chapter for this volume (Chapter 4), neighborhoods of disadvantage are places of poor health and much lower life expectancy.

The negative effects of segregation also occur at the regional level and dramatically affect equality of opportunity, the great promise of American democracy. Raj Chetty and his colleagues (2014), in a landmark study of intergenerational social mobility in the United States, found that income segregation and racial segregation are important barriers to social mobility. They also found that the costs of segregation are borne not only by racial minorities and the poor but by middle-class whites as well. A child raised in a family with income in the lowest quintile and residing in the highest-opportunity metropolitan region in America had a 12.9 percent chance of rising to the highest quintile of family income. A child raised in a family with income in the lowest quintile of the distribution and residing in the lowest-opportunity metropolitan area in America had a 4.4 percent chance of rising to the highest quintile of family income. The difference between low- and high-opportunity regions is a function of socioeconomic differences: places of high opportunity have less residential segregation, lower income inequality, stronger primary schools, greater social capital, and greater family stability.

Segregation has had negative effects on the political domains within American life. As Bill Bishop (2008) described in *The Big Sort: Why the Clustering of Like-Minded America Is Tearing Us Apart*, the sorting of America into increasingly homogenous residential areas contributes to the great polarization that has marked American politics in recent years.

While the last 50 years have confirmed the negative effects of segregation, they have also taught us that segregation is very difficult to solve. Segregation by race is deeply ingrained in an American history that resulted in the genocide and forced location of Native Americans to geographically isolated reservations, and in slavery.

In addition, American incomes have become more polarized, and the percentage of the population that is middle class has declined. This economic polarization is particularly evident in American cities, where we have seen an influx of upper-income residents and an outmigration of middle-income families with children (Hyra 2012). As William Tate notes (Chapter 11), both black and white families tend to move to and prefer areas where members of their race or ethnicity constitute a majority of the population. And the psychology of difference, as summarized by Purnell, suggests that we are intrinsically more comfortable with whomever we define as "our" group.

The difficulty of reducing segregation and its demonstrably negative consequences for most Americans calls for government intervention and a public policy solution. Government, as Richard Rothstein notes (Chapter 2), created much of the racial segregation in America. Without government intervention, we will not reduce racial or economic segregation. Public policy must intervene productively to reduce segregation by harnessing the power of federal, state, and local governments and national and local advocacy organizations.

The chapters in this volume present a clear agenda for an effective government campaign to reduce segregation. Three steps are outlined. The first is promoting integration in high-opportunity neighborhoods by supporting the movement of poor minorities into affluent, usually majority-white areas. The second is redeveloping areas of concentrated poverty as mixed-race, mixed-income neighborhoods. The third is encouraging the maintenance and expansion of existing, economically diverse, middle-income neighborhoods. None of these steps is easy or without risk, but it is the work to be done.

Promoting Integration in High-Opportunity Neighborhoods

There is a very strong case for allowing residents of areas of concentrated poverty to move to high-opportunity areas. Consider, for example, the most recent evidence from the Moving to Opportunity experiment, which offered housing vouchers to randomly selected families in high-poverty housing projects, enabling them to move to middle- and high-income neighborhoods. Children who were below 13 years of age when their family moved had much higher incomes as adults, were more likely to live in better neighborhoods as adults, were less likely to become single parents, and were significantly more likely to attend college (Chetty, Hendren, and Katz 2016). Other studies have confirmed positive effects for individuals whose families moved to stronger neighborhoods when they were young children (Turner, Nichols, and Comey 2012). None of this should be surprising. For generations, middle-income families have moved to better neighborhoods, often in the suburbs, to improve the lives of their children. Such neighborhoods have strong schools, safe streets, and proximity to job centers. Programs like Moving to Opportunity offer poor families a chance to follow the same path.

The challenge is to determine how to further open up high-opportunity areas to racial minorities and those with limited incomes. Expanding the

Moving to Opportunity experiment is one answer. The authors in this volume suggest a variety of other strategies:

- Enforcing housing antidiscrimination laws
- Locating Low-Income Housing Tax Credit projects in low-poverty areas or near high-quality schools
- Making housing vouchers more useful by assisting families to locate in high-opportunity areas, modifying policies to discourage voucher use only in lower-poverty communities, and minimizing jurisdictional barriers to using vouchers
- Interpreting the Community Reinvestment Act to support mixed-income housing in both cities and suburbs
- Promoting scattered-site rehabilitation and preservation of affordable housing in high-income neighborhoods through nonprofit-owned affordable housing or community land trusts
- Adding inclusionary zoning requirements to development incentives
- Eliminating local zoning rules that make affordable housing impossible—for example, rules specifying minimum lot sizes.

Many of these steps are hard to implement and raise substantive issues. Locating Low-Income Housing Tax Credit projects in high-opportunity neighborhoods will increase land costs, raising the cost of the program or reducing the number of new housing units that can be produced. If recipients are to use their housing vouchers in high-opportunity (and, therefore, more expensive) neighborhoods, the values of vouchers must increase. By long tradition, zoning decisions in the United States are made locally. Restricting localities' ability to make these decisions would be difficult. And many minority populations experience marginalization in the white neighborhoods. Despite these concerns, however, a comprehensive set of strategies for eliminating racial and economic segregation must offer low-income and minority populations the option to relocate to high-opportunity neighborhoods (Keene and Padilla 2010).

Redeveloping Areas of Concentrated Poverty

Relocation strategies, for all of their promise, will not eliminate racial and economic segregation. In part, this is an issue of scale. It is very unlikely that sufficient housing can be created in high-opportunity areas to allow the relocation of all who want to live there. It is also a matter of choice. Many low-income residents do not want to leave their neighbors, friends, and family. Public policy should not be about forced removal; it should be about creating options, including the options to remain in one's community of origin and contribute to the improvement of that community.

Neighborhood improvement should be another option supported by public policy. With adequate support, areas of opportunity can emerge in what are now overwhelmingly minority neighborhoods defined by concentrated poverty, weak schools, high crime rates, and other challenges. The investments necessary to effect such transitions are broad and deep. They include efforts to build social capital, improve services, and create housing options. Reducing segregation in these communities requires that neighborhood improvement strategies include efforts to attract middle-class residents. Community improvement can occur without attracting new residents, but reduction of segregation cannot.

In recent years, the most aggressive efforts to rebuild low-income minority communities in the United States have been through federal programs that replace public housing with mixed-income communities, programs such as Hope VI and Choice Neighborhoods. Mark Joseph (Chapter 8) describes the many successes of these programs, including improvements in the quality of housing for the poor, reductions in crime, and revitalization of surrounding neighborhoods. As Joseph notes, Hope VI and Choice Neighborhoods have often led to notable physical transformations of former public housing sites. But creation of such communities is very expensive, and the number of poor residents aided is usually less than the number who previously lived in public housing on the same sites. Evidence suggests that mixed-income development has not led to a trajectory of upward mobility for poor adults. Moreover, as with mobility strategies, the mixed-income approach has left many poor residents feeling marginalized in their new communities.

Much less is known about the net effects of the many efforts to improve neighborhoods of concentrated poverty without the large-scale replacement and rebuilding of public housing that has marked Hope VI and Choice Neighborhoods. In part, the barrier to understanding these effects is methodological. There are so many efforts in so many poor neighborhoods across the country that it is very hard to generalize the results. But there are other issues as well. As Lance Freeman notes (Chapter 3), community improvements in areas of concentrated poverty have been torn between two competing objectives: promoting desegregation and improving living conditions for the poor. Poor minority neighborhoods include some of the worst housing conditions in America. Public policy, particularly the Low-Income Housing Tax Credit, has often been used to build new housing, significantly improving living conditions for residents. As Todd Swanstrom notes in Chapter 9, however, such efforts rarely reduce segregation and can increase neighborhood decline by amplifying the mismatch of housing supply and demand in these neighborhoods. Poor neighborhoods have low property values because there is more housing supply than there is demand. Increasing housing supply, often through well-intentioned efforts to expand the stock of affordable housing, can reduce housing values even further, making neighborhood redevelopment even more difficult.

Reducing segregation requires investing in housing and services that draw middle-class populations to overwhelmingly minority poor neighborhoods. This has been done successfully in many cities. In very-high-growth cities, however, the increased popularity of previously low-income minority neighborhoods has resulted too often in the creation of segregation through gentrification. What begins as an effort to increase diversity becomes, over time, a new form of segregation as poor minority residents are replaced by richer white residents. As John Taylor and Josh Silver argue in this volume (Chapter 7), we must fight segregation and manage gentrification in order to obtain the benefits of neighborhood improvement.

Understanding neighborhood change and managing it to prevent the replacement of one group with another are among the great challenges of urban policy. We are optimistic that such efforts can be successful and are heartened by the many efforts to do so around the country. But this work is hard. It requires careful analysis and planning at the neighborhood level, ongoing interventions in housing markets by government and nonprofit institutions, and the use of such techniques as community land trusts, inclusionary zoning, and permanent affordable housing.

Preserving and Supporting Middle Neighborhoods

The final strategy to encourage economic and racial diversity in housing is to preserve and expand middle neighborhoods. Middle neighborhoods lie between the extremes of wealthy and poor neighborhoods. They are places characterized by a balance of housing supply and housing demand. In most cities, these are neighborhoods of small houses and small apartment buildings, of unremarkable architecture but strong community organizations and religious organizations. There is also evidence that middle neighborhoods are much more racially mixed than low market neighborhoods (Brophy 2016). If middle neighborhoods are allowed to weaken, segregation will increase as racially mixed neighborhoods become predominately minority neighborhoods. Moreover, as Swanstrom notes, these neighborhoods offer the greatest return for public investments aimed at reducing segregation, and the cost of creating affordable housing is much lower in middle neighborhoods than in richer ones. Unfortunately, the science of identifying and supporting middle neighborhoods is not yet well developed. This is a task for future research.

Taking Effective Action to Reduce Segregation

Offering chances for more low-income people to live in high-opportunity areas, revitalizing areas of concentrated poverty, and supporting middle neighborhoods are all positive steps to reduce segregation in America. It is difficult to imagine any of these steps being vigorously implemented, however, unless their proponents make a convincing case for action. Public policy implementation requires political will. We believe strongly that there is a need for a national discussion about why segregation matters, the role of government in creating the current situation, and the governmental action required to reduce segregation. A strong introduction to that discussion is provided in the chapter by Rothstein. He lays out a moral case for extending subsidies to working- and middle-class African Americans as compensation for the government's role in segregation. Rothstein admits that direct subsidies may be fanciful, but he discusses critical issues in presenting his case. Segregation is a drag on America's economy, politics, and sense of fairness. At least one of our national political parties must commit to an active program of reducing economic and racial segregation.

Policy and politics are necessary but not sufficient to reduce segregation in America. We also must invest in the organizational capacity to plan and coordinate the efforts required at the metropolitan and neighborhood level. These strategies will vary in response to local housing markets and the strength of regional economies. In very strong housing markets, for example, inclusionary zoning requires developers of new multifamily housing to set aside affordable units, and the approach does not impose notably adverse consequences in those markets. In weak housing markets, inclusionary zoning without public subsidies will forestall the creation of new housing.

Another strategy for reducing segregation, increasing the value of housing choice vouchers, enables recipients to move to high-opportunity neighborhoods. This strategy is more affordable in weaker housing markets. In each metropolitan region, a coordinating agency must develop an integration strategy that reflects careful understanding of the dynamics of local housing markets and the efficacy of the policy tools available.

The federal Affirmatively Furthering Fair Housing rule of 2015 requires governmental agencies to take affirmative steps to promote fair housing.[5] The rule requires regions to determine the extent of racial and economic segregation every 5 years, to examine in detail the disparities in neighborhood access to opportunity, and to develop concrete goals and strategies for reducing that segregation. The rule's effective date has been extended by the Trump administration until at least 2020,[6] and the rule is not the only way to create such a regional plan. But a plan and regional mechanism to coordinate action are necessary.

Final Issues

In this volume, we present an effective and achievable plan for reducing segregation in America. But at least two vexing issues remain. Each is raised in this volume but not solved. The first is how to promote effective neighboring. There are some benefits to simply living next to diverse neighbors. Yet many of the benefits of economic and racial diversity require integration. The challenge is to break down the barriers of class and race at the personal level and create greater connections. Much of Mark Joseph's recent work is on how to promote interclass ties in intentional mixed-income developments created through Hope VI and Choice Neighborhoods. Jane Jacobs (1961), in her great work on American cities, consistently celebrates neighborliness, the willingness of all of us to intervene to make life better for those we live near. Determining how to achieve neighborliness in communities of great diversity is an ongoing challenge.

The second challenge is to find the right balance between focusing on racial integration and focusing on economic integration. Racial integration requires economic integration, but much economic integration can occur without racial integration. The psychological evidence presented by Purnell suggests that racial integration is a particularly challenging policy goal. But the experience of African Americans, as Rothstein argues, is uniquely disturbing and represents a particularly egregious example of the use of government power to enforce segregation. One tactic, which is worthy of at least discussion, is to analyze how much racial integration could be achieved by various forms of economic integration.

These two challenges and the policy agenda laid out in this volume can be addressed by deep refection and collective action. As in the civil rights movement, tomorrow's housing victories will be won collectively. Collective action must target all levels of government and the private and nonprofit sector. For readers seeking to engage in policy action for housing justice, the organizations of some of the authors of this volume are fitting places to start. The National Community Reinvestment Coalition, the Poverty and Race Research Action Council, and the Center on Budget and Policy Priorities are Washington, DC–based groups working to inform and engage policymakers and the public on these issues. These national groups are joined at the local level by countless groups, such as the Metropolitan St. Louis Equal Housing and Opportunity Council, Dallas's Inclusive Communities Project, and many others. The work of these organizations, the contributing authors, and many others gives us hope that the vision shared in this volume can be realized.

Notes

1. Brown v. Board of Education, 347 U.S. 483, 495 (1954).
2. 42 U.S.C. § 2000d (2016).
3. 42 U.S.C. § 3604 (2016).
4. Estimates from the US Census Bureau's Current Population Survey, Annual Social and Economic Supplements (income in 2014 Consumer Price Index–adjusted dollars), black income only.
5. Affirmatively Furthering Fair Housing, 80 Fed. Reg. 42272 (July 16, 2015) (codified at 24 C.F.R. pts. 5, 91, 92, 570, 574, 576, 903 (2016)).
6. Affirmatively Furthering Fair Housing: Extension of Deadline for Submission of Assessment of Fair Housing for Consolidated Plan Participants, 63 Fed. Reg. 683 (Jan. 5, 2018).

References

Bishop, Bill. 2008. *The Big Sort: Why the Clustering of Like-Minded America is Tearing Us Apart*. New York: Houghton Mifflin.

Brophy, Paul C., ed. 2016. *On the Edge: America's Middle Neighborhoods*. New York: American Assembly.

Chetty, Raj, Nathaniel Hendren, and Lawrence F. Katz. 2016. "The Effects of Exposure to Better Neighborhoods on Children: New Evidence from the Moving to Opportunity Experiment." *American Economic Review* 106 (4): 855–902. doi:10.1257/aer.20150572.

Chetty, Raj, Nathaniel Hendren, Patrick Kline, and Emmanuel Saez. 2014. "Where Is the Land of Opportunity? The Geography of Intergenerational Mobility in the United States." *Quarterly Journal of Economics* 129 (4): 1553–1623. doi:10.1093/qje/qju022.

Hyra, Derek S. 2012. "Conceptualizing the New Urban Renewal: Comparing the Past to the Present." *Urban Affairs Review* 48 (4): 498–527. doi.org/10.1177/1078087411434905.

Jacobs, Jane. 1961. *The Death and Life of Great American Cities*. New York: Vintage.

Keene, Danya E., and Mark B. Padilla. 2010. "Race, Class and the Stigma of Place: Moving to 'Opportunity' in Eastern Iowa." *Health & Place* 16 (6): 1216–23. doi:10.1016/j.healthplace.2010.08.006.

Putnam, Robert D. 2015. *Our Kids: The American Dream in Crisis*. New York: Simon and Schuster.

Reardon, Sean F., and Kendra Bischoff. 2011. *Growth in the Residential Segregation of Families by Income, 1970–2009*. US2010 Project Report. Providence, RI: Brown University, US2010 Project. http://www.s4.brown.edu/us2010/Data/Report/report111111.pdf.

Turner, Margery Austin, Austin Nichols, and Jennifer Comey. 2012. *Benefits of Living in High-Opportunity Neighborhoods: Insights from the Moving to Opportunity Demonstration*. Research Report. Washington, DC: Urban Institute. https://www.urban.org/research/publication/benefits-living-high-opportunity-neighborhoods/view/full_report.

Wilson, William J. 1987. *The Truly Disadvantaged: The Inner City, the Underclass, and Public Policy*. Chicago: University of Chicago Press.

Wodtke, Geoffrey T., David J. Harding, and Felix Elwert. 2011. "Neighborhood Effects in Temporal Perspective: The Impact of Long-Term Exposure to Concentrated Disadvantage on High School Graduation." *American Sociological Review* 76 (5): 713–36. doi:10.1177/0003122411420816.

INDEX

Abyssinian Development Corporation, 48
academic attainment, 223–24
access to opportunity, role of housing as platform for, 84–86
Acs, G., 7
AFFH. *See* Affirmatively Furthering Fair Housing
AFFH Rule Guidebook, 78
Affirmatively Furthering Fair Housing (AFFH), 50, 69, 239
   administrative oversight and compliance, 86–87
   balanced approach, 80–82
   Community Reinvestment Act and, 126, 133
   defined, 81
   history of, 78–80
   Housing Choice Voucher program and, 96
   neighborhood reinvestment in, 80–82
   overview, 77–78
   racially concentrated areas of poverty, 83–84
   role of housing as platform, 84–86
   suspension of compliance with, 88
affordable housing, 35, 51–52, 131–132, 160, 186–88, 207–8, 209–10, 236
Affordable Housing Tax Increment Financing Program, Maine, 208
AFH (Assessment of Fair Housing), 85, 96, 133
African Americans. *See also* siting dilemma
   academic attainment, intergenerational nature of, 223–24
   business development, 226
   church shooting in Charleston, South Carolina, 26–27
   de jure segregation, enduring effects of, 25
   housing in early twentieth century, 36–37
   integration, attitude towards, 29
   market strategy favoring, 189–90
   metropolitan residential segregation of, 216–17
   mixed-income development, social challenges in, 156–57, 158
   modern segregation, development and impact of, 60–65
   psychology of group interaction, 66–68
   public housing for, reactions to, 39–41, 50–51
   public housing policies, segregation through, 17–20
   public policies and practices enforcing segregation, 24
   remedial desegregation, 26–29
   residential segregation, 5
   school composition effects, 218–20, 222–23
   school district segregation, 218
   St. Louis, Missouri, racial disparities in, 58–60
   weak housing markets and, 180
agenda for solving segregation
   concentrated poverty, redeveloping areas of, 236–38
   effective action, taking, 239
   final issues in, 240
   integration in high-opportunity neighborhoods, promoting, 235–36
   middle neighborhoods, preserving and supporting, 238
   overview, 233–35
Allport, G., 70
American Apartheid (Massey and Denton), 63, 69
American ideals threatened by segregation, 7–8
Americans, The (Littell), 26
Analysis of Impediments to Fair Housing, 79, 133
Asian Americans, residential segregation of, 5
Assessment of Fair Housing (AFH), 85, 96, 133
Atlanta, Georgia, 151
attendance-zone gerrymandering, 219

Baltimore, Maryland, 23
banks
   community-based organizations, collaboration with, 131
   CRA exams, 125–26, 134–37
   denials of loans to blacks, 22
   integration in CRA strategy, maintaining, 139
Benner, C., 7, 8
Berands, M., 218–19
Big Sort: Why the Clustering of Like-Minded America Is Tearing Us Apart, The (Bishop), 234
Bischoff, K., 233

Bishop, B., 234
Black Lives Matter movement, 72
black metropolises, 37
blacks. *See* African Americans
brain development, 215–16
brain regimes
   general discussion, 224–26
   strategies for, 225–26
   universities, role of, 226–28
Brentwood, Missouri, 206
Breyer, S., 16
Brown, M., 58
Brown, N., 44–45
Brown v. Board of Education, 218, 233
Budde, A., 217
Burns, J. M., 18–19
Butts, Calvin O., 48

Campbell, H., 7
Capital One National Association, 134–36
caps on rental subsidies, 97–98
Carr Square Village, St. Louis, Missouri, 18
cars, expanding access to, 105
case management, in mixed-income development, 163
Cashin, S., 7–8
Center for Research on Education Outcomes at Stanford University, 222
Center on Budget and Policy Priorities, 240
Charleston, South Carolina, church shooting in, 26–27
charter schools, 221–22
Chetty, R., 92, 122, 234
Chicago, Illinois, 151, 202, 207–8
Chicago Commission on Race Relations, 37
Chicago Daily Defender, 46
Chmielewski, A., 218
Choice Neighborhoods Initiative, 68, 150–51, 159, 237
church shooting in Charleston, South Carolina, 26–27
Citibank, N.A., 137
Citizens Committee of West Chesterfield, Chicago, Illinois, 43
Civil Rights Act of 1964, 3–4, 44, 233
Civil Rights era, public housing in, 44–47
Cleveland, Ohio, 184–85, 206–7
Clinton-Peabody project, St. Louis, Missouri, 18
Coates, Ta-Nehisi, 6
Cohodes, S. R., 225
collaboration complexity of mixed-income transformation, 155–56
Collins, C., 64
community-based organizations, collaboration with banks, 131

community building, proactive approach to, 163–64
community development, 48–49, 126–28
Community Development Block Grants, 132
community groups, participation in fair housing, 138
community land trusts, 131–32
Community Reinvestment Act (CRA)
   AFFH and, 133
   concentrated poverty, trends of, 121–22
   exams, overview of, 125–26
   financing tools and programmatic approaches, 130–32
   gentrification, trends of, 123–25
   overview, 120–21
   Q&A document, 126–29
   recommendations, 138–39
   segregation, combating with, 125–29
   surveys of exams, 134–37, 143–45
concentrated poverty
   CRA exams from bank financing in areas of, 144–45
   gentrification, effect of, 124
   metropolitan areas with high, 145
   redeveloping areas of, 236–38
   survey of CRA exams, 136–37
   trends of, 121–22
Concerned Citizens of the Eighth District, Los Angeles, California, 44–45
consortia of public housing agencies, 100–1
contact theory, 70
Coulton, C., 217
Couture, V., 123
CRA. *See* Community Reinvestment Act
Crowder, K., 217
cultural resources in neighborhoods, 29

Daniel, M. M., 82
Danzer, G. A., 26
Dean, J. P., 21
de facto segregation
   enduring effects, 25
   integration and diversity, 29–31
   overview, 15–17
   public housing, 17–20
   public policies and practices enforcing segregation, 22–24
   remedial desegregation, 26–29
   white suburbanization, 20–21
de jure segregation, 16–17
   enduring effects of, 25
   integration and diversity, 29–31
   public housing policies, 17–20
   public policies and practices enforcing, 22–24
   in public schools, 51

remedial desegregation, 26–29
white suburbanization, 20–21
DeLuca, S., 94
democratic processes undermined by segregation, 7–8
Denton, N., 63, 69, 84
depersonalization, 67
DeSoto-Carr project, St. Louis, Missouri, 18
Ding, L., 123–24
discrimination
  against HCV voucher holders, prohibiting, 102
  social psychology of intergroup relations, 66–68, 69–71
disparate impact, 15, 77, 78
dispersal strategy, 146, 147
dissimilarity index, 65
diversity, 29–31
Divringi, E., 123–24
Douglas, P., 19
Dovidio, J. F., 70–71
Dubois, W. E. B., 37, 216
Dunlap, A. I., 45
durable urban policy, 69

East-West Gateway Council of Governments, 203
economic composition of U.S. population, 5
economic development, redesigning, 206–7
economic exclusion among poor, 156–57
economic growth, effect of segregation on, 7
economic integration, 240
economic polarization, 234–35
economic segregation
  integration, 29–31
  lack of progress in elimination of, 233
  rise in, 4
  social mobility affected by, 8
education. *See also* education triage
  Brown v. Board of Education decision, 218, 233
  housing, effect on access to opportunity, 84–86
  mobility and, 217
  remedial desegregation through, 26–29
  segregation, effect on access to opportunity, 64
education triage
  academic attainment, 223–24
  brain development and learning, 215–16
  metropolitan segregation, 216–18
  regional brain regimes, 224–26
  residential segregation, 216–17
  school composition effects, 218–20
  school district segregation, 218
  triage regime, 220–23
  urban universities as catalysts, 226–28
effective neighboring, 163–64, 240
Ellen, I. G., 123

Elliott, R., 49
employment
  housing, effect on access to opportunity, 84–86
  of nonresident fathers, 226
  segregation, effect on access to opportunity, 64
environmental health hazards, 85
equal opportunity, effect of segregation on, 8–9
equity-efficiency trade-off
  middle market neighborhood strategies, 182–85
  overview, 173–74
  strong and weak housing markets, nature of, 175–77
  strong market neighborhood strategies, 185–88
  weak market neighborhood strategies, 178–82
equity planning, 184–85
ethnic composition of U.S. population, 5
exclusion, in mixed-income development, 153–54
exclusionary zoning ordinances, 28, 62–63

Fair Housing Act, 25, 233. *See also* Affirmatively Furthering Fair Housing
  disparate impact of, 15
  general discussion, 3–4
  Inclusive Communities Project case, 77–78, 83
  strengthening enforcement of, 69
Fair Housing Amendments Act of 1988, 86–87
Fair Housing Initiatives Program, 86–87
Fair Market Rents (FMRs), 94, 97–98
family assistance for voucher use in high-opportunity areas, 101–5
Family Self-Sufficiency program, 163
fathers, income and employment of nonresident, 226
Fauset, A. H., 41
Federal Housing Administration (FHA), 20–21, 25
Ferguson, Missouri, 58, 205–6
Fernandez, S., 7
FHA (Federal Housing Administration), 20–21, 25
financial rewards for voucher use, 96–97
financing of mixed-income development, 155, 160
financing tools, Community Reinvestment Act, 130–32
first refusal right, 132
FMRs (Fair Market Rents), 94, 97–98
Ford, J., 37
For the Sake of All: A Report on the Health and Well-Being of African Americans in St. Louis—and Why It Matters for Everyone, 58–60
Frankenberg, E., 218
Freeman, L., 237
Frey, W., 217

Gaertner, S. L., 70–71
Garboden, P., 94
gentrification
 AFFH and, 133
 benefits of, 125
 community group involvement, 138
 costs of, 124–25
 in mixed-income developments, 153
 Q&A document, 126, 128
 strong market neighborhoods, defining, 177
 survey of CRA exams, 134–36, 143–44
 trends of, 123–25
ghettoization, 22, 37
ghettos, 22–24, 37, 42–44
Gibson, B., 40
Gillborn, D., 220–21
governance, inclusion in, 164
government policy, segregation through. See *de jure* segregation
Grant, Gerald, 219
Great Migration, 36
Gries, J. S., 37
group interaction, psychology of, 66–68
Guryan, J., 218–19

Handbury, J., 123
Harlem, New York, impact of LIHTC in, 48
Harlem River Houses, New York City, 40
harm caused by segregation, 6–9
HCV program. *See* Housing Choice Voucher program
health
 environmental hazards, 85
 housing, effect on access to opportunity, 84–86
 residential segregation, effect on, 64, 65
health insurance, public, 225
Healthy Neighborhoods approach, 183–84
Hendren, N., 92, 122
high-opportunity neighborhoods. *See also* Housing Choice Voucher program
 family assistance for voucher use in, 101–5
 integration in, promoting, 235–36
 LIHTC and, 102, 236
 providing information on units in, 99
 voucher use in, policies supporting, 97–99
Hirsch, A., 51
History Alive!, 26
Hogg, M., 66–67
Hogue, C., 65
HOME Investment Partnerships Program, 132
HOPE SF, San Francisco, California, 151
HOPE VI program, 68, 148, 149–50, 154, 237
Horn, K. M., 50
Housing Act (1949), 19
Housing Choice Voucher (HCV) program
 AFFH, implementation of, 96

agency performance, location outcomes and, 95–96
cars, expanding access to, 105
consortia of agencies, formation of, 100–1
discrimination against voucher holders, 102
dispersal strategy, 146
family assistance for voucher use in high-opportunity areas, 101–5
financial rewarding of agencies for voucher use, 96–97
general discussion, 51, 92–95
higher-opportunity neighborhoods, information on units in, 99
insufficient appropriations in, 28–29
jurisdictional barriers, minimizing, 100–1
landlords, acceptance of vouchers by, 102
location outcomes, incentives for, 95–96
mobility counseling, 102–4
portability moves, promotion of, 101
search periods, extending, 99
subsidy caps, 97–98
voucher use in higher-opportunity areas, policies supporting, 97–99
housing demand, boosting, 180–81
housing market strength
 middle market neighborhood strategies, 182–85
 overview, 173–74
 strong and weak markets, nature of, 175–77
 strong market neighborhood strategies, 185–88
 weak market neighborhood strategies, 178–82
housing mobility, 29–31
Housing Opportunities and Services Together initiative, 162
housing vouchers, 47–48, 51. *See also* Housing Choice Voucher program
HSBC Bank USA, N.A., 134–36
HUD. *See* U.S. Department of Housing and Urban Development
HUD Needs to Enhance Its Requirements and Oversight of Jurisdictions' Fair Housing Plans report, 80–81
Hughes, L., 42
hunkering down, 224
Hunter's Point Dry Dock project, San Francisco, California, 19
Hwang, J., 123–24

Ickes, H., 17, 38
ICP (Inclusive Communities Project), 16–17, 77–78, 83
inclusionary zoning policies, 28, 132, 186, 207–8, 209, 239
inclusion in mixed-income development, 161
Inclusive Communities Project case, 16–17, 77–78, 83

income inequality, 5. *See also* mixed-income development; wealth inequality
income of nonresident fathers, 226
incorporated exclusion, 148, 156–57
Innis, R., 45
integrated public housing, 44
integration, 29–31, 50–51, 70–71, 79, 138–39, 164. *See also* Affirmatively Furthering Fair Housing; mixed-income development, 164–65
  of African Americans, attitudes toward, 29
  in Civil Rights era, 44–47
  in high-opportunity neighborhoods, promoting, 235–36
intergenerational nature of academic attainment, 223–24
intergroup relations, social psychology of, 66–68, 69–71
interstate highways, as tools of segregation, 23

Jacobs, J., 240
Jargowsky, P., 121
Jennings, Missouri, 206
Jobs Plus Initiative, 163
Johnson, J. W., 37
Johnson, L. B., 3–4
Joseph, M., 237
Julian, E. K., 82
jurisdictional barriers impeding relocation, minimizing, 100–1

Katz, L., 92, 122
King, M. L., Jr., 3–4, 58
Kneebone, E., 122
Kramer, M., 65
Kurtz, S., 87

La Guardia, F., 40
landlords, acceptance of HCV vouchers, 102
Lapsansky-Werner, E. J., 26
Latinos
  academic attainment, 223–24
  de jure segregation, 30–31
  residential segregation, 5
  school composition effects, 218–20
  school district segregation, 218
learning
  brain development, 215–16
  school composition effects, 218–20
Lehrer, B., 49
Levin, R., 226–27
Levittown, Long Island, New York, 20, 25, 27
Li, H., 7
LIHTC. *See* Low-Income Housing Tax Credit
limited-equity co-ops, 131
Littell, M., 26

LMI (low- and moderate-income) communities, integration in. *See* Community Reinvestment Act
loans, 22. *See also* Community Reinvestment Act
local housing programs, 132
local public agencies, 138
location
  AFFH, implementation of, 96
  agency performance measurements, 95–96
  cars, expanding access to, 105
  consortia of agencies, formation of, 100–1
  discrimination against voucher holders, 102
  family assistance for voucher use in high-opportunity areas, 101–5
  financial rewarding of agencies for voucher use, 96–97
  general discussion, 92–95
  higher-opportunity neighborhoods, providing information on units in, 99
  incentives for outcomes, 95–96
  jurisdictional barriers, minimizing, 100–1
  landlords, encouraging to accept vouchers, 102
  mobility counseling, 102–4
  policies supporting voucher use, 97–99
  portability moves, promotion of, 101
  school composition effects, 218–20
  school district segregation, 218
  search periods, extending, 99
  subsidy caps, 97–98
long-term sustainability of mixed-income housing, 159–60
low- and moderate-income (LMI) communities, integration in. *See* Community Reinvestment Act
low-income families, housing assistance for. *See* Housing Choice Voucher program
Low-Income Housing Tax Credit (LIHTC), 159, 237
  general discussion, 47–50
  in high-opportunity neighborhoods, 102, 236
  integration through, 131
  limited success of, 51–52
  overview, 36
  in weak market neighborhoods, 178
Luby, J., 215–16

Mallach, A., 130
Manna Inc., 124
market assessments, neighborhood housing, 130
market complexity of mixed-income transformation, 155
market strength. *See* housing market strength
Martin, W. M., 22
Massachusetts, tax increment financing in, 208
Massey, D., 63, 69, 84

McClory, R., 45, 46
medical triage, relationship between educational reform and, 220–21
Meltzer, R., 124
mergers of school districts, 219
metropolitan rental units, 94
metropolitan segregation
  overview, 216
  residential, 216–17
  school composition effects, 218–20
  school district, 218
Metropolitan St. Louis Equal Housing and Opportunity Council, 240
metropolitan-wide Fair Market Rents, 97
Metzger, M., 217
middle market neighborhoods
  defined, 176
  preserving and supporting, 238
  strategies for, 182–85
Miller, K., 37
Milliken v. Bradley, 15–16
Minnesota, tax increment financing in, 208
minorities
  LIHTC, effect on, 50
  school composition effects, 218–20
  social psychology of intergroup relations, 66–68, 69–71
mixed-finance projects, 149–50, 160
mixed-income development. *See also* Community Reinvestment Act
  assumptions regarding, 157–58
  case management and supportive services, 162–63
  Choice Neighborhoods Initiative, 150–51
  city initiatives, 151
  community building, proactive approach to, 163–64
  economic and social exclusion among poor, 156–57
  exclusion at multiple stages of, 153–54
  governance, inclusion in, 164
  history of, 149–51
  HOPE VI program, 148, 149–50
  implementation challenges, 154–56
  inclusion enhancements, design of, 161
  integration approaches, applying insights to other, 164–65
  overview, 146–49
  physical transformation in, 152
  practice and policy, strengthening, 159
  relocation, promoting successful, 162
  resources, financing, and long-term sustainability of, 159–60
  return rates, increasing, 162
  revitalization of neighborhood, 153
  safety and security improvements, 152–53

strategic clarity about goals and approaches, 160–61
structural change, need for, 164–65
upward mobility, focusing on, 163
Mixed-Income New Communities Strategy, 149
mobility
  counseling services, 102–4
  metropolitan residential segregation and, 217
  remedial desegregation, incentives in, 27
  social, 8, 234
mortgages
  denials to African Americans, 22
  federal insurance for, segregation through, 21
Moving to Opportunity (MTO) program, 70–71, 104, 148, 235
Murchison, J., 38–39
Myrdal, G., 84

National Advisory Commission on Civil Disorders, 3, 4, 77
National Association for the Advancement of Colored People (NAACP), 37, 41, 43
National Commission on Severely Distressed Public Housing, 149
National Community Reinvestment Coalition (NCRC), 130
  surveys of exams, 134–37, 143–45
Native Americans, *de jure* segregation of, 30
Negro Renaissance, 37
neighborhood composition rule, 17–18
neighborhood housing market assessments, 130
Neighborhood Progress Inc., 189
neighborhood reinvestment, 80–82
neighboring, effective, 240
neoliberal era, public housing in, 47–50
New Communities Initiative, Washington, DC, 151
New Deal, 17, 38–41
New York
  Harlem, impact of LIHTC in, 48
  Harlem River Houses in, 40
  inclusionary zoning policies, 186–87
  Levittown, Long Island, 20, 25, 27
New York Amsterdam News, 39, 40, 42
New York Times, 78–79
Nixon administration, 46
nonresident fathers, income and employment of, 226

Obama administration, 79–80, 108, 133, 150, 192
Okun, A., 174
operational complexity of mixed-income transformation, 155–56
opportunity hoarding, 6

O'Regan, K. M., 50
Orfield, G., 218
overcrowding of ghettos, 42–44
overlay district, 209

Paine, K., 221
Pais, J., 217
Parents Involved decision, 16
Parker, K. F., 226
Pastor, M., 7, 8
"pay as you go" structure, 199
payments-in-lieu-of-taxes (PILOTs), 199
Penaloza, R., 218–19
people-based subsidies in strong markets, 186
Pettigrew, T., 70
PHAs. *See* public housing agencies
Philadelphia Tribune, 39–40, 43, 44–45
physical transformation in mixed-income development, 152
PILOTs (payments-in-lieu-of-taxes), 199
Pittsburgh Courier, 39–40, 41, 43, 44–45
place. *See* location
Plan for Transformation, Chicago, Illinois, 151
planned shrinkage, 181
polarization, economic, 234–35
police enforcement of racial segregation, 24
political complexity of mixed-income transformation, 155
political economy of place, 147–48
Popkin, S., 163
portability moves, promotion of, 101
positive-negative asymmetry effect, 67–68
postwar years, public housing in, 42–44
poverty
   brain development affected by, 215–16
   racially concentrated areas of, 77–78, 83–84
Poverty and Race Research Action Council, 240
poverty, concentrated
   CRA exams from bank financing in areas of, 144–45
   metropolitan areas with high, 145
   redeveloping areas of, 236–38
   trends of, 121–22
prejudice, social psychology of, 66–68, 69–71
prenatal care, universal, 225
preschool clearinghouse, regional, 225–26
private enforcement of Fair Housing Act, 86–87
private prejudice, 24
project-based housing assistance. *See* public housing
Project-Based Rental Assistance, 93
protests, 4
Pruitt-Igoe towers, St. Louis, Missouri, 19, 46
psychology of group interaction, 66–68
public health insurance, 225

public housing. *See also* Housing Choice Voucher program; Low-Income Housing Tax Credit
   in black communities in early twentieth century, 36–37
   in Civil Rights era, 44–47
   de jure segregation in, 17–20, 30
   in neoliberal era, 47–50
   in New Deal era, 38–41
   in postwar years (1945–1960), 42–44
   siting dilemma, 35–36
public housing agencies (PHAs)
   consortia, formation of, 100–1
   financial rewards for voucher use, 96–97
   higher-opportunity neighborhoods, providing information on units in, 99
   incentives for location outcomes, 95–96
   jurisdictional barriers, minimizing, 100–1
   location outcomes, strategies for improving, 94
Public Housing Program, 35–36
   in Civil Rights era, 44–47
   in New Deal era, 38–41
   in postwar years, 42–44
public schools, 86, 93, 122. *See also* education triage
public transportation policy, 28
Public Works Administration (PWA), 17–18
Purnell, J., 233–34
Putnam, R. D., 224, 233–34
PWA (Public Works Administration), 17–18

question and answer (Q&A) document, CRA, 126–29

race. *See also* racial segregation
   composition of U.S. population, 5
   racial integration, 240
   social challenges in mixed-income development, 156–57, 158
   weak housing markets and, 180
racially concentrated areas of poverty, 77–78, 83–84
racial segregation. See also *de jure* segregation; siting dilemma
   economic growth, effect on, 7
   government policies as cause of, 17
   metropolitan residential, 216–17
   modern, development and impact of, 60–65
   negative effects of, 233–34
   policy implications, 68–72
   psychology of group interaction, 66–68
   public housing policies, 17–20
   public policies and practices enforcing, 22–24
   school composition effects, 218–20
   school district segregation, 218

racial segregation (cont.)
  social mobility affected by, 8
  state-sanctioned housing segregation, elimination of, 44
  in St. Louis, Missouri, 58–60, 205–6
  white suburbanization, 20–21
racial zoning laws, 23
Raleigh, North Carolina, 219
rates of return, 162
Ravo, N., 48
real estate agents, de jure segregation practices of, 23–24
Reardon, S., 218, 233
rebound neighborhoods, in St Louis, Missouri, 187–88
Reeves, R. V., 6
regimes, brain
  general discussion, 224–26
  strategies for, 225–26
  universities, in development of, 226–28
regional brain regimes, 224–26
regional preschool clearinghouse, 225–26
reinvestment, community. See Community Reinvestment Act
relocation, promoting successful, 162
remedial desegregation, 26–29
rental subsidies. See Housing Choice Voucher program
rental units, metropolitan, 94
residential segregation, 5–6, 215–16. See also siting dilemma
  democratic processes undermined by, 7–8
  development and impact of modern segregation, 60–65
  metropolitan, 216–17
  policy implications, 68–72
  psychology of group interaction, 66–68
  reluctance of blacks to desegregate, 29
  in St. Louis, Missouri, 58–60
restrictive covenants, 22, 23
  impediment to housing mobility, 42
  Shelley v. Kraemer, 21, 22–23, 42
  in St. Louis, Missouri, 62
retail, tax increment financing for, 203
reverse migration of white professionals, 5–6
revitalization of neighborhoods, 153
Richards, M., 219
right of first refusal, 132
rightsizing, 181–82
Roberts, J., 16
Robertson-Steel, I., 220–21
Rolen, R., 43
Roosevelt administration, 38–41
Rosenblatt, P., 94
Rothstein, R., 60–62, 189–90
Rubin, H., 190

safety improvements in mixed-income development, 152–53
SAFMRs (Small Area Fair Market Rents), 98
Sampson, R., 217
San Francisco, California, 151
Sarason, S., 220
schools. See also education triage
  Brown v. Board of Education decision, 218, 233
  charter, 221–22
  composition effects, 218–20, 222–23
  education about segregation in, 26–29
  equitable access to, 86, 93, 122
  school district segregation, 218
search periods in HCV program, extending, 99
secondary marginalization, 157
Section 8 vouchers, 47–48, 51
security improvements in mixed-income development, 152–53
segregation. See also specific types by name
  American ideals threatened by, 7–8
  Community Reinvestment Act, combating with, 125–29
  democratic processes undermined by, 7–8
  economic growth stifled by, 7
  harm caused by, 6–9
  historical overview, 3–4
  negative effects of, 233–34
  racial, ethnic, and economic composition of U.S. population, 5
  residential, 5–6
SES. See socioeconomic status
Sharkey, P., 60, 63, 69, 84
Shelley v. Kraemer, 21, 22–23, 42
Sherif, M., 66
Silver, J., 124
siting dilemma
  in Civil Rights era, 44–47
  housing in black communities, historical, 36–37
  in neoliberal era, 47–50
  in New Deal era, 38–41
  overview, 35–36
  in postwar years, 42–44
slum housing, elimination of, 42–44
Small Area Fair Market Rents (SAFMRs), 98
small businesses, effect of gentrification on, 124
Smith, P. H., 43
social capital, 147–48
Social Capital Community Benchmark Survey, 224
social challenges in mixed-income development, 156–57, 158, 163–64
social control, 147–48
social engineering, 29
social exclusion among poor, 156–57
social learning, 147–48

social mobility, 8, 234
social psychology of intergroup relations, 66–68, 69–71
socioeconomic status (SES). *See also* mixed-income development
  academic attainment, effect on, 223–24
  brain development and, 215–16
  effect of segregation on, 64
  social mobility, 8, 234
South, S., 217
spatial-arrangement considerations, in mixed-income development, 161–62
SSI (Supplemental Security Income), 102
Stanford University, 21
Starr, R., 181
state regulatory authorities, segregation practices of, 23–24
Stegner, W., 21
stereotype rebound effect, 66–67
Stewart, P., 15–16
St. Louis, Missouri
  DeSoto-Carr project, 18
  development and impact of modern segregation, 60–65
  market strength measurements, 175
  policy implications, 68–72
  Pruitt-Igoe towers, 19
  psychology of group interaction, 66–68
  racial disparities in, 58–60
  strong submarkets in, 187–88
  tax increment financing in St. Louis County, 202–6
  weak housing markets in, 179–80, 182
St. Louis Argus, 182
St. Louis Real Estate Exchange, 62
strong market neighborhood strategies, 176, 177, 185–88, 189–90
structural change in mixed-income development, need for, 165
subsidies. *See specific programs by name*
suburbanization
  school district segregation, 218
  white, 20–21, 25
Supplemental Security Income (SSI), 102
supportive services, in mixed-income development, 163
surveys, Community Reinvestment Act, 143

TANF (Temporary Assistance for Needy Families), 102
Tate, W., 234–35
tax increment financing (TIF)
  criticism of, 201–2
  equitable use of, 206–9
  history of, 200
  overview, 197
  process, 199–200
  reasoning for, 198–99
  in St. Louis County, 202–6
Team Four, 182
Techwood Homes, Atlanta, Georgia, 18
Temporary Assistance for Needy Families (TANF), 102
Tenant Opportunity to Purchase Act, 132
Texas Department of Housing and Community Affairs v. Inclusive Communities Project (ICP), 16–17, 77–78, 83
Theodos, B., 217
TIF. *See* tax increment financing
Travis, D., 46
triage regime, 220–24
Trump administration, 192, 133–210, 239
Turner, S., 49

underclass, 63
undervalued neighborhoods, identifying, 183
United States History, 26
United States Housing Act, 18–19
universal prenatal care, 225
universities, in development of brain regimes, 226–28
University of Chicago, 22
upward mobility, focusing on in mixed-income development, 163
Urban Center Housing Tax Increment Financing Program, Massachusetts, 208
urban growth paradigm, 182
urban renewal programs, 23
urban universities, in development of brain regimes, 226–28
U.S. Bank National Association, 134–36, 137
U.S. Department of Housing and Urban Development (HUD). *See also* Affirmatively Furthering Fair Housing; Housing Choice Voucher program
  AFFH Rule Guidebook, 78
  Affirmatively Furthering Fair Housing, 50
  moratorium on construction projects, 46
  state-sanctioned housing segregation, elimination of, 44

vacancies, in weak housing markets, 179–80
vouchers. *See* Housing Choice Voucher program

Walker v. HUD, 82, 85
Wallace, G., 58
Washington, DC, 151
weak market neighborhoods
  general discussion, 176–77
  strategies for, 178–82
  strong submarkets in, 187
wealth inequality, 5, 25

Weber, M., 176
Webster, G., 44–45
West Logan Community Civic Association in Philadelphia, Pennsylvania, 44–45
whites
  de jure segregation, enduring effects of, 25
  metropolitan residential segregation, 216–17
  public housing policies, segregation through, 17–20
  public policies and practices enforcing segregation, 24
  remedial desegregation, 26–29
  school composition effects, 218–20, 222–23
  school district segregation, 218
  suburbanization, 20–21, 25

Williams, D., 64
Wilson, J., 68
Wilson, W. J., 233–34
Woofter, T. J., 37
Wright, C., 48
Wyche, P. H., Jr., 45

Yun, J., 218

zip codes, voucher subsidies based on, 98
Zippel, C., 124
zoning policies
  exclusionary, 28, 62–63
  inclusionary, 132, 186, 207–8, 209, 239
Zuk, M., 123